Educational Scholarship across the Mediterranean

Comparative Education and the Mediterranean Region

Series Editor

Ronald G. Sultana (*University of Malta*)

Editorial Board

Abdeljalil Akkari (*University of Geneva, Switzerland*)
Rima Karami Akkary (*American University of Beirut, Lebanon*)
Xavier Bonal i Sarró (*Autonomous University of Barcelona, Spain*)
Hülya Kosar-Altinyelken (*University of Amsterdam, the Netherlands*)
Paolo Landri (*National Research Council, Italy*)
António Magalhães (*University of Porto, Portugal*)
André E. Mazawi (*University of British Columbia, Canada*)
Nagwa Megahed (*Ain Shams University, Egypt*)
Michalinos Zembylas (*Open University of Cyprus, Cyprus*)

VOLUME 3

The titles published in this series are listed at *brill.com/mena*

Educational Scholarship across the Mediterranean

A Celebratory Retrospective

Edited by

Ronald G. Sultana and Michael A. Buhagiar

BRILL

LEIDEN | BOSTON

Cover illustration: Painting by Pawl Carbonaro (https://www.carbonaropawl.com)

All chapters in this book have undergone peer review.

The Library of Congress Cataloging-in-Publication Data is available online at https://catalog.loc.gov

Typeface for the Latin, Greek, and Cyrillic scripts: "Brill". See and download: brill.com/brill-typeface.

ISSN 2667-0046
ISBN 978-90-04-50658-9 (paperback)
ISBN 978-90-04-50659-6 (hardback)
ISBN 978-90-04-50660-2 (e-book)

Copyright 2022 by Koninklijke Brill NV, Leiden, The Netherlands, except where stated otherwise.
Koninklijke Brill NV incorporates the imprints Brill, Brill Nijhoff, Brill Hotei, Brill Schöningh, Brill Fink, Brill mentis, Vandenhoeck & Ruprecht, Böhlau Verlag and V&R Unipress.
All rights reserved. No part of this publication may be reproduced, translated, stored in a retrieval system, or transmitted in any form or by any means, electronic, mechanical, photocopying, recording or otherwise, without prior written permission from the publisher. Requests for re-use and/or translations must be addressed to Koninklijke Brill NV via brill.com or copyright.com.

This book is printed on acid-free paper and produced in a sustainable manner.

Contents

Preface: Back to the Future and the Politics of Hope   IX
List of Figures and Tables   XVIII
Notes on Contributors   XX

PART 1
Regional Focus

1   Socialisation, Learning and Basic Education in Koranic Schools   3
     Abdel-Jalil Akkari

2   Is There a Semiperipheral Type of Schooling? State, Social Movements
and Education in Spain, 1970–1994   26
     Xavier Bonal and Xavier Rambla

3   Toward an Innovative University in the South? Institutionalising
Euro-Mediterranean Co-operation in Research, Technology and
Higher Education   43
     Jorma Kuitunen

4   The Permanence of Distinctiveness: Performances and Changing
Schooling Governance in the Southern European Welfare States   68
     Paolo Landri

5   Gramsci, the Southern Question and the Mediterranean   86
     Peter Mayo

6   Dis/Integrated Orders and the Politics of Recognition: Civil Upheavals,
Militarism, and Educators' Lives and Work   103
     André Elias Mazawi

7   The North African Educational Challenge: From Colonisation to the
Current Alleged Islamist Threat   124
     Pierre Vermeren

PART 2
Country Focus

8 The Circulation of European Educational Theories and Practices: The Algerian Experience 143
Mohamed Miliani

9 State, Society, and Higher Education in Cyprus: A Study in Conflict and Compromise 156
Anthony A. Koyzis

10 Global Discourses and Educational Reform in Egypt: The Case of Active-Learning Pedagogies 171
Mark B. Ginsburg and Nagwa M. Megahed

11 Values in Teaching and Teaching Values: A Review of Theory and Research, Including the Case of Greece 196
Evangelia Frydaki

12 Peace Education in Israel: Encounter and Dialogue 216
Dov Darom

13 The Birth of 'Citizenship and Constitution' in Italian Schools: A New Wall of Competences or Transition to Intercultural Education? 227
Sandra Chistolini

14 Private and Privatised Higher Educational Institutions in Jordan 249
Muhammad Raji Zughoul

15 The Implications of Lebanese Cultural Complexities for Education 272
Linda Akl

16 The Maltese Bilingual Classroom: A Microcosm of Local Society 294
Antoinette Camilleri Grima

17 Multiculturalism, Citizenship, and Education in Morocco 304
Moha Ennaji

18 Conflict and Democracy Education in Palestine 326
Maher Z. Hashweh

CONTENTS

VII

19 Navigating Religious Boundaries at School: From Legitimate to Specious
    Religious Questions   348
        *Maria Esther Fernández Mostaza, Gloria García-Romeral and
        Clara Fons i Duocastella*

20 Human Rights Education: A Comparison of Mother Tongue Textbooks
    in Turkey and France   370
        Canan Aslan and Yasemin Karaman-Kepenekci

PREFACE

Back to the Future and the Politics of Hope

Introduction

Educational Scholarship across the Mediterranean: A Celebratory Retrospective, featuring a selection of articles published in the *Mediterranean Journal of Educational Studies (MJES)*, marks the 25th Jubilee year since the first issue of the journal was published. Launching, managing and editing this journal has been a labour of love, which has taken a number of twists and turns that include its initial format as a biannual print-based publication (Volumes 1 to 12, 24 issues in all between 1996 and 2007), then as an online, open-access journal (Volumes 13 to 15, 6 issues in all between 2008 and 2010), and more recently as a thematic book series produced 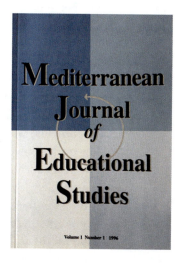 first by Sense (6 volumes in all published between 2011–2017), and now by Brill (3 volumes thus far, including this celebratory publication).

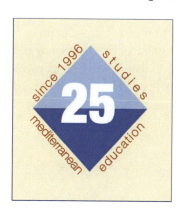

It has been, in many ways, an exciting journey, but also a challenging one, first to carve out a spatial, regional comparative project for Mediterranean educational research, and then to find a sufficient number of scholars ready to help shape the project, enrich it with their contributions, and make it sustainable. It helped that many academics in the region saw this as an opportunity to converse about issues that were close to their concerns, and to work together to address common problems. It also helped that the journal's credentials were endorsed by none other than internationally renowned scholars such as Pierre Bourdieu, Edward Said, and Georges Duby, who were generous enough to acknowledge the journal's efforts, and who were sensitive to the uphill struggles that are likely to be faced by an initiative from the semi-periphery of metropole Europe. Their readiness to associate themselves with the *MJES* project speaks volumes about their largesse of spirit and of mind, and about their awareness of the need for dialogue between the two shores of the Mediterranean, not least on such an important topic as education.

The driving idea behind the *MJES* was the necessity to establish a forum for discussion and scholarly exchange around issues that mattered for education in the region. As declared in the 'Introduction' to the first issue, the aim was 'To develop South-South and South-North dialogue in the field of education, and through this, to enhance the possibility of mutual understanding and co-operation among Mediterranean and other people in the various spheres of life.' Such interaction and collaboration, it was hoped, would help enhance our understanding of some of the key features of our respective education systems, such as how they were marked by shared colonial and post- or neo-colonial histories, by the nature of the relations between state, religious power and formal schooling, by cultural traditions that shaped gender boundaries and life-chances in particular ways, and so on.

Seed funding by the University of Malta and UNESCO served to establish an extensive network of educational researchers from all over the region, creating a database that profiled scholars' academic background and expertise with a view to supporting the *MJES* by submitting papers, reviewing submissions by colleagues, and promoting the journal through their own contacts and networks. Subscriptions to the journal came from as far afield as Australia, Russia, the US, China and Japan, not to mention most of Europe, the Middle East and, to a lesser extent, North Africa. Despite such encouraging international interest, however, it eventually became obvious that those who the editorial team most wanted to engage in our region were the ones with the least resources to subscribe, despite the advantageous fee structures we had put in place for low-income countries. We thus put the journal online, available free to all in an open-access format. When the journal—in its latest iteration as special thematic volumes—was adopted by international publishers, we nevertheless negotiated that the chapters would become available through open access 18 months after their publication.

Mediterranean Comparative Education

Adopting a Mediterranean lens for this new journal was, in many ways, a wager. It involved focusing on an 'imagined community' (Anderson, 1991) which, despite a history of trading and cultural interchange facilitated by a common sea, tends to be seen as riven with misunderstanding at best, and conflict at worst. Mainstream comparative education studies usually focused on one or other of the countries individually, or on regional groupings such as 'South-

PREFACE   XI

ern Europe', the Maghreb countries, the Middle East and North Africa (MENA) countries and territories, and the Arab world. It is therefore not surprising that some comparativists were sceptical about the project, claiming that the many differences in the region called 'the Mediterranean' made it an unlikely and unsuitable object for comparative analyses.

Such concerns are not without justification. It is significant, for instance, that most international aid agencies and development organisations, as well as research institutes, have, at best, a MENA, or a South European studies programme. Even those which do claim to focus on the whole region—such as the Mediterranean Programme of the Robert Schuman Centre at the European University Institute in Firenze—are often mostly interested in studies of Arab states, using the 'Mediterranean' caption interchangeably for 'Arab'. The diversities between—not to mention *within*—countries in the Mediterranean are striking, with significant and cumulative differentials in most aspects of economic and social development indices, whether we are talking about demography, access to power resources, the role and place of religion, the status of individuals and their relationship to inalienable rights, and so on. Diverse colonial histories have led to the development of different educational traditions and systems, as well as to country-specific relations with metropole countries, and with the power blocs present in the region, including the US and the EU.

And yet, one could also present another narrative, one that stresses a different imagery that speaks of resonance, cross-fertilisation, and exchange, if not harmony and *convivienza*. Mediterranean studies, for instance, are common in a range of disciplines including history, anthropology, archaeology, and literature, not to mention tourism studies and the culinary arts. Some scholars have argued that the intensity of contact has carried over from the past, so that 'Over the millennia it has proved impossible for Mediterranean people to ignore each other. They have conquered, colonised, converted ... the contacts are perpetual and inescapable' (Davis, 1977, p. 255). It is this constant factor of interaction, borrowing, diffusion and acculturation that permit us—at least partly—to speak of the Mediterranean as a social system. Anthropologists such as Pitt-Rivers (1963), Peristiany (1965, 1968), Wolf (1969), Gellner & Waterbury (1977), Schneider & Schneider (1976), Davis (1977), and Boissevain (1976, 1979) have shown that adopting a pan-Mediterranean lens is helpful in exploring and identifying the region's distinctiveness around unifying themes. Their studies suggest that a relatively uniform Mediterranean ecology led to an aggregate of sociocultural traits which Gilmore (1982), drawing on a variety of sources, lists (and here we paraphrase) as follows:

> ... a strong urban orientation; a corresponding disdain for the peasant way of life and for manual labour; sharp social, geographic, and economic stratification; political instability and a history of weak states; 'atomistic'

community life; rigid sexual segregation; a tendency toward reliance on the smallest possible kinship units (nuclear families and shallow lineages); strong emphasis on shifting, ego-centred, noncorporate coalitions; an honour-and-shame syndrome which defines both sexuality and personal reputation; ... intense parochialism and intervillage rivalries; communities are marked off by local cults of patron saints who are identified with the territorial unit; general gregariousness and interdependence of daily life characteristic of small, densely populated neighbourhoods, where patterns of institutionalised hostile nicknaming abounds, where the evil eye belief is widespread, and where religion plays an important institutionalised political role, as do priests, saints, and holy men. Marriage patterns, while superficially varied, signal the unity of the Mediterranean through the practice of the dowry. And there are important similarities in politics also, with weak bureaucracies at the national level leading to unstable democratic regimes, often alternating with dictatorships of both Right and Left. At the micropolitical level, this emphasis on informal personal power rather than formal institutions is reflected in the reliance on patronage, with clientage being the preferred form of adaptation to social inequality in the region.

Some attribute the evolution of such 'traits' to internal contacts which are both historical and contemporary, and which tend to germinate around the basin due to a similar eco-environment. Others (*inter alia*, Yachir [1989] and Amin & Yachir [1988]) adopt a political economic approach that considers Mediterranean identity in terms of a shared subjugation to external economic pressures. Here, Immanuel Wallerstein's (2004) world-systems analysis with its emphasis on centre-periphery relations, and Boaventura de Sousa Santos' (2007) theorisation of semi-peripheral societies, help us understand that what is quintessentially Mediterranean is not the result of local or regional conditions, but rather more a direct response to 'de-development' by the core powers.

Adopting a Mediterranean Lens

While the search for foundational legitimacy in adopting the Mediterranean as a unit of comparison is of interest and relevance to the *MJES* and its subsequent iterations and manifestations, the scholarly aspirations also head in a different direction, away from the epistemological and positivist ambition to compare 'like with like'. Rather, the *MJES* represents the effort to find a new standpoint from where to gaze at phenomena and to apprehend them in new

PREFACE

XIII

ways by refracting them through a different lens. A 'Mediterranean perspective', such as promoted by the *MJES*, and now by the Brill thematic volumes, can open up new opportunities for the generation of more context-specific and context-responsive frameworks that help us make sense of educational dynamics. We have discovered, over the years, how bringing together scholars from different parts of the Mediterranean—Israelis and Palestinians; Greeks and Turks (not to mention Greek and Turkish Cypriots); Syrians and Lebanese; Christians, Muslims and Jews of all denominations and persuasions—generates thematic concerns that might not have otherwise surfaced. These include notions of responsibility for future generations who, through the curricular narratives we present, acknowledge and transcend the atrocities piled upon each other across time and space.

Since regions as much as individual states are political constructs, the Mediterranean gaze is nothing more than another faltering step in our effort to widen our associative imagined communities from family to clan, from clan to nation, and from nation to region and to more all-embracing notions of global citizenship. As such, the *MJES* project, through its different reincarnations, recognises the Mediterranean as a space worthy of attention. Its outlook follows in the footsteps and spirit of Braudel (1992), who wrote of the Mediterranean as a geographical theatre, where human dramas have unfolded over millennia 'from the northern limit of the olive tree to the northern limit of the palm tree.' At the same time, however, we understand the Mediterranean as a 'social imaginary', in the manner of Franco Cassano's brilliant *Il Pensiero Meridiano* (2007), a book and an author that recognise that creative and symbolic dimension of the social world through which we, as human beings, create ways of living together and of representing our collective life.

The notion of a 'social imaginary' is important at a historical conjuncture that some have spoken of as an 'interregnum', when old social forms are melting, and yet new ones still have to take shape (Bauman, 2012), a state of affairs that gives rise to a great variety of morbid symptoms, such as populism, obscurantism, and outright fascism. It is precisely at this dangerous and confusing time that the utopic impulse must be set free, with the pandemic serving as a metaphor of the social pathology that the world needs to confront. As old empires die and new ones emerge, the tectonic plates of dominance and influence shift and align themselves around new constellations of power. A potential third space (Bhabha, 2004) opens up, where the oppressed can plot their liberation, where dissent is whispered in the corners of the taverns and bazaars, as much as in citizen uprisings and migratory surges.

The notion of liminality resonates with the way we think of the Mediterranean, itself a liminal, in-between space that is both uncomfortable and troubled, yet laden with possibilities, as habituated structures, roles, and practices dissolve and new ones begin to take shape. Here is where the global North meets the global South in the new 'space of flows' (Matvejevitch, 1992; Chambers, 2008)—here is one of the 'rims' (Cowen, 1998) which provides us with a lens through which we can refract experiences, helping us think through the complexities of our lives in new, provocative, perhaps even startling ways. A focus on our Mediterranean—which, by definition, requires some sort of 'crossing', and indeed multiple crossings—is timely for educators and educational sociologists everywhere, especially if we still define our role in Socratic terms as 'gadflies', that is, an *assemblage* of networked individuals who ask uncomfortable questions, and who, despite all our personal limitations—intellectual, physical, but above all moral—nevertheless still strive to engage with the world as it is, in order to imagine a world as it could and should be. It is thus by bringing together that which many see as incommensurable that a space for emancipatory thinking and for critical education opens up. It is precisely the atonal, ultimately dissonant character of the region that holds out an emancipatory pedagogic promise, disrupting as it does the global and predatory effort to impose a unitary discourse that disciplines, and that has even arrogantly and foolishly claimed the end of history.

Zelia Gregoriou from the University of Cyprus—a philosopher and artist with a keen interest in other sorts of crossings in our region, those of the new 'boatpeople'—captures nicely why a focus on the Mediterranean is important, today perhaps more than ever before. A few days after the Revolution that rocked Egypt on 25 January 2011, she commented in her correspondence:

> Up to a week ago, the major kinds of visual images that would come to my mind of the Mediterranean would be olives and half-empty, half-dry, half-populated Mediterranean landscapes ... the colours of Matisse and the Fauves [...] and then maps of asylum seeker detention camps aligned on the coasts of the Mediterranean basin [...] Today, when I try to visualise the Mediterranean as an idea—and not as a geographical or cultural entity—what comes to my mind is Tahrir square: is it possible that today, after Empire, [...] after the end of the political, the political is staged again in places which were exempted from the European cartographies of political theory? Could the Mediterranean, as an idea, symbolise the return of the political and the other of Europe (because it is already 'other' within, in a way that Europe will never be, cannot be)? What is the place of education in this reclaim of the public sphere as a site for transformation, contestation, revolt, hope?

The *MJES* project is, in our view, even more important today, as it aspires to 'return to the political', embracing the Mediterranean as a unique 'ideoscape'

PREFACE

XV

(Appadurai, 1990) where the global and the local intersect so that social practices, such as education, are negotiated, contested and transformed.

Mirroring the Mediterranean

Since 1996 a good number of authors have contributed articles to general issues of the *MJES*, as well as to thematic volumes (whether appearing under the journal cover or as stand-alone publications) that have broached such topics as higher education (Guri-Rosenblit & Sultana, 1999), special education (Phtiaka, 2001), innovation (Sultana, 2001), multilingualism (Bahous & Thonhauser, 2001), teacher education (Sultana, 2002), science education (Constantinou & Zembylas, 2003), power and education (Sabour & Sultana, 2003), comparative education (Borg, Mayo & Sultana, 2008), critical educators (Sultana, 2011), art education (Baldacchino & Vella, 2013), private tutoring (Bray, Mazawi & Sultana, 2013), representations of the teacher in Mediterranean literature (Galea & Grima, 2014), livelihood and transition to work (Sultana, 2017), socio-emotional learning (Cefai, Regester & Dirani, 2020), and educational leadership (Mifsud & Landri, 2021).

This celebratory retrospective volume features contributions to the journal in its pre-Brill phase—contributions which we consider to be outstanding in terms not only of their content, but also because they still speak to contemporary concerns, to which they bring fresh insights and perspectives. Some cast a comparative eye over the Mediterranean, focusing on sub-regions at times (Southern Europe, the Maghreb, the Arab 'world'), and at times adopting a more comprehensive outlook, drawing our attention to overarching themes and analytic categories, such as to the notions of 'semi-periphery' and the 'global South', or to the Eurocentric referents upon which evaluative judgements of regional educational efforts are unreflexively made. Other papers focus on specific countries, highlighting a whole host of educational concerns that resonate with UNESCO's four pillars upholding education, namely learning to be, learning to know, learning to do, and learning to live together (Delors, 1996). We thus have papers about values and education, the challenges that embracing multicultural and intercultural ways of life represent, the reinforcements of citizenship rights and democratic government through curricula and pedagogy, the efforts to mediate societal conflict through educational interventions, and the globalisation of educational policies and pedagogies. All these papers, even when they have a single country focus, nevertheless open up important opportunities for conversations not only between educators in the region, but well beyond it as well.

It is therefore with pride and a sense of collective achievement that we present this collection of articles to our readers, in the hope that they provide as much inspiration to them as they did to us.

References

Amin, S., & Yachir, F. (1988) *La Méditerranée dans le Monde: Les Enjeux de la Transnationalisation*. Paris: La Découverte.

Anderson, B. R. O. (1991) *Imagined Communities: Reflections on the Origin and Spread of Nationalism* (revised and extended ed.). London: Verso.

Appadurai, A. (1990) Disjuncture and difference in the global economy, *Theory, Culture and Society*, Vol. 7, pp. 295–310.

Bahous, R., & Thonhauser, I. (eds.) (2001) Multilingualism and education in the Mediterranean (special issue). *Mediterranean Journal of Educational Studies*, Vol. 6(1).

Baldacchino, J., & Vella, R. (eds.) (2013) *Mediterranean Art and Education: Navigating Local, Regional and Global Imaginaries through the Lens of the Arts and Learning.* Rotterdam: Sense.

Bauman, Z. (2012) Times of interregnum, *Ethics and Global Politics*, Vol. 5, pp. 49–56.

Bhabha, H. K. (2004) *The Location of Culture*. London & New York: Routledge.

Boissevain, J. (1976) Uniformity and diversity in the Mediterranean: an essay in interpretation. In J. G. Peristiany (ed.) *Kinship and Modernization in Mediterranean Society.* Rome: Centre for Mediterranean Studies.

Boissevain, J. (1979) Toward an anthropology of the Mediterranean, *Current Anthropology*, Vol. 20, pp. 81–93.

Borg, C., Mayo, P., & Sultana, R. G. (eds.) (2008) Mediterranean studies in comparative education (special issue). *Mediterranean Journal of Educational Studies*, Vol. 13(2).

Braudel, F. (1992) *The Mediterranean and the Mediterranean World in the Age of Philip II* (first published in 1949). New York: Harper Collins.

Bray, M., Mazawi, A. E. & Sultana, R. G. (eds.) (2013) *Private Tuition across the Mediterranean Region: Power Dynamics and Implications for Learning and Equity.* Rotterdam: Sense.

Cassano, F. (2007). *Il Pensiero Meridiano*. Roma & Bari: Laterza.

Cefai, C., Regester, D., & Dirani, L. A. (eds.) (2020) *Social and Emotional Learning in the Mediterranean: Cross-cultural Perspectives and Approaches*. Leiden: Brill.

Chambers, I. (2008) *Mediterranean Crossings: The Politics of an Interrupted Modernity.* Durham, NC: Duke University Press.

Constantinou, C. P., & Zembylas, M. (eds.) (2003) Learning in science in the Mediterranean region (special issue). *Mediterranean Journal of Educational Studies*, Vol. 8(1).

Cowen, R. (1998) Thinking comparatively about space, education and time: an approach to the Mediterranean rim. In A. M. Kazamias & M. G. Spillane (eds.) *Education and the Structuring of the European Space: North-South, Centre-Periphery, Identity-Otherness*. Athens: Seirios Publishers.

Davis, S. (1977) *The People of the Mediterranean: An Essay in Comparative Social Anthropology*. London: Routledge & Kegan Paul.

PREFACE

de Sousa Santos, B. (2007) *Another Knowledge is Possible: Beyond Northern Epistemologies*. London: Verso.

Delors, J. (1996) *Education: The Treasure Within*. Paris: UNESCO.

Galea, S., & Grima, A. (eds.) (2014) *The Teacher, Literature, and the Mediterranean*. Rotterdam: Sense.

Gellner, E., & Waterbury, J. (eds.) (1977) *Patrons and Clients in Mediterranean Societies*. London: Duckworth.

Gilmore, D. (1982) Anthropology of the Mediterranean area, *Annual Review of Anthropology*, Vol. 11, pp. 175–205.

Gregoriou, Z. (2011) (personal correspondence with Ronald Sultana).

Guri-Rosenblit, S., & Sultana, R. G. (eds.) (1999) Higher education in the Mediterranean (special issue). *Mediterranean Journal of Educational Studies*, Vol. 4(2).

Matvejevitch, P. (1992) *Bréviaire Méditerranéen*. Paris: Fayard.

Mifsud, D., & Landri, P. (eds.) (2021) *Enacting and Conceptualising Educational Leadership within the Mediterranean Region*. Leiden: Brill.

Peristiany, J. G. (ed.) (1965) *Honour and Shame: The Values of Mediterranean Society*. London: Wiedenfeld & Nicolson.

Peristiany, J. G. (ed.) (1968) *Contributions to Mediterranean Sociology*. The Hague: Mouton.

Phtiaka, H. (ed.) (2001) Special and inclusive education in the Mediterranean (special issue). *Mediterranean Journal of Educational Studies*, Vol. 6(2).

Pitt-Rivers, J. A. (ed.) (1963) *Mediterranean Countrymen: Essays in the Sociology of the Mediterranean*. Paris: Mouton.

Sabour, M., & Sultana, R. G. (eds.) (2003) Education and power in Mediterranean societies (special issue). *International Journal of Contemporary Sociology*, Vol. 40(1).

Schneider, J., & Schneider, P. (1976) *Culture and Political Economy in Western Sicily*. New York: Academic Press.

Sultana, R. G. (ed.) (2001) *Challenge and Change in the Euro-Mediterranean Region: Case Studies in Educational Innovation*. New York: Peter Lang.

Sultana, R. G. (ed.) (2002) *Teacher Education in the Euro-Mediterranean Region*. New York: Peter Lang.

Sultana, R. G. (ed.) (2011) *Educators of the Mediterranean: Up Close and Personal*. Rotterdam: Sense.

Sultana, R. G. (ed.) (2017) *Career Guidance and Livelihood Planning across the Mediterranean: Challenging Transitions in South Europe and the MENA Region*. Rotterdam: Sense.

Wallerstein, I. M. (2004) *World-Systems Analysis: An Introduction*. Durham: Duke University Press.

Wolf, E. R. (1969) Society and symbols in Latin Europe and the Islamic Middle-East: some comparisons, *Anthropology*, Vol. 42, pp. 287–301.

Yachir, F. (1989) *The Mediterranean: Between Autonomy and Dependence*. London: Zed Books.

Figures and Tables

Figures

1.1 The Koranic School from the perspective of situated learning.   12
8.1 The Algerian school system.   153
8.2 The stages of the school system.   154
12.1 Holistic learning: interdependence of processes.   221
13.1 The fundamental theme.   228
13.2 The 'tuning' dynamic quality enhancement circle (from González & Wagenaar, 2003).   239
13.3 Identity of the good teacher in the world.   246
13.4 Definition of the teacher in the world.   247

Tables

1.1 Koranic Schools.   9
1.2 The Koranic School: an original form of learning.   19
2.1 The changing mandates of education policy in Spain (1970–1994).   30
4.1 Population aged 20–24 years with at least upper secondary school level education.   72
4.2 Population aged 18–24 with at most compulsory school level of education and not involved in any education and training.   72
4.3 Adult population (25–64 years) with at least upper secondary level certification.   73
4.4 Adult population (25–64 years) engaged in lifelong learning.   74
4.5 Spending on education as a percentage of GDP.   74
4.6 Average scores on the PISA 2003 survey (average ACDE = 500).   75
9.1 Cypriot students abroad by country.   158
9.2 Enrolment in public and private institutions, 1992–1993.   158
9.3 Enrolment in public and private institutions, 1993–1994.   159
12.1 Children's answers at the end of CTC programme.   223
14.1 Development and growth of Jordanian private universities.   253
14.2 Growth of student enrolment in public and private universities.   254
14.3 Private universities—Arab and foreign student population.   255
14.4 Growth and distribution of faculty members at private universities according to rank.   256
14.5 Distribution of faculty members according to nationality.   257

FIGURES AND TABLES

14.6 Numbers and quantitative growth of administrative and technical staff and their distribution according to qualifications. 258

14.7 Major areas of specialisation offered by private universities. 260

14.8 Distribution of students according to major area of specialisation and percentage to total. 262

16.1 Examples of terminology-switching. 300

16.2 Example of how the meaning of English terms is elaborated in Maltese. 301

16.3 Example of the use of English phrases/terms in Maltese by bilingual speakers. 302

19.1 Number of places of worship per religious tradition. 352

20.1 Dissemination of all the categories in Turkish textbooks according to frequency (f), percentage (%) and intensity score (IS). 378

20.2 Dissemination of all the categories in French textbooks according to frequency (f), percentage (%) and intensity score (IS). 381

Notes on Contributors

Abdel-Jalil Akkari

is professor and the Director of the research group on international and comparative education at the University of Geneva, Switzerland. He is also visiting professor at the Al-Farabi Kazakh National University, Kazakhstan. He was the Dean of research at the Higher Pedagogical Institute HEP-BEJUNE (Bienne, Switzerland) and assistant professor at the University of Maryland Baltimore County (Baltimore, United States). His main experience and major publications include studies on international cooperation, curriculum, education quality and educational planning, multicultural education, teacher training and educational inequalities. His last publications include: *Intercultural Approaches to Education: From Theory to Practice* (Springer) and *Rethinking Education through Indigenous Knowledge* (UNESCO).

Linda Akl (now Crismon)

is the Senior Director of Learning Experience Design for Unicon, Inc., the leading provider of education technology consulting and digital services. Dr. Crismon has over 15 years of international experience in learning and development and in higher education. She is an active academic and researcher, and has been working as a Faculty Associate at Arizona State University since 2013. Her research interests include cross-cultural learning and teaching in higher education, social emotional aspects of education, and strategies for promoting effective student engagement in educational processes. Dr. Crismon earned her EdD in Education from the University of Leicester in the United Kingdom. She has two specialisations, one in Educational Leadership and Management and the other in Learning and Teaching.

Canan Aslan

graduated from the Faculty of Education of Uludağ University in 1995. She completed her master's thesis in 1999, and her PhD dissertation in 2006. She has been working at the Department of Fine Arts Education of the Faculty of Educational Sciences at Ankara University since 2009. Currently, she is the department Chair of the Turkish Education Department. She has also been working as an Assistant Director of the Children and Youth Literature Application and Research Centre at Ankara University since 2010. Her research areas are Turkish and literature education as well as children and youth literature.

NOTES ON CONTRIBUTORS

Xavier Bonal

is professor of sociology at the Universitat Autònoma de Barcelona (UAB) and special professor of education and international development at the University of Amsterdam (UvA). He is the Director of the research group Globalisation, Education and Social Policies (GEPS) at the UAB and Coordinator of the GLOBED Project, an Erasmus Mundus Master on Education Policies for Global Development. He has been member of the EU Network of Experts in Social Sciences and Education (NESSE) and is member of the Editorial Board of several international journals of education policies and educational development. Professor Bonal has published widely in national and international journals and is the author of several books on sociology of education, education policy and globalisation, education and development. He has worked as a consultant for international organisations such as UNESCO, UNICEF, the European Commission, and the Council of Europe. Between 2006 and 2010, he was Deputy Ombudsman for Children's Rights at the Office of the Catalan Ombudsman.

Michael A. Buhagiar

is senior lecturer in mathematics education at the Faculty of Education, University of Malta. His main lecturing and research area is educational assessment, especially in relation to the mathematics classroom. His other research interests include reflective practice, inquiry-based learning, teacher education and lesson study. Dr Buhagiar is a team member of Collaborative Lesson Study Malta (CLeStuM) and is affiliate member of the Euro-Mediterranean Centre for Educational Research (EMCER). Apart from his varied publications, he has participated in a number of EU-funded research projects. Before joining the Faculty in 2008, he was a class teacher in a primary school and later taught mathematics at secondary and pre-university levels.

Antoinette Camilleri Grima

is professor of applied linguistics at the Faculty of Education, University of Malta. She contributed to the international programme of the European Centre for Modern Languages (ECML) of the Council of Europe by co-ordinating projects dealing with intercultural competence, and authored, edited, co-edited and co-authored a number of books and ECML publications, in particular *A Framework of Reference for Pluralistic Approaches to Languages and Cultures.* Her most recent co-edited volume is entitled *Small is Multilingual* (2020) published by Peter Lang. Camilleri Grima has published a number of volumes on Maltese pedagogy and textbooks for the teaching of Maltese, as well as many articles in internationally refereed journals. She is a regular invited speaker at the University of Strasbourg and the universities of Antwerp, Udine, Edinburgh, and Limerick.

Sandra Chistolini

is professor of general and social pedagogy, Department of Education, University of Rome Three, Italy. She is national coordinator of the International Management and Academic Network (Erasmus Plus, Jean Monnet). Her research interests include comparative education, intercultural and citizenship education, teacher education, curriculum development, innovation strategies of teaching and learning, outdoor education. Her latest books are *Decoding the Disciplines in European Institutions of Higher Education: Intercultural and Interdisciplinary Approach to Teaching and Learning* (FrancoAngeli, 2019); *Il Fondo Pizzigoni: Metodo Sperimentale e Scuola dell'Infanzia nei Diari di Sara Bertuzzi* (FrancoAngeli, 2020), and *L'Asilo nel Bosco: La Scuola Aperta alla Comunicazione sul Territorio tra Arte e Comunità* (FrancoAngeli, 2021).

Dov Darom

founded the Social Education programme at Oranim and directed it for many years. He was formerly senior lecturer in education, Oranim, School of Education of the Kibbutz Movement, Haifa University, Israel. He taught, co-ordinated workshops, and wrote on topics such as social education, humanistic education, kibbutz education, classroom climate, interpersonal communication, values education. He was a member of Kibbutz Yassur. Dov passed away in 1998.

Moha Ennaji

is professor of linguistics and cultural studies at Sidi Mohamed Ben Abdellah University at Fès. He has published extensively on linguistics, gender, and migration issues in North Africa. His most recent books include *Muslim Moroccan Migrants in Europe* (Palgrave, 2014) and *Multiculturalism, Cultural Identity, and Education in Morocco* (Springer, 2005). He has also edited several books, the most recent of which are *Multiculturalism and Democracy in North Africa: Aftermath of the Arab Spring* (Routledge, 2014); *Minorities, Women, and the State in North Africa* (Red Sea Press, 2016); *The Maghreb-Europe Paradigm: Migration, Gender and Cultural Dialogue* (Cambridge Scholars, 2019). He has been a visiting scholar at Rutgers University and at the universities of Pennsylvania, Arizona, and Essex.

Maria Esther Fernández Mostaza

obtained her PhD in sociology in 1996. She joined the Faculty of Political Science and Sociology, Universidad Autónoma de Barcelona in 2002, and has been a member (and now Deputy Director) of the research group ISOR (Investigations in Sociology of Religion) for the past 25 years. Recent publications are published in journals such as *EURE: Revista Latinoamericana de Estudios Urbanos Regionales*, *Religions*, and *Salud Colectiva*.

NOTES ON CONTRIBUTORS

Clara Fons i Duocastella

studied sociology at the Universitat Autònoma de Barcelona and is now professionally committed to upholding diversity and cultivating the inner life. She is director of *Dialogal* magazine, founder of Lalè (an editorial project focused on diversity, interiority and social awareness) and Head of Programmes at AUDIR (UNESCO Association for Interreligious and Interconvictional Dialogue). She has published *Malala Yousfzai: Mi Historia es la Historia de Muchas Chicas*, a bilingual illustrated commentary on the experiences of the youngest Nobel Prize laureate (Akiara Books, 2019).

Evangelia Frydaki

is professor in the Department of Educational Studies, School of Philosophy at the National and Kapodistrian University of Athens. She is Director of the postgraduate programme on Theory, Praxis and Evaluation of Educational Work. Her main areas of research interest include educational theory and practice in a postmodern socio-cultural and educational context; teacher's professional development and the development of teachers' personal theory, beliefs, values, and practical knowledge; empowerment of professional identity; literary education and educational practices in the teaching of literature, and dialogism, dialogic education, and interpretive dialogue. Her latest work, entitled *Dialogicity and Literary Education* (KRITIKI Publishing SA), will soon be published in Greek.

Gloria García-Romeral

holds a PhD in sociology and currently works as a researcher and project manager at the Centre for Interdisciplinary Gender Studies at the Universitat de Vic (UVIC-UCC). She is also associate lecturer at Universitat Autònoma de Barcelona (UAB). Her research focuses on the intersection between gender, public policies and religious and cultural diversity. Her most recent publication is published in the journal *Sexualities* (2020).

Mark B. Ginsburg

is a visiting scholar in the International Education Policy programme at University of Maryland (USA), having been a faculty member at other universities: Houston; Pittsburgh; and Teachers College, Columbia (USA); as well as Aston (England); Oslo (Norway); Kobe (Japan); and Ciencias Pedagógicas (Cuba). He also worked for AED/FHI 360 (2006-2016). Previously, he was CIES President (1991-1992) and co-editor of the *Comparative Education Review* (2003-2013). He has (co)authored or (co)edited eight books, four special issues of journals, and over 125 journal articles and book chapters.

Maher Z. Hashweh

is professor of education at the Department of Curriculum and Teaching at Birzeit University and the previous Dean of the Faculty of Education and Dean of the Faculty of Arts. He received his BSc in physics and MA in education degrees from the American University in Beirut, and his PhD in education from Stanford University. Professor Hashweh has published articles and books in science education, democracy education, teacher professional development and research ethics.

Yasemin Karaman-Kepenekci

graduated from Ankara University, Faculty of Educational Sciences, in 1990. She completed her master's thesis in 1993, and PhD dissertation in 1999. She has been working as professor in the Department of Educational Administration of the Faculty of Educational Sciences at Ankara University since 2011. She has also served as Director of Ankara University Graduate School of Educational Sciences since 2018. Her research interests include educational law, human rights and citizenship education, and educational administration. Her recent studies focused on school principals, and have considered legal perspectives in educational leadership, the loneliness of school principals, and meritocracy in educational administration.

Anthony A. Koyzis

currently teaches at several universities in the United States, including Liberty and Wisconsin, among others, and has also served as Dean and Provost. He previously worked for ten years with the Ministry of Education of the Republic of Cyprus, focusing mostly on private higher education. He was Provost at a College in Larnaca, and held a professorial position in Nicosia.

Jorma Kuitunen

is a former social researcher working currently as Country Programme Manager in Iraq for Fida International—a Finnish faith-based organisation working community development and humanitarian aid in 15 countries, with a focus on improving the rights of vulnerable children. Between 2000-2009 he coordinated a project with Iraqi refugees in Amman. He spent four years working as a specialist in global development programme management in the NGO headquarters in Finland, four years as a development consultant, and four years in multicultural training. He is an experienced specialist in social development project management in the global South, focusing in particular on resilience-based empowerment of refugee communities and on capacity development of local NGOs.

NOTES ON CONTRIBUTORS

Paolo Landri

is senior researcher and Deputy Director of the Institute of Research on Population and Social Policies at National Research Council in Italy (CNR-IRPPS). He has recently published Educational Leadership, Management, and Administration through Actor-Network Theory (Routledge, 2020) and *Enacting and Conceptualizing Educational Leadership within the Mediterranean Region* (with Denise Mifsud, Brill, 2021). He is currently Co-Editor in Chief of the European Educational Research Journal (EERJ).

Peter Mayo

is professor and UNESCO Chair in Global Adult Education at the University of Malta. He is co-founding Editor of the journal *Postcolonial Directions in Education* and edits three book series, one for Brill | Sense. His latest books are *Lifelong Learning, Global Social Justice and Sustainability* (with Leona English, Palgrave Macmillan, 2021) and *Critical Education in International Perspective* (with Paolo Vittoria, Bloomsbury Academic, 2021).

André Elias Mazawi

is professor and Head of the Department of Educational Studies, Faculty of Education, University of British Columbia, Vancouver, BC, Canada. His interests are in the fields of sociology of education and higher education, teachers' work, and the geopolitics of higher education and knowledge generation. He has published, among other, on educational policies and reforms in the Arab region, the cultural politics of the schooling of Muslim children in France, and the political history and sociology of teaching in Palestinian society.

Nagwa M. Megahed

is associate professor of comparative education and educational administration at Ain Shams University. She obtained her doctoral degree from the University of Pittsburgh, and since 2018 she joined the Faculty of Education of Yorkville University in Canada. Megahed has gained rich experience in teaching courses, conducting research, and leading and supporting educational research and development projects through her work with Michigan State University, the University of Pittsburgh, the University of Southern Mississippi, and the American University in Cairo. She has published numerous journal articles and book chapters as well as two edited books focusing on educational policy, administration, and reform in local and global contexts.

Mohamed Miliani

is professor of applied linguistics and education at the University of Oran 2. He holds a Diploma in TEFL, a MEd, and a PhD from the University of Wales. His research interests include sociolinguistics, evaluation of education systems, university ethics, and language in education. He has contributed to a number of book chapters on subjects such as preschooling, languages in education, university guidance, and educational leadership. Professor Miliani is research project leader in university ethics at the Centre de Recherche en Anthropologie, member of the textbook accreditation committee, President of the Algerian Technical Committee for Education (UNESCO), and contributes to HERE, an Erasmus Plus programme. His latest publications include chapter contributions to the following edited volumes: *The Politics of Alberia* (Routledge, 2020), and *Enacting and Conceptualizing Educational Leadership within the Mediterranean Region* (Brill, 2021).

Xavier Rambla

is associate professor of sociology at the Autonomous University of Barcelona (UAB). In recent years he has participated in research projects on lifelong learning policies in the European Union, the Civil Society Education Fund, and Education for All in Latin America. Rambla is co-convenor of the Education Policy Network of the European Educational Research Association. He has been a short-term guest lecturer in the areas of social science and education at different universities in Europe and Latin America.

Ronald G. Sultana

is professor at the Faculty of Education of the University of Malta, where he is also founding Director of the Euro-Mediterranean Centre for Educational Research and founding Editor of the *Mediterranean Journal of Educational Studies*. Most of his comparative studies look at the relationship between education and employment. He has recently published an edited volume titled *Career Guidance and Livelihood Planning across the Mediterranean* (Sense, 2017), followed by two related volumes titled *Career Guidance for Social Justice: Contesting Neoliberalism* and *Career Guidance for Emancipation: Reclaiming Justice for the Multitude* (both co-edited with T. Hooley & R. Thomsen and published by Routledge in 2018 and 2019).

Pierre Vermeren

is professor of contemporary history at the University Paris 1 Panthéon-Sorbonne and is a specialist of the Maghreb and the Arabo-Berber world. He has published widely on a range of issues, with his latest books being *On a Cassé la République: 150 Ans d'Histoire de la Nation* (Tallandier, 2020), *Le Maroc en 100 Questions: Un Royaume de Paradoxes* (Tallandier, 2020), and *Déni Français: Notre Histoire Secrète des Liasions Franco-Arabes* (Albin Michel, 2019). He is a regular contributor to the media, and his views on North Africa are solicited by several national and international organisations.

Muhammad Raji Zughoul
was professor of English and applied linguistics at the Department of English of Yarmouk University, Irbid, Jordan. He obtained his BA and MA from the American University of Beirut and his PhD from the University of Texas at Austin. He chaired the Departments of English at Yarmouk, Modern Languages at Yarmouk, Modern Languages at Applied Science University, and Department of English at the College of Basic Education in Kuwait. Professor Zughoul passed away in 2008.

PART 1

Regional Focus

∴

CHAPTER 1

Socialisation, Learning and Basic Education in Koranic Schools

Abdel-Jalil Akkari

1 Introduction

A thorough knowledge of non-Western[1] educators and educational theory remains inadequate in spite of several recent studies (Thành Khoî, 1995; Reagan, 2000; Akkari & Dasen, 2004). A Koranic School system[2] represents an interesting educational model not only because of its longevity but also because of its widespread geographical diffusion throughout the world. Up until now an understanding of Koranic School systems has suffered because of the lack of a deep anthropological study treating Islam as a religion with a novel cognitive system (Colonna, 1984, IIPE, 1984).

Even if comparative education has been open to including culture in its conceptual frameworks, this inclusion has not gone far enough concerning important theoretical debates on the concept of culture in any analysis of educational institutions (Hoffman, 1999, p. 466). The comparison of different educational traditions poses a problem of cultural identity[3] to the researcher as research undertaken within education and anthropology are like all other social and ethno-sciences:

> ... (1) Anthropologist cannot adequately describe, let alone explain, any culture different from their own. (2) For any culture to be adequately described and understood, it must be investigated by an anthropologist who himself has been acculturated in it. (3) For the latter to adequately convey the ideas and institutions of that culture, they must be reported in the native language, for there is no way of rendering the conceptual systems of one culture by the concepts of another ... All science is ethno-science. (Spiro, 1984, p. 345)

In spite of these difficulties, inherent in any comparative analysis, an approach of 'other' conceptions is necessary. As Geertz writes (1994) this necessitates 'entering into an alien turn of mind'. This is what we will try to accomplish in this text devoted to an analysis of the educational foundations of the Koranic School.

© THE EURO-MEDITERRANEAN CENTRE FOR EDUCATION RESEARCH, UNIVERSITY OF MALTA, 2004
DOI: 10.1163/9789004506602_001

2 The Characteristics of Koranic School

The history of Islamic teaching and research on Koranic Schools have been the subject of studies in the Maghreb (Lecomte, 1954; Eickelman, 1978; El-Sayed Darwish, 1981; Colonna, 1981, 1984) as well as in sub-Saharan Africa (Delval, 1980; Santerre, 1973; Santerre et al., 1982; Désalmand, 1983; Brenner, 1993; Meunier, 1997; Lange, 2000). Taken as a whole these studies show that the pedagogical model of the Koranic School contains six basic characteristics which are more or less stable according to the historical period referred to: openness, ritualisation, permanence, flexibility, resistance, and diversity. We will consider each in turn.

2.1 *Openness*

Admission into a Koranic School is a right for any child of a Muslim father with no restrictions connected to birth, age, intellectual level or physical integrity.[4] The normal age of entrance into a Koranic School is around five years. Once the step toward adherence to Islam has been made, opening of the Koranic School to all social groups and cultures makes this an institution of 'basic education' intended for all, and thus by definition egalitarian. The openness of the Koranic School represents an initiative of cultural integration and of full socialisation, and also represents an essential characteristic that differentiates it with any other school system. This ease of access (automaticity), of course, goes with the inevitable corollary: the impossibility of using the Koranic School as a means of social differentiation (Colonna, 1984). The Koranic School embodies a horizontal distribution of basic knowledge that all Muslims are expected to possess.

2.2 *Ritualisation*[5]

The intensive demands on memory, mobilisation of the body by rhythm and voice are exterior signs of the pedagogy of the Koranic School. It is completely permeated by the respect of form and the central role of repetition, both a key category and a central practice of this learning method, which consists in ceaselessly repeating the same recitations, the same motions (Colonna, 1984). 'Learning by heart', larger and larger sections of the Koran have remained a central issue of Koranic School pedagogy in spite of a progressive abandon of this method in other educational traditions. Introduction of reading and writing during apprenticeship of the Koran, executed in Arabic characters irrespective of teachers' and pupils' primary language, is organised around an analytical and progressive approach: letter, word, sentence and meaning.

According to the terminology used by Freire (1973), the Koranic School is essentially depository since it treats students as potential 'recipients' of the Koran. They must immerse themselves in Islamic culture, conform to the established norms and values, and those who wander from these are quickly and severely brought to order. Koranic School can be considered as one in which the students gain access to the universality of the Koran by a transmission-based approach. By imposing constraints (submission/adhesion) it puts in place conditional reflexes, habits built on repetition of a firm programme: the mastery of the Koran. Thus, the traditional Islamic education is characterised by 'rigorous discipline' and a 'lack of explicit explanation of memorised material' (Eickelman, 1985). This rigid pedagogy has certain advantages: speed, low cost and rapid teacher training.

2.3   *Permanence*

The permanence of the Koranic School through the ages should not be explained simply as an archaic cultural heritage. How then can one explain that the Koranic School has been able to survive through many centuries while being present in such a vast geographical area? One possible hypothesis regarding this permanence is the absence in Islam of a hierarchical clergy as within the Catholic Church. In fact, the opening of a Koranic School has no connection to a regulatory institution. The 'authority' to teach depends exclusively on the local community of faith. In the last section of this paper, we will discuss the current vitality of the Koranic School, most notably in Western Africa.

2.4   *Flexibility*

The flexibility and shifting of the Koranic School back and forth from a cultural system to another one is realised on an optimal and subtle combination of oral and written language. This mixed nature allows the Koranic School to come in contact as easily with the greater culture (the written tradition) as with the oral, traditional ones (Colonna, 1984). This ability helps explain the quick implantation of the Koranic School in Western Africa. As Santerre (1973) explained, teachers in Koranic Schools in northern Cameroon are not impeded by their lack of Arabic, as in no way does this lack keep them from playing an important role in the religious socialisation of the children under their responsibility. The mode of operation at the Koranic Schools is non-formal and revolves around the individual operator. Progress of pupils depends on individual ability; they are allowed to progress at their own pace without hindrance. The pupils are first taught the Arabic letters and how to recite the Koran. They then study Islamic jurisprudence and other facets of Islamic education (UNICEF, 1999).

2.5 *Resistance*

The sudden development of the colonial educational system created a situation in which the Koranic School found itself, for the first time in its history, in a position of being dominated. Thus developed a duality, with Western School in charge of educating the children of European settlers and the urban elites and the Koranic School being reserved for the indigenous population and the rural poor. This duality could be seen throughout the colonial period in Northern Africa (Colonna, 1984; Sraieb, 1974). Even in this inferior position, however, the Koranic School was mobilised in the fight against colonisation. While colonial schools (either public or controlled by foreign religious missions) were essentially mobilised for domestication,[6] the Koranic Schools were engaged in a process of cultural resistance against colonisation (Khayar, 1976; Coulon, 1993; Brenner, 1993). Richard-Molard (1954) found that even if the colonisation was able to diminish the influence of Allah, too often this only created people deprived of their cultural roots.

The resistance-transformation of Koranic Schools continued into the postcolonial period where the expansion of modern schooling had become the 'priority of all priorities' of those Western educated elites newly in power. We can note that it took different forms according to the situation:

- devalued against a strong and generalised state system (Tunisia, Turkey)
- incorporated into the state system or at least tolerated within (Iran, Pakistan, Egypt, Morocco)
- complementary with the state system and responding to the needs of marginalised socio-cultural groups (Mali, Senegal, Gambia, Nigeria, Kenya)
- replacing a deficient or totally absent state system (Somalia, Afghanistan).

2.6 *Diversity of the Curriculum, Goals, Space and Time*

To show the curricular diversity of Koranic Schools, Colonna (1984) contrasted different types of schools:

- 'Classical' Koranic School where only the Koran is taught/modernised with a varying degree of secular subjects
- 'Independent' Koranic School under the control of the community/ Koranic School under the control of the state and of village powers (religious confraternities)
- 'Spiritual supplement' Koranic School (similar to Christian catechism)/'Single class Koranic School' which, in certain contexts, remains the only educational institution.

After the development and spread of Western-style schooling throughout the 20th century, the Koranic School lost its central role in a majority of

Islamic regions. It retains, however, a certain influence in the socialisation process. This influence differs in intensity and degree according to the region, the degree of urbanisation, and the strength of what is officially offered as basic education. In the cities in Northern Africa, it offers preschool, before children enter public school, and later weekly catechism classes. Its influence declines when going up the social scale. In rural zones, to the north as well as to the south of the Sahara, the Koranic School remains a central institution in education, sometimes the sole actor because of the deterioration of government services.

In Western Africa, the Islamic educational system has a many-levelled structure, less rigid than Western-style schooling. Currently there exists a traditional branch (Koranic studies only), a formal branch or its 'modern' equivalent (Franco-Arabic schools, often called *madrasa*) and intermediate or hybrid forms often called 'improved Koranic instruction'. While professional training is not an explicit part of the goals of Koranic education, most of the students who continue their studies beyond the elementary level end up working in the community as apprentices with a *marabout*, a craftsman or a shopkeeper (Easton, 1999).

The diversity of the Koranic School can also be seen at the level of:
- The management of class space: Koranic schooling can take place in a mosque, in a single-family home, under a tent, in a shed or under a tree in the open air.
- The management of class time: the temporal organisation of the school does not interrupt the economic and social activities of the community.

3 The Problem of Terminology in the Study of the Koranic School

The diversity of Koranic Schools discussed in the last section can be also analysed on the linguistic level. We observe an enormous multiplicity of denominations: *Kuttab* (Tunisia, Algeria, Egypt), *Katatib* (Kuwait), *Msid* (Morocco), *mahadara* (Mauritania) *Dox* (Somalia), *Khalwa Zawia* (Libya, Sudan), *Madrasa* (Pakistan, West Africa), *Pesantrens* (Indonesia) etc. Thus, a terminological clarification is required even if it is difficult to simplify the complexity of a long-standing institution.

Let us notice initially that the translation of the term 'Koranic School' in Arabic (language of reference in Islamic education) does not make sense. Indeed, nobody speaks about *madrasa kurāniya*. Eickelman (1985) used the expression 'Koranic education'. The common use of Koranic School is probably the consequence of an Eurocentric portrayal of the most stable local, non-formal education providing basic religious and morale instruction to a large number children in Islamic context.

As stated in Table 1.1, we distinguish three major terms used in different Islamic settings in Africa to refer to the so called 'Koranic School': (a) *Kuttab*; (b) *Madrasa*; and (c) *Zawia* (*Khalwa*)

3.1 *Kuttab*

In Arabic root *k-t-b* is expressed as a verbal infinitive as *kataba*, meaning 'to write'. From that basic root we can then get the words *kuttab, kitab* 'book' (with a metaphorical meaning of *Koran*), *katib* 'writer', *maktub* 'written' (with a metaphorical meaning of 'predestined') and *maktaba* 'library'. The use of term *Kuttab* is clearly linked to the development of a culture of literacy. *Kuttab* usually used to name a small learning unit (single classroom) for relatively young children. It is the basic education in Islamic contexts before the intrusion of Western style schooling.

3.2 *Madrasa*

The word *madrasa*[7] generally has two meanings in Arabic. In a common literal and colloquial usage, it means 'school'. This term indicates the current modern schools in Arab countries. In addition, a *madrasa* is an educational institution offering instruction in Islamic subjects including, but not limited to the Koran. Within this religious school, students learn Islamic theology and others philosophical or profane subjects. Generally, the students receive a purse and are placed in the school. *Madrasa* is an institution of education which is bigger, better organised and more structured than the *kuttab*. It offers secondary as well as tertiary education.

Historically, the term *madrasa* is an institution intended for religious elites. It is a 'school of spiritual thinking'. Well known *madrasas* such as Al Azhar in Egypt or A-Zeitouna in Tunisia have been a major instrument for imparting interest in and fostering acquisition of scholarly knowledge and skills in Muslim societies for centuries. As a key element of the social fabric, they also played a major role in shaping the moral and spiritual development of the students in these societies. Eickelman (1985) analysed specifically the *madarasa Yusufia* (the Mosque-University in Marrakech) and traces the transformation of this type of traditional school into what he terms the Religious Institute.

With the interplay of internal and external forces, the role and prerogatives of *madrasas* have changed in many Muslim societies, blurring somewhat the common-sense perception of these institutions. An analysis of *madrasa* could have different implications within various cultural, political, and geographic contexts.

3.3 *Zawiya (Khalwa)*

These expressions usually indicate a small room connected to a mosque used especially for meditation and to learn the Koran. A *Zawiya* is usually founded by a Sufi mystic of sufficient piety. His presence attracts followers forming an informal Islamic study group. In the case of a Sufi saint, his students often confine themselves to the monastic enclave and retreat devoting themselves to prayers, education and charitable works.

TABLE 1.1 Koranic Schools

	Geographical area	Age scope	Size localisation
Kuttab	North Africa Middle East	Young children (basic education)	Small units Rural and urban areas
Madrasa	North Africa West Africa South Asia	Life span	Big structures Urban areas
Zawiya	North Africa	Life span	Small and isolated units Rural and urban areas

Grandin & Gaborieau (1997) show that beyond local and regional specificities, Islamic teaching obeys everywhere and from immemorial time to the same logic. It never seems an autonomous system, but it is included in the general education system. Before the European colonial domination, the knowledge (religious or profane) is an art whose transmission follows a single track, founded on apprenticeship or *suhba* where written teaching and oral teaching are narrowly overlapping. In other words, the process of learning is based on a personal relationship between a master and his disciple. The Master initiates the disciple at the same time with contents of the knowledge and the chain of the guarantors of the knowledge. The itinerancy is the second characteristic of this traditional Islamic education, the disciple moving in the Islamic space in the search of new Masters with the aim of perfecting its initiation.

After the colonial domination of Islamic countries and regions, the Islamic educational system falls under a strategy of survival in the context of cultural and political domination. The adoption of some aspects of Western schooling (system of organisation, formalisation of the master-pupil ratios, establishment of levels of qualification sanctioned by examinations and diplomas, introduction of new subjects, teaching of foreign languages, edition of religious works in vernacular languages, development of the education of the women).

The definition of the 'ideal type' of Koranic School is not possible without taking in account the context in which one wants to explain it. This context is determined by three main factors:
- colonial and post-colonial educational policies
- space left by the current formal education system
- the degree of strength of local religious communities

In most Islamic contexts, the State manages to control the recent revival of Islamic schools by tracking the *wakf* funds and fixing the curriculum of Islamic schools. The recent creation in Morocco of a Department of Traditional Education within the Ministry of Habous and Islamic Affairs aims at extending State control to the network of Islamic schools. El Ayadi (2004) observes that teachers in the public sector play a major role in these new centres of religious training. Today, in the framework of a policy implementation following the development of radical Islamism and the appearance of religious terrorism in the country, the Moroccan authorities are determined to extend the State's control to this private sector.

Luckens-Bull (2001) explores one way in which the Classical Islamic community in Java (Indonesia) seeks to negotiate modernisation and globalisation through the interface of an Islamic boarding school (*pesantren*) and higher education. This negotiation requires imagining and (re)inventing both modernity and tradition.

The two first sections of this paper show that the Koranic School is a paradoxical educational model that is difficult to analyse. On one hand, we find an archaic and depository cognitive system distinguished by extreme ritualisation, rigid discipline and the exclusive focus on rote and decontextualised learning of the Koran, a sacred work, the mastery of which is difficult even for Arabic-speaking children (who represent a decided minority in Koranic Schools). On the other hand, one finds a great diversity in its organisational methods, a flexible arrangement between the written and the oral and a largely successful socio-cultural embeddedness in the local community.

4 The Koranic School: A Case of Situated Learning?

It would seem that situated learning theory[8] is a pertinent educational model with which to analyse and explain the socio-cultural rootedness and lasting quality of Koranic School. Instead of considering learning as the acquisition of a specific knowledge, Lave and Wenger (1991) place learning in the centre of *social relations and co-participatory situations*. In other terms, instead

SOCIALISATION, LEARNING AND BASIC EDUCATION IN KORANIC SCHOOLS   11

of wondering about which *cognitive processes* are mobilised in any learning activity, they tried to identify which type of social engagement provides the best learning context. Learning automatically implies a commitment in a community of practice. Lave & Wenger's model suggests the predominance of the social over the psychological in any act of learning:

> The central grounds on which forms of education that differ from schooling are condemned [in conventional educational argument/policy/discourse] are that changing the person is not the central motive of the enterprise in which learning takes place .... The effectiveness of the circulation of information among peers suggests, to the contrary, that engaging in practice, rather than being its object, may well be the condition for the effectiveness of learning. (Lave & Wenger, 1991, p. 93)

The legitimate peripheral participation and the community of practice (or learning community) are at the centre of the model initiated by Lave and Wenger. The *practices* constitute the whole of social and individual conduct in relation with the norms, content and context of a field of expertise. We are then dealing with the enculturation of novices which easily exceeds the objective of the instilling of a specific knowledge. Figure 1.1 attempts to apply the situated learning model to the Koranic School, where the field of expertise covers the mastery and comprehension of the written Koran. Master and students sat together on the floor in a semi-circle; no desks or other barriers between them; the best regarded seats are those closest to the teacher. Books and writing utensils were viewed as sacred and distinguished tools of knowledge due to the fact that God swears by them in the Koran. Anything that God swears by is regarded in high esteem (Makdisi, 1981). Is learning in Koranic School a legitimate peripheral participation?

Moreover, Koranic School teaching is fundamentally a form of differentiated teaching since the learner goes at his own speed and is only in competition with himself. The pedagogical division of the group/class is based mainly on the degree of expertise of the student and not on the basis of age or degree. The organisation into the large group/class clearly recalls the single-room, rural classroom. The teacher divides the classroom into several levels, which are led by an advanced student. The habitual division consists of two or three groups: *novices, less experienced* and *experienced*, which curiously happens to correspond to the learning cycles which are in vogue in many current school reforms in Europe. Novice students should not be overburdened, but progress should be systematic. Experienced students should not be stuck with easy material. The masters attend to whole needs of students, assisting all students not just the outstanding ones (Makdisi, 1981).

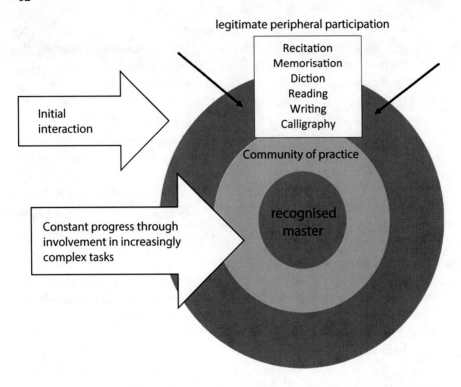

Legitimate: because all participants (students, teachers, parents, local community) accept the position of the children-novices as potential members of the community of Koranic experts (community of believers).

Peripheral: the learners settle in around the teacher by tirelessly repeating the required tasks. In the beginning these tasks are peripheral: preparing the tools (reeds, wooden board, ink etc.), repeating the words of the teacher. The tasks progressively become more important: reading, writing, reciting longer and longer verses of the Koran, comprehension-commentary of the Koran and the application of its precepts in everyday life.

Participation: it is through action that the knowledge is acquired. The knowledge is situated in the praxis of the community of practice and not in a curriculum to be found outside of the community. The dynamics of knowledge acquisition in early Muslim civilisation provided for a concept of Islamic education that placed no barrier between 'religious' and 'secular' learning (Douglass & Shaikh, 2004).

FIGURE 1.1　The Koranic School from the perspective of situated learning

In relation to the Koranic School we can state that:
- Knowledge is defined through doing: 'recite, read, write and understand the Koran', and to behave outside of the school in a way respectful of the precepts of Islam.
- The Koranic School model rejects the separation into social and religious training, religious learning and exercise of the Koran.

– The evaluation and accreditation work toward the command and consolidation of competences.

More precisely, the procedures of accreditation involve the whole community. Mastery of a part of the Koran (subdivided in sixty sections called *hizb*) is subjected to oral notification by the parents to recompense the student and the teacher. If the student is able to read and write a substantial segment of the Koran, a ceremony of ratification of his competences is organised. If the student becomes an expert and is thus able to recite, read and write the Koran in its entirety, the family offers the teacher a remuneration in relation to their economic standing and in relation to the importance of the event for the community. Understanding and higher-order thinking was gradually introduced as the student advanced. Because of the level of mastery required, teachers adjusted the level of instruction to meet the individual abilities of the students. Students varied in ages and rates of instruction. Students 'graduated' when they were able to demonstrate complete mastery over the subject matter to the satisfaction of the teacher. Obviously, this made education a highly personalised experience where every teacher and student became acquainted with one another at an intimate level (Makdisi, 1981).

One needs also keep in mind that the knowledge gained at the Koranic School is theoretically used daily for the five prayers and for other religious ceremonies. It is thus not knowledge for 'professional life' but for 'daily life'. The focus is on the ways in which learning is an evolving, continuously renewed set of relations. In other words, this is a relational view of the person and learning.

Bernstein (1996) uses the metaphor of a mirror and a resonance chamber in which many positive and negative images are projected. The central questions are:

– Who sees oneself as having a *value* in these images?
– In the same vein, one must also ask whose voices are being listened to at school.
– Who speaks?

According to Bernstein, Western school clearly reflects a hierarchy of social class values and a specific distribution of knowledge, which is reflected in the resources, access and acquisition of school culture.

The characteristics of the Koranic School do not enter into Bernstein's analysis as it consists of a non-extractive method of schooling (Serpell, 1999). Thus when, after many years of Koranic study, a student returns to his village, he will be respected since he will be capable of reading and reciting the holy book of the Muslims. This person will then be able to share his knowledge with younger children and thus continue the Koranic tradition.

Nor does the Koranic School model fit with the distinction proposed by Resnick (1978). This author contrasts, on the one hand, individual cognition in school versus shared cognition outside of school, and on the other hand pure mentation in school versus tool manipulation outside of it.

Briefly, despite the seemingly archaic cognitive system (rote memorisation and recitation of the Koran), what is at stake in the Koranic School is the entry into a 'community of Islamic believers'. The knowledge of the Koran is of interest only if the individual is recognised as being worthy of the confidence of the local community.

Coming back to the situated learning model, it should be noted that this model postulates the examination of a type of social engagement favourable for the learning context rather than for cognitive processes. In other words, everything happens as if, in the Koranic School, *the archaism of the cognitive process* is compensated by *the strength of the social engagement*. Looked at in this way, the understanding of literacy mechanisms in the Koranic tradition should be connected to the general debate on the variety of ways to learn to read and write (Goody, 1979; Serpell & Hatano, 1997). According to Gough & Juel (1989), the act of understanding the written word necessitates the mobilisation of two essential components. The first being the recognition of written words and the second the ability to give meaning to language, both written and oral. To put it in Freire's words 'to read the word *and* the world'. Koranic learning, as identified in many studies, is very far from using this pedagogical productive paradigm advocated by Freire.

The most important weakness of the Koranic School is its inability to put meaning and critical thinking in the centre of learning. Fiske (1997) observed in Koranic Schools in Burkina Faso boys learning the Koran by rote memorisation in Arabic. Sometimes memorising major segments of the text without any exegesis or discussion of its meaning—and, it appears, often without much understanding of the Arabic language. So, while certain kinds of schooling may entail a dramatic shift from imitation toward explicit conceptual transmission of declarative knowledge and certain formal skills, the shift may be limited within schools, and may not transform the mimetic transmission of more fundamental cultural practices outside of school.

While the fruitfulness of literacy methods based on 'meaning' needs no more proof, it seems that certain authors push us not to forget that 'access to the meaning of a text depends on the proper functioning of certain mechanisms and especially of their automatism' (Chardon, 2000, p. 116). It is precisely on this second component that Koranic School pedagogy is based. One can thus easily understand how, in spite of the numerous criticisms that can be addressed at the Koranic School, it has shown itself to be very effective in literacy training (Wagner & Lotfi, 1983).

In this vein, in this 'post-September 11, 2001' period where everything having to do with Islam is suspicious, it would be useful to come back to the supposed links between 'Koranic School' and 'Islamic Fundamentalism'. As mentioned in the first section, the Koranic School is characterised by an extreme diversity. The hypothesis which sees the Koranic School as the assimilation of the ancestral educational system for the preparation of future generations of fundamentalists is a hypothesis that does not hold up against a sharp analysis of the political, sociological and economical contexts in which contemporary radical fundamentalism has developed (Algeria, Afghanistan etc.). This is not to say that certain radical groups have not taken advantage of the chaotic situation of certain Islamic countries or of the confusion of the Islamic Diaspora in the West to dispose Koranic Schools for their violent, politico-religious proselytising.

Concerning the habitual exclusion of females from the Koranic School, it should be kept in mind that this is not original to Islam but can be found in all the principle religious traditions (Christianity, Judaism, Hinduism). Reagan (2000) pointed out that traditional Hindu education excludes not just girls but also inferior castes. Certain historical studies even go against common sense about Islamic education. Marty (1921) thus noted that girls are quite numerous in Koranic Schools in Foutu in Guinea. They make up a third and sometimes half of the class. It is quite common for wealthy families to send girls for a year, and even for two or three, to learn the *Fatiha* and the *surats* of the end of the book, and to learn proper prayer techniques. In Northern Nigeria, a survey of UNICEF (1999) found that there are 16,648 Koranic schools with 1,145,111 pupils. Only 184,592 or 16.1% are attending primary school, out of which 38.1% are female.

5   Toward a Mobilisation of the Koranic School for Basic Education?

In many countries in Western and Northern Africa one can witness how the recent expansion of the Koranic School has reduced the phenomena of non-schooling delineated by official statistics and international experts. According to Easton & Kane (2000), the search for alternative solutions has taken many forms: community schools sponsored by the state or by an NGO, pilot schools sponsored by the state (generally traditional elementary schools chosen to try innovative, community-based methods), an increase in interest in Koranic instruction or in hybrid forms that combine Muslim and Western instruction and also private schools created by independent businessmen, especially in urban zones.

In Mali, for example, school attendance figures have been in continual decline since the eighties (30% in 1980, 23% in 1990). This loss of interest in public schooling has been counter-balanced by the growth of 'private' schooling.

Koranic Schools, *madrasa* (schools which give both secular and religious instruction) and community schools have proliferated and have seen their attendance numbers rise (Etienne, 1994). In the rural area of Kangaré in the southwest of Mali, where Etienne (1994) did his research, the number of *madrasa* quadrupled in ten years. While attendance rates in the public sector continually went down over more than a decade, nearly half (49.6%) of all students in the area took Islamic instruction. Unlike Koranic Schools which deal only with religious instruction, the *madrasa* have the distinctive feature of presenting a syncretic and bilingual instruction: given in both Arabic and French, both religious and secular. This type of instruction conveys not only Koranic precepts but also French, reading, writing and mathematics. This combination responds to a double necessity, on the one hand placing the child 'on the road to God' and on the other on the road to 'progress and modernity'. The weakness of the formal educational system, founded exclusively on the Western model, led to the development of an original education, both religious and secular, in which tradition and modernity come together in a new pedagogical and cultural syncretism.

In Niger, the number of Koranic Schools is estimated at around 40,000 in 1990. This number easily surpasses the number of public schools (Easton, 1999). In reality this type of instruction constitutes an alternative to the official, Western-style schools and presents a 'hidden culture' of knowledge that goes against official school culture but which also integrates certain elements.

This reorientation of the social demand for education cannot solely be explained by a repudiation of public schooling. Considered in the past as a way toward social promotion, public schooling, founded on the extractive, Western model inherited from colonisation, no longer fits the expectations of parents. Public schools seem incapable of giving their children a useful base for obtaining a job or instilling them with techniques that they can count on in the future. This observation was made by a working group on informal education, ADEA (Association for the Development of Education in Africa). The credibility granted to the Koranic School has greatly increased in the past few years. Parents choose Koranic schooling because they consider it to be a factor of social integration because of what it teaches (the laws of the Koran and Islamic morality in particular). In a way it would appear that, by means of the educational strategies of the Koranic School, the populations of Western Africa are 'reinventing' basic education. In addition, this school adapts itself to the lifestyle of the population it serves. Thus, in Mauritania, the Koranic School is perfectly established in nomadic life. The educational situation of the country draws its novelty from the association of modern and traditional instruction (Ould Ahmadou, 1997).

Educational difficulties are often connected to the management style of Western-style school, generally centralised and unconnected to village communities. In addition, as Gatti (2001) correctly points out, the greater and more diverse the participation of the community in school management, the easier the children can access the school and the higher the quality of the education.

According to Easton (1999), the practical outcomes of Koranic instruction in Western Africa can be summarised in three points:

1. An introduction to writing, and to a lesser degree mathematics, to a large proportion of the population, men and women, of which a large number would otherwise have had no access to such instruction. Those who continue long enough to learn how to read, write and count well enough for practical daily use (generally in an African language, as a functional understanding of Arabic remains fairly limited) make up a minority, often a large minority in certain cases. Among other things, literacy in Arabic has become a point of reference in many small towns and rural areas, largely considered illiterate according to Western criteria.

2. Training for local leaders, since a solid Muslim education is generally accepted as an indication of morality, honesty and discipline; thus a basic, necessary qualification for holding functions of responsibility in the community.

3. Economic and social promotion, which has always been the case, but even more so recently given the lack of interest for formal instruction. This is possible because of the close connection between relational networks of Koranic Schools and traditional commercial networks of the region. Koranic School graduates are better able to find work or to find an apprenticeship with traditional businesses and in the informal commercial sector.

In Morocco, the revival of the Koranic School is connected to the inability of the state to extend basic education. Thus, Koranic Schools make up the most widespread form of preschool in the country. They provide instruction of a 'renovated traditional' style. Koranic Schools serve 67% of all preschool children. However, the percentage of girls is only 27.1% against 44.6% in modern preschool (Ministry of Education, 2000). Numerous studies on Moroccan village communities and the relationships between teachers and villagers shows that in this rural area the modern school is viewed with distrust and with scepticism regarding its usefulness. Schools and teachers are not chosen by the local community and are clearly seen as culturally outsiders. They are placed by the state and then proceed to impose their lifestyle and their way of thinking, which can be very different from that of the local way (Zouggari, 1991). In

Tunisia, rural farmers show the same mistrust toward agricultural technicians who are supposed to be helping them (Akkari, 1993). In a recent study in the North of Morocco, Tawil (1996, 2000) shows that the Koranic School plays an essential role in the education of the rural poor. It alleviates the absence of official schooling more than it expresses a cultural refusal against this school.

All the signs of a revival of the Koranic School should push states with large Muslim populations, and which are having difficulty at developing basic education, to make attempts to integrate Koranic Schools into their educational structures or to gain inspiration from the pedagogical and social experience, often secular, accumulated by such institutions (Colonna, 1984). Such a position in no way rules out an attentive and critical examination of this form of education, and of how it relates to the local culture and the larger society, in such a way as to create the possibility for 'another school', one which would be socio-culturally appropriate (Wagner, 1988).

Looking at forms of modern schooling introduced in non-Western parts of the world, with very few exceptions, the model is similar to the one that has already been in place since the 19th century in Europe. This model exhibits centralising and urban hegemony, specifically designed to do away with differences, not just on a linguistic level, but more importantly at the level of representations (representations of the world, or time and space and of social relations), thus constituting a form of violence against villagers and also against the developing urban proletariat (Colanna, 1984). Taken outside of the West,[9] these models, while new national powers and the local elite endorsed them, were no less distant from the cultures upon which they were imposed. The Western style schooling is an extractive model, particularly in Africa, where children who succeed go away from their local communities (Serpell, 1999).

By comparison, a Koranic School and the village in which it is located would appear to have a symbiotic relationship, with its temporal rhythm and spatial structure, much more so than the best-intentioned modern school could hope. Tawil (2004) pointed out, on the basis of field research in Northern Morocco, that local communities are resisting the supply of 'secular' basic education from the state and, when asked, declare that they would send their children to public schools if the curriculum took more account of Islamic values and if teachers were hired from within their own communities. The strength of Koranic Schools rests on its community support and the high level of commitment of both parents and teachers. The *Wakf* provides resources to sustain and develop and adapt Islamic schools to modernity. *Wakf* is a social, legal and religious institution which played an important role in the social, cultural and economic way of life of the Islamic world, especially the period, from middle of the 8th century until the end of the 19th century. The Islamic *wakf* (called *habous* in North Africa) can be defined as an action of a member of a Muslim society motivated by an element of the Islamic culture to transform some or all of his personal assets into pious foundations which will serve the public.

To address the problem of basic education in Northern Nigeria, UNICEF (1999) recommends a state policy deliberately and directly addressing the problems of Koranic Schools in terms of integrating elements of basic education, funding and management. Adequate learning materials and equipment should be provided for both Koranic literacy as well as for basic education programme.

6 Conclusion

The Koranic School is a traditional mode of schooling and an introduction into the culture of literacy, an aspect which is usually not taken into account by public education policy. It also represents an original form of learning.

TABLE 1.2   The Koranic School: an original form of learning

	Representation of the learner	Methods of learning	Age-space-time of learning	Social reproduction
Society without schooling	Ethnotheories	Empiric participation in the learning process	Everywhere in the social settings	Limited social reproduction through education
Koranic School	Potential believer	Teaching content coming from divine will	Koranic School and social settings	Limited social reproduction through Koranic School
Society with schooling	Representations of the child, the adolescent and the adult	Imposition of goals and teaching methods Teaching content coming from scientific rationality	Age-space-time of education are centred in schools	Strong social reproduction through the school Social changes through the school

It can be regarded as an alternative to public schooling in some Islamic areas, in particular when the State does not have the human and financial capacities of mass schooling. In some Islamic contexts, Koranic Schools offer formal education which either replaces or complements state-run education. Beyond the apparent pedagogical archaism of Koranic Schools (memorisation, fixed curriculum, etc.), this form of education is making schooling more accessible to local communities. It is a highly personalised experience wherein every teacher and student is acquainted with one another at an intimate level. It is certainly possible that the phenomenon of Koranic School revival, in multiple Islamic contexts, is linked to the efficiency of this institution in the development of literacy skills in the least educated layers of society. For researchers in comparative education, schools linked to the Islamic tradition in many parts of the world may represent a new more rooted form of learning in and through revitalised community, a kind of 'no man's land' neither narrowly 'Westerner' nor 'traditional' (Morah, 2000; Luckens-Bull, 2001). Emerging here is a 'pedagogy of place', a theoretical framework that emphasises the necessary interpenetration of culture, school, community, and environment, whether it's urban, suburban, or rural (Akkari & Dasen, 2004; Sobel, 2004). As an original form of learning, the Koranic School thus deserves to be the subject of future studies in comparative education and anthropology.

Acknowledgement

This chapter originally appeared as: Akkari, A-J. (2004) Socialization, learning and basic education in Koranic Schools, *Mediterranean Journal of Educational Studies*, Vol. 9(2), pp. 1–22. Reprinted here with permission from the publisher.

Notes

1   It should be noted that the opposition between Western and Koranic schools has been contested by Lecomte (1954), who underscored the continuity from the Byzantine School to the Koranic one. Reagan (2000), for his part, considers that the Western and Koranic educational traditions draw from the same religious sources. It is also necessary to add that the Koranic School undertook profound transformations toward the end of the 19th century, such as during the introduction of secular subjects. These changes were halted by colonisation. Makdisi (1981) has argued convincingly for a major Islamic contribution to the emergence of the first universities in the medieval West, showing how terms such as having 'fellows' holding a 'chair', or students 'reading' a subject and obtaining 'degrees', as well as practices such as inaugural lectures and academic robes, can all be traced back to Islamic concepts and practices. Indeed. the idea of a university in the modern sense—a place of learning where

SOCIALISATION, LEARNING AND BASIC EDUCATION IN KORANIC SCHOOLS 21

students congregate to study a wide variety of subjects under a number of teachers—is generally regarded as an Arabic innovation, developed at the al-Azhar university in Cairo. Makdisi has demonstrated that cities bordering the Islamic world (Salerno, Naples, Bologna, Montpellier) developed the first European universities.

2 Unless otherwise noted in this paper, the term 'Koranic School' refers to Islamic schools at the primary and secondary levels.

3 Being an Arabic speaker and a former Koranic School student, I purposely did not use any 'autobiographical' elements in the writing of this text. It is however likely that the tone of this text has been influenced by the researcher's personal experience.

4 One finds a large presence of partially sighted or blind persons among the best 'readers' of the Koran.

5 It should be noted that this ritual dimension is present in other religious educations, for example, Gurugé (1982) in Buddhist pedagogy.

6 It should be noted that this domestication did not always give the desired results for the colonisers. While the first generation of resistance fighters, against the colonisation in Algeria and Tunisia, were taught in Islamic schools, the second generation, which gained independence in Tunisia and which started the war for independence in Algeria, was the product of a double education, 'Arab' and 'French'. A typical example is Bourguiba, who completed his secondary studies in a traditional high school in Tunisia and then went on to obtain a law degree in Paris.

7 See 'Madrasah', in the Oxford Encyclopaedia of the Modern Islamic World (New York: Oxford University Press, 1995).

8 Situated learning depends on two claims difficult to find in Koranic Schools:
   – It makes no sense to talk of knowledge that is decontextualised, abstract or general.
   – New knowledge and learning are properly conceived as being located in communities of practice.

9 Many scholars pointed out that modern schooling in the West contributes to separating children from adults and to make instruction a meaningless activity (Charlot, Bautier & Rochex, 1992; Vincent, 1994).

References

Akkari, A. (1993) *Modernisation des Petits Paysans: Une Mission Impossible?* Tunis: Éditions Éducation & Cultures.

Akkari, A., & Dasen, P. (eds.) (2004) *Pédagogues et Pédagogies du Sud.* Paris: L'Harmattan.

Bernstein, B. (1996) *Pedagogy, Symbolic Control and Identity: Theory, Research, Critique.* London: Taylor & Francis.

Brenner, L. (1993) *Muslim Identity and Social Change in Sub-Saharan Africa.* London: Hurst & Company.

Chardon, S. C. (2000) Expérience de soutien en lecture auprès des élèves faibles lecteurs de fin de cycle 3, *Revue Française de Pédagogie,* Vol. 130, pp. 107–119.

Charlot, B., Bautier, E., & Rochex, Y. (1992) *École et Savoir dans les Banlieues et Ailleurs.* Paris: Armand Colin.

Colonna, F. (1981) La répétition: les Tolba dans une commune rurale de l'Aurès. In Ch. Souriau (ed.) *Le Maghreb Musulman en 1979*. Paris: CNRS Editions.

Colonna, F (1984) *Le Kuttab 'École Coranique': Prime Éducation Islamique et Diversification du Champ Éducatif*. Paris. Institut International de planification de l'éducation.

Coulon, C. (ed.) (1993) *Da'wa, Arabisation et Critique de l'Occident*. Paris: Karthala.

Delval, R. (1980) *Les Musulmans au Togo*. Paris: Publications Orientalistes de France (CHEAM).

Désalmand, P. (1983) *L'Histoire de l'Éducation en Côte-d'Ivoire: 1: Des Origines à la Conférence de Brazzaville*. Abidjan: CEDA.

Douglass S. L., & Shaikh, M. A. (2004) Defining Islamic education: differentiation and applications, *Current Issues in Comparative Education*, Vol. 7(1), pp. 5–18.

Easton, P. (1999) Education et alphabétisation en Afrique de l'ouest grâce à l'enseignement coranique, *Notes sur les Connaissances Autochtones*, No. 11, pp. 1–4.

Easton, P., & Kane, L. (2000) Les savoirs locaux et l'école: le potentiel et les dangers de l'enseignement communautaire dans les régions de l'Ouest du Sahel, *Notes sur les Connaissances Autochtones*, No. 22, pp. 1–3.

Eickelman, D. F. (1978) The art of memory: Islamic education and its social reproduction, *Comparative Studies in Society and History*, Vol. 20(4), pp. 485–516.

Eickelman, D. F. (1985) *Knowledge and Power in Morocco: The Education of a Twentieth-Century Noble*. Princeton: Princeton University Press.

El Ayadi, M. (2004) Entre l'Islam et l'Islamisme: la religion dans l'école publique marocaine, *Revue Internationale d'Éducation*, Vol. 36, pp. 111–122.

El-Sayed Darwish, K. (1981) Developing Koranic Schools to meet the educational needs of the young child. In Notes, Comments. UNESCO-UNICEF, WFP, NS-86, August 1981.

Etienne, G. (1997) *La Tentation du Savoir en Afrique: Politiques, Mythes et Stratégies d'Éducation au Mali*. Paris: Karthala-IRD.

Fiske., A. P. (1997) *Learning a Culture the Way Informants do: Observing, Imitating, and Participating*. Washington, DC: American Anthropological Association Panel.

Freire, P. (1993) *Pedagogy of the Oppressed*. New York: Continuum.

Gatti, C. (2001) Écoles Coraniques au sud du Sahara face à la 'patrimonialisation' de l'UNESCO: problème ou ressource? L'exemple de Djenné (Mali). In *Actes du VIII-ème Congrès de l'Association pour la Recherche Interculturelle* (ARIC), Université de Genève, 24–28 Septembre 2001.

Geertz, C. (1994) The uses of diversity. In R. Borofesky (ed.) *Assessing Cultural Anthropology*. New York: McGraw.

Goody, J. (1979) *La Raison Graphique: La Domestication de la Pensée Sauvage*. Paris: Minuit.

Grandin, N., & Gaborieau, M. (eds.) (1997) *Madrasa: La Transmission du Savoir dans le Monde Musulman*. Paris: Arguments.

Gurugé, A. W. P. (1982) *The Miracle of Instruction*. Colombo: Lake House.

Hoffman, D. M. (1999) Culture and comparative education: toward decentering and recentering the discourse, *Comparative Education Review*, Vol. 43(4), pp. 464–488.

IIPE (1984) *Les Formes Traditionnelles d'Éducation et la Diversification du Champ Éducatif: Le Cas des Écoles Coraniques*. Paris: Institut International de Planification de l'Éducation.

Khayar, I. (1976) *Le Refus de l'École: Contribution à l'Étude des Problèmes d'Éducation chez les Musulmans du Ouaddai (Tchad)*. Paris: Maisonneuve.

Lange, M-F. (2000) Naissance de l'école en Afrique Subsaharienne, *Pour*, No. 165, pp. 51–59.

Launay, R. (1982) *Traders without Trade: Responses to Change in two Dyula Communities*. Cambridge: Cambridge University Press.

Lave, J., & Wenger, E. (1991) *Situated Learning: Legitimate Peripheral Participation*. Cambridge: University of Cambridge Press.

Lecomte, G. (1954) La vie scolaire à Byzance et dans l'Islam. In *Arabica*, T. X., pp. 225–242.

Luckens-Bull, R. A. (2001) Two sides of the same coin: modernity and tradition in Islamic education in Indonesia, *Anthropology and Education Quarterly*, Vol. 32(3), pp. 350–372.

Makdisi, G. (1981) *The Rise of Colleges: Institutions of Learning in Islam and the West*. Edinburgh: Edinburgh University Press.

Marty, P. (1921) *L'Islam en Guinée: Fouta-Djallon*. Paris: Editions Ernest Leroux.

Meunier, O. (1997) *Dynamique de l'Enseignement Islamique au Niger: Le Cas de la Ville de Maradi*. Paris: L'Harmattan.

Ministry of Education (2000) *Statistique Scolaires*. Rabat: Author.

Morah, E. U. (2000) Old institutions, new opportunities: the emerging nature of Koranic Schools in Somaliland in the 1990s, *International Journal of Educational Development*, Vol. 20(4), pp. 305–22.

Ould Ahmadou, E. G. (1997) *Enseignement Traditionnel en Mauritanie: La Mahdara ou l'École 'à dos de Chameau'*. Paris: L'Harmattan.

Plancke, M. (1971) Le kuttab en 'Ifriqiya du VIIe au XIIe siècle: contribution à l'histoire de l'enseignement élémentaire en Tunisie, *Paedagogica Historica*, Vol. 10, pp. 225–242.

Reagan, T. (2000) *Non-Western Educational Traditions: Alternative Approaches to Educational Thought and Practice*. Mahwah, NJ: Erlbaum.

Richard-Molard, J. (1954) *Islam ou Colonisation au Fouta-Djalon*. Paris: Présence Africaine.

Sanneh, L. (ed.) (1997) *Crown and the Turban: Muslims and West African Pluralism*. Boulder, CO: Westview Press.

Santerre, R. (1973) *Pédagogie Musulmane d'Afrique Noire: L'École Coranique Peule du Cameroun*. Montréal: Les Presses de l'Université de Montréal.

Santerre, R., & Mercier-Tremblay, C. (eds.) (1982) *La Quête du Savoir: Essais pour une Anthropologie de l'Éducation Camerounaise*. Montréal: Presses de l'Université de Montréal.

Serpell, R. (1999) Local accountability to rural communities: a challenge for educational planning in Africa. In F. E. Leach & A. W. Little (eds.) *Education, Cultures, and Economics: Dilemmas for Development*. New York & London: Falmer Press.

Serpell, R., & Hatano, G. (1997) Education, schooling, and literacy. In J. W. Berry, P. R. Dasen & T. S. Saraswathi (eds.) *Handbook of Cross-Cultural Psychology* (2nd edition, volume 2). Boston: Allyn & Bacon.

Sobel, D. (2004) *Place-based Education: Connecting Classrooms and Communities*. Barrington, MA: Orion.

Spiro, M. (1994) Some reflections on cultural relativism and relativism with special reference to emotion and reason. In R. A. Shweder & R. A. Levine (eds.) *Culture Theory: Essays on Mind, Self, and Emotion*. Cambridge: Cambridge University Press.

Sraieb, N. (1974) *Colonisation, Décolonisation et Enseignement: L'Exemple Tunisien*. Tunis: Publications de l'Institut National des Sciences de l'Éducation.

Tawil, S. (1996) Poverty and demand for primary education: evidence from Morocco, *Norrag News*, May 1996.

Tawil, S. (2000) Household demand, basis education and exclusion: focusing on out-of-school children in Morocco. In L-E. Malmberg, S-E. Hansén & K. Heino (eds.) *Basic Education for All: A Global Concern for Quality*. Vasa: Faculty of Education, Åbo Akademi University.

Tawil, S. (2004) *Basic Education, Exclusion and Development: Change, Crisis and Reform in Moroccan School Education*. PhD thesis, Graduate Institute of Development Studies, University of Geneva.

Thành Khoî, L. (1995) *Éducation et Civilisations*. Paris: Nathan.

Turin, Y. (1971) *Affrontements Culturels dans l'Algérie Coloniale: École, Médecines, Religion*. Paris: Maspéro.

UNICEF (1999) *Baseline Survey of Qur'anic Schools in Katsina, Kebbi, Sokoto and Zamfara States*. New York: Author.

Vincent, G. (ed.) (1994) *L'Éducation Prisonnière de la Forme Scolaire*. Lyon: Presses Universitaires de Lyon.

Wagner, D. (1988) 'Appropriate education' and literacy in the third world. In P. R. Dasen, J. W. Berry & N. Sartorius (eds.) *Health and Cross-Cultural Psychology: Towards Applications*. Newbury Park, CA: SAGE.

Wagner, D., & Lotfi, A. (1983) Learning to read by 'rote', *International Journal of the Sociology of Language*, Vol. 42, pp. 191–203.

Wenger, E. (1999) *Communities of Practice: Learning, Meaning and Identity.* Cambridge: Cambridge University Press.

Zouggari, A. (1991) *Stratégies des Agriculteurs en Matière d'Éducation: Jbala-Histoire et Société: Études sur le Maroc du Nord-Ouest.* Paris: CNRS.

CHAPTER 2

Is There a Semiperipheral Type of Schooling?

State, Social Movements and Education in Spain, 1970–1994

Xavier Bonal and Xavier Rambla

1   Introduction

If we had to adopt Western standards in educational development as a benchmark or referent, then Spain appears to be behind its continental neighbours, and somewhat a 'late-comer'. A mass school system had not been set up until the seventies, a true state school system had not existed until the eighties, participation in school decision-making had not been defined until 1985, and a system for vocational and educational training is still practically non-existent. These shortcomings have been key issues as far as educational legislation is concerned. The General Educational Act (LGE) of 1970 started a new model of state involvement in education. The school system had been historically dominated by the Church. The LGE 1970 signalled the first step in a change of state intervention culture, aiming to universalise provision of eight years of compulsory education and to extend post-compulsory secondary education. After Franco's death in 1975, democratic governments had to set the conditions for participation. The inheritance of a strong private educational system raised a political right-left contention. In 1981 a right-wing act was passed defending absolute ideological autonomy of schools. When Socialists came into power in 1982, they repealed the act and passed a new one based on a public model of schooling (Act on the Right to Education, LODE, 1985). These struggles have delayed curriculum change until the approval of the 1990 General Educational System Act (LOGSE).

A similar pattern of events can be observed when we look at different dimensions of Spanish social structure. Economic organisation, public services, family patterns, labour markets, social movements, and so on have only recently adopted models prevailing in Western countries (Maravall, 1985; Espina Montero, 1989; Flaquer, 1990; Miguélez & Prieto, 1991). For this reason, many authors argue that Spain is a backward country that is trying to accelerate its modernisation process (Moreno & Sarasa, 1993).

It is our view that these alleged shortcomings must be contextualised within a reality distinct from Western countries, the 'centre' from where sociology normally analyses the phenomena. Other views assert that elements constituting

© THE EURO-MEDITERRANEAN CENTRE FOR EDUCATION RESEARCH, UNIVERSITY OF MALTA, 1996
DOI: 10.1163/9789004506602_002

social structures are articulated in different ways in different states or regions. With respect to education, Green (1990), Dale (1989) and Ramirez & Boli (1987) are supporters of this thesis. They see educational systems and the role of the state as the product of specific historical processes which have salient differences in spite of partial similarities, and therefore cannot be simply compared quantitatively.

In this article we want to ask if some of the issues raised by authors like Tilly (1993), Malefakis (1992), Santos (1990a, 1990b, 1992), Stoer, Stoleroff & Correia (1990) or Correia, Stoleroff & Stoer (1993) contribute meaningfully toward an analysis of state intervention in Spanish educational policy. These authors have tried to sketch a South European region in their consideration of features of social structure or forms of state intervention. More specifically, we want to focus on Santos' theory of semiperipheral social structures and on the related analysis of the educational system in Portugal by Stoer (1994).

2   The Theory of Semiperipheral Societies Applied to Education

According to Santos (1992, p. 109), semiperipheral societies are characterised by a significant articulated mismatch between production and social consumption, that is to say, consumption patterns are closer to central capitalist countries than is development of production. However, two factors enable society to cope with this mismatch. First of all, buffer groups in the social structure help meet the deficits of public provision. They fulfil the needs that markets and the state fulfil in other economies. For instance, and with reference to the Spanish case, we can point out that women's domestic labour has played a key role in substituting welfare state provision; underground economy has complemented income in many areas and has helped many families to survive; and family support is necessary for small businesses, which represent one of the mainstays of the labour market.

State regulation has to be very wide in order to arbitrate these groups' decentralised and scarcely institutionalised practices (Santos, 1990a, 1990b). That is, the state is central in social and economic regulation, even though its direct intervention in production or in service provision is very narrow. For instance, social legislation allows some private institutions to provide education, health or social services, but maintains a bureaucratic control over their organisation. The main consequence of such an articulated mismatch is that the state is internally strong because of its wide field of activities, but it is often weakened by its own regulation: due to the heterogeneity of its policies, its legitimation is continuously strained.

In summary, following Santos, we can argue that in semiperipheral societies the contradiction between accumulation and legitimation is more acute than in central societies. Where a strong state has to deal with many heterogeneous demands,[1] solutions to core problems of the capitalist state often become more contradictory because decisions setting accumulation conditions easily damage state legitimation. Stoer, Stoleroff & Correia (1990), Correia, Stoleroff & Stoer (1993) and Gomes (1994) draw on Santos' ideas when analysing the semiperipheral features of Portuguese educational system and policy. Thus far, this theory has not been applied to the Spanish case: however, some considerations allow us to think that similarities between Spain and Portugal can be analysed from the same theoretical perspective.

We could argue that the main mismatch pointed out by Santos can be translated into the educational field. The fact that the expansion of education and the economic crisis have taken place simultaneously in countries like Portugal, Spain or Greece, may explain the mismatch between educational 'production' (provision) and 'consumption' (demand) (Gomes, 1994). In the case of Spain this can be observed in the surplus of students at the higher education level or in the inefficiency of the grant system to guarantee the continuity of eligible students. The mismatch is also noticeable at other educational levels. For instance, although female activity rates are increasing (Espina Montero, 1989)—and therefore, so is demand for infant schooling, there is a lack of nurseries to facilitate it. Besides, although many teenagers leave school at sixteen or seventeen (Casal, Masjuan & Planas, 1991), there is not a complete vocational education and training system for them.

Buffer groups make it possible to cope with this mismatch. Family networks take care of children or unemployed teenagers and family economies have to pay for indirect costs of higher education. That is one of the reasons why increasingly youngsters leave home later in life (Casal, 1994).

As Santos (1990a, 1990b) suggests, in spite of deficits in educational provision, the state is able to manage the legitimation crisis through the production of legal measures. For instance, the state allows the private sector and local governments (which are not legally in charge) to provide infant schooling or youth training schemes. That is, the state is able to transfer educational provision to other actors when it cannot meet the demands. This type of educational policy broadens state regulation but moves it away from managing the final delivery of its service. Therefore, internal contradictions in educational policy-making are especially acute. For instance, the Act on the Right to Education (LODE, 1985) had to standardise school organisation although half of the schools belonged to the private sector (Boix i Navarro & García Suárez, 1985).

Similarly, the hiring of teachers remains very bureaucratic and centralised (Gimeno Sacristan, 1994), whereas school autonomy has increased.

Stoer, Stoleroff & Correia (1990) and Bonal (1995) have shown how these internal contradictions lead to a specific logic of curriculum policy-making. Stoer, Stoleroff & Correia (1990) draw on Fritzell's (1987) arguments about the education-production correspondence to make a case that negative correspondence is more likely to pattern curriculum policy in semiperipheral societies. That is, due to legitimation problems, the state relies on structural autonomy and promotes democratic values more than industrial values. Bonal (1995) extends this thesis to the analysis of the last Spanish educational reform, arguing how expressive contents are particularly meaningful in curriculum change.

3 The Specificities of Educational Policy in a Semiperipheral Social Formation: The Case of Spain

In this section we try to sketch an explanation of the way in which Santos' arguments can be applied to an analysis of the recent history of the Spanish educational system. It is our view that this historical approach has to introduce the role of agents in order to grasp the formation, the evolution and the consequences of semiperipheral contradictions in educational policy-making. In Giddens' terms (1993), we want to focus on the structuration of educational policy-making, considering both agents and structures. The interplay between agents and structures crystallises in what Dale (1989) refers to as the 'mandate' of an educational system. A mandate is an action programme establishing what is desirable and legitimate to expect from an educational system. At a certain moment, a specific mandate of an educational system is simultaneously shaped by the former mandate, the demands emerging from agents and through the social structure. This interplay fixes the limits of what is achievable and what is not in educational policy-making. In a semiperipheral state such as Spain, the ascendance of the state has become quite relevant, since it has imposed its own dynamics over the link between mandates and contradictions, and has even succeeded—at least temporarily—to model agents pressing over educational policy.

In the recent period of Spanish history several mandates have co-existed, but one of them has tended to predominate. Four periods may be distinguished in relation to the interplay between mandates, contradictions and agents (see Table 2.1 for an overview).

TABLE 2.1 The changing mandates of education policy in Spain (1970–1994)

Mandate	Structural contradictions	Main agents
1970–1977		
Building a meritocratic educational system	Raising expectations vs. low participation and poor facilities	– Technocratic political elites – Religious private sector – Fragmentary anti-francoist opposition
1978–1982		
Democratisation of access to education (cost-free public education, building schools, conditions for participation)	– Previous mandate – Low participation – Unchanging teachers' working conditions – Ideology of economic restrictions	Institutionalisation of demands: – The right represents the interests of the religious private sector – The left absorbs demands from community associations
1982–1985		
– Improvement of the public sector by organising and broadening it – Modernising the educational system according to European standards	– Non-involvement of 'industrial trainers' in educational policy – The existence of a dual educational system	– Religious and private elitist schools – Nationalistic political parties and other sectors – Teachers' union demands
1986–1994		
– Curriculum change – Excellence – New concept of citizenship: an individualistic model	– Low prestige of VET – Scarce resources – Democratic deficits – Bureaucratic assessment vs. de-regulation	– Teachers against labour conditions – Students against numerus clausus – Discreet involvement of new social movements in education

3.1 The 1970–1977 Mandate

From 1970 to 1977 the late Francoist governments tried to redefine the mandate of the educational system in Spain. Since 1857 there had not been an Education Act. The old mandate had just required educating elites and keeping the masses ignorant, because their literacy was openly perceived as a threat (De Puelles, 1986). Some internal (migrations, baby-boom, emergence of technocratic elites) and external (agreement with EEC, foreign investment, tourism) factors provoked the need to legislate on many areas, one of them being education. The new mandate implied, therefore, a formal divide in Spanish history: *it aimed to set conditions for meritocratic reproduction.* Thus new technocratic elites could reproduce their positions and the external image of the regime was improved.

Such a change in the political agenda of Francoism highlighted a *contradiction* that already existed due to the increasing number of students in universities (Lerena, 1986). All of a sudden, the elitist educational system that could not manage massified universities declared it would provide equal opportunities for everybody. The consequence was that expectations were enhanced whereas participation was not allowed and facilities were not provided. Perception of deficits was automatically multiplied as neither primary schooling was guaranteed nor was massified university helped. And what is more, the old monopoly of religious private schools, being based on the accepted and provoked shortcomings of the state system, was challenged.

Of course. implementation of LGE has oscillated from side to side during the twenty years when it has been the basic scheme of the Spanish educational system.

The interests of three main agents—namely, political elites, the Church and opposition movements—should be taken into account in order to understand why a true counter-reform was launched between 1971 to 1977. With respect to political elites, it can be suggested that state auto-rationalisation had begun in 1959 when economic policy had been orientated in line with the OECD pattern. Free exchange rates and wider economic liberalisation eroded the basis over which the Financial Aristocracy had reconstructed its *ancien régime* hegemony in Spain (Moya, 1975). A new bureaucratic elite was born and consolidated around the Catholic movement called *Opus Dei.* Substitution of old factions supporting Francoism (the Party, pro-aristocratic Catholics, and the military) in Ministries, and aristocratic surnames in the main boards of directors attained its peak by 1970. At first LGE aimed to broaden this new rationalistic legitimation.[2]

However, the aims of LGE were not accomplished because resources were diverted and potential support was eroded. Actually, its early implementation consisted of transferring huge subsidies to religious private schools in order to make sure that universal schooling could in fact be provided despite the lack of attention and resources accorded to the public system. Some pro-Church politicians negotiated this arrangement, although Catholic political dissent was notable. Furthermore, some university professors and school teachers withdrew political reformist pressure after the first legal developments (Subirats, 1974).[3]

Social movements increasingly exerted pressure but they failed to constitute a coordinated nation-wide platform. In the educational field social movements drew their strength from three sources, namely the professional class, the working-class, and community associations. But these found expression in a middle class, professionalised movement and a working-class suburb-based movement. The first had its roots in Catalonia and Euskadi, where the middle-classes turned to the school in order to ensure new and academic ways to guarantee social and cultural reproduction (Subirats, 1975). The second one remained restricted to a local context, where educational and labour demands often merged (Balfour, 1990).

In summary, during this mandate the state was able to define a formally meritocratic educational system, but it could not implement it fully because structural contradictions and fragmentary societal demands restricted what was actually achievable.

3.2   The 1978–1982 Mandate

A second period can be distinguished between 1978 to 1982. This is the first democratic period, also known as the phase of political transition. The new mandate tried to respond to former contradictions without substantially changing either the structure of the system or the curriculum. The 1978 Moncloa Agreement between parliamentary parties (Socialists and Communists who represented trade unions as well) defined educational policy as one of the main instruments leading to an equitable distribution of the burden of economic crisis (Bas, 1978). Specifically, the mandate could be summarised by stating that educational policy was entrusted to bridge the gap between the LGE of 1970 and actual policy ever since. The main agenda in educational politics was an ambitious construction programme since several schools had to be built if access to education was to be democratised.

Naturally, the same contradictions highlighted by the late Francoist counter-reform were salient during the period of political transition. But new contradictions emerged too. Firstly, although participation was now not only allowed but also proclaimed, its range and intensity did not increase dramatically (Fernández Enguita, 1993). Secondly, some professional demands—such as teachers' claim for increased status, or young university teachers' lobby consisting of demands about labour conditions and pedagogy—were delayed because Socialist parliamentary opposition blocked the Centrist government project for university autonomy (*Ley de Autonomía Universitaria*, LAD, 1981) and also eroded its act on school organisation (*Ley Orgánica de Estatuto de Centros Educativos*, LOECE, 1981) (De Puelles, 1986). Thirdly, perception of deficits was institutionalised and simultaneously counteracted by official discourse on the grounds of restricting expenditure in times of crisis.

Pluralism was adopted in educational policy-making, thus redefining the role of agents. Both bureaucratic elites and the Church configurated their interests in the new *Union de Centro Democrático*, the party backing the government. Parliamentary opposition, on the other hand, recruited a generation of younger politicians with the goal of developing a new cadre of professional elites and in the hope of striking a new deal with the Church. Thus, the school-building programme and the debate on organisational structures contributed toward the consolidation of new institutional actors. Socialists and Communists were instrumental in channelling social movement demands into this debate, one embracing health and housing as well as education. They convinced the unions that it was important to reach an agreement on these issues, and they co-opted leaders of the community associations movement into local governments. In some ways they absorbed forces from civil society so as to make the agreement possible.

As a consequence, demobilisation followed the institutionalisation of demands (Subirats, 1984; Lope, Jordana & Carrasquer, 1989) and a vague consciousness of consensus became a key but weak element of civic culture (Pérez Diaz, 1991b). It can be concluded that 'consensus', the main motto of political discourse during those years, gave rise to a 'silencer effect' (Orti, 1989). In Catalonia, for instance, the silencer effect may have relied on the split between locally-based demands on the one hand, and the debate on ethnicity on the other. After 1978 schools and primary health care centres became established to such an extent that popular expectations were quantitatively met, and the suburbs had obtained facilities they lacked. On the other hand, 1979 elections for the *Generalitat* autonomous Government galvanised a debate on ethnicity that consolidated a Catalan national consciousness. Political autonomy, abolished by Francoism after the Republic, had been a symbol for all political opposition movements, starting from those defending the immigrants' social rights to those defending Catalan political rights. In education, as in other fields, working-class and community association movements accepted the idea of political autonomy although it was not their priority. After the 1978 Agreement and the 1979 election a double-sided definition of ethnicity became hegemonic. Whereas Catalonia was homogeneously perceived as an oppressed nation within Spain, the meaning of its symbols merged with the perception of social inequalities in the Catalan context (Woolard, 1989). In this way, the abstract definition of ethnicity became the mark of nationhood and social rights were relegated.

We can conclude that democratisation of access was restricted to some quantitative issues during this mandate. Internal qualitative contradictions of schooling became salient and civil society was broken up by political parties.

3.3   The 1982–1985 Mandate

From 1982 to 1985 the new Socialist government brought about a significant change in Spanish education policy. The Socialists had already announced, during the Centrist legislature, their intention to repeal the Schools Administration Act (LOECE) passed in 1981. With the new legislature, Right and Left positions concerning educational policy were more rigidly defined than before. While the Right centred its discourse on school choice and an ideology of autonomy for private schools (even for those subsidised by the state), Socialists were basically supporters of the principle of equality of opportunity and of compensatory policies, and were especially involved in the development of a new education act meant to consolidate the public education sector as well as parental involvement in school administration.

Over and above such goals, educational policy had to start responding to the deep changes in economy and production. An efficient policy was necessary to modernise curricula and to improve teacher training, thus developing a better education system, one that was in synchrony with new societal demands.

Thus, during this period, the education policy mandate was shaped by the need to compensate for historical inequalities between private and public schools, but the educational system also had to avoid obsolescence, and to be closer to European educational systems (Maravall, 1985). Equality and excellence appeared as two simultaneous needs, ones that were in perpetual tension due to a poor educational budget.

But contradictions inside and outside the educational system made it very difficult to attain both goals. Excellence was a rather difficult objective for educational policy to achieve because there were no historical links with the production system. Besides, the very existence of a dual education system and the inheritance of a culture of school choice among the middle-classes constrained the state's attempts to unify criteria and to broaden the public sector. The political struggle over the Right to Education Act (LODE, 1985) illustrates the resistance that private schools could put up to guard themselves against loss of privileges. It was impossible to bring about any curriculum change

IS THERE A SEMIPERIPHERAL TYPE OF SCHOOLING?

before implementing a compensatory policy to correct historical inequalities. In this process of struggle, the ministry had to deal with different interests embodied by different agents. The Church and private elitist schools centred their demands against state interventionism on school ideology. The focus of the struggle was located on the school owner's freedom to hire and fire teachers depending on how close they were to the school ideology and practices. But the Socialist government also had to deal with another private school sector (CEPEPC)—a progressive one, born in Catalonia as an alternative to the national schools during Francoism—whose demands for moving into the public system had not yet been met.

On the other hand, the demands on the part of nationalist parties and other non-public educational organisations for the decentralisation of educational competencies added other difficulties to the development of a uniform policy in favour of equity (Boix i Navarro & García Suárez, 1985). In a context of insufficient funding, a compensatory policy could only be addressed by taking money away from one educational sector and allocating it to the public sector. This zero-sum game was in fact played out in part, and at the cost of private suburban schools, which almost disappeared during the eighties. But it did not affect Church schools or those of the secular bourgeoisie (Mayoral, 1989).

The consolidation of the public educational sector also had to face teachers' demands on labour conditions. Non-civil servant teachers (PNN)—who had begun their struggle in the late seventies—became a huge problem in the early eighties. At the same time, decentralisation processes put pressure on the state in terms of maintaining the same wage level for all Spanish teachers, including those working in regions with full competences on education budget allocations (Iriso, 1990). This process became particularly acute in Catalonia after 1987, since many teachers decided to leave their work places when knowledge of the Catalan language became a prerequisite for teaching in primary schools. Having left their work places, they were also losing some acquired privileges, since Catalan teachers had won a salary increase after 1987.

To summarise, in the 1982–1985 period, the conflictual interests of different agents collided in the discussion of the very controversial Right to Education Act (LODE). Here, the goal of educational equality of opportunity was, for the first time, an objective of educational policy. But this goal implied severe political costs to different social groups. Religious private schools, secular and progressive private schools, parents' associations, regional governments of teachers' unions: all of these had different interests and problems within the educational system. The very different reactions of these sectors during and after the passing of the 1985 LODE shows how impossible it is for the state to go beyond the content of the Act to move in the direction of a more Left-wing educational policy. Thus, a mandate aiming to find a balance between equity and excellence ran into difficulties mainly due to a low correspondence between education and production, and due to resistance from the private sector. Moreover, labour and nationalistic demands entered into the political agenda.[4]

3.4 The 1986–1994 Mandate

The state faced two challenges during the more recent period, 1986–1994. On the one hand, the state had to restructure the educational system in response to different pressures. Among these, one can mention internal decentralisation, European convergence of educational systems, and the implementation of LODE, all of which compelled the state to introduce changes in compulsory schooling and school administration. On the other hand, a curriculum change was particularly urgent. Schools were still under the 1970 General Education Act. Everything was out of date in terms of textbooks, knowledge areas, teacher training programmes, teachers' expectations and mobility, the vocational/academic division, and so on.

These two main challenges have modelled the new mandate of educational policy for the last decade. The state has had to change the structure and the content of the educational system. The most important word in current official discourse is quality of education. Actually, after the failure of Savary's Act in France (Weiler, 1989), Socialists learnt to focus on quality instead of equity.

The new mandate concentrated on excellence in educational provision as a means to achieve European competitiveness and also as a means to guarantee individual development. In this period there is a turn toward a new concern for citizenship. The 'social group' loses ascendance in the discourse in favour of the rights and duties of 'individuals', both as a vehicle for national development and in terms of developing personal potential.

A process culminating with the approval of the 1990 Educational Reform Act (LOGSE) bears witness to the constraints and contradictions which surround the project, and which determine both content and conditions for the implementation of the educational reform.

The contradictions that prevail in the implementation of the new mandate are internal and external to the education system. On the one hand, technical and vocational education has had neither the social status nor the public attention that academic education has enjoyed. Therefore, the 'new vocationalist' policy is used more as a tool for state legitimation than as a direct response to productive needs (Bonal, 1995).

Another problem concerns resources: although LOGSE declares educational expenditure must attain European levels, actual budgets do not (Garzón & Recio, 1992).

Thirdly, the Spanish educational system still has enormous democratic deficiencies which are directly translated into social pressures on the field of educational policy making. It is therefore difficult for the state to speak in terms of excellence of secondary schooling, since this sector has never been a compulsory or a comprehensive one. It is also difficult for the state to promote efficiency measures in school management and administration within a very bureaucratic mode of school assessment and inspection, or to develop a more democratic system of school participation (through school councils[5] included in LODE) whilst encouraging a more enterprise-run culture of school management. Actually, after the 1985 LODE, parental involvement in schools has been a complete failure. Thus, barely ten years later, the first draft of the new act on participation and quality places the responsibility for school administration in the hands of headteachers (MEC, 1994).

Finally, contradictions can also be identified in curricular aspects, and this mainly due to the low correspondence between education and production. Post-Fordist policies lose coherence when considering what labour places are available after vocational training. Contradictions are also located in curriculum decisions. Deregulation only operates at the level of curriculum decisions and practices whilst the state keeps a bureaucratic culture to assess teachers and schools (Gimeno Sacristan, 1994).

Concerning agents, only hypotheses can be advanced at this moment because, to our knowledge, there are no sociological analyses available on this issue. Certainly, demands exist, but they are fragmentary. The 1990 Educational Reform Act (LOGSE) is supported by a wide consensus in comparison to LODE. The only protest came from the Church and the Catholic Parents Associations, who were against the exclusion of religion as a compulsory subject in the curriculum.

Teachers launched a strike in 1989 claiming better wages and improved labour conditions in reaction to a policy favouring their economic proletarianisation. Students' movements protested against numerus clausus regulating access to university. In 1987 they launched another strike against this measure and the protest led to the resignation of the minister. Very particularised conflicts—such as claims against cuts of posts for philosophy teachers in secondary education, or struggles between short-term (*diplomatura*) and long-term (*licenciatura*) professional bodies—are spreading. On the other hand, new social movements have not been very effective in influencing educational policy, or, more specifically curriculum development. Feminist and environmentalist concerns do feature in curricula, but it is difficult to judge the extent to which this is a consequence of pressures from social movements. Moreover, feminist issues have been promoted through institutionalised channels.

However, this segmentation of interests might be overcome as long as civil society realises that LOGSE goals are not met due to budget cuts and delays. *Comisiones Obreras,* one of the main teachers' unions, has campaigned for a new financial act for the educational system. At the same time, there have been since 1994 a number of demonstrations by parents, teachers and students demanding a true implementation of LOGSE.

In summary, although the educational mandate has shifted from equality to quality, similar structural contradictions remain. This time, the state had regulated and contained both Right-wing and Left-wing demands, but potential dissent is noticeable among fragmentary and newly institutionalised interlocutors.

4   Conclusion

Educational policy must be analysed within a broader context that must be defined on theoretical grounds. In this article we have tried to point out the main features of schooling and educational policy in Spain. It is our view that the 'backwardness approach' should be avoided in order to grasp the specificities of a semiperipheral social formation. That implies taking both structural properties and the agents' role into account. Two concepts must therefore be related when analysing a semiperipheral type of schooling: mandate and contradictions influence agents, and conversely agents may raise recursive effects on mandate and contradictions.

Two main conclusions can be stated. First of all, our historical analysis of the Spanish system from 1970 to 1994 has shown the progressive structuring of a public school sector. However, in contrast with central countries, it is a semiperipheral type of schooling because it entails a significant gap between aspirations and provision. Although facilities were provided between 1978 and 1985, remaining qualitative and quantitative deficits have continued to produce structural contradictions. For this reason, Spanish schooling relies on buffer groups, has not been subjected to strong regulation, and keeps a low correspondence with the production system.

Secondly, legitimation through educational policy-making has been confronted with newly institutionalised and very fragmentary demands. The public-private contention has been especially acute between 1970 and 1985, this being the core political issue. With respect to the other demands, the eighties have witnessed the segmentation of the previous anti-Francoist consensus: teachers struggle for improved labour conditions, student movements protest against numerus clausus, a number of private secular schools struggle to

IS THERE A SEMIPERIPHERAL TYPE OF SCHOOLING?

become state schools, regions make nationalistic demands for decentralisation and so on. This kind of pressure has compelled the state to deal with many legitimation problems, and to institutionalise interlocutors for negotiation. These two points contribute to an understanding of the semiperipheral nature of Spanish schooling. Similarities with other Mediterranean countries could make comparison worthwhile for theoretical and empirical reasons.

Acknowledgement

This chapter originally appeared as: Bonal, X., & Rambla, X. (1996) Is there a semiperipheral type of schooling? State, social movements and education in Spain, 1970–1994, *Mediterranean Journal of Educational Studies*, Vol. 1(1), pp. 13–27. Reprinted here with permission from the publisher.

Notes

1 Certainly, every state deals with heterogeneous demands (Dale, 1989), but demands are even more heterogeneous in semiperipheral states because the social structure is much more fragmentary (Santos, 1990a).

2 We support this thesis instead of an alternative one stating that counter-reform can be explained simply by arguing that internationally homologated educational policy foundered because a weak industrial capitalist fraction had not enough strength to back it (Bozal et al., 1975). Agents disappear in this deterministic view since it implies that a necessary process of modernisation is halted because one of its alleged necessary conditions is not fulfilled.

3 In fact, the Church found itself in an ironic situation. On the one hand, state religious confession and generous educational subsidies show that the Church was at the height of its hegemonic power. On the other hand, however and simultaneously, many clerics were questioning their own Church's triumph by pointing out that young people, workers and non-Castilian citizens had been ignored (Pérez Diaz, 1991a), and that the key educational issues raised by these categories had not been dealt with by the LGE.

4 Educational policy during this period might have provided an appropriate context for the take-off of the public education sector. However, more qualitative goals linked to the development of a policy favouring equality of opportunity and including reforms of curricula and of vocational education were not met. The fact that 'industrial trainers' were not involved in educational policy-making—especially in vocational education—did not contribute at all to substitute obsolete content and pedagogical methods. Qualitative changes did take place in the university sector. The universities went through a process of nationalisation, with departments being run by elected directors rather than personal chairs, and market-based degrees set up, for instance. Paradoxically however, access to the non-university sector remained quite undemocratic. Neither was this sector marked by an improvement in quality.

5 School councils are the main decision-making bodies at the school level. Teachers, parents, local government and pupils are represented.

References

Balfour, S. (1990) *The Workers, the City and Dictatorship.* Cambridge: Cambridge University Press.

Bas, J. M. (1978) Pacto de la Moncloa y política educativa, *Cuadernos de Pedagogía*, Vol. 37, pp. 34–37.

Boix i Navarro, M., & García Suárez, J. A. (1985) *La Lode Anàlisi i Comentaris des de Catalunya a una Llei Controvertida.* Barcelona: Universitat de Barcelona.

Bonal, X. (1995) Curriculum change as a form of educational policy legitimation: the case of Spain, *International Studies in Sociology of Education*, Vol. 5(2), pp. 203–220.

Bozal, V., Paramio, L., Alvarez, E., Perez, M., & Perez Galan, M (1975) *La Enseñanza en España.* Madrid: Alberto Corazón.

Calero, J. (1993) *Efectos del Gasto Publico Educativo: El Sistema de Becas Universitarias.* Barcelona: Universitat de Barcelona.

Casal, J. (1994) *L'emancipació Familiar des Joves.* PhD thesis, Universitat Auntònoma de Barcelona, Spain.

Casal. J., Masjuan, J. M., & Planas, J. (1991) *La Inserción Laboral y Social de los Jóvenes.* Madrid: CIDE.

Correia, J. A., Stoleroff, A. D., & Stoer, S. (1993) A ideologia da modernização no sistema educativo em Portugal, *Cadernos de Ciências Sociais*, Vol. 12/13, pp. 25–51.

Dale, R. (1989) *The State and Education Policy.* London: Open University Press.

De Puelles, M. (1986) *Educación e Ideología en España.* Barcelona: Labor.

Espina Montero, A. (1989) La mujer en el nuevo mercado de trabajo, *Economía y Sociología del Trabajo*, Vol. 6, pp. 19–38.

Fernández Enguita, M. (1993) *La Profesión Docente y la Comunidad Escolar: Crónica de un Desencuentro.* Madrid: Morata.

Flaquer, L. (1990) La familia española: cambio y perspectivas. In S. Giner (ed.) *España: Sociedad y Política.* Madrid: Epasa-Calpe.

Fritzell, C. (1987) On the concept of relative autonomy in educational theory, *British Journal of Sociology of Education*, Vol. 8(1), pp. 23–35.

Giddens, A. (1993) *The Constitution of Society: Outline of a Theory of Structuration.* Los Angeles: University of California Press.

Garzón, B., & Recio, M. (1992) Reforma educativa y convergencia europea. *El País*, 3 de marzo.

Gay, J., Quitllet, R., & Pascual, A. (1973) *Societat Catalana i Reforma Escolar.* Barcelona: Laia.

Gimeno Sacristan, J. (1994) La desregulación del currículum y la autonomía de los centros escolares, *Signos: Teoría y Práctica de la Educación*, Vol. 13, pp. 4–20.

Gomes, R. (1994) *O Discurso Educativo e o Poder: Ensaio Analítico das Retóricas Educativa em Portugal (1974–1991).* Paper presented at 'Il Congrés Català de Sociologia', 15–16 April, Girona, Spain.

Gómez Llorente, L. (1983) La política educativa, *Cuadernos de Pedagogía*, Vo1. 100, pp. 12–20.

Green, A. (1990) *Education and State formation: The Rise of Education Systems in England, France and the USA*. London: Macmillan.

Iriso, P. L. (1990) Estructura del estado y relaciones industriales: los sindicatos en la educación pública española. In *Estudios Working Papers*. Madrid: IESA-CSIC.

Lerena, C. (1986) *Escuela, Ideología y Clases Sociales en España: Crítica de la Sociología Empirista de la Educación*. Barcelona: Ariel.

Lope, A., Jordana, J., & Carrasquer, P. (1989) La nova etapa de l'acció sindical a espanya: transformacions laborals i canvis estratègics, *Papers: Revista de Sociologia*, Vol. 32, pp. 89–114.

Malefakis. E. (1992) Southern Europe in the 19th & 20th centuries: an historical overview. In *Estudios Working Papers*. Madrid: IESA-CSIC.

Maravall, J. M. (1985) *La Reforma de la Enseñanza*. Barcelona: Laia.

Mayoral, V. (1989) Dualismo escuela pública-escuela en España. In J. Paniagua & A. San Martín (eds.) *Diez Años de Educación en España (1978–1988)*. Alzira: UNED.

MEC (1994) *Centros Educativos y Calidad de la Enseñanza*. Madrid: MEC.

Miguélez, E., & Prieto, C. (1991) *Las Relaciones Laborales en España*. Madrid: Siglo XXI.

Moreno; L. & Sarasa, S. (1993) Génesis y desarrollo del estado del bienestar en España, *Revista Internacional de Sociología*, Vol. 6, pp. 27–69.

Moya, C. (1975) *El Poder Económico en España*. Madrid: Tucar Ed.

Orti, A. (1989) Transición postfranquista a la monarquía parlamentaria y relaciones de clase: del desencanto programado a la social tecnocracia transnacional. In J. Paniagua & A. San Martín (eds.): *Diez Años de Educación en España (1978–1988)*. Alzira: UNED.

Pérez Diaz, V. (1991a) The Church and religion in contemporary Spain. In *Estudios Working Papers*. Madrid: IESA-CSIC.

Pérez Draz, V. (1991b) La emergencia de la España democrática: la invención de una tradición y la dudosa institucionalización de una democracia. In *Estudios Working Papers*. Madrid: IESA-CSIC.

Ramirez, E. O., & Boli, J. (1987) The political construction of mass schooling: European origins and worldwide institutionalisation, *Sociology of Education*, Vol. 60(1), pp. 2–17.

Santos, B. de Sousa (1990a) O estado e os modos de produçao de poder social. In *A Sociologia de Sociedade Portuguesa nu Viragen do Século*. Lisboa: Fragmentos.

Santos, B. de Sousa (1990b) *State, Wage Relations and Social Welfare in the Semiperiphery: The Case of Portugal*. Paper presented at the Havens Center for the Study of Social Structure and Social Change, University of Wisconsin, Madison, United States of America.

Santos, B. de Sousa (1992) *O Estado e a Sociedade em Portugal (1974–1988)*. Lisboa: Ediçoes Afrontamento.

Stoer, S. (1994) Construindo a 'escola democrática' através do 'Campo de recontextualização pedagógica', *Educação, Sociedade e Cultura*, Vol. 1, pp. 7–27.

Stoer, S., Stoleroff, A., & Correia, J. A. (1990) O novo vocacionalismo na política educativa em Portugal e a reconstrução da lógica da acumulação, *Revista Crítica de Ciências Sociais*, Vol. 29, pp. 11–53.

Subirats, M. (1974) Los primeros cuatro años de la Ley General de Educación, *Cuadernos de Pedagogía*, Vol. 1, pp. 2–5.

Subirats, M. (1975) De la renovación pedagógica a Catalunya, *Perspectiva Escolar*, Vol. 3, pp. 45–52.

Subirats, M. (1984) L'evolució de les forces socials: mobilització i desmobilització, *Papers: Revista de Sociologia*, Vol. 21, pp. 9–26.

Tilly, C. (1993) *Coerción, Capital y los Estados Europeos, 990–1990*. Madrid: Alianza.

Weiler, H. (1989) Why reforms fail: the politics of education in France and the Federal Republic of Germany, *Journal of Curriculum Studies*, Vol. 21(4), pp. 291–305.

Woolard, K. A. (1989) *Double Talk: Bilingualism and the Politics of Ethnicity in Catalonia*. Stanford: Stanford University Press.

CHAPTER 3

Toward an Innovative University in the South?

Institutionalising Euro-Mediterranean Co-operation in Research, Technology and Higher Education

Jorma Kuitunen

1   Introduction

Scientific, technological and educational interaction between Europe and the southern and eastern Mediterranean world has been extensive throughout the long colonial period as well as during the first decades following the achievement of independence of states in the region. This interaction has been mainly marked by asymmetrical relations, with European ideas about science and education being used as a modernising strategy by colonies or nation states.

The focus on asymmetrical patterns of interaction, together with the conceptualisations that underlie such relations, are, however, too limited in scope when one considers the situation over a longer historical perspective. We may, for instance, refer to the golden era of philosophy and science in the Arabo-Islamic world during the Middle Ages. The translations and commentaries about classic Hellenistic science made by such figures like Ibn Sina (Avicenna) were passed on to European scholars. The impact of the Arabic-speaking world on the birth of modern empirical science and scientific-technological culture at large has been crucial (Goichon, 1969; Lindberg, 1978). Moreover, as noted also by Sultana (1999), the institutional history of higher learning is generally much longer along the southern rather than the northern shore of the Mediterranean. The transfer of knowledge, in this perspective, followed rather more a South-North rather than a North-South trajectory.

The Eurocentric view of the history of 'Western' science and technology lacks cultural sensitivity toward the early institutionalisation of higher education and scientific studies in the Arabo-Islamic or, more widely, in the oriental world. The issue of socio-cultural awareness in scientific, technological and educational co-operation between European and Arabo-Islamic Mediterranean states has a long history, and one can indeed tease out continuities between that tradition and the contemporary world. Such continuities can be postulated despite the rapid changes brought about by the globalising economy and its effects on the international system. At the same time, though, we have to have an open mind in order to discern the relevant changes in the

© THE EURO-MEDITERRANEAN CENTRE FOR EDUCATION RESEARCH, UNIVERSITY OF MALTA, 1999
DOI: 10.1163/9789004506602_003

structures and patterns of interaction and co-operation between the North and the South. It is necessary to keep in mind such complexities if we are to understand the state and the nature of co-operative relations in the areas of research, technology and education (hereafter referred to as RTE) and the challenges that have to be faced in the present-day Euro-Mediterranean context.

My focus will be specifically on the more recent developments in the cooperative structures of RTE in the Euro-Mediterranean region. In doing that, I will attempt not to lose sight of the continuity that marks scientific interaction in the region, despite the fact that the concern is with changing structures. Operationally this will mean a moderately critical stance toward current Eurocentrism and the ahistorical ways in which RTE co-operation is both conceptualised and institutionalised. Such an epistemological starting point will also keep at bay an unreflective and sceptical attitude toward new possibilities for socio-culturally sensitive and sustainable institutionalisation of RTE co-operation.

If we are to understand how a new kind of Euro-Mediterranean RTE co-operation policy can be developed and implemented, it is essential to keep a broad outlook on the changing international scene. The newest phase of socio-economic modernisation—what is often referred to as the information era—is changing both the concept and the institutional structures of the major institutions of higher learning. Indeed, one could argue that the ministerial conference held in Barcelona in 1995, when focusing on RTE co-operation policies, had the innovative managerial, financial and pedagogical structures of the universities in the Mediterranean Arab countries keenly in mind. Obviously, this begs the question regarding the extent to which such RTE co-operation policies are marked by socio-cultural awareness, and whether the ideals projected for the university as an idea are congruent with different socio-cultural realities.

2   A Road to a Multilateral Co-operation Concept

As has been noted in several discussions and publications (e.g., Melasuo, 1995; Turunen, 1996), the Barcelona meeting has been regarded as an important turning point in the history of political, economic and (perhaps also) cultural relations between the European Union and the twelve non-member countries in the Southern and South-Eastern Mediterranean. Specifically, the meeting brought to a head the process of change in the EU's Mediterranean policy, a change that had commenced in the latter part of the 1980s. One of the most important challenges in that process has been the end of the Cold War, since it made possible the strengthening of EU integration with Eastern Europe and gave a new strategic meaning to North Africa and the Middle East as a 'neighbourhood' area for an expanding EU macro region (Lorca & Nunez, 1993; Smith & Lahteenmaki, 1998).

The Barcelona declaration and its preparatory EU documents show us that the European Union as well as its partner countries acknowledge the crucial importance of RTE co-operation in the Barcelona process (Kuitunen, 1997). The partnership programme aims at launching a new generation of co-operation programmes, under the comprehensive policy of Euro-Mediterranean relationships. This has facilitated the birth and growth of many other activities outside the immediate patronage of the EU administration.

Despite many encouraging initiatives, the launching of new co-operative activities in the fields of RTE seem to be more difficult than was thought. Simultaneously, the pressure toward realising concrete positive results is increasing. This fact is evident in the Euro-Mediterranean partnership at large. The basic question is how to create new forms of co-operation despite the many obstacles that exist, many of which are directly related to momentous political, economic and cultural issues—such as the complex matter of the Middle East peace process.

This overall situation renders the institutionalisation of co-operation—together with the sensitivity toward the socio-cultural context on which such co-operation is based—major areas of concern for the future of the Barcelona process. This clearly is relevant to the area of RTE co-operation as well. For example, it can be suggested that the science policy dimension of the Euro-Mediterranean co-operation policy has been strongly based on the general lines of the science and technology policy of the EU. If this is the case, then the crucial question is how to build co-operation practices which are socio-culturally more in tune with the specific contexts of the Mediterranean region—in other words, the challenge is how to construct a specific Euro-Mediterranean policy of research and education co-operation that is organic to the prevailing situation. In fact, this tendency toward a regional co-operation concept has gradually increased in the short history of RTE co-operation between the European Community and the Mediterranean South.

The bilateral system of financial and technical aid—one that involves scientific and technological components as well—has, since 1978, been the main framework through which the EU regulated its relations with developing countries (European Commission, 1994). The special focus on scientific and technological development co-operation took off when the Science and Technology for Development (STD) programme was started. In the STD programmes (1982–1994), the Mediterranean region was just one geographical area among many, with co-operation agreements reflecting a more general policy that had no regional specifications apart from some flexibility in country-by-country agreements. An important step toward a region-specific system of co-operation was taken when the ICS (International Scientific Co-operation) programme was established in 1984. It focused geographically on the newly industrialised, developing countries in Asia, Latin America and the Mediterranean region. The European Union has strengthened the economic interaction and development co-operation with those areas and scientific and technological interaction has been one aspect of this general trend.

During the 1990s, a multilateral and regional approach to Euro-Mediterranean co-operation has been introduced in parallel to, and supporting, the dimension of bilateral structures. The development of a regional approach and the multilateral MED-programmes reflecting this—programmes such as Med-Invest, Med-Urbs, Med-Media, Med-Campus, Med-Avicenne—have led up to the Barcelona framework, where key elements have been a focused approach to the Southern and Eastern Mediterranean countries as a whole, and regional integration inside the area.

The turn toward a regional approach to Mediterranean co-operation could be said to have started formally in 1992, as a result of several transformations in the working environment of the international community. In point of fact, the process toward a 'New Mediterranean policy' and even toward Euro-Mediterranean partnership goes back to the latter part of the 1980s, soon after the Northern Mediterranean states of Spain, Greece and Portugal joined the Community. According to the guidelines of the EU's Ministerial Council at the end of 1985, the priority areas of the reform process were to be the promotion of local food production as well as the widening of industrial, scientific and technological co-operation, which were to also include the mutual integration of Southern Mediterranean countries (Niblock, 1997, pp. 122–123).

Scientific and technological co-operation has therefore been regarded as one of the principal strategies in promoting socio-economic development in Southern and Eastern Mediterranean countries and making the Mediterranean co-operation policy more efficient. The pressure for policy reform has increased after the poor economic performance of many Arab countries in the mid- and late 1980s, as well as due to the radical geopolitical transformations taking place at that time. Both economic and security aspects as well as poor results of the former Mediterranean policy gave evidence of the great need for reform. By launching Med-programmes, including those focusing on university networking (Med-Campus) and research and technology (Med-Avicenne), the EU wanted to construct a new kind of cooperative structure and to test its implementative instruments in practice before confirming a major reform of the overall framework. The gradual shift toward a more comprehensive politicisation of socio-economic relations in the Euro-Mediterranean region and the increasing importance given by Europe toward the development of a Mediterranean policy, can be seen as a general trend behind the process of this renewal (see Linjakumpu, 1995; Lahteenmaki & Smith, 1998).

Mediterranean university co-operation within the framework of Med-Campus was divided into four thematic areas. These included: (i) regional, social and economic development; (ii) management in private and public enterprises; (iii) environmental management; and (iv) cultural exchange. There were a number of conditions which had to be fulfilled in order for a country to benefit from financial support. Joint projects were only possible, for instance, in countries which had adopted liberal market politics, and in situations which were marked by institutional stability. There had to be ongoing development projects which could benefit from the new expertise offered by the co-operation agreement. Such conditionalities clearly indicate that university and higher education co-operation was closely linked to a policy of structural adjustment. Such a conclusion is also warranted because the university courses that were generated focused on themes which generally have direct or indirect effects on the development of modern socio-economic infrastructures. Due to the direct relevance of co-operation in the science and technology areas in promoting development, the programme Med-Avicenne had an even more rigorous connection to the aforementioned goal of structural adjustment.

We may therefore conclude that the decentralised Med-programmes foreshadowed the spirit of the Barcelona process. The strengthening of the science and education policy dimension has been one strategic element of that process. Due to administrative problems, however, many of these programmes were terminated soon after the Barcelona meeting. After a long delay, Med-Campus was given a new lease of life in 1998. Med-Avicenne disappeared from the scene in 1994, when it was merged with a new programme of international scientific and technological co-operation between the EU and third countries (INCO).

Following the Barcelona conference, the INCO programme was established in order to co-ordinate all the EU's scientific and technological co-operation with third countries, one section of which is developing countries (INCO-DC). INCO belongs to the EU's framework programme of research and technological development. As with co-operation in terms of the framework programme in general, the INCO-DC is based on a multilateral system. In other words, the joint projects are not organised in terms of bilateral governmental agreements but in a more flexible way between university departments or research institutes and enterprises from three or more partner countries. The national priority areas are, however, agreed upon in negotiations with developing countries.

The thematic focus of INCO-DC has been on four areas: sustainable management of renewable natural resources, improvement of agricultural and agro-industrial production, health issues, and other areas of mutual interest. The last part has increasingly been directed to co-operation in information and communication technology, but non-nuclear energy, biotechnologies as well as material and production technologies have also been supported.

Despite the growing differences between third world countries, INCO-DC has not been specified geographically to the Southern Mediterranean or any other developing regions. The Monitoring Committee of Euro-Mediterranean RTD co-operation has considered this to hinder efficient co-operation. As a result, a special INCO-MED programme has been launched in the fifth framework programme.

More important than INCO's operational modes is, naturally, the overall co-operation policy and politics behind its implementative structures. As a whole, INCO is clearly determined by the EU's RTD co-operation policy in general, the aim of which is to strengthen the European scientific and technological base and, through it, to promote industrial competitiveness in a global economy. INCO is structured around the idea that international scientific and technological co-operation is an increasingly important condition for economic vitality and, moreover, that the increasing co-operation between the EU countries is not sufficient for that purpose.

Information technology has become one of the main areas of co-operation between the EU and developing countries. As explained in the five-year assessment of the INCO programme, the aim is to integrate developing countries—and especially the rising economies of the newly industrialised ones—into the global information society by increasing their information technology expertise, productive capacity, and regional networking (European Commission, 1997). This policy of co-operation can be seen as useful both for local employment and development aims and for European information technology corporations. It is assumed that co-operation will increase understanding of the socio-economic, political and institutional environment in developing societies and the conditions of technology transfer to them. In addition to this, a greater awareness and understanding of the global information society contributes to a deeper commitment to technology on the part of key actors in a developing country. This line of argument may, at first sight, appear to be merely rhetorical, with the intent being to encourage European enterprises to invest in the possibilities of multilateral co-operation. But the logic behind the argument also reflects deeper changes in the interaction patterns of science and technology on the global scene.

3 Science, Technology and Developing Countries in the Era of Global Changes

Global enterprises have not only brought their production to newly industrialised countries but also dispersed some of their RTD activities in them. The opening markets for high technology products in the developing world presuppose sufficient local knowledge about technology as well as a consciousness of the economic and societal functions of research and of the need for the development of appropriately qualified human resources. The globalisation of RID is one aspect of a more general shift toward the vision of a global information society, expectations of profit connected to it, and new kinds of co-operation activities between North and South. It is evident that the EU countries do not want to 'lose' these trends if their aim is to promote the development of their industrial base and to help launch new useful modes of co-operation. According to the prevalent ideology in this regard, this is also what the developing countries need if they want to lessen their economic and social problems and to benefit from global trends.

The INCO programme, like the EU's other RTD programmes, is essentially the result of these kind of trends. The RTD co-operation system of the EU is adapting itself to the restructuring of the international political and economic order after the Cold War. The increasing differentiation of the third world is one result of such radical changes. Many of the developing countries and newly industrialised states have increasingly integrated themselves into the global economy by transforming their economic policy from import substitution and strong public governance to export-oriented free trade and privatisation of state functions. As mentioned by Shinn et al. (1997, p. 18), this turn toward a new paradigm of development is closely connected to globally oriented techno-economic frontiers of telecommunication, microelectronics, informatics, new materials, and biotechnology.

Many countries in Latin America and in South-Eastern Asia (Asian tigers as well as China and India) have, since the 1970s, systematically developed their scientific and technological equipment, as well as their scientific staff and their policy for science and technology. This trend has followed the lines of 'science and technology for development' thinking and can to some degree also be discerned in Arab countries. In the process of global transformations, the expansion of higher education and progress in scientific capacity have appeared to be an important usable resource. Through the globalisation of norms in research and education policy as well as through giving space for other institutional renewal, the developing countries can essentially better their chances to integrate themselves in the global economy (Shinn et al., 1997). However, in the case of Arab countries, many experts of science policy have seen structural problems which have been detrimental to the prerequisites for scientific and technological capacity and its efficient use in societal development (Al-Hassan, 1979; Zahlan, 1980; Khasawnih, 1986; Daghestani, 1993; Qasem, 1996, 1998a, 1999; cf. also Workshop, 1996). Many of these evaluations are not very up-to-date and significant changes are possible. For example, the rapid privatisation of the Jordanian university sector during the last few years is one instance of the opening up to structural change (with its positive or negative results for the various segments of society).

The preconditions for taking part in the global economy, which are increasingly and evidently dividing the third world countries into developing and declining ones, are increasingly seen to be dependent on scientific and technological capacity and ability to adapt research and education systems to the new demands of the global environment. For example, it has been regarded crucial that developing countries have the ability and willingness to adopt a new conception of technological innovation and new kinds of institutional interactions between the academic research community, public governance and private enterprises (in the studies of science and technology policy this has often been called 'triple helix'—see, for instance, Etzkowitz & Leydesdorff, 1995). A few developing countries with strong scientific capacity have shown this kind of will and ability. This seems to be closely connected to the early institutionalisation of strong research centres, science policy organs as well as to the establishment of a research community of science policy studies and educational degrees in science and technology management (Shinn et al., 1997). Unlike some countries with either a Muslim majority or a significant Muslim minority in the Far East, Arab countries seem to have been slow to give strong political priority to science policy or institutional support to systematic studies of science policy as a complex phenomenon, despite the fact that science policy organs were the subject of institutionalisation relatively early.

From the overview above, we can draw the conclusion that there is a common political consensus about the new structure of co-operative activities between developed and dynamic developing countries. They use a common language about science and technology as a precondition for economic success and integration in the global economic space. This will provide new possibilities for international scientific and technological co-operation as compared to the policy of self-reliant development and demand for structural reformation toward a more just world which was inspired by dependency thinking and its tendency toward political criticism. It is important to note that referring to those new possibilities is not a normative commitment to the trend as such but is rather an analytic remark. In order to make a normative evaluation in terms

TOWARD AN INNOVATIVE UNIVERSITY IN THE SOUTH?

of democratic principles one could ask, for example: (i) How comprehensive is the political consensus in the society at large? (ii) What are the short- and long-term effects of the new policy on large segments of ordinary people? and (iii) To what degree has a working balance between global and local been found?

The new consensus of science policy and partnership between North and South is strongly accompanied by a general change of the development thinking in international and national fora. The common vocabulary of development co-operation is neither modernisation in its conventional mode nor dependency tenets. Instead, it is closely connected to a normative construction of a global information technology-based society and a neoliberal politico-economic philosophy underpinning it. The neoliberalist turn has given rise to a new interpretation of relevant societal facts, purposes and practices in almost all sectors of society and the international community (Rothenberg, 1984). What is most important, neoliberalism is an effective ingredient in the change of political and economic climate in which the capitalist system has reacted to the world-wide economic crisis since the first part of the 1970s and gradually rejected the combination of Keynesian macro-economic policy and compensatory social policy typical of the welfare state. In other words, neoliberalism has offered political legitimacy for societal change away from the mass production system of the welfare state, toward the information society and its different conception of the state. The new policy of information society has given more space to the logic of market forces on the local, national, macro regional and global level.

The neoliberal turn is also evident in North-South relations and in the role of developing countries therein. Changing conceptions of economy and government in society as well as in international community have been legitimated by referring to changing realities and to new interpretations of such essentially normative concepts as freedom, rights, justice, and democracy (Boréus, 1997). Accordingly, the explanations for the uneven global development have changed radically. Unlike the propositions of both modernisation theories on the one hand, and dependency theories on the other—both of which put emphasis on the aid coming from international community to the developing countries—neoliberal thinking focuses on the internal structures of a poor country. According to the neoliberal programme, financial aid should be conditional to institutional modernisation in which privatisation of the state sector, opening the markets for foreign trade and development of needed infrastructure for foreign investments should be realised. Societal reforms concerning the productive sector, together with those concerning many purely government-driven social sectors like health and education, are to be realised with the support of the dynamic private sector rather than through public planning and finance. These are basically the same prescriptions which are generally meted out to economies in the developed world.

It has become evident enough that neoliberal development philosophy is closely connected to changes toward the information society and its innovation-based economy. The analysis proposed by van Audenhove and his colleagues (1999) about Africa's Information Society Initiative adopted by the UN Economic Commission for Africa in 1996, refers strongly to the conclusion that the Western information society paradigm has shifted to developing countries without sufficiently problematising its institutional presuppositions and societal relevance. The same argumentative strategy about the positive effects of privatisation of the communication sector in society and investments in the telecommunication infrastructure is used as in Western countries. Moreover, powerful international organisations and multinational enterprises have many possibilities to realise their policies according to the logic of this kind of argument. I agree with the authors that the capability and need of socio-cultural evaluation of the role of information technology in the national policy of a developing country will become a crucial issue.

In dealing with that issue, it is important to note that information technology is not just a sector among technological innovation activities but a very compelling techno-economic and socio-cultural paradigm. As Manuel Castells (1996) has shown in his broad analysis of changes toward global informational society, the information paradigm has led to the rising global network economy on which the competitiveness of local, national and macro regional economies are increasingly seen to depend. That is why this paradigm has such a strong normative and political appeal. It is comparable to the Fordist model of mass industrialism which was the dominant techno-economic paradigm of the welfare state period.

Thus far, I have attempted to give an account of global changes and their effects on North-South relations in scientific, technological and (to a lesser degree) educational co-operation. It is crucial for the purposes of this paper to see how the trends that have been identified will help us understand the science policy dimension of the Euro-Mediterranean partnership framework. The role of science and technology in the globalisation processes and changes in the international political economy are major determinants of RTE co-operation policy in the Mediterranean basin as well. In trying to demonstrate this I will turn, in the following sections, to the analysis of the co-operative policy of various sectors of civil society in the Euro-Mediterranean area.

4 The Co-operative Thinking of Euro-Mediterranean Civil Society Actors

A major new aspect of Mediterranean policy in the Euro-Mediterranean partnership framework was that civil society was regarded as essential to the promotion of the Barcelona process. This represents a qualitative change from the past. As former vice-president of the European Commission Manuel Marin said in 1996, this shift basically reflected a concern with the question of legitimacy. It became clear that the institutionalisation of widening Euro-Mediterranean co-operation could not be sustained unless it received the support of—and was actually implemented by—a wide range of representatives from partner societies. The civil society conference has been a visible counterpart of the ministerial meeting in Barcelona as well as of the follow up conferences in Malta (1997) and Stuttgart (1999). Several other Euro-Mediterranean meetings have also seen the active participation of civil society actors. In this context I will concentrate on the important meeting of Fórum Civil Euromed (hereafter 'Civil Forum') which was organised immediately after the ministerial conference in Barcelona. The meeting was sponsored by the European Commission, Spain's foreign ministry, and UNESCO. Operational preparation and management were carried out by a Spanish institute dealing with Euro-Mediterranean interaction (Institut Catalá del la Mediterrània d'Estudis i Cooperació).

The Civil Forum gathered together about 1200 representatives from business, universities, trade unions, arts and other sectors of society. The meeting was held in, the 'high spirit of Barcelona' in which strong optimism about opening a new era in the Euro-Mediterranean relations was typical. The Civil Forum organised the discussion on ways to promote Euro-Mediterranean partnership around eleven thematic sessions ('working fora') extensively reflecting social, economic and cultural dimensions of co-operation. Many fora addressed issues related to research, technology and higher education. The working groups that focused most directly on these issues were the ones dedicated to 'Technology and co-operation' as well as 'Universities and research'. In addition, the forum on 'Investments' spoke much about educational development and co-operation. Due to limited space and many similarities between the fora, I shall only give an account of, and attempt to analyse, the discussions that developed in the first two fora. The overall aim behind this is to unravel the way Euro-Mediterranean RTE co-operation was conceptualised and, moreover, to understand such a process as a region-specific version of more general trends.

From the methodological point of view, it is important to highlight the fact that the sessions of the Civil Forum represented different actors and interests of significant segments of civil society in the Northern and South-Eastern Mediterranean. Actors from, say, the business or university world, have specific and often contrasting ways of conceptualising and articulating phenomena, that is to say, they have their own ways of 'seeing' and interpreting meaningful facts about the world, and represent norms according to the way they are accustomed to organise their own professional activities.

It is important to delve a little deeper into this methodological point by focusing on the forum dedicated to 'Universities and research'. This workshop gathered together representatives from the academic world in the region. Of 91 participants, an overwhelming majority came from European universities, with only about ten coming from North African or Middle Eastern universities and research institutes. There were also experts from the European Commission and key personnel from the Mediterranean university networks (the Community of Mediterranean Universities and the University of the Mediterranean) as well as a few Med-Campus co-ordinators from a number of European universities. This forum, therefore, was made up of very experienced people reflecting a high level of expertise in Mediterranean research and university co-operation. Compared to the official rhetoric of the Barcelona declaration, the focus on what actors have to say about the concept of co-operation can lead to a more concrete analysis of the promise and pitfalls of co-operation in the region.

The report of the Civil Forum meeting in Barcelona (Fórum Civil Euromed, 1996), which is used as a source (and to which I shall refer only by page numbers), is comprehensive and written with care. It is clear, however, that the report could not possibly mirror every voice that was raised during the discussions at the fora. Rather, it reflects the organisational logic that underpinned the meeting, as well as the thematic and procedural choices and interpretations made by the co-ordinators and secretaries in relation to the discussions as well as to the conclusions of each session. As with any other well-organised meeting, the Civil Forum and its report were produced in a specific way and such a production cannot be strictly separated from the official results of the conference.

5 Technological Cooperation

> The Mediterranean must plot a path towards tomorrow's information society—that takes into account the realities and necessities of the region—as the rest of the world is doing. Geographic proximity will only be converted into vital cultural and economic proximity when there are communication structures and infrastructures that make it possible, and society has integrated this technology into its culture. (Fórum Civil Euromed, 1996, p. 119)

> Intensification of Euro-Mediterranean exchanges and access to the nascent information society will be facilitated by more efficient information and communication infrastructures. (Work programme of the Barcelona declaration)

As the above quotations suggest, the point of departure in the technology forum is the importance of new information and communication technology in a process of transformation toward the knowledge and information society. Like the Barcelona declaration and its work programme, the forum takes this socio-economic and cultural scenario as a common challenge for the Euro-Mediterranean region. Moving to a more operational level, the forum emphasises that the success of supranational co-operation will depend on the will and ability of partners to agree on specified common targets for co-operation activities (p. 120). Those targets and suggestions of concrete projects were produced mainly by actor-specific views of businesses in telecommunication and health technology. Of 97 participants, 15 came from Arab partner countries.

In specifying the crucial role of telecommunications in the Euro-Mediterranean transformation toward the information society and ways to institutionalise co-operation in that frontier of new technology, the forum refers to the same priority areas as those highlighted in the Barcelona declaration: regulation and standardisation of telecommunication networks, regional infrastructures and their connections to European networks, and access to services in the most important fields of application (p. 122). This similarity demonstrates the fact that, concerning information technology co-operation, the forum and the Barcelona framework represent the same agents or at least a common frame of thoughts. However, the Civil Forum discussions permit us to get a much more comprehensive view on that frame.

The specific proposals for developing the Euro-Mediterranean infrastructure in telecommunications arose from two basic issues: the highly uneven development of the infrastructure and ways to promote joint activities among all relevant actors. The key question was the latter one—namely, the efficient institutionalisation of co-operation. It was the topic in which the technology forum made both sophisticated conceptualisations and relevant concrete recommendations.

> Through the proposals for concrete action the forum aims at creating co-operation mechanisms which will ensure continuity, systematic evaluation, and realisation of long-term objectives. This was the idea in suggesting, among other things, the development of Mediterranean telecommunication partnership and preliminary platforms for co-operation which could make proposals for common technical standards, the interoperability of networks, and co-operation in research and technical development strategy or, on the other hand, deal with broader conditions of co-operation like liberalisation of markets. (p. 125)

For the technology forum, the institutionalisation of Mediterranean co-operation is a long-term and gradual process (pp. 129–130). At first, it is necessary to have personal contacts which will help to build up mutual understanding and confidence between the participants and future associates (as the technology forum remarks, the Fórum Civil Euromed had this very function). The next step is to identify areas of common activity and acquire detailed information on the partners as well as the competitive advantages of each of them. Only on this basis is it possible 'to establish the goals of co-operation, in order to work cooperatively in the definition, realisation and evaluation of the project' (p. 130).

Concerning services and applications, the thoughts of the technology forum were focused primarily on human resource development and its essential role in the development of an information society in the Southern and Eastern Mediterranean. In addition to that, the issue of socio-cultural responsiveness was regarded as an important one. The forum felt that the heterogeneity of the Euro-Mediterranean region (i.e., the technological development gap) should not only mean the simple needs of technology transfer but a much broader reflection process and evaluation of differences which would enable the creation of genuine networking of people and organisations. In developing education and training in information technology, it was vital, according to the forum, to take into account the specialities and experiences of all partners and encourage multi-disciplinary and multi-institutional association projects (e.g., between universities and technological innovation centres). The forum also made (pp. 126, 128) many concrete proposals concerning the use of information technology in education and training at all educational levels, hence promoting a broad societal basis for understanding technological innovation.

The technology forum emphasised that technological systems cannot be transferred to different socio-cultural environments without adequate cultural awareness and expertise. By highlighting this point, the forum underscored its agreement with the criticisms that have often been made regarding technical development aid. Several instances have shown the extent to which Western expertise has failed to bring about long-term development in social, economic and technical infrastructure unless there was a strong collaboration with local actors, and unless the latter's cultural knowledge was respected. Such an approach is very much in line with the perspectives adopted by structural dependency theory, which states that technology transfer carries with it the transfer of the socio-cultural codes that underpin it (Morehouse, 1978/79; Rahman, 1978/79). If this is not taken into account, the friction of different socio-cultural frames will destroy or lessen the continuity of co-operation and its overall results.

This wisdom was constitutive of the proposals of the technology forum concerning co-operation in health technology (pp. 134–135, 138). The use of

(European) knowledge and expertise in the development of medical services in the South presupposes the close participation of local officials. According to the forum, it is not enough to transfer medical technology and models of evaluation of medical services. Rather, it is also necessary to promote the relevant cultural values that go along with them. This was operationalised through a proposal which aimed at organising exchange of experts and training for medical service officials in the South.

Despite the thoughtful manner in which the institutionalisation of co-operation was conceptualised at the forum, it can still be said that the model adopted betrayed cultural asymmetry. Socio-cultural responsiveness and partnership with local actors is needed not only to enable the transfer of technology as such, but also to adapt its necessary cultural frame to local environment. The best agents of this acculturation process are not the Western consultants but the local people themselves. They can be encouraged to conceptualise the conditions of co-operation in a socio-culturally reflective way and, thus, promote long-term structural institutionalisation and continuity of co-operation.

The structural acculturation and institutionalisation of partnership is a highly critical issue for the success of the Barcelona process. For the technology forum the previously implicit aim has now been made explicit—it is the scientific and technological culture and the efficient institutions that support such a culture that must be transferred, and not merely their products. The development of RTE capacity and a new kind of comprehensive culture of innovation is a principal instrument in the society that is oriented toward information, and which is in a process of transformation toward a neoliberal framework. In the end, however, we could ask: how has this scenario of meaningful reality been chosen and are there any alternatives in realising it?

6 University and Research Cooperation

The highly academic university forum is self-interested enough to underline the essential role of universities in the social and economic development of a knowledge society. But under the surface there seems to be some uncertainty about the identity of universities in the increasingly demanding environment they have to operate in. As we know, universities have traditionally been seen as autonomous and self-organised communities of scholars in which teachers and researchers have great freedom to focus on seeking new knowledge without outside demands of immediate practical applications. Up to the recent past, it was sufficient for society and state—as major patrons of universities—to believe that academic learning and scientific knowledge were useful in the long run. Although this image of the university does not reflect the actual situation and is—as a reflection of reality—rather more of a myth, it is not wise to deny its effects on the thinking of academics. Neither is its normative relevance and continuity to be underestimated.

In raising this issue, I want to highlight the actual challenges and difficulties that must be faced to find a well-functioning balance between traditional elements and the modernisation tendencies that surround universities. The uneasy transformation from the more or less traditional university concept to an innovative and entrepreneurial one is a global trend and it was the major frame of thought at the Civil Forum as well. The basic question of the university forum was: how does one institutionalise an innovative university in the Mediterranean South and, additionally, how does one organise co-operation policies and practices that promote this aim? This is a special case of a more widespread need to find a balance between traditional university structures and new demands between the local and the global.

As with the technology forum, the problems of the southern university institutions and research work as well their backwardness in relation to the current European norms was a main issue behind the co-operative thinking of the university forum. How these problems were interpreted has a crucial meaning for the conceptualisations of Euro-Mediterranean co-operation of higher education and research. Thus, it is reasonable to focus first on this issue and then move to the second part of analysis concerning the forum's thinking about institutionalisation of university and research partnerships.

Before dealing with that, it would be useful to clarify the issue of the 'Europeanisation' of the concepts of university co-operation. Although a relatively small minority of participants came from Arab countries, we cannot claim that the thinking of the forum was totally organised by European perspectives— that would be tantamount to saying that the Arab participants did not have had any significant impact on the ways problems and proposals were interpreted and articulated. On the contrary, it is my belief that Arab perspectives did have a constitutive effect on the conclusions of the forum, particularly by virtue of their first-hand experience and knowledge of academic structures and cultures in the South. However, this does not deny the importance of the European and global trends in the discussions at the forum. It was clear that the referent and basis for an interpretative consensus during the discussion was the idea of the modernising university, one steeped in a culture of global innovation. As such, the academic forum worked completely in the spirit of neoliberal structural modernisation typical of all the Barcelona framework. Therefore, when speaking about the modes of decentralised co-operation in research and higher learning, the forum states:

TOWARD AN INNOVATIVE UNIVERSITY IN THE SOUTH?

> All these actions should be conducted with the objective of modernising the economic and social structures of the southern Mediterranean countries, increasing their capacity for innovation and their competitiveness and improving their possibilities of adaptation to the conditions of the world market. (p. 166)

The modern innovative university—or rather, a visionary construction of it produced by recent discussion about reform of higher education—worked as a frame of reference of the university forum reflecting mainly the consensus of those of 'us' in the North. The conceptualisation of the problems of 'them' in the South can be seen as the other side of the coin. Those features in the southern universities which will not suit 'our' norms are easily interpreted as 'problems'. It is then possible that the problems are not conceptualised in relation to the socio-cultural environment from which they hail. Rather, the difference as such may sometimes give a sufficient reason to the specification of what is, indeed, a 'problem'. This tendency has been referred to as 'otherness' in certain discussions of the relations between European and Arabic-Islamic cultures.

From the modernisation perspective adopted at the forum on universities, the strict dualism between northern and southern universities appears as essential and constitutive of the discourse. Although the northern universities (i.e., 'our' institutions) evidently have a long way to go in developing their practices toward an innovative university culture, the critical eyes of the forum looked at the failings of the southern university institutes alone:

- Their structures of action have not been sufficiently modernised.
- Their resources are still poor.
- They are too closed in relation to their own societies as well as to universities abroad.
- They have been obliged to fight problems produced by a one-sided policy of democratisation and massive expansion.
- Their quantitative explosion has happened mostly without clarified and internationally up-to-date picture of the mission of higher education in society.
- The performance of their research activities has been low, the research has not given enough support to teaching and, moreover, the studies has been oriented thematically too much to the internal issues of their societies or culture at large especially in the social sciences.
- They have worked without a co-ordinated research policy and, as a result, the research work has not focused on societally relevant topics.

This interpretation of the problems in universities and higher education policies of the South is used as a basis for legitimating the forum's thinking about co-operation, and the strategy for institutionalising it. We may tentatively ask how informative this summary of problems could be. The picture of the problems is supported by the evidence of those reasonably rare (English) research reports which have been made concerning Arab research and science policy or higher education. They have regularly produced very similar conclusions about the rapid expansion of university sector, the lack of societal relevance, the inefficient use of the academic labour force, and so on (Tibawi, 1972; Massialas & Jarrar, 1983, 1987, 1991; El-Sanabary, 1992; Salmi, 1992; Talbani, 1996). On the other hand, the list of problems does not illustrate apparent successes in the educational policy of many Mediterranean Arab partner countries. For example, the democratisation and expansion policy of higher education in Jordan has worked very successfully for many years, when the surplus of educated people found jobs in the oil producing neighbouring countries (Ray & Williams, 1992).

All in all, the massive quantitative expansion of universities in the Arab countries is, despite its shortages, a result of conscious efforts to ease access to higher learning. Without such a policy, scientific, technological and educational capacity would be much lower today. As Antoine Zahlan, the prominent researcher of Arab science and research policy, had already strongly emphasised in 1980, the main problem is not the lack of scientific capacity in Arab societies but, rather, more complex problems concerning the societal roles of science in them (Zahlan, 1980). If the massive growth of the university sector in Arab states (Qasem, 1995) before and after 1980 has not been used enough for the benefit of those societies, this is not only an issue of structures of higher education or science policy but, to repeat, a larger societal question. The participants of the university forum surely knew it, but this point of view was not presented clearly enough in the forum's report. That is why it can easily give the reader an overly one-sided picture of the Arab university sector.

Like the forum 'Technology and co-operation', the forum 'Universities and research' presented a highly developed strategy for institutionalising the Euro-Mediterranean co-operation in its actor-specific fields of operation. The first part of the strategy dealt with higher education and the second one primarily with university research and policy of research.

In the task of programming higher education co-operation, the forum basically expressed the view that the duty of the European partners is to serve the southern universities in modernising their organisation and curriculum. and in developing educational systems which are able to follow (and promote) current economic and social changes. The following proposals have been presented as concrete ways to realise co-operative interventions (pp. 168–169):

– Establishing European universities in the Mediterranean region.

- Offering aid to start specialised studies in the most relevant disciplines.
- Increasing the admission capacity of European universities to PhD students and young teachers from the Southern Mediterranean.
- Co-operation in the design of professional training structures that suit the needs of their businesses.
- Helping southern countries to share their educational resources by increasing mobility of students and professors in South-South and North-South direction and by recognition of diplomas and curricula.
- Creating centres of excellence for the best students of the Euro-Mediterranean region.
- Stimulating distance learning and information gathering of the teaching in each country in the South.

As with the forum 'Investments', the institutionalisation of co-operation in higher learning is conceptualised as an issue of structural harmonisation in keeping with the newest trends toward a more occupationally-oriented policy. Although the norms of this policy emerge from ongoing discussions on university reform in the developed world and, hence, have been produced in certain economic and socio-cultural contexts, the shift of contexts in moving from North to the Mediterranean South does not seem to be the subject of serious reflection (despite some notes on a need for that). As a result, the forum's policy of co-operation appears to be quite Eurocentric and globalistic.

It may be argued that the structure of the forum, made up as it was of mainly European and pro-modernisation elite representatives of Arab universities, can partly explain the consensus in the forum about the relevant facts, concepts and norms of co-operation. This is not to deny the relevance of the structure and the validity of the forum's knowledge base as such. Rather, it is an effort to understand why this interpretative consensus was possible and why other, different opinions and 'truths' failed to emerge. In other words, the actual aim is not to deny the value or legitimacy of the modernisation stance but to ask if there could be other kinds of thoughts which are also important for the institutionalisation of co-operation. This remark may be applied to the research policy dimension as well.

It is evident that a country's science policy, together with the financial backup committed to it, can have a significant effect on the research that is carried out, including the topics that are chosen as a focus and the development of the infrastructure that is necessary to support scientific activities. This is the reason why the science policy dimension has been considered to be fundamental for the institutionalisation of co-operative structures in the context of European Union and in the Mediterranean region as well. The quote below will summarise the university forum's conception of the institutionalisation process and the role of research policy in it:

> To participate in the development of research on the southern shore also implies increasing European means in the region. This could be achieved, as is being demonstrated at the present, thanks to the setting-up of Euro-Mediterranean networks. However, as the debate reflected, trans-Mediterranean scientific research should be institutionalised in order to assure co-operation and in this way achieve overall continuity and coherence, so necessary in the field of the accumulation of knowledge.
>
> Moreover, this institutionalisation effort could favour a beginning of a scientific policy in the southern countries. This means the implementation of a group of coherent projects in the fields that approach social problems, such as .... (p. 170)

The forum's proposals concerning research policy aimed, among other things, at widening the thematic and geographical perspectives of studies and deepening the theoretical level of basic research. More specifically, the forum underlined the fact that studies in southern societies should go beyond the description of those societies and develop conceptual tools whose validity went beyond the geographical area they referred to. The forum also thought that Euro-Mediterranean networks could encourage the researchers of the South to take up the whole Euro-Mediterranean region as an object of research. Moreover, the Euro-Mediterranean networks of fundamental research and the favouring of their localisation in the southern countries also suggested ways to develop the scientific capacity toward international standards and to prevent brain drain (pp. 170–171). As the forum itself puts it, '... in this way co-operation in research matters could advance toward the sharing of research objectives, methods and means within the most varied ambits of the applied and fundamental sciences'. In other words, this was to be a strategy to expand the contact area of researchers through giving more emphasis to the horizons of the common Euro-Mediterranean scientific space.

As it has been repeatedly stated, the recommended ways to promote co-operation between Euro-Mediterranean universities and scientists are basically—and rightly one might add—focused on the institutionalisation of partnership. 'Institutionalisation' has a specific meaning in this context. It refers to the aim to create sustainable modes of co-operation through which the suitable infrastructure and culture of higher education and research work in the South can be developed as a long-term process. What is important to note is that the policy is not to set up unwieldy formal structures but rather to create a flexible co-operative network management with capability for co-ordinated activities and with enough continuity. The opposite would be ad hoc projects without a systematic policy of co-ordination and without taking long-term objectives and results seriously. In the latter case, co-operative projects tend to only bloom during a period of financial support, with very little tending to happen after that.

It is very easy to agree with the university and technology fora that flexible institutionalisation is the basic condition for successful co-operation and that it is necessary if the overall targets, whatever these may be, are to be effectively reached. Moreover, the awareness of—and sensitivity to—the socio-cultural realities of the local environment is evidently one of the crucial presuppositions for long-term partnership between North and South. It is noteworthy that the 'technocratic' technology forum as well as the forum on 'Investments' led by representatives from the business sector took this last issue more seriously than the university forum did, despite the fact that the latter represented what it itself referred to in its final report as the 'humanistic' tradition. Despite some differences, all three fora clearly recognised both managerial efficiency and socio-cultural responsiveness as key institutionalisation strategies leading to mutual benefits of co-operation in research, technology and higher education. There remains, however, one critical issue: the nature of and the basis for this consensus.

7   Conclusions

Certain theoretical aspects have been essential in writing this article about the institutionalisation strategies of scientific, technological and educational co-operation in the context of recent Euro-Mediterranean relations. For example, I chose to review ongoing changes toward a real and normative vision of the global information society as well as changing RTE interaction patterns between North and South. The new generation of the EU's multilateral RTE cooperation essentially reflects those general trends. The institutionalisation strategies have been strongly based on the information society-oriented vision of transformation toward a global economy and society.

Despite the usefulness of explicating linkages of Euro-Mediterranean RTE cooperation and more general trends, this may not be a significant result as such. Otherwise, the conceptualisations and institutionalisation strategies of Euro-Mediterranean partnership programme and participants of Fórum Civil Euromed would not be well-informed about the changing structures of the contemporary world—which is naturally not the case. What I would like to summarise and discuss a little further in this last section is the essence and nature of socio-cultural responsiveness in the institutionalisation strategies of RTE partnership.

It is clear enough that the Euro-Mediterranean cooperation framework reflects a sophisticated cooperation policy. Instead of transferring technology and giving financial aid as such, the aim is to transfer efficient infrastructures as well as a culture and policy of science, technology and higher education. In this framework, RTE cooperation inevitably needs a basis of broad socio-cultural understanding and, hence, more genuine co-operative partnership with local actors. Giving more space for local expertise and actors representing various civil society segments is really an essential strategy (and not only a rhetorical one) for the effective institutionalisation of partnership.

Concerning the nature of RTE partnership and the informative consensus behind it, the question arises as to how broad a legitimation basis exists among civil society actors in the Arab countries. We may ask, for example, what is a concept of an Arab society in this case. As we know, these societies have often strong internal divisions of opinion. The discussion about RTE co-operation could also be widened to include more traditional aspects of civil society—such as the university and science community—which may be critical of Western ideas about science and education and which may not be so eager to follow the newest trends (e.g., the intellectual discourse about Islamisation of knowledge and science). Despite probable differences between frames used, there could also be the space to strengthen the legitimacy and knowledge basis of co-operative strategies.

Widening the scope of civil society partnership may be highly important for the purposes of the institutionalisation process, and mutually beneficial in the long run. In that case the policy could move to a deeper and even more conscious level of structural modernisation by seeking sustainable solutions to the classic tensions between the modern and the traditional, as well as between the global and the local. Cooperation is therefore not necessarily conceptualised as a process of modernisation of southern universities, which are supposed to diminish their development gap according to universalised norms of global trends. Instead of that, the policy of institutional modernisation would go beyond the old historic model of normative acculturation, which has mostly happened without deep consciousness of the nature of the structural asymmetry they represent (Tibi, 1988). In this position, institutional modernisation will neither be realised as an imitation of European (global) norms nor as an uncritical rejection of them. This would mean, for example, the need for more comprehensive knowledge about the traditional structures of science and higher education in Arab countries and in their societal relations (cf. Gottstein, 1986).

As we have seen, the notion of an innovative university in the Mediterranean South is generally in congruence with more general trends concerning a globalising world and changing patterns of scientific, technological and educational interaction. In that sense, the innovative university may be a relevant aim both from the European and the local socio-economic perspective. However, a heavy orientation toward Eurocentric or globalistic frameworks can be counterproductive. Broad and genuine civil society support and regionalism, which are not solely organised according to current global trends, may help to go beyond an 'uncritical dualism' and find a balanced way to facilitate co-operation in the spirit of mutual partnership. One of the major contributions which 'innovative universities' can make in to the development of cooperation policies in both the North and in the South is to cultivate their traditional responsibility for acquiring a broad knowledge basis for 'truths' in society and—what may be an even more demanding and sensitive issue for scholars—about themselves as 'mirrors of society'.

Acknowledgement

This chapter originally appeared as: Kuitunen, J. (1999) Toward an innovative university in the South? Institutionalising Euro-Mediterranean co-operation in research, technology and higher education, *Mediterranean Journal of Educational Studies*, Vol. 4(2), pp. 155–179. Reprinted here with permission from the publisher.

References

Ahmad, M. (1976) Development of nations through science and technology, *Impact of Science on Society*, Vol. 26(3), pp. 203–212.

Al-Hassan, A. Y. (1979) Science in the Islamic world. In C. Moraz'e et al. (eds.) *Science and the Factors of Inequality*. Paris: UNESCO.

Barcelona Declaration (1995) Adopted at the Euro-Mediterranean Conference (27–28 November 1995), Barcelona, 28 November 1995, Final Version 2.

Boréus, K. (1997) The shift to right: neo-liberalism in argumentation and language in the Swedish public debate since 1969, *European Journal of Political Research*, Vol. 31(3), pp. 257–286.

Castells, M. (1996) *The Rise of the Network Society*. Oxford: Blackwell Publishers.

Daghestani, F. A. (1993) *The Arab States: World Science Report*. Paris: UNESCO.

El-Sanabary, N. (1992) *Education in the Arab Gulf States and the Arab World: An Annotated Bibliographical Guide*. New York: Garland Publishing.

Etkowitz, H., & Leydesdorff, L. (1995) The triple helix: university-industry-government relations: a laboratory for knowledge-based economic development, *EASST Review*, Vol. 14(1), pp. 14–19.

European Commission (1994) *Report from the Commission to the Council and the European Parliament on the Implementation of Financial and Technical Cooperation with Mediterranean Non-Member Countries and on Financial Cooperation with those Countries as a Group.*

European Commission (1997) *Five-Year Assessment of the Specific Programme: Cooperation with Third Countries and International Organizations.*

Fórum Civil Euromed (1996) *Towards a New Scenario of Partnership in the Euro-Mediterranean Area.* Barcelona: Institut Catalá del la Mediterrània d'Estudis i Cooperació.

Goichon, A. M. (1969) *The Philosophy of Avicenna and its Influence on Medieval Europe* (translated from French with notes, annotations and preface by M. S. Khan). India: Motilal Banarsidass.

Gottstein, K. (ed.) (1986) *Islamic Cultural Identity and Scientific-Technological Development.* Baden-Baden: Nomos.

Khasawnih, S. A. (1986) Science policy in the Arab world, *International Review of Education*, Vol. 32, pp. 55–70.

Kuitunen, J. (1997) Science and higher education policy as dimensions of Euro-Mediterranean cooperation. In L. Hautamäki, T. Keski-Petäjä & K. Seppälä (eds.) *Society as Orientations* (in Finnish). Tampereen yliopisto: Aluetieteen ja ympäristöpolitiikan laitos.

Linberg, D. C. (1978) The transmission of Greek and Arabic learning to the West. In D. C. Linberg (ed.) *Science in the Middle Ages.* Chicago: The University of Chicago Press.

Linjakumpu, A. (1996) Euro-Mediterranean partnership and the Barcelona Summit 1995. In T. Teoksessa Melasuo (ed.) *Beyond Barcelona: Europe and the Middle East in the Mediterranean International Relations* (TAPRI Research Report No. 66).

Lorca. A. V., & Nunez. J. A. (1993) EC-Maghreb relations: a global policy for centre periphery interdependence, *The International Spectator*, Vol. 28(3), pp. 53–66.

Massialas, B. G., & Jarrar, S. A. (1983) *Education in the Arab World.* New York: Praeger.

Massialas, B. G. & Jarrar, S. A. (1987) Conflicts in education in the Arab world: the present challenge, *Arab World Quarterly*, Vol. 9(1), pp. 35–52.

Massialas, B. G., & Jarrar, S. A. (1991) *Arab Education in Transition: A Source Book.* New York & London: Garland Publishing.

Melasuo, T. (ed.) (1995) *Beyond Barcelona – Europe and the Middle East in the Mediterranean International Development* (TAPRI Research Report No. 66).

Morehouse, W. (1978/79) Science, technology, autonomy and dependence: a framework for international debate. In W. Morehouse (ed.) *Science, Technology and Social Order.* Alternatives IV, 1978–79. Rothenberg.

Niblock, T. (1996) North-South socio-economic relations in the Mediterranean. In R. Aliboni et al. (eds.) *Security Challenges in the Mediterranean: A Southern Viewpoint.* London: Frank Cass.

Qasem, S. (1996) *The Arab States: World Science Report* 1996. Paris: UNESCO.

Qasem, S. (1998a) *The Higher Education System in the Arab States.* Cairo: UNESCO.

Qasem. S. (1998b) *Research and Development Systems in the Arab World.* Cairo: UNESCO.

Qasem. S. (1999) *Research and Development in the Arab States: A New Commitment* (Mimeo).

Rahman, A. (1978/79) Science and technology for a new social order. In W. Morehouse (ed.) *Science, Technology and Social Order.* Alternatives IV. 1978–79. Rothenberg.

Rothenberg, R. (1984) *The Neoliberals: Creating the New American Politics.* New York: Simon & Schuster.

Roy, D. A., & Irelan, W. T. (1992) Educational policy and human resource development in Jordan, *Middle Eastern Studies*, Vol. 28(1), pp. 178–215.

Salmi, J. (1992) The higher education crisis in developing countries: issues, problems, constraints and reforms, *International Review of Education*, Vol. 38(1), pp. 19–33.

Shinn, T. et al. (1997) Introduction: science, technology and society studies and development perspectives in north-south transactions. In T. Shinn et al. (eds.) *Science and Technology in the Developing World.* Dordrecht: Kluwer Academic Publishers.

Smith, C., & Lahteenmaki, K. (1998) Europeanization of the Mediterranean region: the EU's relations with Maghreb. In A. Cafruny & P. Peters (eds.) *The Union and the World: The Political Economy of European Foreign Policy.* The Hague/London/Boston: Kluwer Law International.

Sultana, R. G. (1999) The Euro-Mediterranean region and its universities: an overview of trends, challenges and prospects, *Mediterranean Journal of Educational Studies*, Vol. 4(2), pp. 7–49.

Talbani, A. (1996) Pedagogy, power, and discourse: transformation of Islamic education, *Comparative Education Review*, Vol. 40(1), pp. 66–82.

Tibawi. A. L. (1972) *Islamic Education: Its Traditions and Modernization into the Arab National Systems.* London: Lucac.

Tibi, B. (1988) *The Crisis of Modem Islam: A Preindustrial Culture in the Scientific Technological Age.* Salt Lake City: University of Utah Press.

Turunen, H. (1996) *The EU's Mediterranean Policy and Mediterranean Countries as Market Areas* (Ministry of Industry and Trade, Research Report 25) (in Finnish).

van Audenhove, L. et al. (1999) Information society policy in the developing world: a critical assessment, *Third World Quarterly*, Vol. 20(2), pp. 387–404.

Workshop on the Organization, Management, and Evaluation of Applied Scientific and Technological Research Systems in Arab Universities (1996) Arabian Gulf University, Bahrain, 16–20 November, 1996. An Activity of UNESCO and Arabian Gulf University Joint Programme for the Training on Management of Scientific Research and Transfer of Technology (STEMARN) (Mimeo).

Zahlan, A. B. (1980) *Science and Science Policy in the Arab World.* London: Croom Helm.

CHAPTER 4

The Permanence of Distinctiveness

Performances and Changing Schooling Governance in the Southern European Welfare States

Paolo Landri

1 Introduction

This paper analyses the performances and the emergence of new forms of governance of schooling systems of the countries of the Southern European model of welfare (Ferrera, 1996, 2000). We will see how the process of fabrication of the European space has the effect of pressing isomorphic changes on the patterns of governance of national policies and schooling performances. In some way, this homogenisation can be interpreted as the implementation of the discourse of the knowledge (or the learning) society which seems to diminish the 'force' of national policies within the policies of education. However, a look at the performances of those countries as well as at the attempts to implement new forms of regulation and governance in schooling highlights the *permanence of distinctiveness* in spite of their notable improvements in fulfilling standards, and attempts at reforming their system of schooling. The distinctiveness regards the position of 'low performers' according—to European benchmarking of the wider Lisbon strategy and the endurance of the state tradition in schooling which influences the trajectory of decentralisation (Green, 2002; Prokou, 2008). The paradox of the convergence *and* divergence reveals the complexities of the alignment where the growing relevance of a transnational force (in this case, the EU) develops within the 'light' of the national schooling tradition and leads to a hybridisation of global pressures and tradition of local schooling systems.

The paper unfolds as follows: it first focuses on two homogenising forces in the fabrication of the European education space: performativity and decentralisation. It then will describe how it is possible through these policy technologies to read the common condition of these countries (their condition of 'low-achieving'), and their difficulties in the degree of centralisation-decentralisation in the area of the governance of their school systems. It then aims at discussing the *permanence of distinctiveness* in terms of a *macro-social narrative*, an *institutional perspective* and a *cultural view*.

© THE EURO-MEDITERRANEAN CENTRE FOR EDUCATION RESEARCH, UNIVERSITY OF MALTA, 2008

DOI: 10.1163/9789004506602_004

This is an open access chapter distributed under the terms of the CC BY-NC 4.0 License.

2 Performativity and Decentralisation in the Europeanisation of Schooling

Europeanisation, particularly by means of communitarian politics, activates some trajectories of transformation in the school systems of the member countries, in such a way that, as has been observed by Dale (2000), Europe is increasingly acting as the *agenda-setter* in the field of education. It is notable to consider how this occurs despite the fact that education, and in particular schooling, remains a domain of responsibility of national policies. In this sense, Europeanisation and globalisation converge in a discourse and a common EU engagement to make Europe a 'society of knowledge' and/or learning, capable of increasing its potential of competitiveness in comparison with the USA and Japan.[1] This aim, presented in many European documents (in particular, in the European Commission [1995] White Paper), has then been translated into a series of common targets, explicitly formulated by the documents of Lisbon, Barcelona and Stockholm, which engage the various member states. This common strategy, by showing some elements of the *neo-liberal agenda in the field of education* ('free choice', managerialism, the market)—however mitigated by the inclusion of the criterion of social equity—accentuates the instrumental value of *acquirable school competences* (the link with the labour market). While this implies a strong emphasis on vocational education and training, it affects as a global discourse the differentiation between the areas of education and acts upon these boundaries by diminishing their relevance through the powerful 'umbrella' notion of 'lifelong learning', 'knowledge or learning society' which have a wider currency inside transnational policy discourses and policy educational elites (Lawn & Lindgard, 2002). In that respect, particularly relevant as policy technologies of translation of this strategy are: the market, managerialism and performativity (Ball, 1998). These policy technologies overlap and tend to activate a process of restructuring schooling and practices by affecting subjectivities, identities and practices in the field of education. Here, I would like to draw attention to the principle of *performativity*, that is, the measurability of the results as a discrimination among school performances, and 'good' or 'bad' schools, and the process of *decentralisation* that tends to overcome the bureaucratic government of schools, in favour of a mode of steering educational organisational fields drawing more (at least in principle) on horizontal links among various institutions (what is sometimes called, with some emphasis, 'governance') (Ball, 1998; Magalhaes & Stoer, 2003).

Performativity is a 'technology, a culture and a mode of regulation that employs judgements, comparisons and displays as means of incentive, control, attrition and change—based on rewards and sanctions (both material and symbolic)' (Ball, 1998, p. 45). It implies the setting up of monitoring systems and the production of information in such a way as to produce an ongoing struggle for visualising activities and outcomes, while engaged in the direct practices of teaching and learning, since it supports a view that only what can be measurable and visible is 'good', or worth to consider (the 'terror of performativity' described by Lyotard [1979]). The principle is applied to individuals, organisations as well as to countries, so that European statistics on education and large investigations become increasingly important as a tool to promote competitive performativities among western countries, or if we look at the European Lisbon strategy, among European countries.

Decentralisation accompanies this principle, since it comes through like 'winds of change' across all the educational systems by signalling the demise of state and the role of the state inside the welfare system in favour of greater 'flexibility' and, as suggested in a document of the Organisation for Economic Co-operation and Development (OECD) (1997), a 'devolved environment'. This seems to produce in some way an 'eclipse of the educational bureaucracy' (Benadusi & Landri, 2002), as the dominant mode of organisation of the public provision and regulation of the field of education in nation-states, and the emergence of new mode of governance, where it is possible to experiment, at least in principle, many forms of partnership among the many elements of the organisation field of education.

While these two homogenising forces, and the related elements of the market and managerialism, are well visible in many global discourses and documents of transnational education organisation (OECD and, in particular, European writings and reports since the approval of the Lisbon strategy and the reference to the World Trade Organisation (WTO) as a tool for reaching European benchmarks on education), these principles and technologies do not translate into policy texts and national practices in a direct or automatic way. A useful notion, in this case, is to conceive the re-contextualisation as a translation (not as diffusion) which implies to consider the complex transformation of what is to be displaced and the site where the translation concretely occurs (Czarniawska-Joerges & Sevón, 1996; Ball, 1998). In order to understand how the re-contextualisation occurs and how the alignment develops empirically, I developed here an analysis of performances and of the decentralisation of a selected sample of countries drawing on Eurostat and OECD data as well as on a second-order reflection on the publications derived from Education Governance and Social Integration and Exclusion in Europe (EGSIE) (one of the most relevant European research on the new forms of governance), and the research I am involved in Italy. The cases I will consider are usually classified as belonging to the *Southern European Welfare Model*.

Comparative analysis of the forms of social policies distinguishes different modalities of *welfare capitalism* (Heidenheimer, 1986; Esping-Andersen, 1990). The most successful typology points out three models: (i) the *Scandinavian model*, that includes the North European countries with wider universalistic principles and insurances; (ii) the *Anglo-Saxon model*, drawing on individuals and on capabilities of autonomy, and that comprises the European countries English-speakers; and (iii) the *corporatist model*, where the social inclusion and social assistance are granted *via* work-related schemes and regard European countries of Central Europe. Further analysis led to distinguish the *Southern European Model* (Ferrera, 1996; 2000; Katrougalos & Lazaridis, 2002) by including the countries of then South Europe (Portugal, Spain, Italia, Greece) previously considered a variation of the corporatist model. The presentation of the Southern model was intended to draw attention on the uniqueness of those countries with respect to the other welfare models, and to reduce the possibility of interpretation that considers the difference in terms of backwardness. The debate and the research around the southern difference fed interesting discussions about how to consider the diversity of South Europe and the reason for this distinctiveness. I will explore if this difference applies also to the ways these countries align with the policy technologies of performativity and the process of decentralisation in the field of education. Elsewhere, it has been noted how the dominant mode of state architecture is a relevant aspect in the process of re-contextualisation, so that we have a path dependency from the prevailing institutionalised mode of regulation (Prokou, 2008).

3 Low Performing Systems of Education?

The countries of the Southern European model of welfare appear to be 'low performing' with regard to European benchmarks. Eurostat data induce us to underline the similarity of characteristics in the four countries with reference to five key-indicators: (i) the level of achievement among the youth of the secondary degree of instruction; (ii) the percentage of young people leaving early the education and training system; (iii) the rate of adult population (between 24 and 61 years) who own an upper secondary school leaving certificate; (iv) the percentage of public education expense in reference to the Gross Domestic Product (GDP); and (v) the rate of adult population participating in education and training activities (the rate of participation in *lifelong learning* systems).

With reference to the first indicator (see Table 4.1), the UE27[2] average is that 77.4% of young people aged between 20 and 24 years own at least the school leaving certificate of upper secondary school. In the countries of the

Southern European model—with the exception of Greece, which presents a higher percentage (more than 80%)—the number of young people who own this certificate is inferior (the lowest share refers to Portugal, with a percentage lower than 50%). Throughout the decennium (1995–2005), however, these percentages have been in constant growth, underlining the efforts operated by the countries in raising the degree of completion of upper secondary school for an always-wider quota of young people.

The data concerning early school leavers (see Table 4.2) confirm that there is a high level of school drop-outs in the Southern European model. It means that a high rate of young people, for different reasons, leave education and training opportunities permanently, and, consequently, seem to display a less than sufficient repertoire of competence/knowledge. Here, as before, the best performance is given by Greece, with a portion slightly better than the

TABLE 4.1   Population aged 20–24 years with at least upper secondary school level education

EU/Country	1995	2000	2005
EU		76.6%	77.4%
Greece	73.8%	79.2%	84.1%
Spain	59.0%	66.0%	61.8%
Portugal	45.1%	43.2%	49.0%
Italy	58.9%	69.4%	73.6%

SOURCE: EUROSTAT

TABLE 4.2   Population aged 18–24 with at most compulsory school level of education and not involved in any education and training

EU/Country	1995	2000	2005
EU		17.6%	15.6%
Greece	22.4%	18.2%	13.3%
Spain	33.8%	29.1%	30.8%
Portugal	41.4%	42.6%	38.6%
Italy	32.8%	25.3%	21.9%

SOURCE: EUROSTAT

EU27 average of 15.6%. Portugal, Spain and Italy, instead, register a very high percentage: almost 22% in Italy, almost 31% in Spain and almost 39% in Portugal. These figures indicate that, notwithstanding the efforts carried out in recent years to reduce the phenomenon, there is a range of young people aged between 18 and 24 who, after having reached the end of compulsory schooling, are not involved in any educational and training activity.

The data concerning the school leaving certifications in the adult population (see Table 4.3) confirm that, in the Southern European model of welfare, there is neither an orientation toward the attainment of high school certificates nor a particular interest in formal activities of education and training. In these countries, the range of adult population (25–64 years) with at least the upper secondary school certification is considerably inferior to the EU average (slightly more than 69% in 2005): the lowest result refers to Portugal (26.5%), but low values also concern Spain (48.5%), Italy (50.4%) and Greece (60.0%)—which, although decidedly the highest figure, is still inferior to the EU27 average.

In a similar way, in these countries, the percentage of the adult population, aged between 25 and 64 years, who participate to *lifelong learning* initiatives (see Table 4.4) is quite modest. With the exception of Spain which, in 2005, presented a rather odd figure compared to the decennium trend, we note a percentage oscillating around 5% in Italy and Portugal, and an even lower percentage (around 2%) in Greece.

Moreover, the lack of attractiveness of the school leaving certificate and the functioning difficulties of schools go together with low investments in education as a percentage of public expenditure (see Table 4.5). Among the countries of the Southern European model, Portugal (5.61%) spends more than the EU average on education as a percentage of its Gross Domestic Product (GDP). Comparable figures for Italy and Spain are respectively 4.74% and 4.28%.

TABLE 4.3   Adult population (25–64 years) with at least upper secondary level certification

EU/Country	1995	2000	2005
EU		64.4%	69.3%
Greece	42.6%	51.6%	60.0%
Spain	29.5%	38.6%	48.5%
Portugal	21.9%	19.4%	26.5%
Italy	36.3%	45.2%	50.4%

SOURCE: EUROSTAT

TABLE 4.4   Adult population (25–64 years) engaged in lifelong learning

EU/Country	1995	2000	2005
EU		7.1%	9.7%
Greece	0.9%	1.0%	1.9%
Spain	4.3%	4.1%	10.5%
Portugal	3.3%	3.4%	4.1%
Italy	3.8%	4.8%	5.8%

SOURCE: EUROSTAT

TABLE 4.5   Spending on education as a percentage of GDP

EU/Country	1995	2000	2003
EU			5.17%
Greece	2.87%	3.71%	3.94%
Spain	4.66%	4.28%	4.28%
Portugal	5.37%	5.42%	5.61%
Italy	4.85%	4.47%	4.74%

SOURCE: EUROSTAT

Finally, Greece (3.94%) invests the least in education among the countries of the Southern European model.

A further signal of the 'weakness' of these school systems comes from the PISA 2003 survey, which assessed the competences of students aged 15 at the end of the compulsory school, by focusing on a whole frame of skills (literacy, mathematics and science) considered to be central under the profile of employability and social inclusion. In this survey (see Table 4.6), students from countries of the Southern European model reached average scores that were decidedly inferior to the average score of the other countries participating in the assessment exercise (conventionally fixed at 500).[3] This concerned all three competencies; in this sense, we can say that the performances in Greece, Portugal, Spain and Italy were constantly below average.

In addition, a detailed look at the degrees of achievement of competence indicates that there is a small area of excellent competences (percentages of

THE PERMANENCE OF DISTINCTIVENESS

TABLE 4.6   Average scores on the PISA 2003 survey
(average ACDE = 500)

Country	Literacy	Mathematics	Science
Greece	472	445	481
Spain	481	485	487
Portugal	478	466	468
Italy	476	466	486

SOURCE: OECD PISA 2003

responses more than 7) and a relatively large area of very low competences (percentages of responses less than 1). If we follow this logic, we deal with responses showing the presence of a *relatively extended area of school weakness* and, at the same time, a *rather reduced area of school top performances*. These findings probably suggest a still high degree of *elitism* informing these schooling systems.

At the same time, however, we need to consider the differences and the specificities of the performances. In some cases, the *territorial inequalities* can play an important role in explaining the pattern of data. In the Italian and Spanish cases, they have a valuable relevance; they seem to be less important in the Greek and Portuguese cases, where the signalled characteristics present greater uniformity. The Spanish institutional structure which considers the presence of a vast pluralisation of its autonomies also implies a differentiation in the education levels, with a concentration of educational poverty and of functioning difficulties of the school system in specific areas of the country. In the Italian case, in a similar way, the difference between the North and the South implies a concentration of problematic aspects in the South.

Finally, the performances of the single countries depend also on *different starting conditions*. Among the Southern European countries, Portugal is characterised by very high figures of *early school leavers* (almost 40%), the lowest percentage of young people with an upper secondary school title, and the highest percentage of public spending on education in terms of GDP. Spain and Italy reveal, instead, percentages that place them in a relatively middle situation. But while Greece registers the most positive figure in terms of young people with an upper secondary school title, its percentage of public expenditure on education is the lowest among these countries (the estimate is almost 3.5%) and is considerably inferior to the EU average (superior to 5%).

4   The 'Statist' Legacy

The dynamism of the alignment, in the last ten years, of the countries of the Southern European model with respect to the drive to decentralisation reveals the importance of the architecture of the state in the process of re-regulation. In the following paragraphs, the analysis of the national strategies of each country will allow us to point out, when focusing in greater depth, the *nuances* of this displacement.

5   The Enduring Centralisation in Greece

The case of Greece indicates that the tendency toward the decentralisation of school systems is not a taken for granted end-result of the translation in practice of the knowledge society. We can say that in the European landscape and in the context of the Southern European model, it rather represents a case of persistent *bureaucratic centralism,* still resisting in the face of the considerable expansion of the educational provision and of the efforts carried out during the last 25 years in the democratisation and modernisation of the educational system (Zambeta, 2002; Gouvias, 2007).

An important turning point in the educational policies took place at the end of the 1990s. In the new climate of the 1990s, there was a decisive move toward the keywords of the market and of globalisation: 'flexibility', 'competence', and 'decentralisation'. The reform of 1997, with the approval of Law 2525 and the related decrees of implementation, marked an important step in the restructuring of the Greek school system: the proposal of the institution of the 'integrated lyceum', that is, a form of secondary school aimed at giving the students those abilities which will help the Greek students to gain an easier access, after further training and educational paths, to the job market (Gouvias, 2007). This reform was accompanied, through the communitarian funding in the period 2000–2006 (OPEIVT), by a considerable impulse of financial resources (10 million euro) toward the schools and the universities of the country, multiplying both the private and the public formative provision, and translating itself into schools and courses in the first and second level sectors of Vocational Education and Training (VET), and in the development of a permanent e-learning education.

These fundings tended to create a system of VET. In the emerging system, however, the participation of other *stakeholders* still seemed weak, while the role of central bureaucracies was overrepresented (Gouvias, 2007). As far as decentralisation goes, the 1997–1998 reforms seem not to have produced the

THE PERMANENCE OF DISTINCTIVENESS

effective devolution of powers and competences. Bureaucratic government still prescribes in detail the school timetables, the proceedings of certification and evaluation, salary levels and the mechanisms of the professional careers of the teachers.

6 Decentralisation through School Autonomy

6.1 *The Case of Portugal*

Portugal, instead, represents a case of *decentralisation through school autonomy*. In the last 15 years, according to the results of the research on school governance in Portugal, the most meaningful changes have concerned: (i) the extension of compulsory instruction; (ii) the increase in the rates of participation to the various levels of the school system; and (iii) the programme of education reforms in the 1990s (Alves & Canario, 2002). The democratisation of access to the various levels of instruction has meant an increase in the demand for education and training. The boom started at the primary level with the extension of compulsory schooling to nine years (the compulsory period is now from 6 to 15 years in the *ensino bàsico*), but it also concerned the various segments of the school system up to the upper secondary school. The opening of the system to mass schooling also produced some difficulties due to the deep change of the school audience, now characterised by an heterogeneity of families and by a mixture of social classes, so that, as it has been noted, the advent and the consolidation of mass schooling has also meant, at the same time, its crisis and the need for reforms (Magalhaes & Stoer, 2003). These reforms were, however, developed very late, and meant, according to some scholars, the import of policies already realised elsewhere ten years earlier (Alves & Canario, 2002). Particularly relevant was the intervention to produce changes in the education governance, which focused attention on the schools, and its organisation arrangements.

In this sense, the key-concepts of the reforms have been the autonomy and the *self management* of schools, the participation of social actors, identified as the *stakeholders* of the school service, and the necessity to redefine the role of the state toward the competences of regulation, *mentoring*, monitoring and financing. In Portugal, the school autonomy intersects, at the local level, with the competences attributed to the municipalities.[4] They actually intervene in the institutions of pre-compulsory schools, in the area of *ensino bàsico* (financial investments), in school transportation, in student residencies, and in the sector of adult education. On the efficacy of such a choice of decentring, the positions are diversified: there are some who appreciate the enlargement of the margins for manoeuvre; there are also those who observe that it has not affected the everyday practices of the school service, and that it has translated into an increase in the organisation of work and committees (Alves & Canario, 2002).

6.2   *The Case of Italy*

In the second half of the 1990s, after a long period of normative stability and of practices of *non-decision making*, the Italian education system lived a phase of intense transformation which deeply changed, at least in normative terms, its institutional structure. Probably the development and intensity of such changes originated in the alignment of more *action nets* (Landri, 2002): the process of change in public administration, that is, the reformulation of the role of the state, and the changes in the relationship between public administrations and citizens (Benadusi & Consoli, 2004); the influence of EU policies; and a period of strong government (Ventura, 1998), when the government was able to carry out fundamental political choices in the field of education and training.

In Italy, three are the trajectories along which the process of *policy* change takes place: (i) the attribution of autonomy to the school establishments; (ii) administrative decentralisation; and (iii) the re-shaping of the education curriculum. The discourses supporting school autonomy are similar to those accompanying the decentring route in the other countries of the Southern European model. Therefore, in the frame of a more general process of reform in public administration, single school establishments were attributed financial, organisational and didactic autonomy.

The school autonomy and the re-shaping of the school curricula are accompanied by a reconfiguration of the governance system of education, which redefines the competences of the different institutional involved actors (state, regions, local autonomies, and autonomous institutes) while delineating a new organisational field (Powell & DiMaggio, 1991), the system of education and training, characterised, in comparison with the formula of the preceding government, by a tendency to the pluralisation of its actors (Benadusi & Landri, 2002; Grimaldi & Landri, 2006).

In this case, as in Portugal, the institutional strategy developed in a top-down direction, in the first instance privileging the autonomy of the single school establishment, and only later starting the process of redefining the organisation field with the participation of the other institutional actors. Even more complex seems to be the re-shaping of the curricula. Here, two reforms—the first one promoted by the then minister, Enrico Berlinguer, and a second one by the subsequent centre-right minister, Letizia Moratti, known as *Riforma Moratti*—have not been implemented (Landri, 2002).

THE PERMANENCE OF DISTINCTIVENESS

7   Decentralisation: The Role of Autonomous Communities in Spain

In Spain, decentralisation follows the constitutive elements of the state (the local communities). Actually, the Spanish constitution recognises the role of the autonomous communities; they have a considerable say in different *policies* which they govern with the central state. Here, decentralisation develops in a bottom-up way, since it has been sustained by the different political and cultural components of the diverse communities. Moreover, we can observe that it coincides with the transition to the democratic regime during the 1970s (after Franco's death), and involved the setting up and implementation of mass schooling. In 1990, however, a new act on education (LOGSE) started the democratisation of the system in a decisive manner, through the accentuation of the relevance of compulsory education and the extension of the period of obligatory schooling (up to 16 years). Its rooting in the autonomous communities (and in other fields of *policy-making*) mirrors a linguistic differentiation which is entirely recognised in the school field. This is to say that the institutional field of school in Spain is characterised by a model of governance that considers the distribution of powers and of competences among the state, the autonomous communities, the local administrations and schools. This model of governance has effects on the curriculum content, which can be diversified in the compulsory and post-compulsory schools, in accordance with the autonomous communities. In the case of compulsory schools, for instance, the state determines 55% (in the Spanish-speaking communities) and 65% (in the communities of other recognised languages) of the contents of the central curriculum; the autonomous communities decide on their own the content and curricula of the remaining quota (between 45% and 35%, the first level of responsibility); the schools develop such curricula on the local plane (the second level of responsibility); and, finally, the single classes and the teachers implement and adapt the curriculum to the need of the students. The diversification of the institutional model on the territory produces, in some cases, an excessive emphasis of what is 'unique' in each community, albeit, in a certain sense, counterbalanced by agencies tending the co-ordination, co-operation and collaboration. There are, in this sense, some organisations which are responsible for this task: the *Conferencia de los Consejeros de Educaciòn*; the *Instiuto de la Calidad y Evaluation* (INCE), and the *Consejo Escolar del Estado*. This complex design of governance, however, does not seem sufficient to contrast the social differences in Spain. The presence of a dual system within the compulsory school (a strong sector of private instruction), further reinforces the phenomena of school segregation, while producing vicious circles of 'impoverishment' of the quality of the public service (Pereyra, 2002).

8 Discussion

The analysis of the performances of these countries and of the process of changing governance in schooling indicates the *permanence of distinctiveness*, that is, a 'fatigue' in the re-contextualisation of policy technologies of the Europeanisation of schooling. This has been mainly interpreted along two main lines: a former focusing on *macro-social aspects* and a latter drawing on the conditions of *organisational fields of those countries*. One could add to these reflections the interesting anthropological view which could draw attention on the cultural construction of 'distinctiveness'. These perspectives represent and account for what is occurring while they provide different enactments of the social (Law & Urry, 2004), that is, they are intellectual technologies treating 'distinctiveness' differently (Edwards, 2004).

8.1 *Macro-Social Aspects*

A large amount of literature tackles this issue with regard to these countries' difference in terms of the *regime of social protection* and *welfare state* (Liebfred, 1992; Ferrera, 1996; Katrougalos & Lazaridis, 2002), and extends the debate by including the *family models* and the *care regimes* (Jurado Guerrero & Naldini, 1997; Saraceno, 2000). Other research highlights identity in terms of a 'Southern European social model' (Karamessini, 2007) which refers to a specific mode of social reproduction in a particular national/cross-national/regional context in a given period, which basically includes an employment and a welfare regime. Similarly, Mingione (2002) suggests that South-European countries—notwithstanding national, regional and local differences—belong to the *same model of capitalist development* which gives rise to a labour-market structure whose main characteristics are the strong economic role of the family and a not fully proletarianised condition of workers. These features tend to endure and to create *path-dependency*. If we followed this line of interpretation, the commonalities of the countries in terms of indicators of performance and organisation of school systems, at least in the basic characteristics, should be interpreted as a (natural?) *consequence* (almost a reflection) of this history and common development. Here, the 'low educational orientation' of the population, the underdevelopment of vocational education and training, the elitism of the structures and practices, the attainment of 'on the job' labour market skills, the centralised bureaucracy of the educational system, etc. seem to be characteristic of the capitalist development model or the social model of reproduction of this group of countries.

8.2 *The Institutional Conditions*

This latter interpretation should also be complemented by considering the results of a new institutionalism in education (Meyer & Scott, 1983; Meyer &

Rowan, 2006). This tradition of inquiry has identified the dynamics of educational organisations and, in particular, has framed within the context of 'loose coupling' most of the contribution to education research frequently invoked to explain the weak ties in case of the links between the structure and the practice of schooling, and the not-so-strong relationship between policy and administration. While sometimes the notion of 'loose coupling' has been misused, and is being considered in a reflexive way within the same new institutionalism because of the recent trend in institutional change (Meyer & Rowan, 2006), in our case it draws attention to the conditions which favour the (re) production of the permanence of the distinctiveness, and those dynamics which can alter the *punctuated equilibrium* of an institutional setting. Here, the distinctiveness loses the sense of uniqueness and comes to be interpreted as *institutional inertia*, that is, as a 'difficulty' in abandoning the centralised legacy which is revealed in the fragmentation of the organisational fields disabling school performances and organisations.

Here, the different strategies of decentralisation are affected by the legacy of the state-form: Greece maintains and defends its mainly bureaucratic and centralistic model of organisation, and resists, in a decisive way, what is considered the neo-liberal agenda in the field of educational policies; Portugal and Italy follow the path of autonomy of their school institutes, which can be considered as a strategy maintaining a certain centralisation but which opens up opportunities for co-participation in the sector's *policy-making* process; Spain orientates toward a decentred model of governance, where the local communities play the decisive role in the determination of the educational policies. Such strategies reflect diversity in the more or less decentred and plural *state models* of the different countries; in this sense, the redefinition of the role of the state and of its competences has considerable relevance, because the decentring strategies imply the development of different capacities/competences of governance. In particular, the passage to decentred governance may entail the shrinking of the public sphere (and of the role of the state) with negative effects in the field of social inequalities, which are already well represented in the ordinary performances of the social systems of the Southern European model.

8.3 The Cultural Construction of 'Distinctiveness'

The anthropological view focuses the reflection on the 'distinctiveness' of the system, and about the practical purposes of the reciprocal positionings which lead to the attribution of identity and difference (Varenne & McDermott, 1995). In a *cultural view*, in particular, the focus is on the cultural construction of 'distinctiveness'. The difference of the Southern European countries can be considered in a deficit manner, that is, as a deprivation by assuming European standards and the entire set of benchmarks as 'objective' measures of the imagined European education welfare system. More or less explicitly, the 'deprivation approach' assumes that it is possible to define what a 'good' or a 'bad' educational performance is and an ideal organisation of school governance; this lack is also more or less associated with the idea of an impoverished experience in these countries with regard to the education-work realms. However, the distinctiveness can be regarded simply as a *difference*, and the uniqueness as an expression of cultural diversity: here, we have many cultures of education and learning, and not a dominant European educational culture that defines what a good performance is and what is not. Still, in adopting a cultural approach we draw attention to the *action-nets* which produce situated conditions of assessment where Southern European countries can display their distinctiveness. In other words, we pay attention to how they are made 'distinctive' through a set of arrangements. And this leads us to reflect on the dominant logics of performativity and accountability which emphasises what can be measured and applied to discriminate between 'good' or 'bad' performance of educational systems. In this way, it is possible to analyse the role of transnational actor systems in education, and in particular in what supports the construction of supranational educational space at the European level. This line of inquiry reveals the socio-technical networks attached to the performance of a distinctive Southern European system.

9 Concluding Remarks

The article has analysed the performances and the strategies of decentralisation of governance of schooling in the countries of the so-called Southern Welfare State Model. This reveals a *permanence of distinctiveness*, that is an improvement, yet a persistent gap in aligning with European standards and benchmarks of the Lisbon strategy and a complex drift in moving toward the decentralisation of the schooling systems. Three complementary lines of interpretation (a macro-social, an institutionalist and a cultural approach) may be helpful in understanding and making this difference. Further research is needed to deepen our understanding of the effects of the Europeanisation of schooling in those countries and, particularly, on the influence of the entire 'reform package' for those systems of instruction.

Acknowledgement

This chapter originally appeared as: Landri, P. (2008) The permanence of distinctiveness: performances and changing schooling governance in the

THE PERMANENCE OF DISTINCTIVENESS 83

Southern European welfare states, *Mediterranean Journal of Educational Studies*, Vol. 13(2), pp. 117–135. Reprinted here with permission from the publisher.

Notes

1 Kuhn (2007) offers a vast ranging analysis of *learning society* politics. For the Italian case, see Landri & Maddaloni (2007) in the same volume.
2 The EU expanded to 27 countries in 2004. Consequently, for EU27 data refer to the 2005 entries in the data tables.
3 This paper was completed before the publication of the results of the PISA study of 2006. However, the analysis of these recent results does not modify the main arguments presented here in a substantial way (see www.pisa.oecd.org).
4 In Portugal there are two autonomous regions: Madeira and the Azores Isles, which enjoy a considerable autonomy in the organisation also on the level of school and education politics.

References

Alves, N., & Canario, R. (2002) The new magistracy of influence: changing governance of education in Portugal, *European Educational Research Journal*, Vol. 1(4), pp. 656–666.

Ball, S. (1998) Big policies/small world: an introduction to international perspectives in education policy, *Comparative Education*, Vol. 34(2), pp. 119–130.

Benadusi, L., & Consoli, F. (2004) *La Governance della Scuola*. Bologna: Il Mulino.

Benadusi, L., & Landri, P. (2002) Verso la governance: l'eclissi della burocrazia scolastica e il processo di costruzione del sistema dell'istruzione e della formazione, *Economia e Lavoro*, Vol 36(1), pp. 163–182.

Czarniawska-Joerges, B., & Sevón, G. (1996) *Translating Organizational Change*. Berlin: Walter de Gruyter.

Dale, R. (2000) Globalization and education: demonstrating a 'common world educational culture' or locating a 'globally structured educational agenda'?, *Educational Theory*, Vol. 50(4), pp. 427–448.

Edwards, R. (2004) Intellectual technologies in the fashioning of learning societies, *Educational Philosophy and Theory*, Vol. 36(1), pp. 69–78.

Esping-Andersen, G. (1990) *The Three Worlds of Welfare Capitalism*. Cambridge: Polity Press.

European Commission (1995) *Teaching and Learning, Towards the Learning Society* (White Paper on education and training). Brussels: Author.

Ferrera, M. (1996) Il modello sudeuropeo di welfare state, *Rivista Italiana di Scienza Politica*, Vol. 26(1), pp. 67–101.

Ferrera, M. (2000) Reconstructing the welfare state in Southern Europe. In S. Kuhnle (ed.) *Survival of the European Welfare State*. London: Routledge.

Gouvias, D. S. (2007) The 'response' of the Greek state to global trends of educational policy making, *European Educational Research Journal*, Vol. 6(1), pp. 25–38.

Green, A. (2002) The many faces of lifelong learning: recent education policy trends in Europe, *Journal of Education Policy*, Vol. 17, pp. 611–626.

Grimaldi, E., & Landri, P. (2006) Accordi, conflitti e attese: il governo locale dell'istruzione e della formazione. In M. Colombo, G. Giovannini & P. Landri (eds.) *Sociologia delle Politiche e dei Processi Formativi*. Milano: Guerini.

Heidenheimer, A. J. (1986) Il diritto all'istruzione e alla previdenza sociale in Europa e in America. In P. Flora & A. J. Heidenheimer (eds.) *Lo Sviluppo del Welfare Sate in Europa e in America*. Bologna: Il Mulino.

Jurado Guerrero, T., & Naldini, M. (1997) Is the South so different? Italian and Spanish families in comparative perspective. In M. Rhodes (ed.) *Southern European Welfare States Between Crisis and Reform*. London: Frank Cass.

Karamessini, M. (2007) *The Southern European Social Model: Changes and Continuities in Recent Decades*. Geneva: International Labour Organization.

Katrougalos, G. S., & Lazaridis, G. (2002) *Southern European Welfare States*. London: Palgrave Macmillan.

Kuhn, M. (ed.) (2007) *New Society Model for a New Millennium: The Learning Society in Europe and Beyond*. New York: Peter Lang.

Landri, P. (2002) Oltre la retorica: discorsi, testi ed oggetti dell'autonomia scolastica. In F. Battistelli (ed.) *La Cultura delle Amministrazioni fra Retorica e Innovazione*. Milano: FrancoAngeli.

Landri, P., & Maddaloni, D. (2007) A blurred object: the Italian discourses on learning society. In M. Kuhn (ed.) *New Society Model for a New Millennium: The Learning Society in Europe and Beyond*. New York: Peter Lang.

Law, J., & Urry, L. (2004) Enacting the social, *Economy and Society*, Vol. 33(3), pp. 390–410.

Lawn, M., & Lindgard, B. (2002) Constructing a European policy space in educational governance: the role of transnational policy actors, *European Educational Research Journal*, Vol. 1(2), pp. 290–307.

Liebfred, S. (1992) Towards a European welfare state? On integrating poverty regimes into the European Community. In Z. Ferge & J. Kolberg (eds.) *Social Policy in a Changing Europe*. Frankfurt-am-Main: Campus Verlag.

Lyotard, F. (1979) *La Condition Postmoderne: Rapport sur le Savoir*. Paris: Minuit.

Magalhaes, A. M., & Stoer, S. R. (2003) Performance, citizenship and the knowledge society: a new mandate for European education policy, *Globalisation, Societies and Education*, Vol. 1(1), pp. 41–66.

Meyer, H. D., & Rowan, B. (2006) *The New Institutionalism in Education*. Albany, NY: State University of New York Press.

Meyer, M. W., & Scott, W. R. (1983) *Organizational Environments: Ritual and Rationality*. Beverly Hills: SAGE.

Mingione, E. (2002) Labour market segmentation and informal work. In H. Gibson (ed.) *Economic Transformation, Democratization and Integration into European Union: Southern Europe in Comparative Perspective*. Basingstoke, Hampshire: Palgrave.

OECD (1997) *The OECD Report on Regulatory Reform*. Paris: Author.

Pereyra, M. A. (2002) Changing educational governance in Spain: decentralisation and control in autonomous communities, *European Educational Research Journal*, Vol. 1(4), pp. 667–675.

Powell, W. W., & DiMaggio, P. J. (eds.) (1991) *The New Institutionalism in Organizational Analysis*. Chicago: University of Chicago Press.

Prokou, E. (2008) A comparative approach to lifelong learning policies in Europe: the cases of the UK, Sweden and Greece, *European Educational Research Journal*, Vol. 43(1), pp. 123–139.

Saraceno, C. (2000) Gendered policies: family obligations and social policies in Europe. In T. Boje & A. Leira (eds.) *Gender, Welfare State and the Market: Towards a New Division of Labour*. London: Routledge.

Varenne, H., & McDermott, R. (1995) Culture as disability, *Anthropology and Education Quarterly*, Vol. 26, pp. 324–348.

Ventura, S. (1998) *La Politica Scolastica*. Bologna: Il Mulino.

Zambeta, E. (2002) Modernisation of educational governance in Greece: from state control to state steering, *European Educational Research Journal*, Vol. 6(1), pp. 637–655.

CHAPTER 5

Gramsci, the Southern Question and the Mediterranean

Peter Mayo

1 Introduction

Gramsci's discussion of the Southern Question—which runs throughout his *Quaderni* and is therefore not confined to his essay 'Some Themes regarding the Southern Question' ('*Alcuni Temi sulla Quistione Meridionale*', henceforth 'The Southern Question')[1]—is that which, probably more than anything else, attracted me to the Sardinian's work in the first place. These writings and notes helped shed light on the geopolitical context in which I was born and raised.[2] It is for this reason that I seek to extrapolate from Gramsci's writings, concerning the Southern Question, insights for a greater understanding of some current dynamics in politics and culture in the Mediterranean region at large, a region which I conceive of as an expression of that larger construct referred to as the South.

2 Structure of Argument

The paper opens with some general considerations regarding different conceptions of the Mediterranean, linking the region with the broader South and highlighting issues of subalternity connected with the latter. The Mediterranean is viewed in a manner that takes account of both its Northern and Southern shores. Efforts are made, drawing on Gramsci's own reflections and anecdotal accounts, to avoid romanticising the Mediterranean and the South in general and to capture some sense of the region's complexity. Importance is given, in this context, to the issue of dominant belief systems, with reference to Gramsci's own views on religion. The issue of religion leads to questions concerning ethnicity and religious beliefs of people with different traditions co-existing in the area, especially Southern Europe—the focus of Gramsci's attention. The paper foregrounds one of the major challenges for social solidarity facing people of this region, namely the challenge posed by massive migration from the South to the North in the context of the intensification

© THE EURO-MEDITERRANEAN CENTRE FOR EDUCATION RESEARCH, UNIVERSITY OF MALTA, 2007
DOI: 10.1163/9789004506602_005

of globalisation. The Gramscian theme of regional solidarity, for a revolutionary socialist politics based on knowledge and understanding, and the related themes of misplaced alliances and internal colonialism are taken up. The paper moves from Gramsci's discussion focusing on North-South solidarity (proletariat and peasantry) in the context of a nation state to a broader and trans-national form of North-South solidarity, rooted in political economy and an understanding of colonialism, connected with the issues of migration and inter-ethnic solidarity. Educational strategies, for this purpose, are identified.

3   Different Conceptions of the Mediterranean[3]

Like all regions of the world, the Mediterranean can at best be regarded as a construct. This region is conceived of in different ways by different people according to their location in the North-South axis. There are those in Northern Europe, and possibly other parts of the Western hemisphere, who conceive of the Mediterranean in a colonial, ethnocentric and euro-centric manner. They historically seem to have regarded the Southern part of the Mediterranean as the target of a 'civilising mission'. They also see the division between North and South of the Mediterranean in immutable and therefore essentialist terms. They possibly even see this division as representing the battle line between Christianity and Islam. Pride of place is often given, within this conceptualisation, to those traditions that lie at the heart of 'Western civilisation', notably the Greco-Roman tradition, where explicitly or implicitly any indebtedness of this tradition to civilisations emerging from the Southern Mediterranean is denied. One often finds this conception also among colonised subjects. For as Frantz Fanon wrote:

> The colonialist bourgeoisie, in its narcissistic dialogue, expounded by the members of its universities, had in fact deeply implanted in the minds of the colonized intellectual that the essential qualities remain eternal in spite of all the blunders men [sic] may make: the essential qualities of the West, of course. The native intellectual accepted the cogency of these ideas, and deep down in his brain you could always find a vigilant sentinel ready to defend the Greek-Latin pedestal. (Fanon, 1963, p. 46)

This process of cultural invasion leads one to think of the Mediterranean only in terms of those centres in the region which are directly associated with the Greek-Latin tradition. In this respect, the Rome-based Croat scholar, Predrag Matvejevic, writes 'We need to get rid of this European habit of speaking about the Mediterranean and think only of its northern shore: the Mediterranean has another shore, that of Africa and the Maghreb' (Matvejevic, 1997, p. 119).[4]

4 Avoiding Romanticising the South

Others construct the Mediterranean differently, projecting it as a region having all the characteristics of what can be broadly called the 'South'. Here is a vision of the Mediterranean that connects with a larger and more expansive notion of the South. Needless to say, the South has its contradictions and should therefore not be romanticised. After all, Gramsci, himself a southerner, who reacted strongly to any attempt to caricature the South, criticising even socialists such as Ferri, Nocifero, Sergi and Orano (Gramsci, 1975, p. 47; Gramsci, 1997, p. 183) for their positivist and pathological affirmation of what they perceived as the southerners' 'biological inferiority', never romanticised the region from which he hailed. He regarded most of the unsavoury aspects of life in the South as 'folklore' and did not shy away from underlining the most shocking aspects of his native Sardinia. These included the different forms of superstition from which he, '*Antonu [Ninu] su gobbu*' (Nairn, 1982), suffered as a disabled person, holding his parents responsible for not seeking professional help for what would nowadays be diagnosed as Potts disease and for giving in to the popular myth that anyone born with a disability has a terrible birthmark which has to be hidden from public sight, hence his mother's fabrication that he damaged his spine when falling from a helper's arms (Lepre, 1998, p. 4). His most shocking depiction of the horrors of Southern life is provided in that much cited letter to Tania of 30 January 1933 where he discloses that he once witnessed a disabled young man confined to a hovel fit for animals. The 10-year-old Antonio was taken there by the young man's mother, from whom he was to receive payment on his mother's behalf:

> She told me to accompany her to a certain place and that on returning she would take the crochet work and give me the money. She led me outside the village to a small clearing cluttered with debris and rubble; in one corner there was a hovel resembling a pigsty, four feet high, without windows or openings of any kind and with one heavy door as an entrance. She opened the door, and immediately one heard an animal-like moan; inside was her son, a youth eighteen years old, of very swarthy complexion, who was not able to stand and therefore remained seated and lunged in his seat toward the door as far as the chain around his waist permitted

GRAMSCI, THE SOUTHERN QUESTION AND THE MEDITERRANEAN

him to go ... He was covered with filth and red-eyed like an animal of the night. His mother emptied the contents of her bag, fodder mixed with leftovers from home, into a stone trough and refilled another container with water. Then she closed the door and we went away (Gramsci, in Germino, 1990 p. 3; original in Gramsci, 1996, p. 674) ... I did not say anything to my mother about what I had witnessed given the impression this had on me and that I was convinced nobody would have believed me. (Gramsci, 1996, p. 674; my translation)

It can be argued that Gramsci, an atheist who was the son of a deeply religious woman whose strong spiritual beliefs he respected, even though he did not share them, as manifest in his letters to her, also regards the kind of Catholicism that prevailed in the Southern regions and islands of Italy as another unedifying aspect of life in the *Mezzogiorno* (the South of Italy). The Catholic religion, as Gramsci shows, is tied to strong material interests in the Southern region of Italy. It is connected to land (priests were land administrators, usurers), power structures and folklore; it traditionally served as a buffer against modernising forces and, as the Brazilian thinker Paulo Freire (1995, p. 132) would argue with respect to the 'traditional church' in 'closed societies', such a church would mould the people's 'common sense' along immutable and fatalistic lines. The arrogance of Southern ecclesiastical power was reflected, in Gramsci's time, in the 'morally lax' attitude of priests (in contrast to Northern priests who were perceived to be 'morally more correct') who served as subaltern intellectuals and who were viewed cynically by the peasants themselves ('A priest is a priest on the altar; outside he is a man like all others' [Gramsci, 1995, p. 38; original in Gramsci, 1997, p. 196]). These peasants would nonetheless aspire to see their children join the clergy and therefore move upward within the power structure. This strong connection between religion, hegemony and power, in this part of the world, needs to be borne in mind in a context increasingly being characterised by the influx of immigrants, from outside the peninsula, including immigrants from North Africa who cling to a different belief system. The role of Southern intellectuals, including the dominant 'cosmopolitan' type of Southern intellectuals (who speak a language that cuts them off from the people) as well as the subaltern intellectuals, including the traditional 'pre-industrial society' intellectuals (notaries, doctors, lawyers, priests, teachers), is also analysed for these intellectuals' part in sustaining the agrarian bloc and hence the subaltern status of the southern regions, *vis-à-vis* the North, within the contemporary, post-*Risorgimento*,[5] hegemonic set up. In short, Gramsci does not romanticise the South. He highlights its major shortcomings which, unlike many socialists of his period, he does not attribute to some 'biological inferiority' established 'scientifically', the sort of perception of biological inferiority, presented as 'scientific truth' and 'taught in the universities for over twenty years', that Frantz Fanon (Fanon, 1963, p. 296) decries in *The Wretched of the Earth*. On the contrary, Gramsci attributed such shortcomings to the exploitative 'internal' coloniser-colonised dialectical relation that characterised post-*Risorgimento* Italy.

5 Religion, Ethnicity and Subjugated Knowledge

The alternative conception of the Mediterranean, as an expression of the South conceived of in its broader context, leads to an appreciation of the region's richness and cultural diversity, as well as the many voices and identities it comprises. One can consider many of these voices and identities marginalised, typical of southern voices and identities. In the euro-centric centres of cultural and intellectual production, these voices and identities are constructed as forms of *alterity* and they are often rendered 'exotic', if not demonised,[6] being very much subaltern voices engendering, in Foucault's terms, a subjugated body of knowledge (Foucault, 1980, p. 86). And yet, as I shall attempt to show, also drawing from Gramsci's writings in the *Quaderni* (Prison Notebooks), this body has in the past contributed significantly to the development of what is referred to as the Western tradition.

The Mediterranean gave rise to the three great monotheistic religions, many of which have a hegemonic presence in several countries of the region and therefore feature prominently in Gramsci's analyses throughout his work, notably his prison writings. His insights concerning Catholicism,[7] often enhanced by his reading of *Civilta` Cattolica* (Catholic Civilisation) and papal encyclicals, and Islam[8] are of great relevance to the current situation concerning religion and ethnicity in this conflict ridden and heterogeneous region.

6 Intensified Globalisation and Migration

The link between religion and ethnicity becomes most pronounced in various parts of the region owing to one of the major features (migration by populations from the South to the North) of the intensification of globalisation as it has affected this part of the world, with globalisation, strictly speaking, having always been a feature of the capitalist mode of production characterised by periodical economic reorganisation and an ongoing quest for the exploration of new markets. In fact, it is most appropriate, in the present historical conjuncture, to repeat the term I have just used: the *intensification* of globalisation. This intensification is brought about through developments in the field of information technology. This process 'not only blurs national boundaries but also shifts solidarities within and outside the national state' (Torres, 1998, p. 71).[9]

Mobility is a characteristic of globalisation's 'inner' and 'outer' circuits (Torres, 1998, p. 92). We can speak of mobility in terms of the threat of the 'flight of capital' in a scenario where the process of production is characterised by dispersal and cybernetic control (outer circuit), and mobility of workers within and beyond the region (inner circuit). Migration is an important feature of the Mediterranean. As underlined at the 1997 Civil Forum EuroMed:

> Immigration represents the emerging aspect, probably the most evident, of the wide process which characterizes more and more the whole planet—globalization. Migrations represent more than a phenomenon, a historical certainty that can be found today, though with different features, in all countries and, in particular, in the most developed [*sic. read: industrially developed*]. Migration phenomena are becoming more and more important within the Mediterranean basin. (Fondazione Laboratorio Mediterraneo, 1997, p. 551)

According to Braudel (1992), there was a time when 'exchange' was a prominent feature of life in and around the Mediterranean basin. In this day and age, however, the exchange takes on a different form. In terms of mobility of people,[10] it would be amiss to consider the exchange one that occurs on a level playing field. It can also be argued, with respect to the movement of people from the Southern Mediterranean to the Northern Mediterranean and beyond, that the 'spectre' of the violent colonial process the 'old continent' initiated has come back with a vengeance to 'haunt' it (Borg & Mayo, 2006, p. 151). This process is facilitated by the requirements of the economies in highly industrialised countries concerning certain types of labour and the consideration that these requirements cannot or should not (to minimise labour costs) be satisfied by the internal labour market, despite the high levels of unemployment experienced within these countries (Apitzsch, 1995, p. 68).

7 Colonialism, Hegemony and Misplaced Alliances

The legacy of colonialism and its effect on the migratory movements from the South-Mediterranean to the North-Mediterranean and beyond reflects the similar colonial bind, albeit of an 'internal' nature (Italy's North in a process of colonial domination of the country's Southern regions and islands), that Gramsci emphasised in his writings on the Southern Question. His writings focus for the most part on the need for solidarity among subaltern groups across the North-South divide.

The concept of 'national-popular', so much emphasised by Gramsci, takes on a specific meaning in this context. What is 'national' is often tied to the culture of hegemonic ethnic groups and is related to the whole structure of hegemony. Concepts such as 'national identity', 'national culture' are thus challenged, as part of the process of negotiating relations of hegemony. This applied to relations between different groups within the boundaries of a single nation state, the object of much of Gramsci's analysis. Subaltern groups, involving proletariat and peasants, had to engage in a *historical bloc* to challenge the concept of 'national' and transform the relations of hegemony which it represented. In this regard, one had to challenge misplaced alliances. These included the proposed alliance between exploited Sardinian peasants and their offspring on the island and mainland[11] and the offspring of the exploiting Sardinian gentry, the local (Sardinian) overseers of capitalist exploitation. This is the significance of the episode in 'The Southern Question' concerning the effort of the eight communists to thwart the forming of the *Giovane Sardegna*, a challenge which proved successful and which led to the postponement *sine die* of this proposed Sardinian organisation. The same applies to the episode concerning the role of the *Brigata Sassari* (the Sassari Brigade) with respect to industrial unrest in the North. Here the issue of cultural and ethnic hybridisation is raised by Gramsci who regarded the process of solidarity between proletariat and peasants as likely to be helped by the fact that the former consist, for the most part, of offspring of the latter, given that much of the industrialisation in Italy's North was predicated on internal migration from the industrially underdeveloped and impoverished South. Gramsci highlights the bonding that emerged from conversations between the soldiers and strikers that led to the realisation that both were victims of the same exploitative process. The themes of solidarity therefore and the struggle against misplaced alliances become two of the most important features of his writings on the South, especially the essay on which he was working at the time of his imprisonment in Rome ('The Southern Question'). They have great relevance for the Southern Question when viewed in a larger context, the context of North-South/South-North relations on a regional and transcontinental scale.

8   Renegotiating Hegemony and the National-Popular

One major difference however is that crossing national borders is more difficult and hazardous than crossing regional ones within the same country. As the Slovenian writer Slavoj Žižek rightly argues 'in the much-celebrated free circulation opened up by global capitalism, it is "things" (commodities) which circulate freely, while the circulation of "persons" [*themselves treated as commodities—* author's insertion] is more and more controlled' (Žižek, 2004, p. 34). And yet, often risking life and limb, being at the mercy of unscrupulous 'coyotes', thousands and thousands of migrants cross the 'New Rio Grande' divide between North Africa and Southern Europe, many drowning in the process. If I can play around with Gramsci's statement concerning the North of Italy in relation to the *Mezzogiorno*, Europe with its colonial centre was an 'octopus' (Gramsci, 1975, p. 47) which enriched itself at the expense of the South in its broader context. Long-term victims of the predatory colonial process that led to the ransacking of Africa (see Rodney, 1973), these migrants, often from sub-Saharan Africa who travel via North Africa, attempt to reach the centres of Europe (once again a case of the empire striking back) but often end up at the continent's periphery. The intermeshing of cultures that this brings about leads to further questioning of old hegemonic arrangements and the concepts that reflect them. The concept of 'national popular' takes on a new meaning in this context. Meanwhile, old but still prevalent concepts such as 'national identity' and 'national culture', resorted to by sections of the often self-proclaimed 'autochthonous' population as part of a xenophobic retrenchment strategy, are called into question by those who derive their inspiration from Gramsci and others (more recently Said who draws on Gramsci's 'Southern Question' in his work)[12] and who aspire to a society characterised by social justice. The greater the presence of multiethnic groups and the stronger their lobby, the greater would be the struggle to renegotiate relations of hegemony within the countries concerned.

In this respect, there is relevance, for the current situation, in Gramsci's insistence that the Turin communists in the North of Italy, which, I reiterate, largely included people of southern origin, brought the Southern Question to the attention of the workers' vanguard, identifying it as one of the key issues for the proletariat's national popular politics (Gramsci, 1997, pp. 181–182). Furthermore, the national popular alliance of Italian workers and peasants, advocated by Gramsci and also Piero Gobetti (Gramsci, 1997, p. 204), takes on a larger more global North-South meaning in this age of mass migration from South to North. Any genuinely socialist initiative today must bring to the forefront the issue of the Southern Question in its larger context extending beyond geographical boundaries and territories.

9   North-South Solidarity

This must be done in the interest of generating North-South solidarity and confronting misplaced alliances. I would include, among these misplaced alliances, the false alliance between 'labour' and 'management' against 'the competition'. Globalisation has brought in its wake misplaced alliances based on racist, labour market segmentation strategies. Workers continue to be otherised and segregated on ethnic, national and religious lines, as well as on such lines as those of being refugees, asylum seekers or 'economic migrants'.

Such an anti-racist programme of education and social action can be successful only if rooted in political economy and an understanding of colonialism. These are the elements that Gramsci sought to bring to his analysis of the Southern Question in Italy, placing the emphasis on political economy and a historical understanding of Italy's 'internal colonialism'. Gramsci's use of political economy is most evident in 'The Southern Question' and the notes concerning Italy's post-*Risorgimento* state (see Notebook 1 of the *Prison Notebooks*) where he gives economic reasons for the subordination of the South, reasons that are also supported by the work of economic historians such as Luigi De Rosa (2004). Gramsci writes about the Northern economic protectionist, 'fortress' strategies ruining the southern economy. These strategies include the tariff wars with France that had a deleterious effect on southern agricultural life in Italy (Gramsci, 1975, p. 45). Likewise, economic power blocs such as the EU and the US, today, adopt their 'fortress' economic and agrarian policies that impinge negatively on economic development in Africa and elsewhere. With a daily billion-dollar subsidy provided by the wealthy countries to their farmers, people from poor countries that depend on agriculture will find it hard to feed and educate their children, with migration, often at terrible costs, proving to be their only option.[13]

10   Educating for Solidarity: A Lengthy Process

Using material from Gramsci with respect to the Southern Question and related themes, such as those concerning Arabs and Islam, one can identify some of the ingredients for the kind of work that genuinely socialist parties and other organisations can carry out to generate the consciousness necessary to foster greater solidarity among different subaltern groups in this situation characterised by massive immigration into Southern European countries. This is one of the greatest challenges facing those committed to a socialist politics in this region. The work involved is unmistakably of an educational nature, as was most of the work in which Gramsci was engaged when attempting to generate a truly revolutionary working class consciousness in the Italy of his time. After all, education is, for Gramsci, fundamental to the workings of hegemony itself (Borg, Buttigieg & Mayo, 2002, p. 8). And the kind of educational work in which one must engage, in the contemporary context, is a lengthy one. With local working class people, living in a state of precariousness, being the ones most likely to suffer from the devastating effects of Neoliberal globalisation policies, this work becomes ever so urgent. Unless such an educational strategy is developed, it is more likely that working class people become attracted to the kind of populist right wing and often neo-fascist discourse that plays on their fears and leads to further segmentation and antagonism among workers on ethnic lines. This can result in misplaced alliances and the mystification of the fact that both they and the immigrants share a common fate: that of subalternity and of both being victims of a ruthless process of capitalist exploitation. There have been cases when traditionally socialist parties have been accused of shunning the responsibility of working toward fostering inter-ethnic solidarity among workers. They are accused of doing so for fear of losing electoral votes, a situation which highlights the limits of bourgeois democracy for a genuinely socialist politics predicated on worker solidarity across ethnic and national lines.

11 Elements for an Educational Strategy

My proposal for an educational strategy for greater solidarity in this day and age includes developing a broad terrain of cultural studies which entails:

1. A deep understanding of the culture of 'alterity'. This would include, but of course not be limited to, knowledge of the different religions of the Mediterranean, including the religions which immigrants bring with them from other areas such as sub-Saharan Africa. Once again, as with Gramsci's portrayal of the Southern regions and islands in Italy, one must also avoid romanticising these religions (Christianity, Judaism, Islam and African religions). They should be subjected to critical scrutiny.

2. Avoiding caricatures and exoticisation of the type which Gramsci decried with regard to Northern conceptions of the Southerner's alleged 'biological inferiority' and Northern misrepresentations of legitimate struggles of southerners who were denied land by the Northern 'liberators' (e.g., the references to *brigantaggio*—brigand activity—and the widespread exaggerations surrounding its manifestations).

3. Challenging (mis)representations/conceptions of the other (in this case immigrants from the Southern shores of the Mediterranean and beyond) that reflect a 'positional superiority' on the part of those who provide the representation (Said, 1978).

4. Analysing seriously the relationship between Islam, traditional African religions (many migrants who cross the Mediterranean come from sub-Saharan Africa) and modernity: Gramsci writes about the existence,

before World War 1, of a circle of young Christians in Turin, including Dominicans, who drew sustenance from modernising tendencies in Islam and Buddhism, conceiving of religion as a syncretisation of all the major world religions (Gramsci, 1975, p. 2090).[14]

5. Challenging essentialist (*a la`* Huntington) notions of immigrants, Islam(s), Arabs, Africans, Blacks, etc.—all are much more variegated than Huntington and his like would have us believe, there being no fixed and static cultures but cultures which, on the contrary, have flourished as a result of hybridisation and cultural cross-currents. Gramsci,[15] for instance, writes about key Arab leaders and how they sought to confront a more universalistic Islam with a sense of national unity and adaptation. And he argues that, in many places, the Islam of his times was already different from what it was earlier—it will continue to evolve but not suddenly; he felt that it cannot be substituted by Christianity which took nine centuries to evolve while Islam is forced to run 'dizzily' (Gramsci, 1975, pp. 246–248)—a rather contentious assertion that reflects an 'evolutionary development' model.[16]

12 Cultural Cross-Currents and the 'Clash of Civilisations' Myth

The last point warrants further commentary. Monolithic, essentialist conceptions of Islam are provided by right wing westerners as well as Muslim fundamentalists. In his critique of Samuel Huntington's 'Clash of Civilisations', Edward Said wrote:

> ... Huntington is an ideologist, someone who wants to make "civilizations" and "identities" into what they are not: shut-down, sealed-off entities that have been purged of the myriad currents and countercurrents that animate human history, and that over centuries have made it possible for that history not only to contain wars of religion and imperial conquest but also to be one of exchange, cross-fertilization and sharing. This far less visible history is ignored in the rush to highlight the ludicrously compressed and constricted warfare that "the clash of civilizations" argues is the reality. (Said, 2001, para. 4)

Said made the point, time and time again, about there being no such thing as pure cultures. What we have are hybrid cultures, a point Gramsci demonstrates forcefully in the *Prison Notebooks* and in such works as 'The Southern Question' where he indicates the intermeshing between Southern immigrant workers and Northerners in Italy with the implication being that there is an

GRAMSCI, THE SOUTHERN QUESTION AND THE MEDITERRANEAN

intermeshing of cultures in these regions (e.g., Southern immigrants contributing to Northern culture and *vice versa*). On a broader scale this ought to lead to a consideration of non-European contributions to aspects of what is heralded as 'Western civilisation'.

In this respect, Gramsci echoes many others in highlighting the contributions of Arabs, Islamic culture, and other non-European cultures to the development of so-called 'Western civilisation'. In a note (§5) in Notebook 16, Gramsci makes reference to the work of Ezio Levi and Angel Gonzales Palencia, the latter outlining Arab influences in cuisine, medicine, chemicals etc. (see Boothman, 2007, p. 65). Gramsci furthermore reminds us about the Arab post-1000 influence on European culture via Spain. He states that philosophical and theological disputes in France, during that period, betray the influence of Averroes'[17] doctrine (Gramsci, 1975, p. 642). He also underlines what should be commonplace knowledge and yet which, on the evidence of my own teaching experiences, seems to be ignored, namely the Arab and Jews' reintroduction of ancient philosophy into European civilisation (Gramsci, 1975, p. 644). Also, in Notebook 5, Gramsci mentions the scientific influence of Arabs on the formation of Germanic-roman states, specifically on medieval Spain (Gramsci, 1975, p. 574).[18]

Others have also referred to the work of Miguel Asin Palacios in this context, notably the Italy based Egyptian scholar, Mahmoud Salem Elsheikh who in an article '*le Omissioni della Cultural Italiana*' writes about the 'debtor's syndrome':

> ... the person to whom one is indebted is constantly a hated person; particularly if the creditor, as in this case, is a strange body, rejected by the collective consciousness, hated by the political, social, cultural and religious institutions. If anything, the rage against the creditor, in these circumstances, becomes an almost moral duty and a necessary condition for the survival of that society. (Elsheikh, 1999, p. 38; my translation)

Furthermore, the Turkish writer Ali Hasbi insists:

> The knowledge and technologies which are the shared heritage of humanity were not created *ex nihilo*, but were built up in a lengthy process of accumulation to which every people has made its contribution. Efforts are now being made to give the West credit for a unique and absolute rationality and a creativity, which are seen as consubstantial with it [... *this demonstrates*] amnesia and ethnocentricity. (Hasbi, 2003, p. 378)

The importance of these contributions, including the direct and indirect contributions of black African cultures and other cultures (see, for example,

Bernal, 1987), cannot be overstressed in an educational process intended not only to do justice to a culture or cultures (for instance, those of Islam and Arabs, which are not to be used interchangeably[19]) that have often been denigrated in a process of historical and cultural amnesia predicated on ignorance and prejudice. This process should serve to highlight the hybrid nature of cultures, crisscrossed by 'contrapuntal' (to use the term Said borrows from music and literature[20]) currents, and set the record straight with respect to flawed conceptions of cultures that give one a sense of positional superiority and falsely lead to the construction of cultures and civilisations as being mutually exclusive and antagonistic. In this respect, one must recognise that Christian, Jewish and Muslim fundamentalists are also guilty of a similar historical and cultural amnesia when projecting a fixed notion of their religion and when being reluctant to acknowledge derivations in their religion from other civilisations and philosophical traditions that were in turn indebted to other civilisations and philosophical traditions.

13 Conclusion: Challenging a Contrived World Cultural Order

Over and above an understanding of colonialism and its political economic basis, one must also understand the long-term effects of the imposition of a contrived world cultural order. This work would enable us to foster that sense of solidarity that Gramsci had called for. These are the elements that Gramsci sought to bring to his analysis of the Southern Question in Italy, with his emphasis on political economy, astute cultural analysis and historical understanding of the *Risorgimento* (a passive revolution) and the process of 'internal colonialism' it brought about.

Much of the published literature, at least in English, concerning Gramsci's ideas and education, have hitherto focused on such themes as the Unitarian School, the education of adults (including ideas connected with the Factory Councils and the issue of industrial democracy), hegemony in its broader context, the role of educators as organic intellectuals and the educational role of revolutionary parties. The writings concerning the Southern Question, however, deserve greater treatment in educational debates. I hope therefore that this initial effort to engage some of Gramsci's writings on the issue will lead to further debates in the field since the 'Southern Question' is not a thing of the past but very much a contemporary reality. It is a question which, as I hope to have shown, continues to have implications for socially transformative educational and cultural work in this day and age. May the debate continue.

GRAMSCI, THE SOUTHERN QUESTION AND THE MEDITERRANEAN

Acknowledgements

Earlier drafts of this piece were presented at: (i) the international conference, *Gramsci, le Culture e il Mondo* (Gramsci, Cultures and the World), Fondazione Istituto Gramsci, Rome, 27–28 April 2007; (ii) seminar with PhD students, 'Religion and Cultural Hegemony', Faculty of Sociology and Political Science, Goethe Universität, Frankfurt Am Main (modified version incorporating the discussion about Catholicism and Islam), 26 June 2007; and (iii) public seminar 'Gramsci, The Southern Question and the Mediterranean' organised by the Global Education Network, Department of Education Policy Studies, University of Alberta, Edmonton, Canada, 23 July 2007. I am indebted to the various participants at these seminars for their insights on the paper and the issues raised. I am also indebted to Godfrey Baldacchino, Carmel Borg, Joseph Buttigieg, Joseph Gravina and Michael Grech for their comments on earlier drafts of the article. I have taken up and incorporated some of their suggestions. I also thank the reviewers and copy editor for suggestions regarding modifications. Joe Gravina and Michael Grech wrote numerous insightful comments in the margins which, I feel, helped me improve the text, clarify some of my statements and provide a more nuanced perspective on things. Any remaining shortcomings are my sole responsibility.

This chapter originally appeared as: Mayo, P. (2007) Gramsci, the Southern Question and the Mediterranean, *Mediterranean Journal of Educational Studies*, Vol. 12(2), pp. 1–17. Reprinted here with permission from the publisher.

Notes

1 Gramsci uses 'Quistione' instead of 'questione', a word which would nowadays be considered archaic. According to Verdicchio (in Gramsci, 1995, p. 16), it was written in response to an article that appeared in *Quarto Stato* (an important neomarxian journal whose founding editors were Carlo Rosselli and Pietro Nenni) which refers to Guido Dorso's assessment, in *La Rivoluzione Meridionale* (The Southern Revolution), of the Italian Communist Party's position on the Southern Question.

2 I was born, raised and still live in the Mediterranean and typically *Meridionale* island of Malta which historically has shared strong cultural affinities with the Italian *Mezzogiorno* (South) to which it is geographically also very close—96 kilometres off the Sicilian coast.

3 I have reproduced in this section material from chapter 5 of my book *Liberating Praxis* (Mayo, 2004). Permission granted by Praeger Publishers.

4 Personal translation from Predrag Matvejevic's address, in Italian, at the II Civil Forum, Euromed, Naples, 1997.

5 Italian unification (called in Italian the *Risorgimento*, or 'Resurgence') was the political and social process that unified different states of the Italian peninsula into the single nation of Italy.

6　In the words of Egyptian writer, Nawal El Saadawi: 'Perhaps the problem of the world has always been the 'objectification', the nullification, of the 'other'. For the West or the North, the South is the other which exists only as an object to be exploited and oppressed. Christianity or Western culture sees Islam and Arab culture as the other. And in all religions, all that does not belong to God is seen as emanating from the devil. The problem of our world is to ignore, to dismiss, to destroy the other. To do this, the other must be satanised' (El Saadawi, 1992, p. 137).

7　It has a strong presence in the Italian Southern regions and other countries such as Spain, Croatia, Malta and Portugal (it strictly speaking lies on the Atlantic but shares a southern European/Mediterranean culture).

8　Islam is very strong throughout the South Mediterranean as well as in Turkey, the Turkish Republic of Northern Cyprus, Bosnia-Herzegovina, and other parts of Southern Europe given the strong migratory waves across the Mediterranean basin.

9　This process continues to have a strong influence on identity, especially with regard to communities that have traditionally not been organised along individualist lines as has been the case with most Mediterranean and non-Western communities. This, together with other previous modernising forces, seems to be at odds with the fundamentally religious way of life experienced in certain regions of the Mediterranean and also tends to destroy that sense of mystery so much cherished in several non-Western societies. I am indebted to Michael Grech for this point.

10　I have been inspired, in discussing the very important contemporary issue of migration across the Mediterranean, by Pasquale Verdicchio's concise and excellent introduction to his annotated translation of *The Southern Question* (Verdicchio, 1995).

11　'Il continente'—'the continent', as Sardinians refer to the Italian mainland.

12　See Said (1994, pp. 56–59).

13　I am indebted to the late Professor M. Kazim Bacchus, Professor Emeritus, University of Alberta, Canada, for this point.

14　When discussing the relationship between Islam and liberalism, Palestinian peace activist Nahla Abdo had this to say in an interview: 'If and when Islam is conceived of as a religion, I see no reason why one cannot speak of liberal Muslims, the same way they would speak of liberal Christians or liberal Jews. Muslim liberal discourses have firmly been entrenched in the legal system of some Arab/Muslim countries like Tunisia for example. Moreover, Sheikh al-Qaradawi, often featured on al-Jazira and the well-known Sheikh Al-Azhar from Egypt are well known for their liberal interpretations of social and gender phenomena' (Nahla Abdo in Borg & Mayo, 2007, pp. 29–30).

15　Points 4 and 5 draw from Boothman (2007, pp. 65–66).

16　In this respect, I would refer to an interview by Michael Grech with Antonio Dell'Olio, coordinator of the Italian branch of Pax Christi International. Dell'Olio refers to a conversation he held with a Muslim professor from a Cairo university. The latter is reported to have told Dell'Olio 'Give us time … in the Islamic world we had neither a French revolution, which led to social reforms as a result of its separation between church and state, and its cry of Liberty, Equality and Fraternity, nor a Vatican Council which led to religious reforms. These two important events led to a situation when, after so much resistance, denial of progress by the Church and giving up [on the possibility of reform], the Catholic Church and Catholicism began to renew themselves. When we have events such as these we will make a leap forward' (in Grech, 2006, pp. 64, 65; my translation from Maltese).

17　Abū l-Walīd Muhammad ibn Rushd.

18　I am indebted to Boothman (2007) for these points.

19 Derek Boothman states that Gramsci uses 'Arab' almost interchangeably with Muslim: 'In the paragraphs cited here it is always the case that when Gramsci writes 'Arab' the term is also understood to refer to the larger category of Muslim' (Boothman, 2007, p. 65; my translation) If Gramsci does that, then this is unfortunate. Not all Arabs are Muslim. Furthermore, Arabs constitute only one tenth in a milliard of Muslims while Islam is a world religion which therefore knows no ethnic boundaries.

20 See for instance Said in Viswanathan (2001, p. 211).

References

Apitzsch, U. (1995) Razzismo ed atteggiamenti verso gli immigrati stranieri: il caso della Repubblica Federale Tedesca, *Quaderni dei Nuovi Annali*, Vol. 33, pp. 67–76.

Bernal, M. (1987) *The Black Athena: The Afroasiatic Roots of Classical Civilisations*. London: Free Association.

Boothman, D. (2007) L'Islam negli articoli giornalistici gramsciani e nei Quaderni del Carcere, *NAE*, Vol. 6(18), pp. 65–69.

Borg, C., Buttigieg, J. A., & Mayo, P. (2002) Introduction: Gramsci and education: a holistic approach. In C. Borg, J. A. Buttigieg & P. Mayo (eds.) *Gramsci and Education*. Lanham, MD: Rowman & Littlefield.

Borg, C., & Mayo, P. (2006) *Learning and Social Difference: Challenges for Public Education and Critical Pedagogy*. Boulder, CO: Paradigm.

Borg, C., & Mayo, P. (2007) *Public Intellectuals, Radical Democracy and Social Movements: A Book of Interviews*. New York: Peter Lang.

Braudel, F. (1992) *The Mediterranean and the Mediterranean World in the Age of Philip II, Vol. I*. London: Harper Collins.

De Rosa, L. (2004) *La Provincia Subordinata: Saggio sulla Questione Meridionale*. Bari: Laterza.

El Saadawi, N. (1992) *The Nawal El Saadawi Reader*. London: Zed Books.

Elsheikh M. S. (1999) Le omissioni della cultura italiana. In I. Siggillino (ed.) *L'Islam nella Scuola*. Milan: Editore FrancoAngeli.

Fanon, F. (1963) *The Wretched of the Earth*. New York: Grove Press.

Fondazione Laboratorio Mediterraneo (1997) *Obiettivi e Mezzi per il Parternariato Euromediterraneo: Il Forum Civile EuroMed*. Naples: Magma.

Foucault, M. (1980) *Power/Knowledge: Selected Interviews and Other Writings, 1972–1977*. New York: Pantheon Books.

Freire, P. (1995) *The Politics of Education*. South Hadley, MA: Bergin & Garvey.

Germino, D. (1990) *Antonio Gramsci: Architect of a New Politics*. Baton Rouge, LA: Louisiana State University Press.

Gramsci, A. (1975) *Quaderni del Carcere* (critical edition edited by V. Gerratana, IV volumes). Torino: Einaudi.

Gramsci, A. (1995) *The Southern Question* (translated and annotated by P. Verdicchio). West Lafayette, IN: Bordighera.

Gramsci, A. (1996) *Lettere dal Carcere 1926–1930, 1931–1937* (edited by A. Santucci). Palermo: Sellerio Editore.

Gramsci, A. (1997) *Le Opere: La Prima Antologia di tutti gli Scritti*. Rome: Editori Riuniti.

Grech, M. (ed.) (2006) *Knisja tat-Triq* (Street Church). Malta: Pubblikazzjonijiet AWL.

Hasbi, A. (2003) Introduction to the open file, *Prospects*, Vol. 33(4), pp. 375–384.

Lepre, A. (1998) *Il Prigioniero: Vita di Antonio Gramsci*. Bari: Laterza.

Matvejevic, P. (1997) Address. In Fondazione Laboratorio Mediterraneo, *Obiettivi e Mezzi per il Parternariato Euromediterraneo: Il Forum Civile EuroMed*. Naples: Magma.

Mayo, P. (2004) *Liberating Praxis: Paulo Freire's Legacy for Radical Education and Politics*. Westport, CO: Praeger.

Nairn, T. (1982) Antonu su gobbu. In A. Showstack Sassoon (ed.) *Approaches to Gramsci*. London: Verso.

Rodney, W. (1973) *How Europe Underdeveloped Africa*. London: Bogle-L'Ouverture Publications.

Said, E. (1978) *Orientalism*. New York: Random House.

Said, E. (1994) *Culture and Imperialism*. London: Vintage.

Said, E. (2001) The clash of ignorance, *The Nation*, 22 October. Available online at: https://www.thenation.com/article/archive/clash-ignorance/

Torres, C. A. (1998) *Democracy, Education and Multiculturalism: Dilemmas of Citizenship in a Global World*. Lanham, MD: Rowman & Littlefield.

Verdicchio, P. (1995) Introduction. In A. Gramsci, *The Southern Question* (translated by P. Verdicchio). West Lafayette, IN: Bordighera.

Viswanathan, G. (ed.) (2001) *Power, Politics and Culture: Interviews with Edward Said*. New York: Vintage Books.

Žižek, S. (2004) *Iraq: The Borrowed Kettle*. London: Verso.

CHAPTER 6

Dis/Integrated Orders and the Politics of Recognition

Civil Upheavals, Militarism, and Educators' Lives and Work

André Elias Mazawi

1   Problematic

The burgeoning literature on education in conflict and post-conflict contexts identifies the powerful intersections among schooling, civil upheavals, and militarism as expanding areas of scholarly research and policy making. The literature also underscores the recognition of schooling and education as central to a 'humanitarian response' organised by states, international governmental and non-governmental organisations that undertake post-conflict reconstruction (Retamal & Aedo-Richmond, 1998; Aguilar & Retamal, 2009). This expanding interest has been recently actualised in several special issues in the field of comparative education. A special issue of *Research in Comparative and International Education,* guest edited by Julia Paulson (2007), focuses on the tensions that underpin the provision of education in contexts marked by civil and military upheavals. Contributions highlight the role education plays in constructing people's engagement in violent civil and armed upheavals, such as in the Great Lakes region in Africa (Bird, 2007). More particularly, Chelpi-den Hamer (2007) investigates how the administrative structures that regulate schooling are affected in countries torn apart by civil wars, such as in Côte d'Ivoire. Pushing one step further, a special issue of *Comparative Education Review,* guest edited by Lynn Davies & Christopher Talbot (2008), offers a series of ethnographic field studies that illuminate the role schools play in the social re-integration of former child soldiers in Sierra Leone (Betancourt et al., 2008), the inclusion of Burmese ethnic refugees in Thailand (Oh & van der Stouwe, 2008), and the enhancement of children's well-being in Afghanistan and Africa (Dicum, 2008; Winthrop & Kirk, 2008).

In a particularly compelling study, Hromadžić (2008) clarifies how civil war and militarised conflict result in the institution of 'new' types of school within multi-ethnic and deeply divided societies. Studying Bosnia and Herzegovina, Hromadžić describes the 'collision' between two groups—international actors intervening in the conflict and the Croat political community—over

---

© THE EURO-MEDITERRANEAN CENTRE FOR EDUCATION RESEARCH, UNIVERSITY OF MALTA, 2008
DOI: 10.1163/9789004506602_006
This is an open access chapter distributed under the terms of the CC BY-NC 4.0 License.

the integration of 'national minorities'. This clash of principles resulted in the creation of a high 'school [which] now has a unified management, while preserving ethnic segregation and the ethos of segmental autonomy' (p. 542). As Hromadžić explains, the 'materialization of a new form of school that is concurrently 'shared' and 'separated' creates a new type of school geography in [Bosnia and Herzegovina], one based on the ideology of ethnic symmetry and polarization of youth' (p. 542). In striking contrast to this perspective, a special issue of *Comparative Education*, guest edited by Larsen & Mehta (2008), turns the problematic of conflict and geopolitical military upheavals around. It focuses on 'the manifestations, implications and effects of insecurity and desire across the field of education in North America' (p. 256) and how these shape educational discourses and practices in Canada, the US, and Mexico in the post-9/11 period.

Notwithstanding the examples mentioned above, and despite educators' vulnerability when it comes to civil and military upheavals, studies that delve into educators' lives and work remain rare. Curiously, this is particularly so in teacher education and educational leadership journals.[1] Kirk & Winthrop (2007) conclude, 'teachers working in emergency and post-conflict contexts have so far received little attention from researchers' (p. 721). Perceived by military apparatuses and insurgent groups alike as bearers of knowledge deemed ideologically threatening, the location of educators within schools emphasises their potentially subversive actions, as was the case, for instance, in Vietnam in the 1970s-1980s (Cassidy, 2006, p. 156). During the decolonisation of Algeria in the 1950s, teachers were located at the juncture of comprehensive social and political transformations (Le Sueur, 2005). Still, for embattled regimes, school teachers and university professors present a readily available group that can be drafted into the army as was the case, for instance, during the Iraq-Iran war of the 1980s (Hiro, 1991, p. 175; 'Allaq, 1997, p. 96). Not least, in post-conflict contexts, educators—particularly history teachers—act as 'critical' witnesses in the 'public construction' of memory. They create spaces of remembrance and 'memory making' that are crucial in the process of reconciliation and reconstruction (Dreyden-Peterson & Siebörger, 2006; see also Baranović, Jokić & Doolan, 2007).

In all this, the virtual absence of systematic studies that explore the impact of military conflicts and civil upheavals on schooling in the Arab region is striking, and more precisely and particularly so against the backdrop of the region's turbulent military and political histories. At different points in time, schools across the Arab region have operated (and some continue to operate) despite the collapse of the state or disintegration of central political authority. This would apply to societies that experienced (or are experiencing), at different points in time, extended periods of upheaval, such as in Jordan (Sirriyeh, 2000), Lebanon (Frayha, 2003), Algeria (Cheriet, 1996), the Sudan (Graham-Brown, 1991), the Occupied Palestinian Territories (Al-Zaroo & Hunt, 2003), and Iraq (Velloso de Santisteban, 2005), to name but a few. While it is true that schools across the Arab region have become part of highly differentiated national systems of education, there is hardly a contemporary society across the Arab region that has not experienced a radical, and often violent, upheaval of its civil and political orders at least once since the end of World War II. In some societies across the region, social, political, and military upheavals are the norm rather than the exception; entire generations recognise civil and military upheaval as the only order. Yet, the few sources available allow only fragmented insights into what educators who toil under such conditions do, and how they engage a collapsed or collapsing socio-political order, or the militarisation of daily life within schools and communities.

The following question remains therefore largely unexplored with regard to the Arab region: how do educators pursue their understandings of education and schooling when the civil order and political regimes collapse, disintegrate, or are violently reconfigured through military operations? In this paper, I address this particular question and discuss its underpinnings and ramifications, as well as its ontological and epistemic implications for studies of educators' lives and work in the Arab region and beyond.

2 Conception

The study of educators' lives and work during periods of upheaval faces conceptual, methodological, and logistical challenges. Some of these challenges are associated with access to and availability of archival materials, community-based records, and, not least, witnesses (see, for example, Suleiman & Anderson, 2008). Makkawi (2002) also cautions that interviewing educators about matters that are politically sensitive may expose them 'to undue harm' (p. 51).

One should not belittle conceptual challenges facing such an endeavour. The current dominant themes of studies concerned with educators' work revolve around school effectiveness and student learning within stable national systems. A heavy emphasis is placed on 'best practices', identifying professional standards and accountability mechanisms for educators (see, for example, World Bank, 2008), and international comparative studies of student learning (e.g., TIMSS, PISA) (Stack, 2006). This leaves little space for studies that explore the actions and judgments of educators during periods of social, political, and military upheaval. The latter are perceived as structurally transitory circumstances, devoid of specific and long-term value for our understanding of educators' work.

Here, it is useful to invoke Goodson's (1997) observation that 'at precisely the time the teacher's voice is being pursued and promoted, the teacher's work is being technicised and narrowed' (p. 111). The 'paradox' Goodson refers to is well reflected within certain strands of educational research by rigid lines of demarcation drawn between the private and public spheres that separate educators' lives and work. Articulated in the form of accountability regimes, these lines of demarcation recognise educators' performance skills exclusively within classrooms and schools, to the exclusion of other forms and spaces of engagement and pedagogical action. These distinctions operate as regimes that ultimately 'discipline' educators into pre-inscribed and surveilled roles (Anderson, 2001) while 'trivialising teacher education' (Johnson et al., 2005). And yet, when social and political orders collapse in the midst of military and armed conflicts, and state surveillance and regulative power dissipate, educators may become engaged in myriad sites of action, outside the direct regulative power of established accountability regimes. This can occur within and outside communities, schools, and classrooms; as part of social and political movements, and organisations; and as part of newly constituted social groups (refugees, internally displaced persons, volunteers, community leaders, insurgency groups, and so forth). This suggests that under upheaval circumstances the private lives of educators acquire public political overtones, and vice versa, thus offering new configurations within which educators pursue their understandings of themselves and of their work. Several questions thus arise: how do civil and military upheavals reconfigure the distinctions between the private and public dimensions of educators' roles? How are these shifting distinctions leveraged into emergent 'modes of being' and 'relational identities' (Mouffe, 2005, pp. 6–8)? How do they shape not only educators' work, but also the alternative horizons and spaces through which citizenship, affiliation, and professionalism in subsequent periods of reconstruction are articulated?

The questions posed above identify educators' lives and work under upheaval conditions as critical spaces, worthy of sustained exploration. They allow a critical interrogation of educators' engagement in relation to a broader political theory of action. They also problematise the arbitrary distinctions between educators' lives (private) and work (public), avoiding their articulation as a Manichean set of opposites. Furthermore, they highlight the need to understand how educators locate themselves and the meanings of their lives and work outside the exclusive framework of state apparatuses and regulatory regimes. These questions open up new spaces to explore both how educators enact their subjectivities within the context of specific historical, social, and political circumstances, and how these subjectivities are then re/inscribed in the field of power in relation to which the school, as a dispenser of education, acquires its meanings.

With regard to the Arab region, addressing these questions would offer a corrective to the over-emphasis placed on the role of the Arab state (Ayubi, 1995) as the exclusive framework within which educators operate and from which they draw the meanings they attach to their work. Such an exercise would also clarify, in the words of Starrett (1998), 'how scholarship, in creating the objects of its study'—in this paper: educators' lives and work—'often acts to reproduce the very intellectual categories it argues explicitly against' (p. 59). Equally, it would unsettle the policy spaces that are currently being narrowed as a result of neo-liberal policies implemented in the field of education and social welfare (see, for example, Baylouny, 2008). In these spaces, educators are represented through uniform and essentialised discourses which claim that '[g]roup work, creative thinking, and proactive learning are rare' among educators in the Arab region (World Bank, 2008, p. 88). Not least, exploring these questions repositions educators across the region within their multi-faceted contexts of practice, and clarify the 'political anatomy' (Foucault, 1979, p. 28) through which educators mediate power and its cultural underpinnings.

3 Contexts

To illustrate the issues and challenges facing educators' lives and work in contexts of upheaval, I draw upon the distinct cases of the Palestinian society and the southern Sudan. The case of the stateless Palestinian society offers insights into educators' lives and work under continued colonisation and military occupation. The contrasting case of the southern Sudan provides an opportunity to reflect on educators' lives and work under conditions of internal colonialism and prolonged civil war within a deeply fragmented multi-cultural and multi-ethnic state.

3.1 Palestinian Society

The lives and work of educators in Palestinian society continue to be powerfully intertwined with the socio-political and military upheavals experienced by Palestinians since the early 20th century. Tibawi's (1956, pp. 193–212) account of the British administration of the Arab school system in Palestine (1917–1948) documents the roles many Palestinian educators played in organising community insurrection, as well as devising texts that by-passed government censorship and administrative control as the Palestinian national movement gathered momentum in the late 1930s and 1940s. If these years saw the emergence of educators as a professional group and as a 'leadership class', it is also true that educators represented the ideological backbone of a rising middle and middle-upper class, particularly in the urban centres of mandatory Palestine (Mazawi, 1994).

The 1948 *Nakba*, or Catastrophe, witnessed the territorial dismemberment of mandatory Palestine, the displacement of several hundred thousand Palestinian refugees across the Middle East and beyond, the destruction of over 400 villages, and the depopulation of the major urban Palestinian centres (Khalidi, 2007). As a result, between 1948 and 1967, Israel, Jordan (West Bank), Egypt (Gaza Strip), and the United Nations controlled school systems that served Palestinians.[2] Following the occupation of the West Bank and Gaza Strip by Israel in 1967 and until the signing of the 'Oslo accords' in 1993,[3] Israel controlled both the schooling of Palestinian citizens of Israel through the Israeli Ministry of Education, and of Palestinians in the occupied West Bank and Gaza Strip through the apparatuses of the military administration. In both contexts, the textbooks in the fields of history, geography, literature, and civics reflected this political control through the marginalisation, if not exclusion, of references to Palestinians as a nation with rights to their land (see, for example, Al-Haj, 2005; Moughrabi, 2001).

The year 1948 and the period that followed irremediably transformed not only the experiential realities, lives, and work of Palestinian educators—and of Palestinians in general—but also the social class composition of the teaching profession. From that time forward, educators represented the largest professional group in Palestinian society, and a proletarianised one at that. Many teachers originated from refugee and/or lower socio-economic class backgrounds (Brand, 1988, p. 145).

Within Israel, the citizenship of Palestinians is still contested terrain, in a state defined by its legislators as 'Jewish and democratic'. This definition leaves unsettled the spaces open to all citizens to participate in shaping the public good, regardless of their ethnicity or cultural affiliation (Jamal, 2007a). It also narrows, according to Jamal (2007b), the scope and breadth of legitimate political action, leaving the citizenship of Palestinians 'hollow' and 'devoid of substantive meaning'. Palestinian educators in Israeli schools that serve Palestinians are thus subject to clearance by the General Security Services (GSS), with the latter being involved in matters of hiring, dismissal, or promotion (Adalah, 2004). Moreover, deeply entrenched policies and practices discriminate against Arab schools in resource allocation and educational opportunities (Human Rights Watch, 2001; Golan-Agnon, 2006). Notwithstanding such inequities, Makkawi (2002) observes that, despite their structural dependency, 'Palestinian teachers have developed unique techniques to attend to the cultural and national expectations of their community and students without putting their jobs in jeopardy' (p. 51). According to Nasser & Nasser (2008),

> Teachers may use implicit messages to make students doubt the validity of knowledge presented in textbooks but, simultaneously, they have to emphasize that these textbooks are required for passing examinations and for academic success ... The end result of this complex situation is lack of trust in the school curriculum and the textbooks' cultural, historical, and political messages. (p. 643)

In the Israeli occupied West Bank and Gaza Strip, the lives and work of educators (as that of Palestinians in general) were subject to military administration until the coming into being of the PNA. Educators' work and classroom behaviour was heavily controlled by the Israeli military. Attempts to unionise teachers were often curtailed ('Assaf, 2004). Moreover, distinctions between government schools, private (church) schools, and UNRWA schools meant that educators were subject to differential work conditions and incentives, as well as to different regulations concerning their terms of service. These institutional distinctions—which persist in Palestinian society—are also powerfully associated with social class distinctions.

With the eruption of the first *Intifada* (Uprising) in the West Bank and Gaza Strip in December 1987, educators and communities in some localities in Palestinian society organised educational provision as part of a widespread and prolonged civil insurrection against Israeli occupation.[4] With schooling banned by the occupying Israeli military, teaching was organised in alternative locations (Mahshi & Bush, 1989). Graham-Brown (1991) notes that, during the *Intifada*, the 'educational system in the Occupied Territories, from kindergartens to universities, has been shut down for many months at a time over a period of more than three years, effectively punishing the population by withdrawing opportunities for education' (p. 56). More recently, under the second *Intifada*, following the collapse of the 'Oslo accords' in 2000, Sultana (2006) and Shalhoub-Kevorkian (2008) undertook compelling field studies into the multiple ways through which educators, students, and communities organise the schooling experience in the occupied West Bank and Gaza Strip.[5] These authors document how Palestinians (including educators) resist and attempt to circumvent the militarisation of daily life, and how they confront check points, arrests, killings, bombings, continued colonisation, and widespread settler violence in order to maintain school routine.

Yet, even following the creation of the PNA in 1994, schooling remained affected by continuing Israeli intrusions, the intensive expansion of settlements, the recent construction of a separation wall on the West Bank (which fragments Palestinian communities from within), a deteriorating economy, and vehement intra-Palestinian struggles over the emerging structures of a Palestinian state bureaucracy. Clashes over work conditions between the PNA and teachers' unions led to strikes and to punitive measures against some teachers, including transfers to different schools (Nicolai, 2007, pp. 104–105). Within this larger context, the lives and work of educators have been devastated, making it 'impossible' for educators 'to discuss moral education in the case of Palestine while the conflict is still there' (Affouneh, 2007, p. 354). With children and youth in Palestinian society representing well over half the total population, this means that educators—as family members, income providers, and as professionals—stand at the junction of intense economic, political, organisational, and curricular challenges. These challenges are felt particularly in schools located in rural areas (villages), in which educators often work in rudimentary conditions and inadequate buildings, lacking support and basic resources. Due to a severely overburdened infrastructure, some schools must operate in two shifts, particularly in the Gaza Strip where an already precarious infrastructure was destroyed by Israeli bombardments and air raids in December 2008–January 2009. Educators toil in overused and dilapidated facilities; they are underpaid, and must function with less than minimal physical and professional spaces, despite efforts and projects to the contrary. One young Palestinian teacher, transferred as a counsellor to a rural primary school, poignantly reflected on his working conditions, observing that the school 'actually resembles a tomb' (Al-Khawaja, 2009, p. 9).

For many Palestinians, either in Israel or in the West Bank and Gaza Strip, teaching is a major occupational outlet. This reflects the relative inaccessibility of labour markets to Palestinian workers, whether as a result of occupational discrimination and marginalisation in Israel (see, for example, Sa'di & Lewin-Epstein, 2001), or as a result of the dire state of the Palestinian economy in the West Bank and Gaza Strip (Perlo-Freeman, 2008). Differences in gender participation in the teaching profession among Palestinians are mediated by class-based, political, economic, and geographic factors. Moreover, intra-organisational factors mediate women's relative visibility and access to power positions within schools.[6]

3.2   *The Sudan*

The Sudan offers quite a different context within which educators and schools operate, a context marked by internal colonialism and secession of some southern provinces as part of a two-decade struggle over the distribution of political power and national resources. Since its independence in 1956, civil and armed conflicts have not abated, leaving over two million people dead and massive displacement among diverse ethno-cultural, regional, and religious communities. The formation of the Sudan Peoples' Liberation Army (SPLA) in the early 1980s, and the subsequent emergence of its political wing, the Sudan Peoples' Liberation Movement (SPLM), should be understood against this backdrop. The conflict is often perceived as pitting a dominantly Arab Muslim north against an ethnically, religiously, and culturally diverse south. However, military and armed conflicts and struggle over power transcend these broad lines of demarcation and extend within groups and regions (Lesch, 1998; Dean, 2000; Deng, 2005).

In the late 1980s, the Sudan's ruling elite promoted the Arabisation of instruction and the Islamisation of curricula in all educational settings, thus exacerbating existing ethnic and regional tensions (Breidlid, 2005; Lesch, 1998, pp. 143–145). Constitutional legislation in 1998 attempted to mitigate the pervasive effects of continued political instability by introducing a scheme for the devolution of powers. In the field of education, responsibility would be shared between federal and provincial (state) governments. Within this framework, southern communities and their organisations introduced curricular changes to preserve their identity, heritage, and rights to difference and self-determination in relation to the Sudanese state. A peace agreement was subsequently signed between the federal government and the SPLM in 2004, recognising the right of the southern region to self-determination (Deng, 2005).

However, a protracted civil war took its toll on schools and on the work of educators. Public services have collapsed in the Sudan's southern and western regions, including in Darfur. Sommers (2005) refers to 'educational islands, as well as the immensity of educational emptyness that has arisen between them' (p. 24). The material poverty, the displacement and dismemberment of communities, as well as the fragmented intervention of international aid agencies and non-governmental organisations: all these leave little space for educators to provide a meaningful schooling. Described as 'an educational disaster' (Sommers, 2005, p. 251) that left a school system 'in shambles' (Joint Assessment Mission, 2005, p. 7), two decades of civil war 'have robbed a generation of their opportunity for education' (Joint Assessment Mission, 2005, p. 16). Surveys report an overwhelming absence of qualified teachers (only 6% are qualified), dilapidated school facilities, and a widespread lack of school textbooks and any form of organisational support.[7] Moreover, teaching is a provisional placeholder as '[g]ood teachers have left the profession to join NGOs that pay better salaries' (Joint Assessment Mission, 2005, p. 10).[8] Particular challenges face the education of refugees and persons displaced either within the Sudan or in refugee camps in adjoining countries. Warring factions are also implicated in the forced mobilisation of both teachers and students (child soldiers) into the armed conflicts (Sommers, 2005), thus further weakening the already limited capacity of relief organisations to sustain school facilities over time. Not least, significant disparities exist between ethno-cultural and religious communities in the southern Sudan in terms of their capacity to pool material resources through local churches and indigenous community institutions and organisations, with the view of maintaining a meaningful educational provision.

Kirk (2004) reports that women represent about 6% of all teachers in the southern Sudan, despite a women to men ratio of 2:1 in the general population, due to war-related mortality (see also Joint Assessment Mission, 2005, p. 16). In some provinces, women represent not more than 2% of all teachers. Within men-dominated schools, women are employed in conditions of cultural and organisational peripherality; they are assigned heavy workloads, and have very few prospects of assuming positions of responsibility or even receiving meaningful payment for their work. Kirk's (2004) paper raises important questions about the impact of wars and armed conflicts on the gendering of teachers' opportunities within schools. It also suggests that teachers are embedded within the larger conflicts in ways that further exacerbate the workings of schools.

3.3   *Reflections*

Four main observations emerge from the discussion so far. First, educators play a significant role in processes of decolonisation and national emancipation. Educators' engagement is part of larger processes of urbanisation and class formation, which underpin the broader struggle of colonised societies. *Qua literati*, they play a significant role as public intellectuals or politically engaged members of their communities, and as bearers of liberation ideologies and constructors of national identity. Yet, the capacity of educators to engage social and political upheavals is significantly challenged under conditions of internal colonialism and prolonged civil wars that occur among unequally organised ethnic/cultural communities living largely in rural areas dependent on agriculture or seasonal pastoralism. In this context, educators' work falls between relief intervention and social-economic development, with all the ensuing competing demands placed on educators and on the operation of schools. On the one hand, educators are perceived as front-line actors providing humanitarian assistance, particularly to children and youth (who represent the largest age group in society), and to impoverished and marginalised communities. On the other hand, educators' work is perceived as an important institutional medium through which refugees, displaced persons, and child soldiers can be re-integrated into their communities through the acquisition of skills and knowledge (Kirk & Winthrop, 2007, p. 715). Within this 'double bind', educators struggle with competing social and economic agendas in relation to which schools need to position themselves in order to remain viable in periods of upheaval.

Second, under civil and military upheavals educators' lives and work are radically reconfigured in terms of their geographic locations and the physical and social spaces within which schooling operates. Here, one thinks particularly of conditions of refugeedom, displacement, and spatial relocation. These processes assume transnational dimensions and dynamics, taking place across geopolitical regions and national borders. Moreover, educators are involved in the appropriation and/or construction of new sites of action, within homes, shelters, refugee camps, and new (urban and rural) communities. Educators' engagement also becomes embedded in new institutional and social forms that span organisational lines. These processes remain the least studied and understood, however, despite their critical importance for the ways through which educators negotiate meanings regarding their lives and work outside the framework of state support.

Third, in the illustrations above, educators are far from being exclusively engaged in front-line routinised teaching within the classroom, as is so often depicted in the literature (see, for example, Massialas & Jarrar, 1991, p. 143; Berger, 2002, p. 37; World Bank, 2008, p. 88). Rather, they emerge as engaged both within and outside classrooms and schools, within and in relation to their communities of reference, interacting with particularly complex, challenging, and highly unrewarding socio-political and geographic environments. And yet, depictions of educators in the Arab region have systematically cast aside these larger contexts of engagement in understanding educators' lives and work. Moreover, educators in contexts of upheaval often show resourcefulness and engagement within particularly harsh conditions (see, for example, Al-Khawaja, 2009, and other contributions in the same issue). Notwithstanding, studies of educators' lives and work have remained adamant in fixing their gaze on educators' work exclusively in relation to formally mandated curricular texts within classrooms. Educators' voices in other areas of practice that are part and parcel of their daily lives and work are thus effectively silenced. The argument advanced here should not be interpreted as claiming that processes of resistance/engagement are representative of all teachers within all contexts, not even at the same point in time. Rather, I argue that an examination of the engagement of educators in contexts of social and political upheavals provides evidence of alternative modes of educational leadership that transcend the narrow confines of the classroom and go beyond 'frontal' teaching. It is important to capture these nuanced facets in educators' work across the region. Only thus is it possible to appreciate the positioning of educators in relation to the larger dynamics operating within the field of power, and the impact this has on the provision of schooling during civil and militarised upheavals.

Fourth, rare are the studies that unpack how the experiential gender and class-based realities of educators impact their lives and work in diverse contexts of practice across the Arab region. All particularly, voices of women educators remain largely excluded and their 'contrapuntal readings' of schooling left unheard. This denial of voice is further exacerbated when it comes to understanding how intersections of patriarchal, social class, ethnic, cultural, and spatial-geographic forces *differentially* mediate the impact of conflicts on educators' practice; how these forces are actualised through the construction of gendered and class-based 'discursive practices' within schools; and how these discourses in turn amplify the effects of civil war and military upheavals on the operation of schools and on teachers' lives and work.

4   Horizons

Researchers have largely marginalised the experiential realities of educators' lives and work in the Arab region, as selectively illustrated above. Moreover, a cursory review of Arab scholarly publications and journals, as well as studies published in English by researchers working in the region, reveals that studies of educators' lives and work are, with some notable exceptions (Nuwayr, 2001; 'Assaf, 2004), entrenched in the measurement of attitudes, skills, and knowledge of educators in relation to school efficiency or effectiveness (see, for example, Saleh & Kashmeeri, 1987; Al-Jaber, 1996; Halawah, 2005; World Bank, 2008). This state of affairs does not only reify educators' professional judgment. It also prevents the articulation of a praxis framework through which educators in the Arab region can best understand themselves, the work they perform, and the challenges they face in relation to larger power struggles.

Not least, the uncritical extension to the Arab region of educational leadership models developed in Western societies dismisses vital cultural dimensions of local contexts and their political and geopolitical underpinnings. This effectively detracts attention from the core social and political issues that impact schooling in the Arab region. It also constructs educational leadership in ways that operate an ontological and epistemic disjuncture between the experiential realities of educators and the formal ways through which their professional judgments and performance are assessed. For instance, in one reform initiative carried out by American consultants in the United Arab Emirates (UAE), not less than the Interstate School Leaders Licensure Consortium (ISLLC), Standards were adopted in order to 'provide a profile of a person intended to lead the reforms to school management' (Macpherson, Kachelhoffer & El Nemr,

2007, p. 67). While the authors do state that they have adopted the standards 'not uncritically' (p. 65), and that they were ' "indigenized" by the authors in consultation with Arab and Islamic colleagues' (p. 67), the 'intended learning outcomes' do not provide a clear idea how this was done.[9] The authors remain particularly silent on how the ISLLC standards were 'indigenised' at the light of the social, political, cultural and economic transformations brought about by a UAE workforce composed overwhelmingly of expatriates, in a context in which citizenship is the preserve of the very few. In making sense of this paper, one may find some consolation in Thomas (2007) who reminds us that the 'lack of appropriate contextualization' in studies of educational leadership in Gulf Arab societies 'may lead researchers to incorporate ethnocentric attitudes and perspectives into their studies ..., inadvertently reinforcing the bias they claim to counter and leading to further false conclusions and consequent inappropriate policy implementation' (p. 212). He further explicitly warns that failure to conceptualise properly the extension of educational leadership models from one cultural context to another 'has led to claims that many findings are confused because they use cultural terms arbitrarily, ignore appropriate levels of analysis and fail to deal with conceptual and methodological problems arising from how cultures are measured and leadership assessed' (p. 214).[10]

Opening up new spaces for research on the civil and military upheavals that affect educators' lives and work in the Arab region requires therefore the articulation of contextualised conceptual approaches that build, epistemologically and ontologically, on local, national, and community histories and on educators' experiential realities and voices in relation to which their work could be meaningfully engaged. This approach would require, if one draws on Goodson (1997), that educators' voices, and the stories they give rise to, 'should not only be *narrated* but *located*' (p. 113) within their contexts of practice, in ways which ultimately enable educators to 're-write domination' (p. 114). 'Locating' stories means, if one extends Brighenti's (2007) conceptualisation, that researchers must strive to articulate an 'epistemology of seeing' through which the ethnographic and temporal (historical) richness of community, national, and regional circumstances are 'made visible' in their contribution to a grounded understanding of educators' lives and work.

It is worth signalling here the wealth of data that has only rarely been used in studies of educators' lives and work in the Arab region, and which offers new opportunities for research. It includes autobiographies, biographies, novels, personal diaries of activists, politicians, and community leaders, as well as photographs and other records kept in archival collections, international organisations, newspapers, and local communities (see, for example, Endersen & Øvensen, 1994). These repositories contain primary documents and visual materials regarding how educators in public and private schools, in war torn societies and in refugee camps organised themselves and their students in ways that transcend the immediate circumstances of political and civil upheaval.[11]

More importantly, however, opening up new spaces hinges on a critical interrogation of dominant conceptual and methodological paradigms through which educators in the Arab region are constructed, and all too easily dismissed, as an inefficient, incompetent and agent-less public, denied a dissenting voice (see, for example, the observation by Berger, 2002, p. 37). Embarking on such an undertaking highlights therefore the challenge for researchers to incorporate in their work communicative and participative methodologies that engage educators and locate their standpoints, voices, and discourses within their multi-faceted contexts of practice, and the conflicts and upheavals within which they act and work (see, for example, Herrera & Torres, 2006; Thomas, 2008). This entails, as Goodson (1997) suggests, 'develop[ing] stories of action within theories of context ... which act against the kinds of divorce of the discourses which are all too readily imaginable' (p. 117). Hence, developing a multiplicity of emic[12] languages that capture the contradictory articulations of educators' lives and work throughout the Arab region emerges as a crucial—and yet to be undertaken—project.

If one wants to attune research on educators' lives and work with their 'modes of being', as an agentic public engaged in a diversity of contradictory locations and fields of power across time and space, then it is crucial to unpack critically the contextual articulations of their practice. This would allow researchers and educators to transcend 'the forms of apartheid' (Goodson, 1997, p. 117) that are erected between educators' stories and the 'vernaculars of power' (p. 117) that are used to control educators' work and subjugate them as a public.

Acknowledgement

This chapter originally appeared as: Mazawi, A. E. (2008) Dis/integrated orders and the politics of recognition: civil upheavals, militarism, and educators' lives and work, *Mediterranean Journal of Educational Studies*, Vol. 13(2), pp. 69–89. Reprinted here with permission from the publisher.

Notes

1 The positional distinctions between 'school teachers' and 'school administrators' (principals, vice principals, department heads, etc.) are acknowledged. In the present paper they are both referred to as 'educators'.

DIS/INTEGRATED ORDERS AND THE POLITICS OF RECOGNITION 117

2 The United Nations is still in charge of the schooling of Palestinian refugees through UNRWA (United Nations Relief and Works Agency for Palestine Refugees in the Near East). This agency operates schools and welfare programmes in Palestinian refugee camps across the West Bank and Gaza Strip, Lebanon, Syria, and Jordan.

3 The 'Oslo accords' are known formally as the Declaration of Principles on Interim Self-Government Arrangements. Signed in September 1993 by the State of Israel and the Palestine Liberation Organization (PLO). They institute the basis upon which the Palestinian Authority—commonly known as the Palestinian National Authority (PNA)—came into being during the following year.

4 What is commonly referred to as the first Palestinian *Intifada* erupted in the Israeli occupied West Bank and Gaza Strip in December 1987 and abated toward the signing of the 'Oslo accords' in 1993. According to Al-Zaroo (1988), before the *Intifada*, between 30 October 1968 and 7 April 1988, 30 teachers (of whom five were women) were exiled by the Israeli occupation (p. 306). Between July 1970 and 5 July 1987 (the eve of the first *Intifada*), 17 teachers (of whom five were women and one a university professor) were placed under house arrest (p. 305). During the first six months of the *Intifada* alone (between 27 October 1987 and 6 July 1988), 77 teachers were arrested, of whom three were women (pp. 98–100). Nicolai (2007) further reports that 'as many as 1,600 teachers were removed during the period of the first *intifada*' (p. 97).

5 What is commonly referred to as the second Palestinian *Intifada* erupted in the Israeli occupied West Bank and Gaza Strip following the collapse of the negotiations on a final status agreement between the PLO and the State of Israel in 2000. Nicolai (2007, p. 111) reports that in the period 2000–2005 alone, 27 teachers were killed, 167 detained, and 53 injured.

6 While women in Palestinian schools in Israel and the West Bank and Gaza Strip represent slightly over half of all teachers, their representation is significantly lower in post-primary education (junior high and high schools). In 2007–2008, women represented about 75%, 56%, and 44% of all teachers in primary, junior high, and secondary Arab schools in Israel, respectively (State of Israel, 2008, p. 410). In the PNA's jurisdiction, the percentage of women among all teachers stood at 55.4%, with a significantly lower percentage for the Gaza Strip compared to the West Bank. In private (mainly church) schools, the percentage of women reached almost 73% (Palestinian National Authority, 2008, p. 304).

7 Deng (2006), a senior SPLM education official, writes that according to UNESCO, '[m]ost schools opened during the current civil war in southern Sudan are 'bush schools' with outdoor classrooms and only 12 per cent of the classrooms are permanent buildings made of bricks or concrete ... [T]he number of schools with concrete buildings was only less than 200 schools compared with 800 primary schools that were permanent buildings during pre-war periods. This clearly shows the considerable destruction inflicted on schools facilities and structure during the current civil war' (p. 11). ... 'While about 70 and 46 per cent of the primary schools in southern Sudan do not respectively have latrines and [a] source of safe drinking water such [as] a borehole or well, about 57 per cent of schools do not have health facilities nearby' (p. 12). A Joint Assessment Mission (2005) report states that in 'South Sudan 38% of classes are taught outdoors and 51% in local materials structures in variable states of repair' (p. 9).

8 A Joint Assessment Mission (2005) report in the field of education notes that most teachers are paid 'at rates averaging $290 per annum. Teacher commitment is variable and this is reflected in absenteeism and shortening of the academic year' (p. 9). NGO stands for 'non-governmental organisation'.

9 Moreover, the authors' discussion of the critique of the ISLLC is perfunctory. It disregards sustained critiques that have been raised about the standards in the US (see, for example, Anderson, 2001).

10 Refer, for example, to the arguments debated by Richardson (2004) and Clarke & Otaky (2006) regarding the cultural underpinnings of reflectivity in relation to the education of teachers in the Gulf Arab societies.

11 For instance, a study undertaken by Bashkin (2007), and which focuses on Iraqi schools during the interwar period, aptly illustrates the multiple ways through which these primary and secondary sources can be used to explore teachers' engagement during political upheaval. By using a wide array of 'newspaper articles, novels, and short stories' (p. 41), Bashkin shows how the competing claims to jurisdiction, legitimacy, and authority played out between senior state officials and the vehement opposition levelled by Iraqi intellectuals and educators during the formative stages of the formation of the Iraqi state. The study also shows how in many instances educators and school administrators introduced into their classrooms alternative (though short-lived) textual materials to those mandated by the state. Bashkin also shows that while 'the state suffered from tribal revolts and ethnic tensions' (p. 42) during the formative period of its consolidation, educators played a central role in mediating competing political agendas, curtailing the impact of state policies and promoting alternative political and ideological platforms.

12 Thomas (2007) points out that '[e]mic approaches examine behaviours within one culture that cannot be transferred to others as concepts are defined differently and, therefore, cannot be commonly measured or claimed to be universal' (p. 220).

References

Adalah (The Legal Centre for Arab Minority Rights in Israel) (2004) Petition demanding end to GSS intervention in appointments of Arab educators – Supreme Court orders Attorney General to respond within 30 days, *Adalah's Newsletter*, No. 5.

Affouneh, S. J. (2007) How sustained conflict makes moral education impossible: some observations from Palestine, *Journal of Moral Education*, Vol. 36(3), pp. 343–356.

Aguilar, P., & Retamal, G. (2009) Protective environments and quality education in humanitarian contexts, *International Journal of Educational Development*, Vol. 29(1), pp. 3–16.

Al-Haj, M. (2005) National ethos, multicultural education, and the new history textbooks in Israel, *Curriculum Inquiry*, Vol. 35(1), pp. 47–71.

Al-Jaber, Z. (1996) The leadership requirements of secondary school principals in Kuwait: a post-invasion analysis, *Journal of Educational Administration*, Vol. 34(4), pp. 24–38.

Al-Khawaja, Y. (2009) Tajribat "mashru' al-madiya .. mashhad jughrafi thakafi min zawiya irshadiya" (The experimental project of "Al-Madiya .. a geographic and cultural representation" from a counseling point of view), *Ru'a Tarbawiya* (Educational Vision), Issue 28, pp. 8–11.

'Allaq, 'A. J. (1997) The dialogue of ink, blood and water: modernity and higher education in Iraq. In K. E. Shaw (ed.) *Higher Education in the Gulf: Problems and Prospects*. Exeter: Exeter University Press.

Al-Zaroo, S. (1988) *Al-Ta'lim Taht Al-Ihtilal 1967–1987* (Education under Occupation 1967–1987). Al-Khalil, West Bank: Rabitat Al-Jami'iyin.

Al-Zaroo, S., & Hunt, G. L. (2003) Education in the context of conflict and instability: the Palestinian case, *Social Policy and Administration*, Vol. 37(2), pp. 165–180.

Anderson, G. L. (2001) Disciplining leaders: a critical discourse analysis of the ISLLC national examination and performance standards in educational administration, *International Journal of Leadership in Education*, Vol. 4(3), pp. 199–216.

'Assaf, 'O. (2004) *Harakat Mu'alimi Al-Madares Al-Hukumiya Fil-Daffa Al-Gharbiya 1967–2000* (The Palestinian Public School Teachers Movement in the West Bank, 1967–2000). Ramallah, West Bank: Muwatin – The Palestinian Institute for the Study of Democracy.

Ayubi, N. N. M. (1995) *Over-Stating the Arab State*. London: I. B. Tauris.

Baranović, B., Jokić, B., & Doolan, K. (2007) Teaching history in a postwar social context – the case of the Croatian Danube region, *Intercultural Education*, Vol. 18(5), pp. 455–471.

Bashkin, O. (2007) 'When Mu'awiya entered the curriculum' – some comments on the Iraqi education system in the interwar period. In W. Kadi & V. Billeh (eds.) *Islam and Education: Myths and Truths*. Chicago: The University of Chicago Press.

Baylouny, A. M. (2008) Militarizing welfare: neo-liberalism and Jordanian policy, *Middle East Journal*, Vol. 62(2), pp. 277–303.

Berger, A. E. (2002) *Algeria in Others' Languages*. Ithaca, NY: Cornell University Press.

Betancourt, T. S., Simmons, S., Borisova, I., Brewer, S. E., Iweala, U., & de la Soudière, M. (2008) High hopes, grim reality: reintegration and the education of former child soldiers in Sierra Leone, *Comparative Education Review*, Vol. 52(4), pp. 565–588.

Bird, L. (2007) Learning about war and peace in the Great Lakes region of Africa, *Research in Comparative and International Education*, Vol. 3(2), pp. 176–190.

Brand, L. (1988) *Palestinians in the Arab World*. New York: Columbia University Press.

Breidlid, A. (2005) Education in the Sudan: the privileging of an Islamic discourse, *Compare: A Journal of Comparative Education*, Vol. 35(3), pp. 247–263.

Brighenti, A. (2007) Visibility: a category for the social sciences, *Current Sociology*, Vol. 55(3), pp. 323–342.

Cassidy, R. M. (2006) *Counterinsurgency and the Global War on Terror: Military Culture and Irregular War*. New York: Greenwood.

Chelpi-den Hamer, M. (2007) How to certify learning in a country split in two by a civil war: governmental and non-governmental initiatives in Côte d'Ivoire, *Research in Comparative and International Education*, Vol. 2(3), pp. 191–209.

Cheriet, B. (1996) The evaluation of the higher education system in Algeria. In R. Cowen (ed.) *The Evaluation of Higher Education Systems* (World Yearbook of Education Series). London: Kogan Page.

Clarke, M., & Otaky, D. (2006) Reflection 'on' and 'in' teacher education in the United Arab Emirates, *International Journal of Educational Development*, Vol. 26(1), pp. 111–122.

Davies, L., & Talbot, C. (eds.) (2008) Education in conflict and postconflict societies (special issue). *Comparative Education Review*, Vol. 52(4).

Dean, R. (2000) Rethinking the civil war in Sudan, *Civil Wars*, Vol. 3(1), pp. 71–91.

Deng, L. B. (2005) The challenge of cultural, ethnic and religious diversity in peace-building and constitution-making in post-conflict Sudan, *Civil Wars*, Vol. 7(3), pp. 258–269.

Deng, L. B. (2006) Education in Southern Sudan: war, status and challenges of achieving Education For ALL goals, *Respect: Sudanese Journal for Human Rights' Culture and Issues of Cultural Diversity*, Issue 4, pp. 1–27.

Dicum, J. (2008) Learning, war, and emergencies: a study of the learner's perspective, *Comparative Education Review*, Vol. 52(4), pp. 619–638.

Dreyden-Peterson, S., & Siebörger, R. (2006) Teachers as memory makers: testimony in the making of a new history in South Africa, *International Journal of Educational Development*, Vol. 26(4), pp. 394–403.

Endersen, L. C., & Øvensen, G. (1994) *The Potential of UNRWA Data for Research on Palestinian Refugees: A Study of UNRWA Administrative Data* (Report 176). Oslo: FAFO.

Foucault, M. (1979) *Discipline and Punish: The Birth of the Prison*. New York: Vintage.

Frayha, N. (2003) Education and social cohesion in Lebanon, *Prospects*, Vol. XXXIII(1), pp. 77–88.

Golan-Agnon, D. (2006) Separate but not equal: discrimination against Palestinian Arab students in Israel, *American Behavioral Scientist*, Vol. 49(8), pp. 1075–1084.

Goodson, I. F. (1997) Representing teachers, *Teaching and Teacher Education*, Vol. 13(1), pp. 111–117.

Graham-Brown, S. (1991) *Education in the Developing World*. London & New York: Longman.

Halawah, I. (2005) The relationship between effective communication of high school principal and school climate, *Education*, Vol. 126(2), pp. 334–345.

Herrera, L., & Torres, C. A. (eds.) (2006) *Cultures of Arab Schooling: Critical Ethnographies from Egypt*. New York: State University of New York Press.

Hiro, D. (1991) *The Longest War: The Iran-Iraq Military Conflict*. London: Routledge.

Hromadžić, A. (2008) Discourses of integration and practices of reunification at the Mostar Gymnasium, Bosnia and Herzegovina, *Comparative Education Review*, Vol. 52(4), pp. 541–563.

Human Rights Watch (2001) *Second Class: Discrimination Against Palestinian Arab Children in Israel's Schools*. New York: Author.

Jamal, A. (2007a) Strategies of minority struggle for equality in ethnic states: Arab politics in Israel, *Citizenship Studies*, Vol. 11(3), pp. 263–282.

Jamal, A. (2007b) Nationalizing states and the constitution of 'hollow citizenship': Israel and its Palestinian citizens, *Ethnopolitics*, Vol. 6(4), pp. 471–493.

Johnson, D. D., Johnson, B., Farenga, S. J., & Ness, D. (2005) *Trivializing Teacher Education: The Accreditation Squeeze*. Lanham, MD: Rowman & Littlefield Publishers.

Joint Assessment Mission (2005) *The Education Sector Plan of the New Sudan for the Pre-Interim Period and January 2005–December 2010*. Khartoum & Nairobi: Author.

Khalidi, R. (2007) *The Iron Cage: The Story of the Palestinian Struggle for Statehood*. Boston: Beacon Press.

Kirk, J. (2004) Promoting a gender-just peace: the roles of women teachers in peace-building and reconstruction, *Gender and Development*, Vol. 12(3), pp. 50–59.

Kirk, J., & Winthrop, R. (2007) Promoting quality education in refugee contexts: supporting teacher development in northern Ethiopia, *International Review of Education*, Vol. 53(5–6), pp. 715–723.

Larsen, M. A., & Mehta, S. (2008) Insecurity and desire: North American perspectives on education's contested ground, *Comparative Education*, Vol. 44(3), pp. 255–263.

Lesch, A. M. (1998) *The Sudan: Contested National Identities*. Bloomington & Oxford: Indiana University Press & James Currey.

Le Sueur, J. D. (2005) *Uncivil War: Intellectuals and Identity Politics during the Decolonization of Algeria*. Lincoln, NE: University of Nebraska Press.

Macpherson, R., Kachelhoffer, P., & El Nemr, M. (2007) The radical modernization of school and education system leadership in the United Arab Emirates: towards indigenized and educative leadership, *International Studies in Educational Administration*, Vol. 35(1), pp. 60–77.

Mahshi, K., & Bush, K. (1989) The Palestinian uprising and education for the future, *Harvard Educational Review*, Vol. 59(4), pp. 470–483.

Makkawi, I. (2002) Role conflict and the dilemma of Palestinian teachers in Israel, *Comparative Education Review*, Vol. 38(1), pp. 39–52.

Massialas, B. G., & Jarrar, S. A. (1991) *Arab Education in Transition: A Source Book*. New York & London: Garland Publishing.

Mazawi, A. E. (1994) Teachers' role patterns and the mediation of sociopolitical change: the case of Palestinian Arab school teachers, *British Journal of Sociology of Education*, Vol. 15(4), pp. 497–514.

Mouffe, C. (2005) *The Return of the Political*. London & New York: Verso.

Moughrabi, F. (2001) The politics of Palestinian textbooks, *Journal of Palestine Studies*, Vol. XXXI(I), pp. 5–19.

Nasser, R., & Nasser, I. (2008) Textbooks as vehicle for segregation and domination: state efforts to shape Palestinians Israelis' identities as citizens, *Journal of Curriculum Studies*, Vol. 40(5), pp. 627–650.

Nicolai, S. (2007) *Fragmented Foundations: Education and Chronic Crisis in the Occupied Palestinian Territory*. Paris & London: UNESCO & Save the Children.

Nuwayr, 'A. S. (2001) *Al-Mu'alimun Wal-Siyasa fi Masr* (Teachers and Politics in Egypt). Cairo: Centre for Political and Strategic Studies.

Oh, S., & van der Stouwe, M. (2008) Education, diversity, and inclusion in Burmese refugee camps in Thailand, *Comparative Education Review*, Vol. 52(4), pp. 589–618.

Palestinian National Authority (2008) *Statistical Abstract of Palestine* (No. 9; Publication code 1526). PNA: Central Bureau of Statistics.

Paulson, J. (ed.) (2007) Policy, education and conflict (special issue). *Research in Comparative and International Education*, Vol. 2(3).

Perlo-Freeman, S. (ed.) (2008) Symposium: Palestine – an economy in conflict. *The Economics of Peace and Security Journal*, Vol. 3(2). Available online at: http://www.epsjournal.org.uk/Vol3/No2/issue.php

Retamal, G., & Aedo-Richmond, R. (eds.) (1998) *Education as Humanitarian Response*. London: Cassel.

Richardson, P. M. (2004) Possible influences of Arab-Islamic culture on the reflective practices proposed for an education degree at the Higher Colleges of Technology in the United Arab Emirates, *International Journal of Educational Development*, Vol. 24(4), pp. 429–436.

Saba-Sa'di, S. (2008) *The Disputed Role of a Traditional Intellectual Group: The Case of Arab Women Teachers in Israel* (EUI Working Papers, RSCAS 2008/23). Florence: European University Institute, Robert Schuman Centre for Advanced Studies.

Sa'di, A., & Lewin-Epstein, N. (2001) Minority labour force participation in the post-Fordist era: the case of the Arabs in Israel, *Work, Employment and Society*, Vol. 15(4), pp. 781–802.

Saleh, M. A., & Kashmeeri, M. O. (1987) School administration factors associated with distress and dissatisfaction, *Education*, Vol. 108(1), pp. 93–102.

Shalhoub-Kevorkian, N. (2008) The gendered nature of education under siege: a Palestinian feminist perspective, *International Journal of Lifelong Education*, Vol. 27(2), pp. 179–200.

Sirriyeh, H. (2000) Jordan and the legacies of the civil war of 1970–71, *Civil Wars*, Vol. 3(3), pp. 74–86.

Sommers, M. (2005) *Islands of Education: Schooling, Civil War and the Southern Sudanese (1983–2004)*. Paris: UNESCO, International Institute for Educational Planning.

Stack, M. (2006) Testing, testing, read all about it: Canadian press coverage of the PISA results, *Canadian Journal of Education*, Vol. 29(1), pp. 49–69.

Starrett, G. (1998) *Putting Islam to Work: Education, Politics, and Religious Transformation in Egypt*. Berkeley, CA: University of California Press.

State of Israel (2008) *Statistical Abstract of Israel* (No. 59). Israel: Central Bureau of Statistics.

Suleiman, Y., & Anderson, P. (2008) 'Conducting fieldwork in the Middle East': report of a workshop held at the University of Edinburgh on 12 February 2007, *British Journal of Middle Eastern Studies*, Vol. 35(2), pp. 151–171.

Sultana, R. G. (2006) Education in conflict situations: Palestinian children and distance education in Hebron, *Mediterranean Journal of Educational Studies*, Vol. 11(1), pp. 49–81.

Thomas, A. (2007) Self-report data in cross-cultural research: issues of construct validity in questionnaires for quantitative research in educational leadership, *International Journal of Leadership in Education*, Vol. 10(2), pp. 211–226.

Thomas, A. (2008) Focus groups in qualitative research: culturally sensitive methodology for the Arabian Gulf?, *International Journal of Research and Method in Education*, Vol. 31(1), pp. 77–88.

Tibawi, A. L. (1956) *Arab Education in Mandatory Palestine: A Study of British Administration*. London: Luzac & Company.

Velloso de Santisteban, A. (2005) Sanctions, war, occupation and the de-development of education in Iraq, *International Review of Education*, Vol. 51(1), pp. 59–71.

Winthrop, R., & Kirk, J. (2008) Learning for a bright future: schooling, armed conflict, and children's well-being, *Comparative Education Review*, Vol. 52(4), pp. 639–662.

World Bank (2008) *The Road Not Traveled: Education Reform in the Middle East and Africa*. Washington, DC: Author.

CHAPTER 7

The North African Educational Challenge

From Colonisation to the Current Alleged Islamist Threat

Pierre Vermeren

1 Introduction

This article presents a summary of my thesis in contemporary history, *Des Nationalistes aux Islamistes: La Formation des Élites Tunisiennes et Marocaines de 1920 à 2000*, which has been published in France and in Morocco, but has not been translated into English (Vermeren, 2002). The thesis argues that in order to understand how the governments of the region's post-colonial nations reached the situation they are presently in and the challenges they have to face today, one must first focus on the ideological and historical context of the building of colonial elite's education system. We will therefore show how, after independence, nationalism failed to build a new, democratic high school system. We will also try to understand the main challenges facing North Africa today, related to overcoming the profound educational crises, and to addressing the social consequences of the regional elite's reproductive system.

2 The Ideological and Historical Context of the Creation of the Colonial Elite's Education System

Education was not a major preoccupation of early French colonisation. In the 1830s, when the conquest of Algeria began, and for some decades after that, the policy regarding 'indigenous' people centred on matters of control, diplomacy and war. Over this long period, amounting to almost 30 years, education was only a concern for the families of the French military and civil servants.

As the French began to control the tribes through a policy of indirect rule, 'indigenous affairs' officers were primarily interested in being able to communicate clearly with Berber and Arab leaders. Officers learnt indigenous languages, and gave a few 'Muslims' some basic training to enable them to understand what was expected of them and to facilitate obedience from the locals.

Colonising settlers soon dominated the political scene. They supported the Second Republic in 1848, and obtained the creation of three '*départements*'— i.e., French metropolitan administrative districts—in Africa. Algeria formally

© THE EURO-MEDITERRANEAN CENTRE FOR EDUCATION RESEARCH, UNIVERSITY OF MALTA, 2009
DOI: 10.1163/9789004506602_007
This is an open access chapter distributed under the terms of the CC BY-NC 4.0 License.

became a part of the French Republic, which meant that French laws also applied in Algeria's civil territories. During the Second Empire (1851–1870), some officers and counsellors convinced Napoleon III to set up a specific policy for indigenous populations. The first indigenous schools, with French curricula and modern teaching methods, emerged in North Africa, though there were also some Christian schools. In 1865, indigenous people, who had been French by law since 1848, were granted the possibility to obtain French citizenship if they accepted to renounce their personal (i.e., religious) laws. Only a few of them did do so over a period of one hundred years.

With the final reinstatement of the Republic in France, in the 1870s, the settlers obtained the permission to extend so-called 'pro-indigenous' policies. In the 1880s, complete 'assimilation' with the French population and administration was granted—rights which were not shared by the *'indigène'*—to the locals. For example, the education laws promulgated by the Jules Ferry, which imposed *'une école laïque, gratuite et obligatoire'* (a secular, free and compulsory education for all), were also adopted in Algeria. However, these laws only applied to French citizens. The 'indigenous' schools that existed subsisted as if by chance.

One has to wait for the *Recteur* Jeanmaire in Algiers, who, at the end of the century, promoted a new educational policy for 'Muslims' in Algeria. He set up 'indigenous schools', created four *'medersas'* for the instruction of both Muslim and Republican civil servants in Islamic affairs, and a university was created in Algiers after 1895. But the latter, while in principle open to all, was in fact reserved for European students. By 1914, fewer than 2% of Algerian children were attending school, even if this lack of access was in complete contradiction with assimilationist policies.

Consequently, at the turn of the century, there was no intellectual elite conversant in the ways of the metropole and of the coloniser among native Algerians. If a lot of Algerian people did speak French in urban business, in the army, or on the farms with settlers, they were far from able to compete on an equal footing with the French colonial elite, whether educated in France or locally.

The situation in Tunisia was quite different. Here colonisation took place at the time of Ferry's laws (1881–1883), and consequently, the colonial system was heavily influenced by these developments. A small, indigenous graduate elite emerged before 1914. It was easier for 'Tunisians' than for Algerians, because Tunisia was not France, and the Protectorate treaty was supposed to pave the way for the self-government of Tunisia by its elite. Tunisia had moreover introduced some school and administrative reforms in the mid-19th century, initiated by the Ottoman regime. In the beginning of the Protectorate, several young, brilliant subjects of the Bey went to Paris to study. They returned to Tunisia, where they worked to develop the local administration and education (e.g., the Khaldounia Association). But it is only after 1918 that a second wave of student migration to France took place, beginning with the future President, Habib Bourguiba.

Algeria's colonial history shows that, as we can read in the classical French historiography about this period (Turin, 1983), there was no global approach to education. Academic education was reserved for the European pupils and students, and there was no public conception of education of and for the locals. We can thus observe three different points of view concerning the objectives and systems of colonial education in French North Africa.

The first group interested in the education of the locals was made up of army officers. The way the educational project was conceived is similar, whether we refer to the first decades of colonial Algeria, or to the Sherifian Empire (Morocco), when the French Resident General Lyautey embarked on the task of setting up the Protectorate's administration. For General Lyautey, as for General Bugeaud—who had created the 'Bureaux des Affaires Indigènes' (Bureaus of Indigenous Affairs) in Algeria eighty years before—the main questions were: how to use the traditional elite to control society, and how to recognise an honorific role to this elite in order to keep it peaceful and respectful of the new authorities (Azan, 1948).

The second group that articulated a view on the education of the locals is symbolised by the settlers, representing the views holding sway in Europe at that time. In their view, the indigenous population had to be controlled. Given that the function of the locals was to constitute a working class providing manual labour, the settlers considered that education was not necessary for them. Indeed, schooling could even be dangerous if it taught the democratic principles of freedom and equality, or promoted mastery of French language, rhetoric and history. In the view of the settlers, therefore, the locals—and mostly males—had only to be educated to respect some rules, to understand a few French words, to comply with sanitary laws, and to learn some technical skills (agriculture for men, and dress-making for women).

The European settlers, who were a minority among the indigenous population, had always been afraid of the 'Arab' threat. They were physically afraid of being submerged, and politically threatened by the principle of democracy. If the Muslims claimed their right to equality, the settlers would lose their leadership. It was therefore necessary to exclude the locals not only from French citizenship, but also from state schools. The best the locals could hope for was vocational schooling.

A third view on the question of the education of the locals was promoted by Republican and Socialist school teachers—or 'moniteurs', as they were then known. For some of these, there was no contradiction between their mission of state school teaching and the colonial principle of assimilation. As civil

THE NORTH AFRICAN EDUCATIONAL CHALLENGE

servants, they were often sent to Algeria for some years by their Ministry—as was the case, for instance, with the young Fernand Braudel, and then Pierre Bourdieu. At the end of the century, an increasing number of local teachers were trained in the *'Ecole Normale de la Bouzareah'* in Algiers. Among them were an increasing number of Muslim teachers who, during the 1920s, created a magazine called *'La Voix des Humbles'* ('The Voice of the Poor'). Several contributors to this magazine tried to reconcile French republican values with their own origins, personal history, and bicultural identity.

This evolution took place in a faster and more vigorous manner in Tunisia than in Algeria. In the former country, some schools for Muslim pupils were set up as 'Franco-Arab' institutions as from the very first years of the Protectorate. Like European people in their own schools, after passing the primary certificate, these young Tunisians were able to enrol in *'Sadiki College'*, a former Ottoman school which became a French Arabic *'collège'*, or high school. By the WWI, Tunisian professors and teachers had succeeded in securing a beneficial educational policy for the indigenous local population, building on it right up to the time of decolonisation.

Nevertheless, the French colonial system tried to maintain the indigenous upper class—i.e., the former elite—under its domination, a fate that upper classes rarely submit to willingly. This may be the reason why this project failed at the end of the colonial period. In fact, the main result of the French colonial legacy in North Africa is probably the constitution of a small native elite base which was essentially Francophile. The colonised forgot their own aristocratic and pre-modern model, and instead looked up to the settler elite of French army officers, doctors, lawyers, teachers, and journalists. At the end of the day, what they seemed to be interested in doing was copying them.

The public service was out of bounds for indigenous people in Algeria because only French citizens could be employed in it, and in the Protectorates because these were foreign countries. The young elite was trained in 'Sadiki College' in Tunisia, in the *medersa* in Algeria, in the two 'Muslim Colleges' in Morocco. But these institutions only led to such subaltern employment as translators, clerks, junior officers, and so on. So, step by step, the 'independent professions' became considered as the only way to social promotion and autonomy. But these careers were reserved for a very few of the locals, which explains why a lot of parents and families thought that independence would promote a new order, since the school would be open to their sons.

To recapitulate, therefore: France built in North Africa three different educational systems, each one bearing the mark of its colonial model and its local actors. The first model is the Algerian one. Here two separate systems subsisted after several experiments. On the one hand, some children of Muslim high society, of Muslim soldiers lost in action, or of Muslim civil servants were incorporated with French pupils and students in French schools. Before WWI, only a very few of them obtained the *Baccalauréat*, and went on to the university in Algiers or in Paris (Pervillé, 1999). On the other hand, some other Muslim children were admitted in bilingual schools, and after the obtaining the *Certificat* at the end of lower secondary schooling, they became civil servants or students in the *medersas*. Here, therefore, we have a double model of schooling, even if very few of the Muslim children actually went to school—less than 8% around WWII.

The second model is the one we find in Tunisia, where two sections cohabited. The first was the Arabic section. The best graduates were accepted in Sadiki College (Sraïeb, 1994). Until WWI, this *Collège* was an important place for the reproduction of elites. But since this period, an increasing number of students came from the '*Sahel*' (South of the capital), allowing some promotion for the 'Sahelian' and Tunisian small bourgeoisie. At the same time, Tunis's aristocracy sent its sons to the French '*Lycée Carnot*', a state High School where the European and the Jewish elite prepared for the *Baccalauréat* to study in Paris or Marseille.

The third model is Morocco, where General Lyautey tried, as much as possible, to separate the European and the Muslim ways (Rivet, 1988). He created some '*fils de notables*' schools for locals in the main cities. After obtaining the primary school certificate, students could go to the '*Collège Musulman*' in Fes or Rabat (Merrouni, 1983). After six years, they could get a Certificate in Islamic Studies, on the basis of which General Lyautey tried to allocate some honorific positions. However, if families were ambitious and realistic, they understood that the only way to gain access to university was by obtaining the *Baccalauréat*. Some rich and powerful families therefore enrolled their sons in the '*Lycée Gouraud*' in Rabat, the French High School in Morocco.

After some years, the Protectorate created a special education section for the sons of tribal and Berber leaders and chiefs. This was the Berber College of Azrou in the Middle Atlas (Benhlal, 2005), which prepared a few students for the Military Officer's School of *Dar El Baïda* in Meknes. This case was unique in the French Colonial Empire, preparing a real competition between the Arabic and nationalist elite in the cities and the Berber officers at the head of the colonial (then national) forces.

3 Why Did Nationalism Fail to Build a Democratic Educational System?

When nationalist movements took to the street to fight against the colonial power, in Algeria as elsewhere, a key aspiration was to gain not only independence, but

THE NORTH AFRICAN EDUCATIONAL CHALLENGE

also the right for young people to gain access to school and to the university, thus facilitating social mobility. National independence was equated with the promise of mobility, and 'hope' was the key slogan that drove the movement toward independence.

When independence was secured, the new national elite that filled the top positions vacated by the colonisers considered that the French educational model was the one to be preserved. While they had promised citizens and militants a return to Islamic and Arabic education, they had themselves been completely transformed by their own Francophile education, and by their experience of study in Paris or some other city in France. For the new political class, therefore, the French system of education, from which locals had been excluded during the colonial period, had to become the new national model. Most of the new leaders entertained strong feelings of identification with—and gratitude for—their former colonial school teachers. Both Habib Bourguiba (Lacouture, 1961), the Tunisian President, and Hassan II, the King of Morocco (Ganiage, 1994), for instance, expressed such feelings about their own school teachers.

For twenty years after decolonisation, the educational policies led by 'nationalist' governments produced the largest francophone generation North Africa had ever seen. Under colonisation, French or Arab-French education had only concerned a minority. When, in 1955, France left Morocco and Tunisia, and Algeria's War of Independence started in earnest, only 12% of Moroccan children were enrolled at school, with the corresponding figures for Algeria being 21%, and 33% for Tunisia (Ganiage, 1994). These percentages reflect the three different points of view concerning the objectives and systems of colonial education in French North Africa that we considered earlier, and which, like a complex alchemy, had an impact on each country and on the whole Maghreb region. Tunisia was more affected by the school teachers' point of view, Algeria by that of the settlers (Ageron, 1968), and Morocco by the military.

A turning point in colonial educational policies took place after the WWII. For ten years, an effort was made to develop schooling quickly in the three countries. Independent regimes in Morocco and Tunisia pursued with such voluntarist plans, attempting implementation at an even faster rate. After fifteen years, toward 1970, the percentage of those attending schools came near to 50%, and was even higher in Tunisia thanks to the efforts of Mahmoud Messaadi, who served as Education Minister for a whole decade (Sraïeb, 1974).

It was quite different in Algeria, where the eight-year-long war between the French army and the 'FLN' (National Liberation Front) changed the deal. In an effort to convince the Algerian people to keep their French nationality, the army developed education as it had never done before. In a few years, two million Algerian children and young people learned the French language, in civilian as well as in military schools (Branche, 2005). For a long time, Algeria became the most important francophone country in North Africa, all the more so since Arabic culture was very weak after 130 years of French colonisation.

After some hesitations by nationalist governments, colonial educational policies were extended, this time toward 'all' children. Nationalist governments in Morocco and Algeria could not implement alternative policies because both countries had very few Arabic teachers and graduates. To avoid being in contradiction with their ideology, first Morocco, then Algeria, imported hundreds of Arabic teachers and imams from the Middle East—with General G. Nasser exploiting this opportunity to send members of the Society of Muslim Brothers to the Maghreb. Despite this, however, the number of such Arabic teachers could never compare with the thousands of French teachers who had been sent to secondary schools during the 1960s and 1970s.

At this time, educational policy regarding elites was very similar to the model prevailing in France. In two decades, new national universities and some selective 'Grandes Écoles' were created in North Africa. Their professors were mostly French, and, with the exception of Islamic departments, the curriculum and teaching methods and models were French. Some Schools, such as the French 'Ponts et Chaussées' for civil engineers, were completely integrated with small sister schools, such as the 'Hassania School of Ponts et Chaussées' in Rabat. In other cases, the French administration received a lot of students from the newly independent countries, offering them short-, mid- or long-term specialist training.

Consequently, for a long time after independence, the new administrators and leaders in science, industry, university, research, trade, administration, security and so on, worked according to French standards and usually spoke French at work. In France, this new political model became known under the name of 'cooperation', which followed on from 'colonisation'.

For many political and social reasons, the turning point of cultural decolonisation took place after the mid-1970s. In a few years, educational policies changed completely, and this had a long-term impact on the training system of the elite.

Three years (1976–1979) marked the end of educational 'cooperation'. Lesser qualified Islamic graduates replaced foreign francophone teachers everywhere, particularly in mathematics and the sciences. At the same time, the Arabic language became the language of instruction in all subjects except the natural sciences and some postgraduate courses (Grandguillaume, 1983). However, the changes are not reducible to just language. During the 1970s, the new nationalist and Islamic conservative approach is supported, or symbolised, by Mohamed Mzali in Tunisia, Taleb Ibrahimi in Algeria, and Azeddine Laraki in

THE NORTH AFRICAN EDUCATIONAL CHALLENGE

Morocco. Islamic culture generally replaced philosophy, sociology and French literature in high schools as well as in universities.

At this time, the Islamic traditional approach was considered by governments and leaders—such as King Hassan II, President Habib Bourguiba, and President Houari Boumédiène—as the best way to eradicate the revolutionary threat. After a deep crisis caused by Socialist contestation and demonstrations, the pacific and traditional role of Islamic religion appeared as the best way to eradicate the modern, revolutionary and political roots of youth movements. Arabisation was the cultural face of this religious movement. And last but not least, the old Islamic school methods of memorisation—what the 2008 World Bank Report refers to as 'outdated methods of teaching'—became the dominant pedagogic paradigm. The French 'esprit critique' had become a synonym for subversion in North Africa. It had to be eradicated by all means, even it meant destroying the elitist model left by the French. Mass university education also signalled the end of such a model.

The effects of this academic revolution slowly gained ground with the new generation. By the mid-1980s, the worldview of young students and graduates had changed quite radically. While this is not the place to discuss the language question in North Africa—a central issue in relation to both education and society more generally—it is nevertheless important to highlight the fact that Arabisation, in this region, is not only a question of words and symbols, but a fundamental question concerning the very conception of the world (Krichen, 1986), the place of religion, and political behaviour (Grandguillaume, 1983).

Mass higher education and Arabisation are, however, not the only ways by means of which society is reformed. Everywhere, and specifically in science, the elite has maintained small and selective ways aimed at reproducing the existing model. This is the case with medicine, engineering, business administration, and international law, for instance. In each country, francophone high schools became the best way to succeed in these professional careers.

All the prestigious and selective schools or sections still use the French language—and occasionally English or Spanish—in contrast with the rest of the educational institutions, which use Arabic. As human science researchers have consistently observed for a long time, linguistic competence is a social, economic and intellectual privilege. This is a reality everywhere, but perhaps especially so in North Africa, given that here linguistic discrimination is very strong (Anonymous, 1989). It is necessary to speak three or four languages at least, if one wants to succeed in your higher education and your professional life (Benrabah, 1999).

In North Africa, a student speaks his or her mother tongue, which is frequently the North African vernacular version of Arabic. Both French and standard Arabic are used as languages in teaching. Then, students typically learn English or Spanish as foreign languages. As for the Berbers, who are a strong minority in Algeria and Morocco, there is one additional linguistic hurdle. In conditions such as these, it is quite impossible for most students in Morocco or in Algeria to be truly fluent in French and in Arabic if they attend ordinary state schools. For such students, there is practically no possibility to succeed at university, since all the scientific disciplines and medicine are exclusively taught in French. And yet, despite this situation, Medicine and Engineering faculties have been, as in the Middle East, the main areas where the Islamist opposition started and grew during the 1970s and 1980s.

Each country has its own elite schools. In Algeria, the most prestigious field is oil engineering (National School of Petroleum Engineers), followed by the Military Academy (Kadri, 1992). However, new Business and Management schools have recently appeared. In Tunisia, the main schools are Engineering schools (such as the National School of Engineers of Tunis—ENIT). However, Medicine and Management also rank highly. Since the Ben Ali regime, the 'Ecole Nationale d'Administration' (ENA) has seen its role and importance increase.

In Morocco, engineering is still the most important way to attain high positions in administration and corporate management, in the government, and in state agencies. King Mohammed VI is even more deeply interested than his father was in a technocratic vision that gives pride of place to engineering and technology. The 'Makhzen'—i.e., the head of state, composed of families and counsellors around the King—seems to consider that, because they have graduated in Law, these technocrats are far from politics. In addition, they generally know how the Makhzen functions, and they understand that their career strictly depends on their fidelity to the Throne.

What is certain is that, in Tunisia as in Morocco, the most prestigious and powerful engineers are graduates from the French 'Grandes Écoles', and sometimes from North American universities (Benhaddou, 1997).

4   Which Way out of the Deep Educational Crises and the Social Consequences of Elite Reproduction?

During the 1990s, the political and cultural make-up of the new generations changed radically. After the Islamist 'avant-garde' of the 1970s, the new generations were more homogenous in their Islamic conformism. Furthermore, young people were competent in new computer technologies, which are now part of daily life in North African cities. This contradiction resulted from the impact of international dynamics, though it was also a result of local and specific educational trends.

The fact remains that a separate lite was part of this generation, or more exactly, lived next to it. Only a small tranche of a generation—probably less than 1% of an age group (Wagner, 1998)—was able to reach notable corporate and state positions, or to work outside Morocco. With only around 20% of a generation obtaining the *Baccalauréat*, the majority of young people were disqualified from further opportunities due to inadequate studies. The situation was worse than in the 1980s and, with the exception of Tunisia, resembled that which had prevailed in Western Europe during the 19th century.

During the 1960s and the 1970s, independence provided a great opportunity for urban youth to enrol in high schools and universities. At this time, the social reproduction of the former pre-colonial and colonial elites was able to constitute the new state class. After independence, as in all the new independent states in the developing world, there was a significant dearth of military and civil servants, engineers, doctors and executives. As the pre-colonial elite was very small, and as the colonial power structure tried for a long time to reserve key positions to its own elite, the children of these groups were far from constituting the majority of the emerging state class. Indeed, these first decades constituted a big opportunity for young, urban, literate men (Ben Salem, 1968). They were the 'independence generation'. In modern North African History, there had never been such a favourable period for social mobility.

At this time a mixed elite emerged, incorporating *'héritiers'* (inheritors) from the former pre-colonial elite (Bourdieu & Passeron, 1970), some from the colonial elite, and some new elements. The former pre-colonial elite was more important in Morocco than in Tunisia, where the colonial elite had replaced the pre-colonial one. In the Kingdom of Morocco, for instance, the new state administration had, in one decade, grown from a few thousands to 200,000 civil servants, while the number of corporate executives rose from a few hundreds to several thousands. This fact helps explain why revolutions failed during this period in North Africa.

From the mid-1970s onward, the effects of this massive recruiting, together with the economic crises, led to a halt in state employment policy. At the same time the social effects of the new school policies started to be felt.

After 1978–1980, the new configuration was an explosive one: state administration was reaching saturation point, and a whole bevy of reforms had transformed the elitist school system into a mass institutional one. The turning point for graduate unemployment in Morocco was 1979. But social conditions were deteriorating in the whole region: in Tunisia and Morocco since 1978, and in Algeria after 1986, due to the collapse of the price of gas. In a few years, the social situation led to a political change in Tunisia (1987), to a revolution and a civil war in Algeria (1988 and 1992), and to riots (1981, 1984 and 1990) and then to a political liberalisation in Morocco during the 1990s (since 1991).

North Africa is now confronted with a divided society, with on the one hand one group looking to the Middle East and its fundamentalist ideologies, and on the other hand, a small elite addicted to a Western way-of-life and culture. It may not be too far-fetched to talk about an intellectual and social rift segregating the majority of young people on the one hand, and a globalised elite minority on the other.

Is there any alternative to this situation for governments? If they want to safeguard their societies from subversion and violence, they are obliged to use violence themselves. In this way, they will perhaps preserve the present system, which works in favour of their own children. However, if they want to uphold their societies in the long term, they have to rebuild educational systems, or at least, they have to provoke debates about educational reform. Up to 2008, Tunisia really tried to rebuild its school system. Morocco and Algeria, however, seemed to baulk in front of this Herculean undertaking.

Educational reform was tested at the beginning of the 1990s by Ben Ali's government, at a time when he was still supported by the Francophile and open-minded elite. Between 1989 and 1994, the Minister of Education was Law Professor Mohammed Charfi (1936–2008), a Francophile intellectual. Charfi's reform tried to fund a new educational pact. He supported a reform in philosophy, in literature, and in the approach to policies regarding language and culture. His clear intention was the eradication of the roots of cultural Islamism. Even before this reform, which strengthened bilingualism, Tunisia had a diversified school system which formed its own elites. In Morocco, however, elites are formed outside the system—especially in French schools—while Algerian elites are formed outside the country.

Since 1999, with the ascent to the throne of King Mohammed VI, educational reforms seemed to be the order of the day in Morocco. However, despite that, as in Algeria, the government understands the necessity of such reforms, there is a fear of the political consequences of such change. The governing elite refuses to appear as if they were supporters of the West or of the French, because the general expectation is that they uphold the nationalist and Arabic programme. They are moreover afraid of the reactions of the conservative elite, whose influence largely exceeds that of the Islamists.

The civil war in Algeria did not provide a promising context for such educational reforms. Since the end of the war in 2001, the government and its institutions have remained under the ideological pressure of the Islamists. Algerian society has increasingly adopted conservative and religious behaviours. On the

THE NORTH AFRICAN EDUCATIONAL CHALLENGE

political scene, the Francophile camp ('*hizb's frança*' for its enemies) has been weakened.

Benjamin Stora (2001), a French historian of contemporary Algeria, underlines the fact that the civil war began by attacks against French high school pupils. During the war, francophone and French schools were closed, and a lot of young students from the 'best' families were enrolled in selective schools in France, Switzerland, England and elsewhere. During this period, state schools in Algeria were an open field for Islamist propaganda.

Since the end of the conflict, a lot of francophone private schools have reopened in different cities. As in Morocco, and then in Tunisia, the main target of this free school movement has been to offer a French alternative, as a response to the policy of Arabisation. Just by way of example, in the year 2000, there were more than 1,000 private schools in Casablanca alone. But such private education alternatives were not as easy to establish in Algeria, where nationalism consists in refusing French culture and its symbols. Following his re-election, President Bouteflika decided in 2004 to close all the Francophone private high schools. This, of course, does not prevent some rich young people from pursuing the studies they want in the country of their choice. Nor does it stop thousands of young pupils from learning French at home, as their mother tongue, which is the best way to prepare for their economic future. In such a context, however, there is no chance of voting for deep reforms.

Since the mid-1990s, Morocco has become the new frontier of high school and university reform in North Africa. In 1995, a World Bank report underlined the catastrophic situation in Moroccan education: the illiteracy rate approached 60% of the adult population, and only 1% of the youth were university graduates. Furthermore, the new UNDP international rating, i.e., the Indicator of Human Development, which incorporates the educational level attained by different countries, ranked Morocco last in North Africa.

Similar indictments of Morocco's educational system have been made by internal reports, such as the one commissioned by the Royal Cabinet. Engineer Abdelaziz Meziane Belfqih, counsellor of King Hassan II, headed the Orientation Commission for Teaching and Research (COSEF) and, working with a large panel of experts, drew up a report on education in the Kingdom, delivering the outcome of its deliberations some days before the death of King Hassan II. The Commission concluded that education was the main weakness in Morocco. A 'National Council for Education' was established in order to propose concrete reforms, and to enforce them.

The period between 1999 and 2002 saw the failure of the 'alternation government', which was in charge of the proposed educational reforms until 2002. Changes were restricted to small or symbolic reforms, such as the introduction of the Berber language in the initial years of the primary school, or the reinstatement of philosophy at high school and university levels. The claim was that such reforms had helped Moroccan children obtain improved scores at school, though it seems that there was little evidence and substance behind such claims, which served a political purpose in the main.

The next government, led by Prime Minister Driss Jettou (2002–2007), was more interested in economic and investment affairs. The main objective in the educational camp was to adapt the Moroccan university to the new European model, thus triggering an important reform in 2007. This reform, however, was more technical than intellectual in nature, and while representing new challenges for the special counsellor, engineer A. M. Belfqih, the central problems in education persist. More than a reform of the higher education system, the *makhzen*'s main concern seems to be to adapt it to the economy—a fact that is reflected in Belfqih's reform programme, titled *10,000 Engineers for Morocco*.

That the reform will not have a deep impact on Morocco's higher education system has been confirmed again recently. A private 'Governance High School of Rabat' was created in 2008, after an agreement with 'Sciences PO Paris'. This was in response to strong local demands for higher business administration courses, which were much in demand among the small upper class. However, it proved to be easier to create new and external institutions than to reform the system from the inside.

Again, in the winter of 2008, the World Bank provoked a strong reaction from government when a new and controversial report on Arab education titled *The Road Not Travelled: Education Reform in the Middle East and North Africa*, drew attention to the fact that the Moroccan economy was still suffering due to a weak education system, and that reforms were urgently needed. Like thirteen years before, special counsellor M. A. Belfqih was once again called to the rescue.

5   Conclusion

During the colonial period, the French colonial power relegated the former North African elite to the position of middle-men between the colonial authorities and the indigenous population. With this purpose in mind, they set up a new education and training system—including such institutions as the Islamic *colleges*—to develop a subaltern elite. The new young urban and educated elite ('*les évolués*', as the French said) and the '*héritiers*', however, refused this relegation. On the one hand, they tried, and obtained, the right to access the French university, and on the other hand, they built a long-term political movement, nationalism, to re-appropriate state power.

THE NORTH AFRICAN EDUCATIONAL CHALLENGE

In Paris, the 'AEMNAF' (Muslim North African Students' Organisation in France) combined both approaches from 1932 until the granting of independence. When this new, narrow, composite elite came to power in 1956 and in 1962, it had to recruit a lot of civil servants and army officers to build the new state administrative apparatus. As the French had implanted a new selection process for the elite, schools, high schools and the university had become the keys to land a leadership position in administration, in government, or in a corporation. During this first period immediately after independence, i.e., during the 1960s and 1970s, social mobility became a reality in the region for those who were capable to take up this challenge.

However, after two decades, and due to the saturation of posts within the state apparatus, as well as thanks to the global economic crises, this period of opportunities was over. A new period began, marked by educational reforms, the process of Arabisation, mass higher education, and graduate unemployment. The crises marking this period are cultural, social, and educational. The meritocratic school model was eclipsed, with the system being transformed into a dualist and closed one. In the 1990s, a large part of the graduates, especially those in the best universities and aiming for the most prestigious careers, hoped to reproduce the fortunes of their parents, who had graduated and taken up key posts in different sectors in the 1970s. For the post-1990 graduates, however, the era of meritocracy was over.

Who really wants a democratic reform of elite education and class formation in North Africa today? And how can one reunify the higher education system, which, right now, looks like a caricature of the French one, but with more danger if we consider the political risks at stake? For three decades, the new educational policy has completely transformed the young generations. The cultural contexts they are living in, together with their intellectual and linguistic make-up, have provoked a complete change in mentalities, in worldviews, and in qualifications.

Today, North African graduates, up to the age of 45, while less francophone than their elders, and less fluent in any language, are nevertheless more connected with the rest of the world through the new technologies. Despite this, they experience feelings of fear and helplessness in front the world, a situation which tempts them to retreat into their Islamic culture. The only exception to this is a small, internationalised elite who have left the region: more than 2,000 former Moroccan students from the 'Grandes Écoles' live in Paris, while thousands of Tunisian graduates live in the Western world.

In these persistent conditions, the challenge is crucial for North African elites and their Northern partners. Either they are capable of changing the ideological and practical substance of the educational policies, or they have to face a radical change in their societies, a permanent risk of Islamist subversion and an increasing gap with European societies.

Acknowledgement

This chapter originally appeared as: Vermeren, P. (2009) The North African educational challenge: from colonisation to the current alledged Islamist threat, *Mediterranean Journal of Educational Studies*, Vol. 14(2), pp. 49–64. Reprinted here with permission from the publisher.

References

Ageron, C. R. (1968) *Les Algériens Musulmans et la France (1871–1919)*. Paris: Presses Universitaires de France.

Anonymous (1989) Une génération sacrifiée, *Les Cahiers de l'Orient*, No. 15.

Azan, P. (1948) *Par l'Épée et par la Charrue: Ecrits et Discours du Général T-R. Bugeaud*. Paris: Presses Universitaires de France.

Ben Salem, L. (1968) Démocratisation de l'enseignement en Tunisie, *Revue Tunisienne de Sciences Sociales*, Vol. 16, pp. 81–135.

Benhaddou, A. (1997) *Les Élites du Royaume*. Paris: L'Harmattan.

Benhlal, M. (2005) *Le Collège Berbère d'Azrou*. Paris-Aix: Karthala-Iremam.

Benrabah, M. (1999) *Langue et Pouvoir en Algérie – Histoire d'un Traumatisme Linguistique*. Biarritz: Séguier-Atlantica.

Bourdieu, P., & Passeron, J-C. (1970) *La Reproduction*. Paris: Les Éditions de Minuit.

Branche, R. (2005) *La Guerre d'Algérie: Une Histoire Apaisée?* Paris: Points Seuil.

Ganiage, J. (1994) *Histoire Contemporaine du Maghreb de 1830 à nos Jours*. Paris: Fayard.

Grandguillaume, G. (1983) *Arabisation et Politique Linguistique au Maghreb*. Paris: Maisonneuve & Larose.

Kadri, A. (1992) *Le Droit à l'Enseignement et l'Enseignement du Droit*. PhD thesis, School for Advanced Studies in Social Sciences (EHESS), Paris, France.

Krichen, A. (1986) La fracture de l'intelligentsia: problèmes de la langue et de la culture nationales. In *Tunisie au Présent: Une Modernité au-dessus de Tout Soupçon*. Paris: Éditions du CNRS.

Lacouture, J. (1961) *Cinq Hommes et la France*. Paris: Éditions du Seuil.

Merrouni, M. (1983) *Le Collège Musulman de Fès (1914 à 1956)*. PhD thesis, Montréal University, Canada.

Pervillé, G. (1999) *Les Étudiants Algériens de l'Université Française – Populisme et Nationalisme chez les Étudiants et Intellectuels Musulmans Algériens de Formation Française*. Paris: CNRS Éditions.

THE NORTH AFRICAN EDUCATIONAL CHALLENGE 139

Rivet, D. (1988) *Lyautey et l'Institution du Protectorat Français au Maroc 1912–1925*. Paris: L'Harmattan.

Sraïeb, N. (1974) *Colonisation, Décolonisation et Enseignement: L'Exemple Tunisien*. Tunis: Publications de l'Institut National des Sciences de l'Éducation.

Sraïeb, N. (1994) *Le Collège Sadiki de Tunis 1875–1956: Enseignement et Nationalisme*. Paris: CNRS Éditions.

Stora, B. (2001) *Algeria, 1830–2000: A Short History*. London: Cornell University Press.

Turin, Y. (1983) *Affrontements Culturels dans l'Algérie Coloniale: Écoles, Médecins, Religion 1830–1880*. Algiers: Entreprise Nationale de Livre.

Vermeren, P. (2002) *Des Nationalistes aux Islamistes: La Formation des Élites Tunisiennes et Marocaines de 1920 à 2000*. Paris: La Découverte.

Wagner, A-C. (1998) *Les Nouvelles Élites de la Mondialisation*. Paris: Presses Universitaires de France.

World Bank (2008) *The Road Not Travelled: Education Reform in the Middle East and North Africa*. Washington, DC: Author.

PART 2

Country Focus

CHAPTER 8

The Circulation of European Educational Theories and Practices

The Algerian Experience

Mohamed Miliani

1 Introduction

On an historical plane, Algeria has for a long time been the land of invasions of several peoples and tribes, namely the Vandals (429–535), the Ottomans (1554–1830), the Spanish (1504–1792), and the French (1830–1962), but she has also been the crucible of several civilisations: Berber, Phoenician, Carthaginian, Roman, Byzantine, Arab-Muslim, Turkish, Spanish and French. If, on the one hand, the Algerians' resistance at this level has been fierce and successful, on the other hand, it has been tougher, sometimes quasi-insuperable, if not quixotic (others would say counter-productive), to fight against the incursion of more elusive, though less visible, and yet more invading opponents: i.e., ideas and theories, particularly on educational matters, which were or are still produced in foreign contexts and applied in Algeria.

After their political freedom, few developing countries achieved economic independence, and very few have been able to attain their total cultural freedom. Besides, the weight of the colonial heritage concerning the school system has been particularly heavy, and its consequences catastrophic. Thus:

> ... what the Europeans' departure is going to bring about is the sudden promotion of a certain number of civil servants on the spot, and a massive entry of those who have benefited from their schooling in French, as well as men—mainly "political" cadres of the struggle (for independence)—who benefit from a loosening of the regulations concerning recruitment. (Glasman & Kremer, 1978, p. 26)

This is true of all sectors of the state, but education has been particularly hit. Therefore, when developing countries tried to improve their educational structures, they experienced multi-faceted problems which prevented education from playing its role in the overall development of the nation. This is no less the case of Algeria.

© THE EURO-MEDITERRANEAN CENTRE FOR EDUCATION RESEARCH, UNIVERSITY OF MALTA, 1996
DOI: 10.1163/9789004506602_008

The aim of this paper is to study the circulation of certain European educational ideas or theories and their application in the school system whose major aim, whether in formal or informal education, is to prepare and help people to reach, through training, a better standard of living, of literacy and health. The present debate centres on the assessment and quantification of the importance of the impact of these ideas on the system, and their role in the improvement of the educational structures, and the possible attribution of failure, admitted or not, in the implementation of the above-mentioned thoughts and practices.

Two broad periods can be identified in the history of educational ideas and thoughts in Algeria. They correspond roughly to the application, very often misapplication, of a major educational theory or practice (home-produced: rather rare; or imported or borrowed from foreign countries: very often the case, and the object of our concern in this paper). The two identified periods tie with the educational philosophies which pervaded the Algerian educational system for decades. In the first period (1962–1970), Algeria went through a mimicry phase, due more to objective factors than well thought-out decisions. Then, in the second period (1971–1995), she started to develop its own idiosyncratic vision of, and strategy in, education and pedagogy.

2 'The Colonial Hangover' (1962–1970): The Impossible Emancipation

The first period can be qualified as the era of '*impossible emancipation*' because of the rather restrictive political, social, economic and educational factors present shortly after independence in 1962. Besides, any national culture retreats or even fades away when foreign cultures invade a given country with ease or with force, and where little resistance is developed against the intruder. This is certainly true of Algeria which failed to generate the conditions for success in general growth or those for a steady development. In addition, the skilled manpower and adequate financing necessary to allow the country to free itself from the long-standing bonds with metropolitan France were scarce or absent. Once again, the limited means (human: lack of teachers; infrastructural: few schools, *lycées* or colleges, and only one university in Algiers; financial: Algeria was then an agricultural country; and organisational: lack of managers) and an absence of expertise in educational matters made the task of bringing about a 'true' Algerian educational system difficult, if not impossible to achieve.

After independence, and despite an ultra-nationalist ideology, the educational authorities had to make do with a hybrid school system resulting, on the one hand, from the lukewarm reforms undertaken by the French during colonisation, and on the other, the embryonic educational framework consisting of hundreds of koranic schools and *medersa,* the equivalent of the European colleges providing religious teaching. With independence, Algeria inherited problems from colonial rule: a rigid school curriculum and a very selective system of examinations strewn with formal tests like obstacles throughout the school system: first, *La Sixième,* sixth year primary school; second, the BBPC (*Brevet d'Etudes du Premier Cycle*), fourth year secondary school; third, the *Probatoire,* or first part of the *Baccalauréat,* sixth year secondary school; and finally, the *Baccalauréat* or its second part, seventh year secondary school. This obstacle race, of course, led to a very high school drop-out level.

From 1962, the Algerian government felt the need to develop an authentically Algerian system of education able to satisfy the country's plans for rapid economic growth, and also to face the ever-growing demand of the public for a substantial increase in education provision. To face this demand, but also to stop the human haemorrhage from the schools due to the departure of teachers of French stock, educational institutions called upon teachers from traditional structures, namely koranic schools and *medersa.* This had bad effects on the quality of teaching. Educational authorities had to reverse this decision (Grandguillaume, 1983) in order to avoid the entrenchment of a very low level of educational provision. Since then, the school system has undergone a series of reforms to re-shape the educational structure, basing its philosophy on ideas originating mainly from Europe, either directly imported from European countries or through people who were completely behind these ideas because of their education or training.

The first period in the history of education in Algeria is characterised by the reproduction of European school models. Indeed, the Algerian educational system remained, for a long time, a carbon copy of the French one. French policies of centralism, in synchrony with the *democratic centralism* of the Algerian regime, and secularism, since religious teaching was not as systematic as it is presently, were carried on without change, deviation or alteration. The educational authorities had, as a priority, to take over from the French manpower at all levels of the school system (as teachers, course designers, educational institution managers, inspectors, etc.). It is partly thanks to foreign expatriates' know-how that all sorts of problems were handled more or less adequately.

The application of such borrowed theories and practices has led de facto to a centralising and standardising monolithism which, in the long run, has discredited or rather ignored, the indigenous traditional values and attitudes to make room for modernism as determined by the *developed centre* (as opposed to *underdeveloped periphery* to which Algeria belonged). One must add that this educational monolithism was in harmony with political monolithism advocated during the 1960s and 1970s by the anti-imperialistic and socialist leaders who ruled the country. People endured the rigours of this new yoke. In some ways this was not new to them, but this time they bore this version of the burden with more understanding and even fatalism: a well-known attitude Algerians develop in the face of strong adversity or a catastrophe. Amid this profusion of thoughts and theories originating from Europe, Algerian educationists were more concerned, consciously or not, with the preservation of the school infrastructure, the provision of sufficient but not necessarily qualified manpower, and the development of a centralised administrative system, partly because of a need to maintain their own status and privileges, due to their lack of expertise and know-how, or because of an absence of intellectual courage to tackle real problems at the root of the ills.

Besides, the Algerian educationists were then engaged in action as technocrats, busy with the technicalities of the school system. They did not take up the role of intellectuals and failed to generate theoretical debates in order to develop an indigenous philosophy of education to inform their policy-making. This failure can be partly attributed to the insufficiency, quantitatively and qualitatively speaking, of Algerian cadres, but also to the tight control of the political authorities (or rather the ruling party) over educational matter and change in the school system.

Despite its socialist regime, Algeria turned quite often toward the developed centre for an expert's view or help to solve the numerous problems she experienced in all fields. However, maybe due to the Algerian regime, there was a certain western European reluctance to co-operate and help the country meet its economic, political, and educational needs. Consequently, the Algerian state looked eastward, toward the Eastern block and the Middle Eastern countries, and although without the proper financial or human resources, adopted a voluntarist policy to reduce, among other things, the level of illiteracy. Such was the priority of the first government, intent to meet the demands of the school system and the economy. However, there was an additional problem: a marked opposition between the productive sector and the system of education. Each of them seemed to be living in total isolation from the other. Thus:

> ... the educational system produced degree-holders in the scientific and technical fields, less and less called upon by industry, and whose job, when they are recruited, has nearly nothing to do with the expressed needs. As for the productive sector, it met its own needs in technological competences in a quasi-autonomous way, on the one hand by equipping itself with its proper structures of training, and on the other by drawing heavily and from the start on foreign technical aid. (Djeflat, 1993, p. 43)

In the first decade of its independence, Algeria became the field for the experimentation of foreign theories brought by individuals (experts, teachers) or groups (companies, research units). from Europe, the USA, or the Middle East. Strangely enough, this burgeoning life of ideas prevented the educational authorities from freeing themselves from too narrow a cooperation with 'friendly' states. The ideas applied were not always for the good of the country nor of the people. Algeria badly needed hundreds of experts in education, industry and economy in general. Unfortunately, the expatriates were not always as expert as it was claimed, to say the least. Moreover, this cacophony of conflicting views did not help the authorities to find a happy medium between some extreme opinions. All this gave a heterogeneous and unorganised character to the whole educational system, which reinforced its lack of organisation and coherence.

Meanwhile, the solving of the economic (until the oil boom of the 1970s) and political problems (military coup in 1965) was the first item on the government's agenda. Education was not, practically speaking, a priority for politicians except in speeches and slogans. In the political sphere, the only concern was the number of millions of dinars to give to education, which meant little, when we know that over 70% of the budget was devoted to salaries.

Under such adverse conditions (intellectual, human, political, and financial), it was almost impossible for the educational system to come of age. It was rather too early to have some kind of tradition established, as it was also imaginary or illusory to see total change occur overnight. The agents of change (Algerian experts, teachers, etc.) were at that time few, untrained, or ignored. On the other hand, one should not forget the force of inertia constituted by some groups or individuals who felt endangered by certain educational measures, and who were thus more interested in preserving or getting a status, a profit, or a privilege to the detriment of the school system or the nation. During this first decade of its rather short history, if one considers 1962 as the starting date of modern Algeria, decision-makers, more often than not, affected a simple transplantation of ideas. Besides, they had very little if any capacity to adapt these theories to the environment, let alone create or invent ideas suitable to the educational setting. The motto of educationists seemed to be: 'Adopt, do not adapt'.

But this state of affairs could not go on forever. Deeper reforms were needed in order to change the whole face and structure of the school system. Besides, it was important to shed the vestiges of 132 years of colonialism and build a socialist society that would move vigorously to the 21st century, and at the same time prepare the country to obtain the autonomy and emancipation which it had failed to achieve in the first years of its independence. This was a highly difficult, if not utopian goal. However, that did not mean that Algeria had to live in autarchy. Development does not mean 'reinventing the wheel', but going beyond all the advances achieved in science and technology, rather than being tied by them.

3   'The Paradigm Shift' (1971–1995): The Era of Inconsistencies

Once the economic (thanks to the oil boom of the 1970s) and political problems (disappearance of strong opposition and strengthening of one-party socialist system) were somehow handled, the government turned toward the educational structure to reform it. Reforms were more carefully planned and most of the time were based on imported theories. However, this period was characterised by a gap between wishful thinking of the authorities, and a reality rarely apprehended in its entirety. Real problems on the terrain were very often not well grasped, if not totally ignored. Therefore, any change was very remote from the problem area it was supposed to remedy, either because the objectives were not realistic or the means to attain these objectives absent or insufficient.

The intention of the political as well as the educational authorities was first to strengthen the socialist approach to education (provision of equal opportunity to all, free schooling, school for all, scholarships awarded to the majority of pupils, or nominal fees in all cases). One other way of bringing change to the philosophical aspect directing the school system was to adopt the Polytechnical Curriculum Theory (East German model) for the first nine years of schooling. Hence, 1978 saw the setting up of the Foundation School based on the fundamental principles of socialist education, namely:

- Compulsory schooling up to the age of 16, in order to ensure literacy and faithfulness to the Constitution and the National Charter;
- Fusion between primary and middle schools to avoid the problem of dropouts;
- Scientific and technological literacy, given that an important objective of education was to produce citizens capable of adapting themselves not only to socio-economic and cultural, but also to technical and technologic transformations taking place. Literacy electives were encouraged less and less; and
- Tightening of the bond between schooling and work, since education needed to be conceived and planned as an integral part of the development of the country, and had therefore to be intimately linked to the planning of other sectors (such as agriculture and industry).

The introduction of Foundation School has diminished the number of years of compulsory education from ten (in the old French-type system) to nine. French as a medium of instruction has disappeared from the school curricula. It is now considered as the first foreign language, a slight privilege over the other foreign languages, namely Spanish, English, German and Russian. Besides, the pupils can be oriented either toward vocational training or toward the secondary school. Entrance to university is subject to the award of the *baccalauréat*. Another institution was recently created: the University of Further Training (*l'Université de la Formation Continue: UFC*), for those who leave school without the *baccalauréat*. While no one would dispute its contribution, there is one criticism that is often made: it is a 'shadow university' with nearly the same programmes as can be found at the traditional universities without, however, the necessary human resources.

The *Ecole Fondamentale et Polytechnique* was the result of the pressure for more and better education. It supposes the reconversion of the middle cycle and its combination with the primary cycle which precedes it. Its aim is to become progressively polytechnical, combine theory with practice, and bridge the gap between academic and practical studies. Foundation School came about to put the whole system back in its qualitative context with the hope that it would solve the problem of drop-outs, which has become somewhat catastrophic in proportion.

We have avoided speaking of higher education, because it is our feeling that only cosmetic changes were brought about by the 1971 Reform of Higher Education. Among such changes was the transformation of faculties into institutes. On the other hand, Foundation School was thought to revolutionise the system, and at the same time satisfy the demands of modernism, which meant that the Algerian system of education had to support an industrial revolution. This it did not always do and indeed a number of harmful and counter-productive decisions were taken. Thus, 1979 saw the end of the technical colleges (*Collèges d'Enseignement Technique: CET*) in a period when industry needed large numbers of skilled and semi-skilled workers (Djeflat, 1993).

This paradigm shift (i.e., from a highly selective school system to a school for all through a democratisation of education) could not be completely realised because the triptych of the government's educational policy was far from being achieved. This threefold policy included:

– The 'Arabisation' of all curricula and medium of instruction (most scientific subjects are still taught in French);
– 'Algerianisation' of the teaching staff (now standing at about 80%); and
– The democratisation of education.

Results were mainly achieved in the democratisation of education. There has been in fact a quantitative development of education to mitigate the limited and selective opportunities provided by colonial masters. The benefits include the replacement of an elitist system by a more balanced one with equal opportunities for all, and the reduction of social stratification (Miliani, 1991). There has been a shift, therefore, in that education went from a phase where it was highly selective and competitive, to a stage where it became considered as an inalienable human right for the benefit of all. This swing of the pendulum was not supported by the pedagogical, didactic and human resources necessary to provide a quality education for all. Furthermore, a new phenomenon appeared with mass schooling: school drop-outs. These drop-outs and other young unemployed who developed a kind of anti-establishment attitude, became known as *Hittiste* (those who lean on walls).

The type of school advocated was therefore more concerned with political principles in line with the socialist regime than with other types of organisation or ways of functioning of the educational system. However, the role of education is now increasingly being seen as a promoter of growth and as an investment for the future.

Despite the everlasting slogans, the situation on the terrain was totally different. In reality, there was also a continuation of a French centralist orientation and of the dominance of degrees over expertise. Degrees were and are still valued more than the level of expertise of teachers. The other problem came from the fact that the educational authorities were, and are still, looking for the help of foreign training research units, i.e., *Bureaux d'études*, mostly French, American and British, in order to have access to technologies, an assumption which proved with time to be false. Most of the time these very companies of educational engineering were focusing their efforts on obtaining contracts which excluded the national expert from the control or mastery of the knowledge or know-how they sold. Indigenous experts were mostly concerned with administrative affairs.

> The intervention of the research unit means the coherent use of methods and techniques of capitalistic management: experts, profitability, computer, everything there is to impose the image of a superior rationality, and therefore not questionable. (Glasman & Kremer, 1978, p. 127)

The result of this profusion of ideas and theories was an incoherent set of structures and practices. This was partly due to the antagonistic nature of the theories or experiences applied, for there was not only diffusion of a knowledge and/or know-how, but also the laying of an ideological superstructure upon a culture alien to it. This melting-pot of ideas gave birth to educational institutions (Foundation School, *Lycée*, *Collège*, University, University Centres, etc.) that are placed side-by-side without being integrated into a whole. This atomistic vision of school could not logically lead to a well-integrated educational system.

Furthermore, there was then a blatant contradiction between the so-called anti-imperialistic position of the country, as expressed in official speeches, and the use of capitalist methods of management recommended by these research units. The latter's educational theories and proposals were supposed to be adapted to the 'national realities' of the country. However, content-wise the system was similar to that of many European nations, while the local teaching methodologies left a lot to be desired. In fact, what is still advocated is a quantitative approach to the development of education despite supposedly future-bound policies whose intent is focused more on quality. This concern for quality exists, but reality in the field is wrongly apprehended. To the real problems diagnosed (problem of drop-outs, medium of instruction, large class size, lack of qualified or well-trained teachers, foreign language learning, etc.) in all educational areas, the authorities respond by launching sporadic, unsystematic and incongruous actions. Changes are always conceived in a limited and localised stage of the system, never as part of a whole where transformation at a level may have impacts on others. Besides, decisions for change seem to come out of the blue. The idea of long-term planning, of thinking in terms of decades, is something that decision makers do not seem to be capable of.

4 Perspectives: Between Social Fracture and Economic Crisis

Several individuals' personal and/or political ambitions have driven the country to its present social predicament. Even schooling has contributed greatly to the present social and cultural plight as Carlier (1995, p. 406) notes, the 'Foundation School has provided the managerial staff, the troops and lexis, if not the syntax of neo-fundamentalism'.

The disappearance of social values has led the country to a fracture among members of the population which used to be united against one common enemy, colonialism. Since then, it has lost faith in the future and in itself, and has also lost its sense of direction. The problems are all the more insuperable now that the country is suffering economically from the diktat of the International Monetary Fund: the influence of the world economy is being felt more and more, as Algeria progressively adopts a market economy.

This tragedy has many faces: economic, because Algeria relies too much on trade with Europe; social, since over one million Algerian emigrants live in

France; political, given the strong links with the European Community and the USA; and technical/technological, due to the reliance on European know-how and expertise. All these facts will always facilitate the circulation of foreign ideas, notwithstanding the speeches of educational/political authorities who increasingly advocate an open resistance to change initiated '*extra muros*' to make room for intramural initiatives. By way of reply to change generated from European thoughts, there is still a strong move to return to 'primeval roots', a favourite slogan of the conservatives. Among these are the *Salafists* who since the 1970s have advocated a puritan reformism toward 'authenticity', a concept rarely explained or defined. In fact, a clarification of these roots is neither needed nor desired, because this would mean tackling very controversial aspects, where very opposed views are expressed. Foremost among these would be the discourse on national identity, the writing of the history of Algeria, and so on.

Today the government has decided, once again, to develop the ethos of a national system of education (see Figure 8.1 and Figure 8.2 for details regarding its structure). It has thus decreed in April 1995 that a Higher Council for Education be created in order to structure the educational system in a more efficient way. The objective of the Council is to link the work of the ministries of Education, of Higher Education and of Employment. Will this be another hope nipped in the bud? My feeling is that this top-down approach to solving problems is not the way to face the numerous demands of the school system. For over thirty years, education has tried many theories, most of them of European origin, but what seems to be essential is not only which educational theory to implement, but also whether the approach advocated is a systemic one or not. Most of the time, failure seems to be due to a micro-analysis of problems, forgetting their relationships with and in the whole.

Furthermore, I see a major point of contention which will block the implementation of European ideas in the Algerian school system: the notion of progress and growth the educational system should aim at. There is now a marked difference between those who favour the western view of development, and those who hold strong religious opinions. If the latter's vision had been subterranean but always present, even before independence and especially during the last ten years, it has now emerged as a major force to be reckoned with. The problem now is that the ideas and positions held by these opposite standpoints are at both ends of the theoretical and practical spectrum. What is unfortunate is that extremism characterises both positions and a happy medium seems very unlikely to be found. In any of the considered cases, when there is a possible change, there is no ecological consideration for the system of education. On the other hand, it is also my belief that education will always suffer from a primary monolithism of the decision-makers which is the expression of the fear of the alien, the other, except if the other is of Arab or Muslim origin. This tendency toward sameness sends back to us the everlasting problem of our national identity, a problem not yet solved. Very few governing authorities, political, cultural or educational, have dared tackle the thorny problem of Algerian identity. Many subterfuges have been used, but the problem remains untouched. Talking about this, Grandguillaume (1983) posits that

> ... it is necessary (for the Algerians) to forge a myth of origin, a discourse on the origins which is also ... a discourse on identity ... the heroic struggle (against France) can create this myth ... the nation must be symbolised, it cannot be this way permanently by negation only, by opposition to the other, by the sole discourse on war. (p. 155)

The pluralism (or rather richness) of the country (linguistic, regional, ethnic, and intellectual) is thus ignored, denied or fought against, first by the ruling class, and then by several cultural and educational bodies, and this in favour of some supposedly unifying notions like *qawmiyya:* supra-nationality, one great Arab nation, instead of the more limiting and yet identifiable *wataniyya:* nationhood (Lacheraf, 1988), or entities (Pan-Africanism, Pan-Arabism, Pan-Islamism etc.) which thus far have been ephemeral myths:

> Arab nationalism and socialism on one side and Islamism on the other have in Algeria taken on forms more uncompromising, ostentatious and authoritative than anywhere else, in a kind of caricatured excess imposed by an image of the self by constantly calling upon the past. (Carlier, 1995, p. 408)

This monolithic approach to development is not the only problem experienced by the school. On the other side of the spectrum, the circulation of

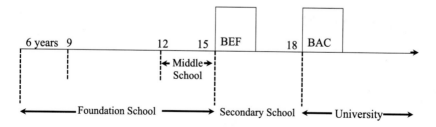

(BEF: *Brevet d'Enseignement Fondamental*)
(BAC: *Baccalauréat*)

FIGURE 8.1   The Algerian school system

Age Level	2–5	6–9	9–12	12–15	16–18	19–25	Educational Institution
Pre-school	Not systematic						Kindergarten
Foundation School		compulsory & free					1st Cycle (basic stage)
			compulsory & free				2nd Cycle (awakening stage)
				compulsory & free			3rd Cycle (training stage)
Secondary School					free		Lycées & Collèges
Higher Education						free	Universities & Grandes Écoles

FIGURE 8.2   The stages of the school system

foreign ideas will always be detrimental to the Algerian system of education if endogenous and exogenous factors are not looked at carefully and changes brought about progressively. The need or obligation to graft foreign theories onto the system will always pose a problem because these are imposed on an alien set without a consideration for the whole, putting into question the ecological validity of these theories. The following points show the complexity of the intellectual debate the circulation of European theories can generate:

- Does not mimicry of educational thoughts, whatever their origin, harm social behaviours and cultural habits specific to countries of the periphery?
- Does Occidentalism (following western ideas) mean modernism/development as defined by the countries recipient of the mentioned theories and ideas?
- Does not Occidentalism, which pretends to tend toward universalism, mean uniformalism in its negative sense? Does not sameness then mean the end of progress, development and possibly creativity?

But this is another debate. And the Algerian educational system is not yet there.

Acknowledgement

This chapter originally appeared as: Miliani, M. (1996) The circulation of European educational theories and practices: the Algerian experience, *Mediterranean Journal of Educational Studies*, Vol. 1(1), pp. 1–12. Reprinted here with permission from the publisher.

References

Carlier, O. (1995) *Entre Nation et Jihad*. Paris: Presses de Sciences PO.

Djeflat. A. (1993) *Technologie et Système Educatif en Algérie*. Algiers: OPU.

Glasman, D., & Kremer, J. (1978) *Essai sur l'Université et les Cadres en Algérie*. Paris: CNRS.

Grandguillaume, G. (1983) *Arabisation et Politique Linguistique au Maghreb*. Paris: Françoise Maspero.

Lacheraf, M. (1988) *Écrits Didactiques sur la Culture: L'Histoire et la Société*. Algiers: ENAP.

Miliani, M. (1991) Algeria. In *Handbook of World Education*. Houston, TX: American Collegiate Service.

Further Reading

Ageron, C. R. (1983) *Histoire de l'Algérie Contemporaine (1830–1982)*. Paris: PUF.

Boutefnouchet, M. (1982) *La Culture en Algérie*. Algiers: SNED.

Colonna, F. (1975) *Instituteurs Algériens (1883–1939)*. Paris: Presses de la Fondation Nationale des Sciences PO.

Lacheraf, M. (1978) *Algérie, Nation et Société*. Algiers: SNED.

Necib, R. (1986) *Industrialisation et Système Éducatif Algérien*. Algiers: OPU.

CHAPTER 9

State, Society, and Higher Education in Cyprus

A Study in Conflict and Compromise

Anthony A. Koyzis

1 Introduction

When in 1992, the first public university in Cyprus opened its doors, the institution was heralded with high expectations. As the university of a small island republic, this university was also in the midst of the island's on-going division along ethnic lines. The occupied North is inhabited by Turkish-Cypriots, and the Republic is predominantly Greek-Cypriot. Since the internationally recognised Republic of Cyprus is the focus of this paper, only development in this part of the island will be primarily focused on.

Apart from the fact that the university is located in the midst of a divided island, from its very inception it was faced with a series of challenges coming from both ideological foes, as well as ideological friends. What in fact was happening in Cyprus since the fall of 1992 and even before the opening of the University of Cyprus, was an on-going debate over what the university would teach, in what language, and whether students would pay or not. How would it be governed and organised? And what role would the state play in university affairs? This along with other issues became fundamental reasons not only for debate, but also for an enduring conflict regarding what Cypriots were defining as worthwhile knowledge to be taught in institutions of higher learning, and conflict over the role of higher education in society.

This paper will begin by focusing on the major structural features of the Cypriot system of higher education as well as its slow but steady expansion over the last twenty years. Following structural features, the paper will develop a construct of the various knowledge traditions which have dominated Cypriot notions of higher education. These knowledge traditions have been a by-product of the influencing effect of both decades of reliance by Cypriots on overseas study as well as the ensuing expansion of the private English language sector of higher education. These private institutions in particular have been bringing to Cyprus knowledge tradition constructs from British and North American sources. Following the discussion in knowledge traditions is a section on future implications and the future development of higher education in Cyprus in light of Cyprus' desire to enter the European Union.

© THE EURO-MEDITERRANEAN CENTRE FOR EDUCATION RESEARCH, UNIVERSITY OF MALTA, 1997
DOI: 10.1163/9789004506602_009

STATE, SOCIETY, AND HIGHER EDUCATION IN CYPRUS

2 Nature and Structure of Higher Education in Cyprus

The first institutions of post-secondary education established in Cyprus were two teacher training colleges, one for male students in 1937, and a second one for female students in 1940. Both of these institutions were started by the then British Colonial Office of Education. It enrolled both Greek and Turkish students. The language and curriculum were exclusively English. These institutions' goal was to prepare elementary teachers for the government elementary schools.

On January 1958 both the above-mentioned institutions were combined in the co-educational Pedagogical Academy of Cyprus, and by 1959 the institution was turned over to the Greek community of Cyprus preparing for independence from Britain in 1960. In 1960 an equivalent Turkish Teacher's College also began. In 1958 the Pedagogical Academy had adopted the two-year curriculum of the pedagogical academies of Greece. A third year was added to the curriculum in the early 60's. At this time mandatory teaching of English was added to the curriculum.

By 1992–1993, the Republic of Cyprus was providing post-secondary education to 33% of all Cypriot students in post-secondary education. These students were 58% of all secondary school graduates who continued beyond the secondary level. The remaining 25% were studying abroad. This was a significant decline in the percentage of students studying abroad compared to the students studying abroad in the mid-1980s. This was primarily due to the founding of the public university in 1992, and the expanding of the private sector of higher education. The number of students studying abroad was still relatively high: 9,066 in 1992–1993, which has dropped from 10,312 in 1985–1986 (see Table 9.1).

The 33% of the students attending post-secondary institutions in Cyprus were attending 31 public and private institutions with a total enrolment in 1992–1993 of 6,263, compared to 5,952 in 1991–1992. At this post-secondary level in 1992–1993, 29.6% were enrolled in public institutions and the remaining 70.4% in private institutions. Males accounted for 50.7%, and females for 49.3% (see Republic of Cyprus, 1993, p. 21).

It should be noted that the 1992–1993 academic year was the first full year for the University of Cyprus. The university's enrolment was purposely kept at 486, and by 1993–1994 had increased to 974. It is estimated that by 1996–1997 the enrolment would increase to slightly over 1000 students. In addition, the Pedagogical Academy has been absorbed by the university. This has resulted in the creation of the Department of Educational Sciences. The 1992–1993 statistics show the last year of enrolments at the Academy (see Table 9.2).

TABLE 9.1 Cypriot students abroad by country

Country	1985–1986		1992–1993	
	Number	%	Number	%
Greece	4027	39.1	3581	39.5
UK	1668	16.2	2391	26.4
Other Western Europe	1825	17.7	908	10.0
USA	2231	21.6	1775	19.6
Eastern Europe	443	4.3	322	3.5
Other	118	1.1	89	1.0
Total	10312	100.0	9066	100.0

SOURCE: REPUBLIC OF CYPRUS (1986, 1993)

TABLE 9.2 Enrolment in public and private institutions, 1992–1993

Public	Males	Females	Total
University of Cyprus	58	428	486
Higher Technical Institute	500	117	617
Pedagogical Academy	49	174	223
School of Nursing-Midwifery	77	218	295
Hotel-Catering Institute	76	35	111
Forestry College	34	0	34
Mediterranean Institute of Management	20	7	27
Cyprus International Institute of Management	47	15	62
Total	**861**	**994**	**1855**
Private			
Total	2314	2094	4408
Grand Total	**3175**	**3088**	**6263**

SOURCE: REPUBLIC OF CYPRUS (1993)

What is significant about higher education in Cyprus is the large private sector of higher education which enrols three times more students than its public sector (see Table 9.2 and Table 9.3). This is not anticipated to change in the future, unless fewer Cypriots choose to study abroad, which may in effect

STATE, SOCIETY, AND HIGHER EDUCATION IN CYPRUS   159

TABLE 9.3   Enrolment in public and private institutions, 1993–1994

Public	Males	Females	Total
University of Cyprus	132	842	974
Higher Technical Institute	495	127	622
Pedagogical Academy	—	—	—
School of Nursing-Midwifery	88	342	430
Hotel-Catering Institute	51	47	98
Forestry College	48	1	49
Mediterranean Institute of Management	16	7	23
Cyprus International Institute of Management	49	20	69
Total	**879**	**1386**	**2265**
Private			
Total	2249	2218	4467
Grand Total	**3128**	**3604**	**6732**

SOURCE: REPUBLIC OF CYPRUS (1994)

increase private enrolments even further. The significance of the private sector is that it not only enrols three times as many students as the public sector, but it exclusively provides higher education to Cypriots in English and models its curricula and courses of study on British and North American institutions.

These 23 private sector institutions rely exclusively on British or North American accreditation and degree validation auspices and offer programmes in business studies, computers and information sciences, hotel management, engineering and technology, secretarial studies. and to a very limited extent social sciences (see Koyzis, 1989).

The public sector of higher education includes the University of Cyprus which includes: Schools of Humanities and Social Sciences (with Departments of Greek Studies, Turkish Studies, Foreign Languages, Educational Sciences, Social and Political Sciences), a School of Pure and Applied Sciences (with Departments of Mathematics/Statistics, Computer Science, and Natural Sciences), and the School of Economics and Administration with a Department of Economics, Public and Business Administration (see Koyzis, 1993). Other public sector institutions include a School of Nursing and Midwifery, which offers two- and three-year certificate programmes in nursing or midwifery. The Hotel and Catering Institute offers short-term programmes in a variety of areas such as cooking, waitressing, front office management, and so on. The Higher

Technical Institute founded in 1966 provides three-year programmes in various engineering and technology fields and is the largest public institution on the island.

The Forestry College is a rather small institution focusing on training foresters. The Forestry College trains foresters from all over the Middle East. The two Management Institutes also offer specialised programmes for Cypriot and Middle Eastern managers. Courses are offered in short-term managerial training, much like American post-graduate management programmes similar to the MBA. It should also be noted that the Nursing School and the Hotel and Catering Institute conduct their classes in both Greek and English. The Forestry College, the Higher Technical Institute, and the two Management Institutes offer most of their courses only in English.

The University of Cyprus' official languages of instruction are Greek and Turkish as primary languages, and English as the secondary language. But due to the political situation on the island, Turkish is only used in the Turkish Studies Programme. Since 1992 Greek has become the de facto language of the University of Cyprus. However, all programmes require some English instruction as well.

The University of Cyprus' enrolments shows a high number of female students in education (primary and early childhood), which is a carry-over from the Pedagogical Academy with business, computer studies, and economics following. Sciences and mathematics are a close third, with the humanities and social sciences fourth. English language studies attract most students classified as humanities students (Republic of Cyprus, 1993, 1994, 1995).

The relatively large private sector of higher education developed in Cyprus since the mid-1970's. Most institutions were set up by individual academic entrepreneurs. Many institutions were originally English language institutes or examination preparation centres (for GCE's, TOEFL, and so on). Responding to increasing social demand for higher education in the late 1970's and 1980's, these institutions began offering 'post-secondary' level programmes. These 'post-secondary' programmes were initially connected to various British professional licensing bodies (such as the Institute of Marketing, UK, Institute of Bankers, UK, Association of Certified Accountants, UK). Later some institutions began offering programmes preparing students for course and degree examinations given by the State of New York Regents Universities (USA), Thomas Edison State College (USA), University of London External Studies (UK), and so on.

Other institutions functioned as Cyprus campuses for American institutions, such as Intercollege's connection with the University of Indianapolis, or Frederick Polytechnic's connection with Empire State College of New York. In

STATE, SOCIETY, AND HIGHER EDUCATION IN CYPRUS

addition, institutions like Cyprus College were able to begin as autonomous institutions, giving their own degrees, and seeking accreditation and legitimacy from American and other institutions and accrediting agencies (see Koyzis, 1989).

As of early 1996, private institutions of higher education were in a semi-permanent limbo, awaiting a re-institution of a once failed accreditation process. The originally instituted Council of Accreditation has been disbanded. New legislation is underway. The issue of legitimacy for the private sector is at stake here with the government and institutions seeing the accreditation issue as a potentially conflicting endeavour with enormous political implications.

3   'Knowledge Traditions' and Notions of the 'Educated Cypriot'

Cypriot Greeks have been relying on overseas study for attaining post-secondary qualifications since the advent of universities in medieval times. Numerous Cypriots would travel to Constantinople, Alexandria, Salamanca, Venice, Rome, and Paris for higher education during the years following the fall of Constantinople to the Ottomans in 1453. Cypriot Greeks would continue this tradition even more with the creation of modern Greece in 1830. With the founding of the University of Athens in 1837, many Cypriots travelled to Athens for an education in the 'national ideals'. This was especially true since Cyprus was under Ottoman control long after the creation of the modern Greek state. Even after Cyprus became a British colony in 1878, Cypriot Greeks continued looking toward Greece for education and culture (Persianis, 1978). Even though in the more recent past the percentage of Cypriots going to Greece stayed at a relatively steady rate (35%–40% of the students studying abroad), more Cypriots have been going elsewhere for post-secondary education (Republic of Cyprus, 1993).

Cypriots receiving their education in Greek universities have traditionally had the exclusive monopoly on positions in Greek secondary schools in Cyprus, in the Inspectorate, and in the Ministry of Education. A one-time favourite area of study was philology. The term 'philology' was a catch-all area combining classical Greek literature, philosophy, and history, a concept which the University of Athens developed from the German concept of *bildung*. Philology became an influencing factor of Cypriot knowledge tradition (McClelland, 1980).

The education of a philologist in the School of Philosophy at the University of Athens blended a concept of what is worthwhile knowledge with a uniquely Greek version of educational humanism. This Greek version of educational humanism combines Greek Orthodoxy, classical Hellenism, and an emphasis on literary humane studies. A goal of this Greek educational humanism is to create the 'Greek Christian person'. This Greek Christian person sees himself/herself as an adherent to this modern Hellenic authenticity. Modern Hellenic authenticity combines classical Greek ideals with Greek Orthodox Christianity. According to McLean (1990):

> The School of Philosophy of the University of Athens (where languages, literature, and history are taught as well as philosophy) has been the centre for the preservation of the humanist tradition. It has maintained links with the secondary school teachers' union, whose members have been trained largely in this university school. There is also a wider consumer for humanist education. The School of Philosophy at Athens retains the highest prestige. (p. 108)

Even though based on today's data, when less Cypriots attending universities in Greece specialise in philology, the influence of the philologist is felt in a number of ways (Republic of Cyprus, 1993). First and foremost, up to 85% of all secondary school teachers in the Greek secondary schools are graduates of Greek universities, with philologists making up over 60% of all secondary teachers. These teachers teach in a variety of areas. They do not teach exclusively in literature and classics, but also in the social sciences, foreign languages, and occasionally religious classes. Philologists also make up the majority of secondary principals. In addition, these philologists make up to 70% of the personnel in the Ministry of Education. Claire Angelidou, a philologist, was appointed Minister of Education with the election of the Clerides administration in 1993 (Republic of Cyprus, 1993).

This philologist-humanist knowledge tradition has effectively become a dominant factor in the state's conception of what is worthwhile knowledge. This is particularly crucial in the way that the Ministry of Education sees its role as a major player in formulating Cypriot higher education policy. Of importance is the Ministry's view of the role of the University of Cyprus. In particular, someone from a philologist-humanist knowledge tradition sees the role of the University of Cyprus as an institution committed to reproducing a Hellenic national character by emphasising classical humanistic learning. A philologist-humanist would include 'Hellenic ideals' in all aspects of the university's curriculum. In many ways this position tends to be anti-modern and authoritarian. The philologist-humanist perceives such 'modern' Western ideals as liberalism, academic freedom, and critical inquiry as antithetical to the role of the university. The philologist idea sees the university as an arm of the state, and wants the institution to reproduce the disciplined, cultured, and moral Christian-Greek (Maratheftis, 1992).

Another knowledge tradition which has influenced Cypriot intellectual life and invariably the development of higher education has been English essentialism. Even though English essentialism resembles Greek humanism, it does not share its ethnonationalist flavour. This knowledge tradition has been influential in Cyprus, through the influence which Britain had over Cypriot life during colonial times (1878–1960), and continuing to the present. This is especially true due to the fact that Cypriots continue to go to Britain (primarily England) for post-secondary studies. According to Holmes & McLean (1989),

> The continued domination of essentialist views in the secondary school curricula has been aided by the survival of a narrow and élitist system at higher education and by forms of technical/vocational education which remain specialised and separate from mainstream education. (p. 32)

The English essentialist tradition which Cypriots encounter tends to be highly specialised. It either fits the tradition of educating civil servants, lawyers, and accountants or in the more recent years the more vocationalised version found in the education of engineers and technologists at colleges of further education, polytechnics, or technological universities.

The English essentialist knowledge tradition comes to Cyprus, both in the form of a remnant of a colonial legacy, and also through Cyprus' continuous reliance on England as a major trading partner, a source of overseas study, a major source of tourism, a place for Cypriots to emigrate to, and a political guarantor of stability on a divided island. This knowledge tradition tends to create a non-articulate Anglophilia among more urbane middle-class Cypriots. These Cypriots prefer things that are 'English' and cosmopolitan to things that are 'Greek' and thus perceived as more parochial. Anglophilic Cypriots tend to argue that English liberalism, free markets, and English culture are more natural to middle class Cypriots than the sentimental 'backward' Greek-Christian Hellenic ideals (Attalides, 1979).

Another group of Cypriots influenced by the English essentialist knowledge tradition sees the role of English language as a potential unifying force for Greek and Turkish Cypriots. This group of Cypriots tend to be critical of educational philosophies which are ethno-nationalistic. These Cypriots argue that the role of the university would be to provide a specialised curriculum to students by focusing less on classical and nationalist issues. and more on 'modern studies'. Other than a curriculum emphasising specialised study, it would also incorporate moral education and individualism (McLean, 1990).

Keeping with the English essentialist tradition of separating academic from vocational education, another segment of higher education (i.e., technology institutes, colleges, etc.) would provide a specialised higher education in such fields as engineering, technology, business, and so on. Cypriots influenced by English essentialist knowledge traditions see higher education in Cyprus as a system of institutions which function independently from the state and tend to respond to professional associations, labour markets, and social demand as only one guiding force in the provision of higher education. It does not rely on them exclusively. Academic tradition, professional and guild associations are also important players in shaping higher education.

A third knowledge tradition which influenced the development of higher education in Cyprus is North American educational utilitarianism. This influence has been quite marked in recent Cypriot circles. It has been a product of the last two decades where increasing numbers of Cypriots have been studying in the USA (see Table 9.1). This knowledge tradition has also entered Cyprus through the American-style private colleges which emphasise American-modelled programmes and curricula (Koyzis, 1989). This American educational utilitarianism resembles less the American liberal arts tradition of utilitarianism found in US or Canadian undergraduate programmes, but resembles more the vocational/professional school version of North American educational utilitarianism (see Rothblatt & Wittrock, 1993).

This knowledge tradition sees higher education and higher learning directly linked to the needs of occupations and labour market requirements. It also accepts the fact that voluntary accrediting agencies such as the ones accrediting business, engineering, education, and other programmes are the major curricular guiding forces. This implies of course that these voluntary accrediting bodies respond to occupational and labour market needs. In most cases this version of educational utilitarianism sees as worthwhile knowledge the combining of general 'core' knowledge to more specific skill-based knowledge (see Rothblatt & Wittrock, 1993).

Cypriot educational utilitarians who are graduates of North American institutions based either in Cyprus or abroad, tend to see the role of higher education as one preparing persons for occupations. Voluntarism, free markets, and choice are stable concepts in their views of curriculum for higher education. Many Cypriot educational utilitarians tend to prefer education in general to be less tied to 'national' and 'ethno-national' interests, and more concerned with economic and social development.

Some Cypriot educational utilitarians tend to support private sector institutions of higher education which have been accredited by voluntary accreditation entities. Some of these accreditation entities have been from the USA.

They tend to mistrust fellow Cypriots as accrediting/evaluating entities. The University of Cyprus for educational utilitarians should be much like North American state or private institutions, which are autonomous, and voluntarily accredited institutions receiving public funding with few strings attached (Lanitis, 1990).

In addition to the three above mentioned knowledge traditions found in Cyprus, other traditions such as the polytechnic one, from the ex-Soviet bloc, a version of French encyclopaedism, and German naturalism, are found among some Cypriots. The influence of these traditions remains limited, since their particular voice has not surfaced in the recent debates over education in Cyprus.

The Higher Technical Institute, the Forestry College, and the two other Management Institutes are not under the jurisdiction of the Ministry of Education. The existence of these institutions has reinforced the prominence of the educational utilitarian knowledge tradition. The Higher Technical Institute and the two post-graduate Management Institutes are public institutions under the auspices of the Ministry of Labour, whereas the Forestry College is under the control of the Ministry of Agriculture and Natural Resources. All four of the above-mentioned institutions use English as their language of instruction. This leads to a set of inter-related questions: What role does the state play in the development of higher education? And how have knowledge traditions become a point of conflict over what is perceived as worthwhile knowledge and the definition of the 'educated Cypriot'? More broadly, what is the role of higher education in Cypriot society? These questions are addressed in the next section.

4   State, Markets, and Higher Education

Many of the recent debates over higher education in Cyprus—whether they have to do with the role of the state as an accrediting/evaluating entity, the role of Greek language and the university, the incidents involving Parliament's education committee members questioning the role of Turkish textbooks at the university, or the debate over the incident surrounding the exclusion of the Greek Orthodox Archbishop from the opening ceremonies of the university— all invariably have to do with the role of the state and higher education. More specifically it tends to reflect the conflict between Cypriots who see higher education as an arm of the state versus Cypriots who want higher education to respond to the presumed needs of labour market and occupational needs.

Without entering into the long debate over what is the Cypriot state (Attalides, 1979; Polyviou, 1980) one can assume that the liberal democratic nature of Cypriot politics has developed a state relying on elites and elite structures for survival (Attalides, 1979). According to Dale (1989),

> The state, then, is not a monolith, or the same as government, or merely the government's executive committee. It is a set of publicly financed institutions, neither separately nor collectively necessarily in harmony, confronted by certain basic problems deriving from its relationship with capitalism, with one branch, the government, having responsibility for ensuring the continuing prominence of those problems on its agenda. (p. 57)

In particular, the nature of the Cypriot elite tends to be two-fold. On the one hand there is the cultural elite, and on the other is the economic elite. The economic elite tend to be urban and associated with business and professions (Persianis, 1981). The cultural elite is primarily made up of Cypriot Greeks who have either been educated in Greece, or have adhered to the dominance of Greek culture (language and religion) as the driving force behind the Cypriot state. In its most symbolic sense this cultural elite supported, and was in turn upheld by the late Archbishop Makarios, who was both the President of the Republic as well as the head of the Greek Orthodox Church of Cyprus (Panteli, 1990).

Due to historical circumstances, this cultural elite dominated and dominates Cypriot Greek public education as well as the educational bureaucracy. But their influence has primarily remained up until 1992 at the elementary and secondary educational level (Persianis, 1981, 1994). It stemmed from the fact that since the late 1890s, Greek secondary education (Gymnasium) was in the hands of the Greek Orthodox Church. On the other hand, post-secondary education, with the exception of teacher education, was neither under the auspices and influence of the educational bureaucracy (Ministry of Education) nor under the influence of cultural elites. Furthermore, as mentioned earlier, post-secondary institutions under other than Ministry of Education auspices, were influenced by economic elites (Persianis, 1981). In addition, the large private sector of higher education was an exclusively market driven sector, and undoubtedly under the auspices of the economic elite.

Under these circumstances, the Cypriot higher education experience resembles the experience of the public-private conflict over higher education found in some Latin American nations (e.g., Brazil) with large private market driven higher educational sectors (Levy, 1986). Specifically, economic elites in the recent past have opted to argue that:

1. The University of Cyprus should be free from the influence of the educational bureaucracy and the cultural elites' insistence on Hellenocentric higher education;

STATE, SOCIETY, AND HIGHER EDUCATION IN CYPRUS

2. University and higher education in general should be market-driven, rather than culture-driven. In this regard they would favour English language instruction and a more utilitarian curriculum since it would presumably lead to economic development;

3. Private higher education is a necessary sector which needs to be allowed to be flexible in order to respond to labour market needs;

4. Private higher education needs to be legitimised through state recognition, (i.e., accreditation) but should not be regulated. Its regulation comes from market forces, as well as connection with British and North American post-secondary institutions;

5. Cypriot higher education has not and should never be perceived as a part of higher education in Greece since the Cypriot state and Cypriot society are separate and distinct from the Greek state and Greek society (Koyzis, 1989, 1993; Persianis, 1994).

On the other hand, cultural elites in the recent past have tended to argue that:

1. The University of Cyprus is a state institution and it should serve and respond to the needs of a Greek-Cypriot state;

2. Market-driven higher education would lead to an over-emphasis on narrow utilitarian ends, rather than the preservation of Hellenic identity and culture;

3. Private higher education is an anomaly since it solely depends on American and British imported curricula, and undermines the Hellenic character of Cypriot society;

4. Private higher education should be either tightly regulated by the Ministry of Education, or as in the case of Greece, simply not recognised;

5. Cypriot higher education, much like Greek-Cypriot society, should see itself as part of the broader Hellenic world. This is imperative in order to survive in Europe and against cultural enemies. This may entail regulation and control of curriculum, extra-curricular activities, and the overall post-secondary experiences (Koyzis, 1993; Persianis, 1994).

It appears that the conflict between the economic market proponents versus the state cultural proponents tends to also be overshadowed by their perceptions of what should be taught at institutions of higher learning. This then takes us back to the question already discussed earlier in this paper when discussing the issue of 'knowledge traditions'. It also appears that at the moment neither the economic market proponents nor the state cultural proponents have a thorough understanding of issues such as academic freedom, institutional autonomy, and other characteristics found in a more mature system of higher education. Furthermore, Cyprus' bid for European Union membership will force the higher educational sector to re-adjust to broader European realities. It may imply redefining the role of the state and higher education as well as the private sector's consumerist market orientation.

Cypriot higher education is still relatively young, and it will take several decades before both the state and society as a whole begin seeing it as separate from school education. or something beyond simply education for vocational preparation. In addition, due to the relative newness of higher education, Cyprus lacks an authentic intellectual culture which would be uniquely developed on Cypriot soil, which means that Cyprus will still rely on 'importation' rather than autonomous creations (Persianis & Polyviou, 1992). In addition, higher education in Cyprus would inevitably have to deal with the issue of the role to be played by Turkish-Cypriots in higher education. This has been overshadowed by the division and the narrower 'ethno-nationalist' feelings projected by the current administration. This is an imperative dilemma in the light of any future settlement of the 'Cyprus problem', regardless of how it turns out.

5   Conclusion

Cypriot higher education, even though it is in an embryonic state when compared to the higher education systems of Germany, Britain, or the US, is facing a series of dilemmas. As a society Cyprus has been ready for a full system of higher education, but due to political circumstances, it was not until 1992 that a public university opened its doors. This university found itself amid not only problems stemming from the aftermath of the 1974 Turkish invasion, but also amid conflicts within Cypriot society. These conflicts have been explored in this paper, by being categorised as either conflicts stemming from the different 'knowledge traditions' (or what is perceived as worthwhile knowledge in higher education) existing in Cyprus, or as conflicts between proponents of state versus market control in higher education.

Underlying both sets of conflicts are questions that relate to culture. Among such questions are: What is the nature of Cypriot society? Should this be perceived as an extension of Greek society? Or rather is it unique and pluralistic enough to be able to be considered as a separate entity? Private and public higher education appear to be in the middle of this debate.

With the absence of a full system of higher education, Cyprus has not yet developed traditions of intellectual and academic culture, or perhaps a cadre of academic mandarins, similar to the German mandarins that Ringer (1990) writes about, which could articulate the role of higher education in Cypriot society.

Acknowledgement

This chapter originally appeared as: Koyzis, A. A. (1997) State, society, and higher education in Cyprus: a study in conflict and compromise, *Mediterranean Journal of Educational Studies*, Vol. 2(2), pp. 103–117. Reprinted here with permission from the publisher.

References

Attalides, M. (1979) *Cyprus: Nationalism and International Politics*. New York: St. Martin's Press.

Dale, R. (1989) *The State and Education Policy*. Milton Keynes: Open University Press.

Holmes, B., & McLean, M. (1989) *The Curriculum: A Comparative Perspective*. London: Unwin Hyman.

Koyzis, A. (1989) Private higher education in Cyprus: in search of legitimacy, *Higher Education Policy*, Vol. 2(2), pp. 13–19.

Koyzis, A. (1993) The University of Cyprus: questions and future implications, *International Review of Education*, Vol. 39(5), pp. 435–438.

Lanitis, G. (1990) Universities in Cyprus? *The Cyprus Weekly*, 15 February.

Levy, D. (1986) *Higher Education and the State in Latin America*. Chicago: University of Chicago Press.

Maratheftis, M. (1992) *The Cypriot Educational System*. Nicosia: Pedagogical Institute of Cyprus.

McClelland, C. (1980) *State, Society, and University in Germany 1700–1914*. New York: Cambridge University Press.

McLean, M. (1990) *Britain and a Single Market Europe: Prospects for a Common Curriculum*. London: Kogan Page.

Panteli, S. (1990) *The Making of Modern Cyprus: From Obscurity to Statehood*. Nicosia: Interworld Publications.

Persianis. P. (1978) *Church and State in Cyprus Education*. Nicosia: Violaris Publishers.

Persianis, P. (1981) *The Political and Economic Factors as the Main Determinants of Educational Policy in Independent Cyprus (1960–1970)*. Nicosia: Pedagogical Institute of Cyprus.

Persianis, P. (1994) *Facets in Cypriot Education at the End of 19th and Early 20th Centuries*. Nicosia: Pedagogical Institute of Cyprus.

Persianis, P., & Polyviou, G. (1992) *History of Education in Cyprus*. Nicosia: Pedagogical Institute of Cyprus.

Polyviou, P. (1980) *Cyprus, Conflict and Negotiation 1960–1980*. London: Duckworth.

Republic of Cyprus (1986) *Statistics of Education 1985–1986*. Nicosia: Government Printing Office.

Republic of Cyprus (1993) *Statistics of Education 1992–1993*. Nicosia: Government Printing Office.

Republic of Cyprus (1994) *Statistics of Education 1993–1994*. Nicosia: Government Printing Office.

Republic of Cyprus (1995) *Statistics of Education 1994–1995*. Nicosia: Government Printing Office.

Ringer, F. (1990) *The Decline of the German Mandarins.* Hanover: Wesleyan University Press.

Rothblatt, S., & Wittrock, B. (1993) *The European and American University since 1800.* New York: Cambridge University Press.

CHAPTER 10

Global Discourses and Educational Reform in Egypt

The Case of Active-Learning Pedagogies

Mark B. Ginsburg and Nagwa M. Megahed

1   Introduction

In recent years comparative educators and other social scientists have engaged in extensive debates about 'globalisation' (Burbules & Torres, 2000; Stromquist & Monkman, 2000; Carnoy & Rhoten, 2002). And while world-system or global-level dynamics are by no means new phenomena, these debates have helped to call attention to the ways in which *economic, political,* and *cultural* features of a given society—including *educational reform*—can be understood as being shaped by global as well as national and local processes (Ginsburg, 1991; Daun, 2002).

Some have argued that globalisation represents an *imposition* on nation states and their citizens by dominant countries and elites who control the workings of international financial, trade and other organisations, thus reducing citizens' capacity to determine educational and other social policies and practices (Arnove, 1980; Berman, 1992; Brown & Lauder, 1996; Ismael, 1999; Tabb, 2001). Others have characterised the processes that have led to convergence of educational policies and practices in terms of local and national actors voluntarily *borrowing* or *adapting* 'good', though foreign, ideas to which they have been exposed, including other countries' offers to *lend* such policies and practices (Meyer & Hannan, 1979; Inkeles & Sirowy, 1984; Steiner-Khamsi, 2004). There are at least three limitations to the way the issues are framed above. First, the global discourses (statements and practices), which could be imposed or borrowed, contain important contradictions, as is the case with other ideologies and practices. This not only means that the global discourses can be 'read' differently at different times, in different places, by different people, but also that these ideas and practices may lead to different outcomes.

Second, these portraits either diminish the role of nation-states or treat states as relatively autonomous, rational-choice actors. While viewing the state as autonomous is fraught with theoretical and political problems (see Dale, 1989; Willinsky, 2002), we should note that even semi-peripheral and peripheral nation-states within the world system (Hopkins & Wallerstein, 1979) have

---

© THE EURO-MEDITERRANEAN CENTRE FOR EDUCATION RESEARCH, UNIVERSITY OF MALTA, 2008
DOI: 10.1163/9789004506602_010

This is an open access chapter distributed under the terms of the CC BY-NC 4.0 License.

some influence on global dynamics and have some capacity to filter, if not deflect, the penetration of global discourses (e.g., see Berman, 1992, p. 59).

Third, these portraits relegate to the shadows the full range of national and international actors. For example, Robertson, Bonal & Dale (2002, p. 472) argue that 'globalization is the outcome of processes that involve real [global organization] actors ... with real interests' and Suarez (2007, p. 7) indicates how intergovernmental organisations (IGOs) and international nongovernmental organisations (INGOs) serve as 'receptor sites for transnational ideas ... promot[ing] and diffuse[ing] new ideas in education' (see also Terano & Ginsburg, 2008). Thus, we should note that various intergovernmental organisations, whether bilateral or multilateral, may have different interests and assumptions, and thus the global reform agendas that these organisations seek to promote may not always be the same or, if similar, may not be pursued in ways that reinforce each other.

In this paper we offer an analysis—based on a review of published scholarship as well as documents published by multilateral organisations (i.e., UNDP, UNESCO, UNICEF, World Bank), bilateral agencies (US Agency for International Development), and international NGOs (e.g., Academy for Educational Development, Aguirre International, American Institutes for Research, CARE)—of the global discourses on the reform of teaching, with particular attention to ideas/practices of active-learning pedagogies. In addition, in order to better understand how such discourses inform and are informed by a range of national-level actors, we focus our lens also on discourses of the government of Egypt, which is one of the nine most populous countries in the world, has one of the largest education systems (UNESCO, 2006), and plays a central strategic role 'in determining the stability of the Middle East and southern Mediterranean area' (Sayed, 2005, p. 67).

2   Discourses of the Community of Scholars

'Active-learning' (or 'student-centred') pedagogies represent a model of teaching that highlights 'minimal teacher lecturing or direct transmission of factual knowledge, multiple small group activities that engage students in discovery learning or problem solving, and frequent student questions and discussion' (Leu & Price-Rom, 2006, p. 19; on student-centred instruction, see Cuban, 1984, pp. 3–4). 'Active-learning' pedagogies can be contrasted with 'formal' or 'direct instruction' approaches emphasising teacher lecturing or direct transmission of factual knowledge, coupled with 'recitation and drill' (Spring, 2006, p. 6).[1] Thus, there are both behavioural and cognitive dimensions on which

GLOBAL DISCOURSES AND EDUCATIONAL REFORM IN EGYPT 173

active-learning, student-centred pedagogies can be contrasted with formal or direct instruction (see Mayer, 2004; Ginsburg, 2006; Barrow et al., 2007). The behavioural dimension of active-learning pedagogies focuses on the degree to which instructional practices enable students to engage in verbal or physical behaviour, while the cognitive dimension highlights the degree to which teaching strategies enable students to engage in various forms/levels of thinking. Thus, we can identify different theoretical and philosophical notions that have contributed to how the differences between these pedagogies are framed.

The *behavioural dimension* is perhaps most frequently traced to American philosopher/educator, John Dewey (1859–1952), who developed a pragmatist philosophy, popularised 'progressive' or 'experiential' education, and promoted learning by experimentation and practice, learning by doing (e.g., Dewey, 1938). However, one can also trace a concern for (especially verbal) behaviour in learning to: (i) Confucius (551–479 BC), who argued for 'individualized instruction through discussion'; (ii) Socrates (470–399 BC), who emphasised involving individual learners 'in a philosophic dialogues'; (iii) Johann Heinrich Pestalozzi (1746–1827), who encouraged 'firsthand experience in learning environments'; and (iv) Friedrich Froebel (1782–1852), who argued for learning via 'free self-activity ... [which] allows for active creativity and social participation' (Treat et al., 2008). Furthermore, we should note the more recent theoretical contribution of scholars and educators associated with the Humanist Movement, for example, Carl Rogers (1969, p. 162), who argued that 'much significant learning is acquired by doing' and that 'learning is facilitated when the student is a responsible participant'.

The *cognitive dimension* is generally traced to the work of the French psychologist, Jean Piaget (1896–1980), who 'suggested that, through processes of accommodation and assimilation, individuals construct new knowledge from their experiences' (Wikipedia, 2008, para. 1). Another source of influence is the work of Lev Vygotsky (1896–1934), whose writings focused on 'the relationship between language and thinking' as well as 'the roles of historical, cultural, and social factors in cognition' (Wikipedia, 2008, para. 3). Moreover, although qur'anic schools have tended to emphasise rote learning and memorisation (Boyle, 2006; Spring 2006), alternative pedagogical traditions associated with Islamic scholars stress students' active cognitive role in learning. For example, Al-Jahiz (776–868) promoted using 'deductive reasoning' as well as 'memorization' and Abu Nasr al-Farabi (870–950) encouraged 'instruction ... that ... ensures that both teacher and student participate actively in the process ..., allow[ing] the instruction to be student-centered' (Günther, 2006, pp. 375–376). Finally, a more contemporary cognitive psychologist of education, Merl Wittrock (1979), explains that 'learners have active roles in ... learning. They are not passive consumers of information ... Even when learners are given the information they are to learn, they still must discover meaning' (p. 10).

3 Discourses of International Organisations

Beeby's (1966) book, *The Quality of Education in Developing Countries*, was 'widely influential' internationally 'in the late 1960s and early 1970s' in efforts 'to improve the quality of teaching by changing teaching styles ... toward liberal, student-centered methods' (Guthrie, 1990, pp. 220–221). And in a chapter in *The Quality of Education and Economic Development: A World Bank Symposium* (Heyneman & White, 1986) Beeby restated his earlier argument that as education systems (particularly primary schools) progress toward higher stages of development 'teaching becomes less rigid, narrow, and stereotyped and less dependent on mass methods of instruction and rote memorization' (Beeby, 1986, p. 39). In the introduction to this volume, based on a symposium organised by the World Bank in May 1983, Heyneman (1986) explains:

> Previously most educational loans from the World Bank were directed at expanding educational systems by building more schools, hiring more teachers, and providing access for more students. ... [Now the focus is on quality. And,] although classroom pedagogical style may be locally determined, the ingredients required to make classrooms function properly are not. (p. 3)

The late 1980s, the 1990s and the 2000s witnessed an explosion of international research reports and policy documents focusing on reforming teachers' behaviour toward active-learning pedagogies. Perhaps one of the most internationally visible policy statements was the document ratified by the World Conference on Education for All (EFA): Meeting Basic Learning Needs, jointly organised by UNDP, UNESCO, UNICEF and the World Bank, in Jomtien, Thailand, 5–9 March 1990. The *World Declaration on Education for All* states that 'active and participatory [instructional] approaches are particularly valuable in assuring learning acquisition and allowing learners to reach their fullest potential' (Inter-Agency Commission, 1990, Article 4).

In the following year, the World Bank published a research-based policy report (Lockheed & Levin, 1991), in which the editors conclude

> by summarizing the areas of accord [across cases in book] as a basis for considering generic approaches to developing schools that will become

GLOBAL DISCOURSES AND EDUCATIONAL REFORM IN EGYPT   175

more effective ... The emphasis on student learning is to shift from a
more traditional passive approach in which all knowledge is imparted
from teachers and textbooks to an active approach in which the student
is responsible for learning. (pp. 15–16)

UNICEF helped to channel this global pedagogical discourse into Egypt,
when in cooperation with the Egyptian Ministry of Education (MOE) and the
Canadian International Development Agency it launched the Community
School project in 1992. As a key UNICEF staff member (Zaalouk, 2004) later
recounted, the 'community-school education model in Egypt was established
during the period following the [1990] *Jomtien Education for All* (EFA) world
conference' (p. 31):

> The contract signed [with the MOE] stipulated that ... community schools
> would provide innovative pedagogies for quality education [especially for
> girls] that would focus on active learning, acquisition of life skills, values-
> based learning (with an emphasis on practicing rights), and brain-based
> learning that would awaken all the child's intelligences, including his or
> her spiritual and emotional ones. (Zaalouk, 2004, p. XI)[2]

Moreover, UNESCO and UNDP helped to diffuse the discourse on pedagogical reform by funding an assessment of educational reform efforts in Egypt
between 1991 and 1996. The authors of that report, which was widely and
prominently circulated in Egypt, state that:

> By all standards, the initial phase of the basic education reform in Egypt
> (1991–1996) has been successful. ... [However,] a number of capacity-
> building initiatives are needed to strengthen the reform in the follow-
> ing areas: (1) teacher education, both in-service and pre-service, so as
> to broaden the teachers' capacities to deliver the new curriculum and
> [interactive instructional] methods. (Spaulding et al., 1996, cited in MOE,
> 2002, pp. 169–171)

The World Bank also helped this pedagogical discourse to travel to Egypt,
when in cooperation with the Egyptian Ministry of Education and the European Union it initiated the Education Enhancement Programme in 1996.
According to the *Project Information Document* (World Bank, 1996), this project sought to 'significantly increase students' achievement of basic skills and
help improve their critical thinking skills' (p. 2). This would be accomplished
by 'improving the quality of teaching and learning' (p. 2) and introducing

educators to 'new methods of teaching' (p. 8). While this brief document is somewhat ambiguous about how teaching quality and new teaching methods were conceived, the programme evaluation conducted a decade later clarifies a preference for active-learning, student-centred versus formal transmission, and teacher-centred instruction approaches. Variables studied included:

- *Educational Techniques* to meet the needs of low achievers ..., for example, giving them a large number of questions ...
- *Frontal Teaching* represents the time the teacher, on average, spends on frontal teaching.
- *Group work* represents the time the teacher, on average, spends on group work ...
- *Teacher classroom management* refers to ... giving pupils the opportunity to express their opinions, distributing roles and responsibilities among pupils, encouraging pupils to depend on themselves ...
- *Learning strategies* ... refers to the extent to which teachers divide pupils into 'cooperative working' subgroups, take into consideration to develop pupils' critical thinking, train pupils in problem solving ... (Programme and Project Monitoring Unit [PPMU], 2006, pp. 48–49).

The US Agency for International Development also began to promote pedagogical reform toward active-learning methods in the mid-1990s. For instance, the 'amplified description' of a proposed (but not implemented) Strategic Objective Agreement between the Arab Republic of Egypt and the United States of America for Girls' Education states: 'The Parties to this agreement will advance this process [by training] ... teachers to apply the interactive teaching methodologies and encourage problem solving by learners. ... Technical assistance will support the development of ... [teachers] using student-centered methodologies and emphasizing problem-solving and analytic skills' (USAID/Egypt, 1996, p. 10).

Ten years after the World Conference on Education for All, UNDP, UNESCO, UNICEF and the World Bank co-sponsored a meeting in Dakar, Senegal, attended by representatives from most governments from around the world, including Egypt. The 'Dakar Framework' from this 2000 meeting reiterates an international policy commitment to active-learning pedagogies: 'Governments and all other EFA partners must work together to ensure basic education of quality for all, regardless of gender, wealth, location, language or ethnic origin. Successful education programmes require [among other things:] ... well-trained teachers and active-learning techniques' (UNESCO, 2000, p. 17).

In the same year USAID/Egypt initiated the New Schools Programme (NSP), which in many respects mirrored the ideas contained in the (non-implemented)

Strategic Objective for Basic Education grant. Based on USAID/Egypt's request for proposals, CARE, the Education Development Centre, World Education and several local NGOs submitted the following as part of their NSP proposal, in reference to one of the expected intermediate results—'Improved Teaching and Learning Practices in USAID-Supported Schools: The CARE Team will develop an effective training program for teachers and school officials ... in single-grade NSP schools, ... emphasiz[ing] active, child-centered learning methodologies that help students develop strong problem-solving skills' (CARE et al., 1999, p. 16). Such reform pedagogies were also mentioned in the mid-term evaluation of NSP (Aguirre International, 2003): 'To meet its goal of improving educational quality', the New Schools Programme provided 'teachers with support for trying new ideas, ... [including:] cooperative learning, some forms of active learning' (p. x) and for 'changing ... their teaching practice from traditional, rote learning to one in which children are working together, participating actively in their own learning' (p. 18).

And in March 2001, USAID/Egypt (2001) committed to supporting the Alexandria Education Reform Pilot Project designed to 'improve the quality of education in the Governorate of Alexandria ... through [among other things] ... enhanced training of teachers and school administrators' (p. 1). The Concept Paper for this project observed that 'most teachers ... over-emphasize the skill of memorization. ... [and need to be] trained for using alternative methods encouraging student interaction' (pp. 4–5). In the Status Report on the Alexandria Pilot, which was distributed half way through the second school year of the project, USAID/Egypt (2002, p. 8) calls positive attention to the training courses provided for teachers, including: Effective Teaching Methods, Student-Centred Methods, Advanced Student-Centred Training—(conducted in the) US, and Supervising Student-Centred Classes.

Also in 2002, in preparation for requesting proposals for the Education Reform Programme (see Academy for Educational Development et al., 2004; American Institutes for Research et al., 2004), USAID/Egypt commissioned a study. The study report sketched a number of cross-cutting themes, including: 'Classroom Learning Environment. ... Egyptian public schools ... emphasize memorization and rote learning of the exam-driven curriculum. ... There is little ... [use of] new methodologies that encourage and enable students to become active, enthusiastic participants in their own learning' (Aguirre International, 2002, pp. 11–12).

USAID/Egypt's growing and increasingly explicit enthusiasm for active-learning pedagogies is evident in its September 2003 Programme Descriptions used to request applications for ERP: 'Quality improvements are required to ensure that universal enrollment is accompanied by the acquisition of critical-thinking skills. ... Extensive training is required for tens of thousands of Egyptian educators to adopt modern methodologies and promote active learning' (USAID/Egypt, 2003a, p. 4; USAID/Egypt, 2003b, p. 7). Furthermore, USAID/Egypt (2003a, pp. 19–20) specified two of the sub-intermediate results expected to be achieved by the Classrooms and Schools component ERP: (2.4) 'teachers receive pre-service education and in-service training in learner-focused teaching and assessment methods' and (3.1) 'students engage in participatory learning, critical thinking and problem-solving'.

Then, in 2005, USAID (2005) published its global *Education Strategy*, which argued that '[i]mproving instruction is a complex task that entails a wide range of interventions. ... supporting improved teacher training ... [toward] adoption of *teaching* methods that involve students in the learning process' (p. 9). That same year, USAID/Egypt agreed to extend the New Schools Programme through 2008. In its application for the extension, reflecting its perception of USAID/Egypt's priorities, CARE (2005) highlighted that: (a) 'over 1,500 teachers and facilitators are using active, student-centered learning methodologies as a result of their training with NSP' (p. 5) and (b) 'active learning methods ... create a dynamic, interactive environment in which girls and boys have a voice and an opportunity for hands-on educational activities' (p. 9).

Also, in 2005, USAID/Egypt commissioned an evaluation of the Alexandria Pilot Project, which focused in part on the goal of improving teaching and learning. The evaluation report mentions:

> [T]he introduction of new teaching-learning methods to the schools most directly addresses educational quality. The central premise is that students optimize their acquisition, mastery, and retention of new skills when they are actively involved in their acquisition. ... Most pilot-school teachers understand at least the fundamental nature of active-learner pedagogy. ... Although classroom observation was not possible, evidence suggests that pilot-school teachers have introduced interactive methods into their classrooms to a modest extent. (Tietjen et al., 2005, p. VII)

More recently, in 2007, in its Request for Proposals for a new initiative, entitled Girls Improved Learning Outcomes, USAID/Egypt (2007) observed that 'ineffective instructional methods and other dimensions of school quality also limit the capacity of the school system to prepare students, particularly girls, with basic skills needed for a modernizing society' (p. 6), and then outlined the purpose of one of the components of the project, 'improving the quality of teaching and learning: ... to support the implementation of a standards-based model for quality education in targeted schools and communities ... [through]

GLOBAL DISCOURSES AND EDUCATIONAL REFORM IN EGYPT 179

a focus on ... active and meaningful student learning and assessment [as well as] ... girl friendly educational materials and pedagogical practices' (p. 8).

Given the volume—in the sense of amount and loudness—of the multi-lateral organisation discourse promoting active-learning pedagogies during the previous two decades, we should not be surprised that UNESCO's (2008) *EFA Global Monitoring Report* concludes that 'country case studies ... indicate a trend to revise curricula to make classroom interactions more responsive and centred on the child. There is a move away from traditional 'chalk and talk' teaching to more discovery-based learning and a greater emphasis on outcomes that are broader than basic recall of facts and information' (p. 131).[3]

4 Egyptian Government Discourses

When Mohamed Ali assumed political leadership of 'modern' Egypt in 1805, he established a secular education system alongside the Islamic al-Azhar system, though both systems seem to have been dominated by teacher-centred, knowledge-transmission pedagogies. During Egypt's period of 'semi-independence' (1922–1952), following British colonisation (1882–1922), 'great [quantitative] advances took place in public education at all levels' (Cochran, 1986, p. 1; see also Williamson, 1987, p. 107), but there was less progress in achieving quality. For example, Radwan's (1951; cited in Erlich, 1989) research concluded that 'teaching in the schools ... consisted mainly of inculcating abstract or factual information, learned by rote in the traditional way' (p. 97).

Following the 1952 Revolution, the Egyptian government headed by Gamal Abdel Nasser (1954–1970) continued to focus on quantitative growth in schooling, 'expanding access to education at all levels' (Williamson, 1987, pp. 118–119), as did Anwar Al-Sadat's government (1970–1981). However, in September 1979, the Ministry of Education during the Sadat period published *A Working Paper Concerning the Development and Modernization of Education in Egypt*, which focused some attention on quality issues: 'This paper ... argued that ... [there is] an urgent need to change and update Egyptian education ... [because]: a) curricula do not prepare students for practical, productive lives; b) rote memorization dominates the learning-teaching situation; ... [and] e) low teacher qualifications' (MOE, 1979; discussed in USAID/Egypt, 1981, p. 5).

And when Mohammed Hosni Mubarak (1981–2001) became president, his government initially emphasised quantitative expansion, including extending compulsory education from 6 to 9 years. However, in 1991, at the end of his first decade in office, in the wake of the World Conference on Education for All, and in the context of Egypt negotiating a structural adjustment programme with the World Bank, Mubarak (in a speech before the joint session of the People's Assembly and the Shura Council; see MOE, 1992) called attention to what he termed 'the crisis in education ... Education continues to suffer from a predominant focus on quantity rather than quality' (p. 5). The volume in which his speech was published, *Mubarak and Education* (MOE, 1992), articulated the Egyptian government's conception of improving educational quality:

> Education should, therefore, change from an outdated mode of teaching dependent on memorization and repetition to a new form of instruction, which would include the student as an active participant in the educational experience and an active partner in the learning process. ... Emphasis on rote learning and memorization has produced individuals who are easily programmed and vulnerable ... contributing to the prevalence of many social problems, such as drug dependency, extremism, and fanaticism. (p. 43)

Similarly, in its *Implementing Egypt's Educational Reform Strategy*, the Egyptian Ministry of Education (1996) elaborates its conception of educational quality, when discussing education being a 'national security' issue: 'The democratic framework also necessitated that students through all stages of the educational ladder be exposed to different types of learning tools and materials, and taught necessary democratic skills, such as debate, tolerance for other opinions, critical analysis and thinking, and the significance of participating in decision making' (p. 22). And in his book, *Education and the Future*, Hussein Kamel Bahaa El Din (1997), who served as Egypt's Minister of Education from 1991 to 2004, echoes points made earlier by Mubarak when discussing the continuing 'crisis in education': 'It is imperative for us to change from a familiar system that emphasized rote memorization and passive learning to a new system that emphasizes active participation, with the learner a significant partner in the process' (p. 107).

While (as discussed above) multilateral and bilateral organisation discourses can be seen to have been channelled to Egypt through technical assistance projects and evaluation studies, we should also note how Egyptian discourses have been a part of, and likely informed, such international organisation discourses. For instance, Egyptian President Mubarak spoke at the 2000 Dakar EFA conference, stressing: 'As the ninth decade of the last century witnessed determination that education is for all, the first decade of the twenty-first century must witness, with more determination and insistence, strenuous efforts to achieve a new vision, i.e., *Education for Excellence and Excellence for All*' (see MOE, 2002, p. 67). The phrase 'education for excellence and excellence for all' was repeated in the MOE publication, *Mubarak and Education: Qualitative*

Development in the National Project of Education (MOE, 2002), calling this 'a major national target that directs its march according to the criteria of total quality in education' (p. 6). This MOE (2002) publication also identifies the following as two key elements of the 'future vision of education in Egypt': (a) 'Achieving a Learning Community ... Moving forward from a culture of memorization and repetition to [one] of originality and creativity. ... marked by the individual's active role in the teaching/learning process' (p. 140) and (b) 'Revolution in the Concepts and Methods of Education ... The student's role is not that of a *passive receiver*, but of a knowledge-producing researcher' (p. 148).

In 2003, the Ministry of Education published a key document, the *National Standards of Education in Egypt*, following an intensive effort involving many educators. According to the introduction to this document: 'Having succeeded in achieving ... [the objective of 'education for all'], the state is now inspired by the President's vision which is represented in his [1991] call for a qualitative change in education' (MOE, 2003, p. 4). The standards and indicators for the 'educator' domain, entitled 'learning strategies and classroom management', provide evidence of how central active-learning, student-centred pedagogies had become within at least the official Egyptian discourses:

– First Standard: Utilizing educational strategies that meet student needs. [Indicators:] Teacher involves all students in diverse educational experiences suitable to their skills and talents. Uses different strategies to present concepts, introduce skills and explain the subject. Gives students open-ended questions and facilitates discussion to clarify and motivate the student's thinking.
– Second Standard: Facilitating effective learning experiences. [Indicators:] Teacher provides independent and cooperative learning opportunities. Divides students into groups to promote interaction and learning. Encourages positive interaction and cooperation among students.
– Third Standard: Involving students in problem-solving, critical thinking and creativity [Indicators:] Encourages students to apply what they have learnt in educational and life situations. Encourages students to be inquisitive, have initiative and show creativity. ... Involves students in problem-solving activities and encourages various ways to reach solutions. Encourages students to put forth critical questions. ...
– Fifth Standard: Effective utilization of motivation methods. [Indicators:] Creates a favorable educational and learning climate to encourage classroom interaction ... (MOE, 2003, pp. 75–76).

During his relatively brief period as Minister of Education, Ahmed Gamal Eddin Moussa (July 2004–December 2005) downplayed somewhat the role of standards, though the Ministry and the Egyptian government more generally maintained a clear focus on improving educational quality and active-learning. For instance, in its September 2004 publication, *Reforming Pre-University Education Programs*, the Ministry outlines the latest plans for reform, which included as two of its five main pillars for reform: 'assuring education quality' and 'training and improving teachers' conditions' (MOE, 2004; cited in El Baradei & El Baradei, 2004, p. 5). Moreover, the Minister of Education articulated the following during a newspaper interview: '[More important than] having thick books [and] a huge number of courses ... is that students interact with what they are learning in order to simply gain knowledge and acquire useful skills. ... Quality is more important than quantity, and if we have a lot of schools without qualified teachers or proper equipment, then we haven't solved anything' (Moussa, 2005).

Soon after Yosri Saber Husien El-Gamal was appointed Minister of Education in December 2005, he stated in an interview: 'The third pillar is professional development—focusing on raising teachers capabilities ... [including using] modern educational methods ... The second challenge is about the quality of education ... based on national standards. ... [and focused on] ... develop[ing] students' mental skills and creativity' (El-Gamal, 2006). The Minister also mentioned similar points, while highlighting teachers' use of student-centred and active-learning teaching methodologies as well as students' engagement in critical thinking and problem solving, during a presentation made in March related to the Ministry's strategic planning initiative:

- The Educational Vision is built upon sector-wide, total quality approach, based on six main domains: 1) Effective School, providing quality education for every learner, in an untraditional student-centered environment, using technology and active-learning methodologies to enable the student acquiring self learning, problem-solving, critical thinking and life skills. ... 3) Curricula that are relevant, based on active learning, [and] support critical thinking [and] problem solving ... (MOE, 2006, slides 6–7).
- Strategic Directions: 2. Quality: ... a) opportunities for on-going training and professional development ... [and] d) curriculum and teaching will be diverted from rote-learning mode to active learning, building the knowledge base of the learner and enhancement of higher skills (MOE, 2006, slides 15–16).

MOE's *Strategic Plan* (2007, part IV, chapter 2) continued to stress the importance of active-learning pedagogies: (a) 'there are 4 key factors that contribute to educational quality in what and how students are taught: standards-based content, integration of IT, integration of assessment, and adopting an active learning methodology' (p. 1); (b) 'the ... curriculum documents/frameworks

GLOBAL DISCOURSES AND EDUCATIONAL REFORM IN EGYPT 183

[should] ... reflect the move away from a traditional rote memorization approach with a strong focus on content to one that is focused on application of skills and critical thinking and problem solving' (p. 4); and (c) 'to insure effective implementation of the new curricula and instructional materials, teacher professional development programs in the area of student-centered, active-learning methodology and assessment are essential elements' (p. 7).

Finally, in 2007 Egypt's National Centre for Educational Research and Development (NCERD, 2007) published a *Mid-Term EFA Evaluation*, reporting on progress in achieving the goals set out in Egypt's *National Plan for Education for All, 2002/2003–2015/2016* (NCERD et al., 2004). The report summarises the qualitative shift in which the Egyptian government in engaged, including a focus on active learning: 'The MOE works on achieving a qualitative shift in education, and improving the quality of the educational process through the following efforts: ... (2) moving from achieving quantity to quality aspects in education; (3) ensuring excellence for all and achieving total quality education through students' active involvement in the educational process ...; [and] (4) promoting teachers' professional development and improving teaching methods' (NCERD, 2007, p. xi)

5 Conclusion

In this paper we sought to illuminate how the global and national/local interact with respect to educational reform. Our focus was on the discourses of multilateral organisations (UNDP, UNESCO, UNICEF and World Bank), bilateral agencies (viz., USAID), international NGOs (e.g., Academy for Educational Development, Aguirre International, American Institutes for Research, CARE), and the Egyptian government with respect to promoting active-learning, student-centred pedagogies as a key element of improving educational quality.

While our focus here is on reform rhetoric, readers may also be interested in whether such rhetoric corresponds to classroom practices. That is, to what extent have active-learning teaching methods been fostered through professional development activities and to what extent have Egyptian teachers implemented this pedagogical reform? There is, indeed, evidence that within the context of pilot projects teachers acquired the commitment and competence to at least move along the continuum from teacher-centred and transmission/memorisation-oriented to student-centred and active-learning pedagogical approaches. This is the case, for example, for the Community School Programme in Egypt (1992–2004) supported by UNICEF and the Canadian Development Agency (see Zaalouk, 2004), as well as for three USAID-supported projects in Egypt: (a) the New School Programme (2000–2007) (see Aguirre International, 2003); (b) the Alexandria Pilot Project (2002–2004) (see Tietjen et al., 2005); and (c) the Education Reform Programme (2004–2009) (see Ginsburg et al., 2008; Megahed et al., 2009). However, reformed teacher behaviour appears not to have been generalised either by 2002 or by 2007[4]:

> Egyptian public schools ... emphasize memorization and rote learning ... [and] there is little ... [use of] new methodologies that encourage and enable students to become active, enthusiastic participants in their own learning. (Aguirre International, 2002, pp. 11–12).

> [D]espite ... effective implementation of components targeting changes on factors of the teaching-learning process in Egyptian schools, there is not much evidence of ... impact on pedagogical practices. (World Bank, 2007, p. 47)

With respect to the relative strength of influence of local/national versus global actors, Sayed (2006) argues, for example, that

> the reform initiatives had already been conceived internally within Egyptian government schemes ... before the launch of the Jomtien Education for All Campaign in 1990. The MOE assimilation of the EFA goals allowed it to jump on a moving wagon ... [and] secure funding for education projects. (p. 148)

We believe that this represents only part of the picture. The report of discourses presented above reflects neither a simple dynamic of national/local actors making unfettered choices in a free market of ideas nor a simple process of international actors imposing ideas on unwilling national/local actors. The complex dialectic between the global and local (see Arnove & Torres, 1999) may be seen from the following statements by the Egyptian government. First, reflecting a more voluntary choice perspective, the MOE (2002) identifies what it terms *its* own objectives in the field of international cooperation and partnership:

1. To benefit from world experiences and international co-operation that Egypt has approached through openness to different cultures.
2. To set up new partnerships with the international organizations concerned with education (e.g., UNESCO, UNICEF, the World Bank, European Union, USAID, CIDA, Japanese Aid, Finnish Aid, and some others).
3. To get foreign aid and international expertise to participate in carrying out different education projects.

4. To develop education cadres capable of coping with international developments.
5. To get acquainted with international standards that help to achieve quality education (p. 128).

Second, portraying an external-influence perspective, Egypt's National Centre for Educational Research and Development (NCERD et al., 2004, p. 30) states that the 'National Plan for EFA, 2002–2016' was informed by 'the goals of 'Education for All' as approved by the International Forum on Education (Dakar, April 2000)'—an 'external' international document, though developed during a meeting attended and perhaps influenced by Egyptian government representatives. At the same time NCERD et al. (2004) mention the following, which might seem to be internal sources, but in fact were often produced with international technical assistance:

a. The National Plan for Social and Economic Development (2002–2007) in Egypt.
b. The Ministry of Education's five-year plan (2002–2007).
c. The Program of National Modernization—Egypt in the 21st Century—education as the base for human development and future modernization (2002–2012).
d. Structural modeling of a national plan for "Education for All" ... (p. 30).

In addition, in this paper we outlined some of the global discourses of the community of scholars focused on active-learning, student-centred pedagogies versus more formal teacher-centred, transmission-oriented instructional approaches. Whether focusing on the behavioural or the cognitive dimension to distinguish these teaching methods, these discourses can be traced back at least to the beginning of the 20th century (e.g., John Dewey, Jean Piaget), but appeared much earlier in Asia (Confucius: 6th–5th century BC), Europe (Socrates: 5th century BC), and the Islamic world (Abu Nasr al-Farabi, 9th century AD). Thus, it should be clear that the ideas were available—and, at least to an extent, circulating—long before they punctuated the discourses of either:

a. international organisations (first identified in the mid-1980s, but increasingly more audible beginning in the early 1990s); or
b. the Egyptian government (first catalogued in the late 1970s, but increasingly visible beginning in the early 1990s).

Finally, our examination of global and national discourses of active learning invites further research to explore why the volume of active-learning pedagogical reform discourses (rhetoric and actions) increased when it did. Although it is important to analyse the theoretical and research discourses through which this was accomplished, here we point to political and economic developments that may have not only facilitated such discourses but also enabled active-learning pedagogies to become increasingly taken for granted as part of notions of educational quality. According to the World Bank's (1999, pp. 1–2) *Education Sector Strategy*, two of the 'five drivers of change' in the field of education are (a) 'global democratization and the growth of a powerful civil society which requires education for citizen participation' and (b) 'globalization of markets resulting in employers pursuing the best and least expensive workers by shifting their operations from country to country' (see also Spring, 2004, pp. 45–46).

With regard to *global democratisation*, Spring (2006) has argued that '[f]ormalistic forms of education are often used to prepare students to accept and fit into existing ... systems ... [while p]rogressive forms of education are considered a means for preparing students to actively influence the direction of ... political and social systems' (pp. 6–7). Thus, *at least at a rhetorical level*, there may be a link between promoting active-learning pedagogies and supporting political democratisation. Interestingly, however, while the Egyptian Ministry of Education argued the connection between pedagogical and political reform in the mid-1990s—'the democratic framework also necessitate[s] that students ... be ... taught necessary democratic skills, such as debate, ... critical analysis and thinking and ... participating in decision making' (MOE, 1996, p. 22)—we did not detect this argument explicitly within the educational reform discourses of international organisations during the time period we investigated. Moreover, we need to be cautious in accepting uncritically the idea that real democratisation—as opposed to the ideology of democracy—is spreading around the world (see Diamond & Plattner, 1993). We also need to consider that although the 'Egyptian state has formally recognized the importance of and need for democratization ever since the 1970s, ... the state approaches democratization with prudence, ... particularly since national security and political stability are 'endangered' by fundamentalist terrorist movements and external conspiracies' (Sayed, 2006, p. 79).[5] Thus, in his critical analysis of reforms promoting 'democracy of learning' in Egypt, Badran (2008) observes that one meaning of this phrase is 'giving the students a great deal of freedom and responsibilities' for learning, but notes that such 'efforts ... to improve ... the educational system ... will be fruitless unless they occur in ... a context where the spirit of democracy prevails ... [in] the social and political relations taking place outside the school' (pp. 6, 9; see also Hargreaves, 1997).

In terms of *globalisation of the economy*, Carnoy (1999) notes that the goal of 'competitiveness-driven reforms' (in contrast to 'finance-driven reforms' and 'equity-driven reforms') are primarily to improve economic productivity by improving the 'quality' of labour. In practice, this philosophy translates into expanding the average level of educational attainment among young workers and improving the 'quality' at each level—where quality is measured mainly by student achievement, but also by education's relevance to a changing world of work. (p. 137)

This, of course, could lead to a privileging of formal, teacher transmission-oriented pedagogies. However, as Mattson (2008) comments in relation to higher education in the US: 'Increasingly, justifications of active learning seem less interested in questions of democracy and active citizenship ... than in the 'new' realities of the American economy. Active learning is necessary because employers need people who can retool quickly' (para. 6). And clearly the international and national documents reviewed above often articulated at least an implicit link between pedagogical reform and economic development, in that the rationale behind improving educational quality was framed in relation to international competitiveness. This link is made even more explicitly in the following excerpt from a volume entitled *Strengthening Education in the Muslim World*:

> The teacher-focused learning and authoritarian teaching styles that prevail in most Egyptian classrooms promote passive learning. ...It is clear that Egypt will need a more sophisticated education system that *produces students with* critical thinking skills and the *ability to enter the competitive job market.* (USAID, 2004, p. 11, emphasis added)[6]

But why did the discourses favouring active-learning pedagogies reach such a crescendo beginning in the 1990s? While technological developments like the 'information revolution' (World Bank, 1999) certainly reshaped the world economic system, we need to consider as a major contributing factor the restructuring of the global political economy that resulted from the 'revolutions' in Eastern Europe in 1989 and the 'collapse' of the Soviet Union in 1991. The move from a bi-polar world (plus non-aligned nations) to basically a uni-polar world (though with important divisions in terms of wealth and religious/ideological dimensions) has enabled the rise of at least the ideologies of 'democracy' and the ascendance of multinational corporatist capitalism.

Acknowledgements

This is a revised and abridged version of keynote presentation at the Mediterranean Society of Comparative Education (MESCE) conference, Malta, 11–13 May

2008. The research on which this article is based was undertaken, in part, in relation to work funded through the Educational Quality Improvement Project (EQUIP1) Leader Award and the Egypt Education Reform Programme (ERP).

Both authors have been involved with the USAID-funded Education Reform Programme (ERP), one of the international organisation-supported projects discussed in this paper. Mark Ginsburg initially served as director of the Faculties of Education Reform division of ERP (2004–2006), and subsequently contributed short-term technical assistance for 'documentation for reform diffusion' activity of ERP's Monitoring and Evaluation division, while based at the Academy for Educational Development in Washington, DC (2006–2008). Nagwa Megahed served as programme specialist for Action and Decision-Oriented Research within ERP's Faculties of Education Reform division (2004–2006), and subsequently worked as a senior technical advisor in ERP's Monitoring and Evaluation division (2006–2008). The research reported in this article represents an extension of a documentation study of ERP-supported reform in the area of professional development (see Megahed & Ginsburg, 2008). The article also builds on the research undertaken as part of the Leader Award for USAID's (global) Educational Quality Improvement Programme (EQUIP1) (see Ginsburg et al., 2008; Megahed et al., 2009).

This chapter originally appeared as: Ginsburg, M. B., & Megahed, N. M. (2008) Global discourses and educational reform in Egypt: the case of active-learning pedagogies, *Mediterranean Journal of Educational Studies*, Vol. 13(2), pp. 91–115. Reprinted here with permission from the publisher.

Notes

1 Guthrie (1990) notes that 'the schools of lesser-developed countries are littered with remnants of attempts to change the quality of teaching. ... [based on] Western philosophies of education that denigrate the formalistic teaching' (p. 219); 'while many modern educationalists do not approve of formalism, it is desirable and effective in many educational and cultural contexts' (p. 228). Furthermore, noting the paradox that rote learning tends to be more dominant in Asian than Western schools, but students in Asian countries tend to outperform their Western country peers on international achievement tests, Watkins (2007, p. 309) calls our attention to 'cultural differences in the perception of the relationship between memorizing and understanding', commenting that Asian students 'frequently learn repetitively, both to ensure retention *and* to enhance understanding'.

2 Approximately ten years after this UNICEF- and CIDA-supported project was launched, the author of a UNDP and UNESCO reform assessment mission in Egypt recognised favourably the 'innovative models of institutions, such as One-Classroom Schools and Community Schools ... [which have] introduce[ed] appropriate learning materials and teaching practices for multi-grade teaching' (Spaulding, Manzoor & Ghada, 2003, p. 12).

GLOBAL DISCOURSES AND EDUCATIONAL REFORM IN EGYPT 189

3   The EFA *Global Monitoring Report* mentions that the People's Republic of China 'introduced a new curriculum in 1999, focusing on active learning ... It was in place across the country in primary and junior middle schools by 2005' (UNESCO, 2008, p. 131). Interestingly, China adopted such progressive pedagogies as government policy in 1999, apparently as a result of World Bank (as well as UNDP, UNICEF, and UNESCO) discourses, but in the 1920s, before the rise and fall of the Mao-led communist revolution, 'John Dewey introduce[ed] progressive education ideas that had a major impact on Chinese educational theory' (Spring, 2006, p. 7).

4   In fact, part of the basis for assessing the impact of professional development activities undertaken within the context of the Education Reform Programme (ERP) was to observe systematically that teachers involved in the programme exhibited a higher degree of reform pedagogies than those in the same governorates who had not participated in ERP-supported activities (see Abd-El-Khalick, 2006, 2007).

5   Sayed (2006) explores in more detail how the Egyptian government and international organisations (bilateral and multilateral intergovernmental as well as nongovernmental) have faced and tried to deal with 'conspiracy'—whether theories or realities—in relation to foreign assistance in education and other sectors. For example, international projects focused on developing 'the 'international orientation of the curriculum' is the element that is most contested and gives weight to conspiracy theory arguments' (Sayed, 2006, p. 110). However, pedagogical reform does not seem to have been caught up in the politics of conspiracy, perhaps, as discussed below, because economic development (versus democratisation) was emphasised by international organisations and the Egyptian government in its discourses about active-learning pedagogies.

6   Reinforcing the point that international organisation discourses focused on economic (versus political/democratic) benefits of pedagogical reform, a subsection of this USAID document devoted to 'civic participation' actually highlights the economic dimension, quoting the *Arab Human Development Report* (UNDP, 2002): 'The most worrying aspect ... is education's inability to provide the requirements for the development of Arab societies. ... If the steady deterioration in the quality of education in the Arab countries ... [is] not reversed, the consequences for human and economic development will be grave' (cited in USAID, 2004, p. 12).

References

Abd-El-Khalick, F. (2006, 20 December) *Educational Quality Baseline Study: SCOPE II Data Analysis Report.* Cairo: Education Reform Program.

Abd-El-Khalick, F. (2007, 4 November) *Educational Quality Baseline Study: SCOPE III Data Analysis Report.* Cairo: Education Reform Program.

Academy for Educational Development (AED), ORC Macro, Michigan State University (MSU), Research Triangle Institute (RTI) & University of Pittsburgh's Institute for International Studies in Education (IISE) (2004) *EQUIP2 Proposal for ERP, 2004–2009.* Washington, DC: AED.

Aguirre International (2002) *Quality Basic Education for All: Strategy Proposal* (submitted to USAID/Egypt). Washington, DC: Author.

Aguirre International (2003) *New Schools Program: Mid-Term Evaluation* (submitted to USAID/EGYPT). Washington, DC: Author.

American Institutes for Research (AIR), Educational Development Center (EDC) & World Education, Inc. (2004) *EQUIP1 Proposal for ERP, 2004–2009.* Washington, DC: AIR.

Arnove, R. (1980) *Philanthropy and Cultural Imperialism: The Foundations at Home and Abroad.* Boston: G. K. Hall.

Arnove, R., & Torres, C. A. (eds.) (1999) *Comparative Education: The Dialectic of the Global and the Local.* New York: Rowan & Littlefield.

Badran, S. (2008) *Diversity in a Frame of Unity: The Democracy of Education and Cultural Diversity in Egypt: A Critical Study.* Unpublished paper, Alexandria University, Egypt.

Bahaa El Dinn, H. K. (1997) *Education and the Future.* Kalyoub, Egypt: Al-Ahram Commercial Press.

Barrow, K., Boyle, H., Ginsburg, M., Leu, E., Pier, D., & Price-Rom, A. (2007) *Cross-National Synthesis of Educational Quality Report No. 3: Professional Development and Implementing Active-Learning, Student-Centered Pedagogies* (EQUIP1 research report). Washington, DC: American Institutes for Research.

Beeby, C. (1966) *The Quality of Education in Developing Countries.* Cambridge, MA: Harvard University Press.

Beeby, C. (1986) The stages of growth in educational systems. In S. Heyneman & D. White (eds.) *The Quality of Education and Economic Development: A World Bank Symposium.* Washington, DC: World Bank.

Berman, E. (1992) Donor agencies and third world educational development, 1945–1985. In R. Arnove, P. Altbach & G. Kelly (eds.) *Emergent Issues in Education: Comparative Perspectives.* Albany, NY: State University of New York Press.

Boyle, H. (2006) Memorization and learning in Islamic schools, *Comparative Education Review,* Vol. 50(3), pp. 478–495.

Brown, P., & Lauder, H. (1996) Education, globalization, and economic development. In A. Halsey, H. Lauder, P. Brown & A. Stuart Wells (eds.) *Education, Culture, Economy, and Society.* New York: Oxford University Press.

Burbules, N., & Torres, C. A. (eds.) (2000) *Globalization and Education: Critical Perspectives.* New York: Routledge.

CARE (2005) *Technical Application for Extension of New Schools Program* (submitted to USAID/Egypt). Cairo: Author.

CARE, Education Development Centre & World Education (1999) *Technical Application for New School Program* (submitted to USAID/Egypt). Cairo: CARE.

Carnoy, M. (1999) *Globalization and Educational Reform: What Planners Need to Know.* Paris: UNESCO International Institute for Educational Planning.

Carnoy, M., & Rhoten, D. (eds.) (2002) Meaning of globalization for educational change (special issue). *Comparative Education Review*, Vol. 46(1).

Cochran, J. (1986) *Education in Egypt*. London: Croom Helm.

Cuban, L. (1984) *How Teachers Taught: Constancy and Change in American Classrooms, 1898–1980*. New York: Longman.

Dale, R. (1989) *The State and Education Policy*. Milton Keynes: Open University Press.

Daun, H. (ed.) (2002) *Educational Restructuring in the Context of Globalization and National Policy*. New York: RoutledgeFalmer.

Dewey, J. (1938) *Experience and Education*. New York: Macmillan.

Diamond, L., & Plattner, M. (1993) *The Global Resurgence of Democracy*. Baltimore: Johns Hopkins University Press.

El Baradei, M., & El Baradei, L. (2004, December) *Needs Assessment of the Education Sector in Egypt* (report conducted under contract with the German Development Cooperation Agencies). Cairo: Author.

El-Gamal, Y. (2006) An electronic revolution in the Ministry of Education: based on interview with the Minister. *El Akhbar*, 14 January, p. 1.

Erlich, H. (1989) *Students and University in 20th Century Egyptian Politics*. Totowa, NJ: Frank Cass & Co.

Ginsburg, M. (ed.) (1991) *Understanding Educational Reform in Global Context: Economy, Ideology and the State*. New York: Garland.

Ginsburg, M. (2006) *Challenges to Promoting Active-Learning, Student-Centered Pedagogies* (EQUIP1 issue paper). Washington, DC: American Institute for Research. Available online at: http://www.equip123.net/docs/E1-IP-ChallengesPromotingActiveLearning.pdf

Ginsburg, M., Megahed, N., Abdellah, A., & Zohy, A. (2008) Promoting active-learning pedagogies in Egypt. In N. Popov, C. Wolhuter, C. Heller & M. Kysilka (eds.) *Comparative Education and Teacher Training* (volume 6). Sofia: Bureau for Educational Services and the Bulgarian Comparative Education Society.

Günther, S. (2006) Be masters in that you teach and continue to learn: medieval Muslim thinkers on educational theory, *Comparative Education Review*, Vol. 50(3), pp. 367–388.

Guthrie, G. (1990) To the defense of traditional teaching in lesser-developed countries. In V. Rust & P. Dalin (eds.) *Teachers and Teaching in the Developing World*. New York: Garland Publishing.

Hargreaves, E. (1997) The diploma disease in Egypt: learning, teaching and the monster of the secondary leaving certificate, *Assessment in Education: Principles, Policy and Practice*, Vol. 4(1), pp. 161–196.

Heyneman, S. (1986) Overview. In S. Heyneman & D. White (eds.) *The Quality of Education and Economic Development: A World Bank Symposium*. Washington, DC: World Bank.

Hopkins, T., & Wallerstein, I. (1979) *World-Systems Analysis: Theory and Methodology* (volume 1). Beverly Hills: SAGE.

Inkeles, A., & Sirowy, L. (1984) Convergent and divergent trends in national educational systems. In G. Lenski (ed.) *Current Issues and Research in Macrosociology.* Leiden: E. J. Brill.

Inter-Agency Commission (1990) *World Declaration on Education for All* (document adopted by the World Conference on Education for All: Meeting Basic Learning Needs, Jomtien, Thailand, 5–9 March, 1990). New York: Inter-Agency Commission.

Ismael, S. (ed.) (1999) *Globalization: Policies, Challenges and Responses.* Calgary: Detselig.

Leu, E., & Price-Rom, A. (2006) *Quality of Education and Teacher Learning: A Review of the Literature.* Washington, DC: USAID.

Lockheed, M., & Levin, H. (1991) Creating effective schools. In H. Levin & M. Lockheed (eds.) *Effective Schools in Developing Countries.* Washington, DC: World Bank.

Mattson, K. (2008) Why "active learning" can be perilous to the profession, *Academe,* Vol. 91(1), pp. 23–26.

Mayer, R. (2004) Should there be a three-strikes rule against pure discovery learning? The case for guided methods of instruction, *American Psychologist,* Vol. 59(1), pp. 14–19.

Megahed, N., & Ginsburg, M. (2008) *Documentation Study of Professional Development Reform in Egypt.* Cairo: Education Reform Program.

Megahed, N., Ginsburg, M., Abdellah, A., & Zohy, A. (2009) *Active Learning Pedagogies as a Reform Initiative: The Case of Egypt* (EQUIP1 research report). Washington, DC: American Institute for Research.

Meyer, J., & Hannan, M. (1979) National development in a changing world system: an overview. In J. Meyer & M. Hannan (eds.) *National Development and the World System: Educational, Economic and Political change, 1950–70.* Chicago: University of Chicago Press.

Ministry of Education (MOE) (1979, September) *Working Paper Concerning the Development and Modernization of Education in Egypt.* Cairo: Author.

Ministry of Education (MOE) (1992) *Mubarak and Education: A Look to the Future, 1992.* Cairo: Author.

Ministry of Education (MOE) (1996) *Implementing Egypt's Educational Reform Strategy, 1996.* Cairo: Author.

Ministry of Education (MOE) (2002) *Mubarak and Education: Qualitative Development in the National Project of Education: Application of Principles of Total Quality.* Cairo: Author.

Ministry of Education (MOE) (2003) *National Standards of Education in Egypt* (volume 1). Cairo. Author.

Ministry of Education (2004) *Reforming Pre-University Education Programs* (in Arabic). Cairo: Author.

Ministry of Education (MOE) (2006, March) *Strategic Planning for Educational Development* (PowerPoint Presentation).

Ministry of Education (MOE) (2007) *National Strategic Education Plan, 2007/08–2011/12* (English Version). Cairo: Author.

Moussa, A. G. (2005) Mission impossible: interview with the Minister by Shaden Shehab. *Al-Ahram Weekly*, 27 January – 2 February (Issue No. 727), p. 1.

National Centre for Educational Research and Development (NCERD) (2007) *Mid-Term EFA Evaluation, 2000–2007* (requested by UNESCO). Cairo: Author

National Centre for Educational Research and Development (NCERD), UNESCO (Cairo and Beirut offices) & Ministry of Education (Arab Republic of Egypt) (2004) *The National Plan for Education for All, 2002/2003–2015/2016*. Cairo: NCERD.

Programme and Project Monitoring Unit (PPMU) (2006) *Education in Egypt Longitudinal Study Report: Education Enhancement Programme*. Cairo: PPMU & MOE.

Radwan, A. F. (1951) *Old and New Forces in Egyptian Education*. New York: Columbia University.

Robertson, S., Bonal, X., & Dale, R. (2002) GATS and the education service industry: the politics of scale and global re-territorialization, *Comparative Education Review*, Vol. 46(4), pp. 72–96.

Rogers, C. (1969) *Freedom to Learn*. Columbus, OH: Charles Merrill.

Sayed. F. H. (2005) Security, donors' interests, and education policy making in Egypt, *Mediterranean Quarterly*, Vol. 16(2), pp. 66–84.

Sayed. F. H. (2006) *Transforming Education in Egypt: Western Influence and Domestic Policy Reform*. Cairo: The American University in Cairo Press.

Spaulding, S., Klaus, B., Binayagum, C., & Nader, F. (1996) *Review and Assessment of Reform of Basic Education in Egypt*. Cairo: UNESCO (with support from UNDP).

Spaulding, S., Manzoor, A., & Ghada, G. (2003) *Educational Reform in Egypt, 1996–2003: Achievements and Challenges in the New Century* (semi-final draft, 1 April). Cairo: UNESCO.

Spring, J. (2004) *How Educational Ideologies are Shaping Global Society: Intergovernmental Organizations, NGOs, and the Decline of the Nation-State*. Mahwah, NJ: Lawrence Erlbaum.

Spring, J. (2006) *Pedagogies of Globalization: The Rise of the Educational Security State*. Mahwah, NJ: Lawrence Erlbaum Associates.

Steiner-Khamsi, G. (ed.) (2004) *The Global Politics of Educational Borrowing and Lending*. New York: Teachers College Press.

Stromquist, N., & Monkman, K. (eds.) (2000) *Globalization and Education: Integration and Contestation across Cultures*. Lanham: Rowman & Littlefield.

Suarez, D. (2007) Education professionals and the construction of human rights education, *Comparative Education Review*, Vol. 51(1), pp. 48–70.

Tabb, W. (2001) *The Amoral Elephant*. New York: Monthly Review Press.

Terano, M., & Ginsburg, M. (2008) Educating all for peace: educating no one for (physical or structural) violence. In J. Lin & C. Bruhn (eds.) *Transforming Education for Peace*. Greenwich, CT: Information Age Publishing.

Tietjen, K., McLaughlin, S., El Said, M., & M. (2005) *Evaluation of the Alexandria Education Reform Pilot Project* (draft: prepared for the United States Agency for International Development/Egypt, Project No. 4333-001-49-06). Washington, DC: Management Systems International.

Treat, A., Wang, W., Chadha, R., & Hart Dixon, M. (2008) *Major Developments in Instructional Technology: Prior to the 20th Century*.

UNDP (2002) *Arab Human Development Report 2002*. New York: Author.

UNESCO (2000) *The Dakar Framework for Action: Education for All: Meeting Our Collective Commitments* (text adopted by the World Education Forum, Dakar, Senegal, 26–28 April).

UNESCO (2006) *Decentralization of Education in Egypt* (Country Report on the UNESCO Seminar on EFA Implementation: Teacher and Resource Management in the Context of Decentralization, Administrative Staff College of India, Hyderabad, India, 6–8 January 2005). Paris: Author.

UNESCO (2008) *EFA Global Monitoring Report, 2008: Education for All by 2015: Will We Make It?* Oxford: Oxford University Press and UNESCO Publishing.

USAID (2004, April) Egypt. In *Strengthening Education in the Muslim World: Country Profiles and Analysis* (PPC issue Working Paper no. 1). Washington, DC: USAID Bureau of Policy and Programme Coordination.

USAID (2005, April). *Education Strategy: Improving Lives through Learning*. Washington, DC: Author.

USAID/Egypt (1981) *Egypt Basic Education* (project paper: project #263-0139, FY1981-FY1986). Cairo: Author.

USAID/Egypt (1996, September) *Strategic Objective Agreement between the Arab Republic of Egypt and the United States of America for Girls' Education*. Cairo: Author.

USAID/Egypt (2001, 13 June) *Concept Paper: The Pilot Education Initiative in Alexandria*. Cairo: Author.

USAID/Egypt (2002, 16 December) *Alexandria Education Pilot Reform Project: Status Report*. Cairo: Author.

USAID/Egypt (2003a) *Program Description for ERP* (request for application to EQUIP1). Cairo: Author.

USAID/Egypt (2003b) *Program Description for ERP* (request for application to EQUIP2). Cairo: Author.

USAID/Egypt (2007) *Request for Proposal (RFP) No. 263-07-003 Girls' Improved Learning Outcomes (GILO)*. Cairo: Author.

Watkins, D. (2007) Comparing ways of learning. In M. Bray, B. Adamson & M. Mason (eds.) *Comparative Education Research: Approaches and Methods*. Hong Kong: Comparative Education Research Centre and Springer.

Wikipedia (2008) *Constructivism (Learning Theory)*. Available online at: https://en.wikipedia.org/wiki/Constructivism_(philosophy_of_education)

Williamson, B. (1987) *Education and Social Change in Egypt and Turkey: A Study in Historical Sociology*. London: Macmillan.

Willinsky, J. (2002) The nation-state after globalism, *Educational Studies*, Vol. 33(1), pp. 35–53.

Wittrock, M. (1979) The cognitive movement in instruction, *Educational Researcher*, Vol. 8(2), pp. 5–11.

World Bank (1996, 19 August) *Project Information Document, (Egypt) Education Enhancement Program*. Washington, DC: Author.

World Bank (1999) *Education Sector Strategy*. Washington, DC: International Bank of Reconstruction.

World Bank (2007, 29 June) *Arab Republic of Egypt: Education Sector Policy Note 2007, Improving Quality, Equality, and Efficiency in the Education Sector: Fostering a Competent Generation of Youth*. Washington, DC: Author.

Zaalouk, M. (2004) *The Pedagogy of Empowerment: Community Schools as a Social Movement in Egypt*. Cairo: The American University of Cairo Press.

CHAPTER 11

Values in Teaching and Teaching Values

A Review of Theory and Research, Including the Case of Greece

Evangelia Frydaki

1   Introduction

The discourse on educational values, and specifically in the teaching process, is not new. In each era there seems to be a renewed dialogue on this issue raising specific questions. Our late modern era expanded the relevant discussion on this matter, posing questions such as: What kind of meanings did education attribute to the concept of values in order to be treated in teaching? Have these meanings been modified? Should, nowadays, teachers infuse values in their instructional settings, or should they abstain from such a task? In addition, what kind of values should teachers infuse: the values of a shared value system or values of their own preference and belief system? Furthermore, is there a common ground on which a shared value system may rest? Is such a system desirable (Butroyd, 1997)? The different and sometimes confusing answers to these questions engender from time to time a new need for a review, particularly seeing that emerging situations create new needs, both social and educational; the current society of late modernity needs members which are able to identify and choose their values with increasing autonomy, in an increasingly complex social environment.

To survive, society itself needs high degrees of tolerance, acceptance of difference (be it cultural, religious, or value-related) and, simultaneously, some sort of social commitment from its members. As eloquently put by Bruner (1990), in a democratic culture, broadness of mind is the 'willingness to construe knowledge and values from multiple perspectives without loss of commitment to one's own values' (p. 30). Consequently, even though education's traditional socialisation role seems to be limited in an open pluralistic society, it is the position of this author that teachers ought to support the efforts of youth to develop their own values in a process which takes place in different socio-cultural contexts, and under different circumstances. In such a complex context, teachers as well as prospective teachers need updated information deriving from theoretical frameworks and research findings, which could facilitate them to broaden their concepts, expand their perspectives, strengthen

© THE EURO-MEDITERRANEAN CENTRE FOR EDUCATION RESEARCH, UNIVERSITY OF MALTA, 2009
DOI: 10.1163/9789004506602_011

This is an open access chapter distributed under the terms of the CC BY-NC 4.0 License.

their awareness, in order to gain a thoughtful sensitivity to the concrete situations of practice.

Under this perspective, the present paper aims to review: (i) the ways in which education attributed meaning to values and treated them during teaching in the second half of the 20th century, including the case of Greece; (ii) the relationship between values and education with respect to three educational movements of different underlying theoretical traditions; and (iii) recent research focusing on how teachers integrate their values in the teaching process, thus influencing the development of their students' own values. In this manner, this paper aims at shedding light on the terms of this pedagogical discourse, and to contribute to the review, diffusion, and enrichment of relevant thinking, both for education researchers and for active practitioners. Lastly, it seeks to suggest new perspectives for the education of future teachers.

2   Meanings Attributed to Values And Instructional Treatments

In the 1950s and 1960s, western societies considered as values the socially and culturally acceptable models and behavioural norms. Not only were society's goals and needs considered more important than the individuals', but they could also determine the latter's respective goals and needs (Parsons, 1951; Whiting, 1961). Consequently, the teaching of values was the process by which students came to identify, accept, and internalise social values in their own value system. Apart from this perspective of the individual as a servant of social needs, a contrary position viewed the individual as a free participant in society, contributing only to the degree society ensured the individual's own self-fulfilment. According to the latter view, deriving from Rousseau's tradition, school curriculum should teach values like freedom to learn, human dignity, creativity, justice, self-exploration and personal development. The work of Maslow (1970, 1979) and Rogers (1983), belonging to humanistic psychology, provided a useful starting point in the above orientation. Maslow used the popular term *self-actualisation* to describe a desire that could lead a person to realising his/her capabilities, and to reach personal growth, which takes place once lower order needs have been met. People that have reached *self-actualisation* are spontaneous, open-minded, and they accept themselves and others. Rogers (1961), like Maslow, was interested in describing the healthy person. His term is *fully-functioning,* which includes qualities such as openness to experience, trusting, responsibility for one's choices, and creativity. In the comparative overview of a survey of 26 countries concerning values education in Europe, several values emanating from the work of Maslow and Rogers were often mentioned (see Consortium of Institutions for Development and Research in Education in Europe [CIDREE], 1994, p. 41).

Another aspect of values education in the early 1980s concerned the specific ways in which the institution of education in general, and the process of teaching in particular, taught values. Values were perceived as absolute, universal, eternal entities that could be neither negotiated nor challenged. The only conceivable problem concerned the process and framework of their legitimisation; for some, values were considered theological (pre-modern discourse), for others, they were viewed as natural orders, and for others still, related to varied theories or ideologies. The above debate had little impact on the mission of teaching, which adhered to one task: to 'transmit' values via the appropriate subject matters, which in most cases included the humanities, without any discussion, critical reflection, or questioning (Huitt, 2004). During the same period, Massialas (1975) suggested a new approach to values in teaching in the framework of humanistic education. His perspective concerned 'human learning through social inquiry', which included a flexible pattern of questioning through which teachers could encourage students to clarify, support and justify with evidence their ideas, values, judgments and emotions that were relevant to the problem under examination.

During the following years, education was dominated by technical and instrumental thinking, for a period culminating in the 1980s. Emphasis in education was given to goal oriented curriculum, skill development, and on effective teaching; values were cast aside, perhaps because it was believed that they belong to a precarious non-scientific realm, marked by normative, moralistic, or ideological perspectives. By the 1990s, a renewed interest in the ways in which values could be re-integrated in the educational process appeared again in the academic and research world. This interest is presently revamped given the social innovations and changes, the weakening of cohesive traditional value systems, the expansion of the cultural continuum to which individuals are exposed today, and the plethora of choices available in the context of a globalised society (Veugelers & Vedder, 2003).

As far as the Greek educational system is concerned, it has not set clearly its priorities regarding values in teaching due to various and often conflicting factors. At first, the turbulent history of the Greek nation state, the need for creating, or recreating, its national identity, the spiritual and moral values of Christianity, as expressed by the Greek Orthodox Church, are some of the reasons contributing to an overemphasis on nation-centred values (Flouris, 1997). Besides the fact that up to 1976 the cultivation of nation-centred and religious values constituted a crucial educational target (Cidree, 1994). Up until the previous decade, Greek curricula were still dominated by traditional and

VALUES IN TEACHING AND TEACHING VALUES

nation-centred values, and teachers were authorised to fill the students' minds with predetermined sets of values (Massialas & Flouris, 1994; Flouris, 1995). This was the period when the teaching of any literary or Ancient Greek text should emphatically promote the text's 'eternal meanings'; Greek history was a pantheon of heroes, martyrs, and glorious achievements; finally, in Philosophy and Ancient Greek Literature, the conflict between Socrates and the sophists was only taught in order to compare the former's morality to the latter's immorality. On the other hand, as some scholars support, Greece is in a transitional stage and at a technocratic period, with a 20-year lag (Kassotakis, 2004), which brings up more the issue of effectiveness of teaching rather than its value laden aspects. In parallel, many scholars call for the ideal of an informed, active, socially responsible and probably universal civil citizen, which is also promoted by the European educational policy. This citizen is to be equipped with skills, such as literacy, technological literacy and foreign languages as well as with attitudes and values, such as the respect of human dignity and human rights, the tolerance for those from a different cultural background, etc. (Massialas & Flouris, 1994; Flouris, 1997; Koutselini, 1997; Xochellis, 2001). Hence, the Greek educational system has not demonstrated a systematic discourse either on common acceptable values to be taught in schools, which would not necessarily be the desirable orientation, or on the moral groundwork of an open, pluralistic society.

The issue of teaching values in Greece has been expanded at present, as it is supported by the Pedagogical Institute (PI), the main investigatory and advisory institute concerning educational matters, which was established in 1964 and falls directly under the aegis of the Minister of Education. The PI claims that students ought to adhere to 'a strong sense of responsibility towards the nation and the universal and multicultural perspectives of present and future' (PI, 2000, p. 162). The value-related recommendations of the current curriculum for the teaching of Literature and History cover a wide range, including both the goals of traditional humanities and postmodern objectives (respect of difference, multiple perspectives) (Frydaki & Mamoura, 2007). Furthermore, in Social Studies, objectives refer to a growth of students' awareness of the equality of persons, of the interdependence of people in society, of the rights of family and education (Papoulia-Tzelepi, 1997). As fortunate as these may seem, they do not enjoy sufficient support by schoolbooks, teaching materials and guidelines, nor do they illuminate what actually takes place under real school conditions (Flouris, 1995). Likewise, a considerable difference has been already pointed out between the values that a school proclaims and those which in fact underpin teachers' practice (Halstead, 1996). In this slightly confused context, as already mentioned, teachers seem to need extra help to realise their own value-commitments in order to support students to develop their own values. With regard to this need, a theoretical framework, including some different perspectives on the teaching of values, is discussed in the following section of this paper. This framework is not intended to uphold some perspective against the others. Instead, it is intended to initiate a dialogue which could generate fruitful and reflective thinking about the positions and contradictions of all perspectives so that teachers can be assisted in locating themselves within value contexts and gain awareness of the essential role that their own options play in the process of value communication.

3 Three Perspectives on Teaching Values

Among the variety of trends on values in education, three distinct movements stand out: Value Education, Moral Development, and Critical Pedagogy (Veugelers, 2000).

The concept of Value Education or Character Education refers to the teaching of social, political, religious, cultural, aesthetic, or other types of values, predetermined as necessary for shaping the students' character (Linkona, 1993, 1997; Noddings, 1995; Wynne, 1997). Many researchers concur on the great difficulties in reaching a consensus on universal, non-relative values that transcend the needs of specific societies and constitute a multicultural world society. Thomas (1992) points out that not everyone defines the moral domain in the same way, and he substantiates the complexity of such a definition using the following three patterns that highlight three controversial dimensions of values: (i) universal versus relative moral values; (ii) permanent versus changeable values; and (iii) absolute versus conditional values (pp. 69–74). This complexity is perhaps one of the reasons why Value Education is linked with basic values, considered as non-controversial by their advocates, which ground character formation and peaceful co-existence, that is, trust, participation, care, fairness, respect and collective responsibility (Cohen, 1995). Some describe these values to be as *meta-moral* (Berkowitz, 1997), since they represent an individual's attribute supporting his/her moral functioning. Value Education programmes aim to reinforce the teaching of such values in the educational process, not only through the curriculum (that is via direct teaching of specific subject matters), but also through the school's communication conditions and moral environment. Relevant criticism focuses on the following points: Firstly, no research so far has demonstrated direct correlations between taught values and their impact on students' behaviour. Secondly, notions such as *fairness*, *participation* and *trust* can be very controversial issues, in the sense that all these concepts may have different connotations in different contexts, that is, in an abstract humanistic framework or in a socio-political context. However, the advocates of this Value Perspective avoid highlighting this point and they present these concepts in their most abstract and normative sense. Thus, given the normative character of this approach, there seems to be a risk of becoming oppressively moralising, instead of involving students actively in meaning making, decision-making, and reflecting on their lives (Lockwood, 1997; Wardekker, 2004).

The movement of Moral Development differs from the first one in two crucial determinants: the types of values and the way they are developed. Regarding value types, this movement revolves not around personal, social, or aesthetic values, but around 'basic moral concepts' (Kohlberg, 1969, 1984), which, in Kant's tradition, morally establish any individual or collective action. They include honour, justice, equality, human dignity, responsibility and any value that directly promotes others' rights and well-being (Prencipe & Helwing, 2002). In terms of value development, this is based on the development of cognitive processes, as defined by Piaget's cognitive development stages. Cognitive development can also support the development of moral reasoning, the skill of thinking and reflecting on issues related to moral values. The ideal strategy recommended (and implemented) for developing such skills may be via small group discussion. This encourages students to take a stand on value dilemmas, as presented in real or imaginary situations and/or stories. The stories should clearly represent a main character's 'real conflict', contain a certain number of moral issues, and facilitate differentiated student reactions. The teacher should firmly guide the discussion toward the development of moral reasoning. In practice, this means encouraging students to express their views freely, urging them not only to share their views with others, but also to discuss the reasoning behind their views and choices; student discourse should be structured and based on arguments, without necessarily leading to a 'correct' or acceptable answer (Gailbraith & Jones, 1975). Relevant criticism focuses on the movement's tendency to overestimate cognitive processes and underestimate the emotional and social factors involved in the development of values (Lovat & Schofield, 1998; Wardekker, 2004). Gilligan (1977, 1982), based on her studies of women, suggested that females' moral decisions relate more to relational and affective factors rather than to abstract principles, as Kohlberg has proposed. Hence, Gilligan (1993) developed a 'care version' of moral reasoning arguing that moral dilemmas are to be placed in a relational and emotional context.

The movement of Critical Pedagogy has had an impact on Greek educational discourse during the recent years. According to the principles of Critical

Pedagogy, every form of social reproduction or reform is the result of political and cultural struggle. In education, this struggle is reflected in the curriculum, the teachers' goals, and their teaching practices (Giroux & McLaren, 1989). That is, it is reflected not only in the transfer of knowledge, but also in the development of values. Willing or not, teachers cannot retain a neutral stance toward this political and cultural struggle, nor can they remain neutral in terms of value transfer. For instance, by teaching their students on their role as citizens in a democratic society, teachers influence shifts either toward social reproduction or toward social reform. Thus, Critical Pedagogy theorists argue that teachers' involvement with values ought to correspond to their socio-political or socio-cultural practice, and the way they do it contributes to social justice (McLaren, 1994). Critical Pedagogy theorists are more explicit regarding the values they deem important: critical reinforcement, the right to difference, self-determination in political terms, and social justice. Such an orientation by the teacher could help students listen to the voices of the oppressed; understand the degree to which they themselves may be the victims of inequality, and develop a sense of justice and empowerment, which is central to becoming moral persons. However, according to relevant criticism, the rhetoric of Critical Pedagogy is hardly helpful for thinking through and planning classroom practices to support the political agenda (Ellsworth, 1989). Moreover, there is a lack of skills required by teachers to critically reflect on their values, integrating them more consciously in their socio-political or socio-cultural practices, so that their students become co-players in the pedagogical game of signification (Veugelers, 2000). Therefore, teachers seem to be allowed to deal with the topics promoted by Critical Pedagogy in any way they themselves see fit.

According to Wardekker (2004, p. 189), the first two movements seem to ignore that the individuals' (i.e., teachers' and students') values are seldom developed as product of an individual rationality, but rather tend to conform to existing rules and moral qualities of the social contexts in which individuals live. One could infer that Critical Pedagogy seems also to emphasise the individual rationality, in case it remains restricted to its political rhetoric. Moreover, teachers who implement the principles of Critical Pedagogy by confining themselves to the transmission of its rhetoric, run the risk of being considered as inculcators. On the other hand, Critical Pedagogy could highlight the relatedness between the micro and the macro, the personal and the political. That is, it could help students develop a sense of critical and emancipatory empowerment on the understanding that it tackles topics which emerge from students' own lives as well as that teachers foster a genuine reflective dialogue about the existing societal values, possibly internalised by the students. Such reflective dialogue should relate the abstract value concepts to real students' experiences and practices in order for the students to understand that they

VALUES IN TEACHING AND TEACHING VALUES   203

themselves have choices that would permit them to change their own lives and
social life as well (Ball, 2000).

Although the dialogue between the three perspectives on the teaching of
values can generate a fruitful and reflective relevant thinking, another thing
remains to be considered for the topic to be better illuminated: How do teachers deal with values within actual classrooms nowadays? What kind of values
do they infuse and in what way? Thus, the following section attempts to classify some currently available research findings on how teachers themselves
infuse their own values in their classrooms, including the case of Greece.

4   Indirect Diffusion of Values in Teaching

Despite long-standing consensus regarding the inevitable embedding of values in teaching (Dewey, 1964), there has been little research on how teachers incorporate their values in the design and practice of their teachings, their
behaviour toward students, and their teaching discourse. However, significant
evidence, mainly from small-scale qualitative research projects, indicates that
teachers' underlying values are crucial regarding how they transform curriculum into practice in the classroom. According to Veugelers (2000), teachers
cannot avoid influencing students, even if they strive to strictly confine themselves to the learning processes. For learning is a process of meaning making,
of attributing a particular personal meaning to the subject matter taught and
to the world in general. Inevitably, every such process involves elements of the
teachers' and students' own identity, and therefore explicit or implicit value
orientations.

In reviewing the literature on teaching values from 1990 to 2008, some studies were identified regarding the way teachers' values permeate the teaching process. Reference databases (ERIC and HEAL-LINK) were searched for
potentially relevant studies published since 1990. Two groups of descriptors
have been used (including synonymous and related terms). The first group of
descriptors was: values, moral, ethical. These descriptors were combined with
terms such as: teaching, teachers, teachers' beliefs, teachers' dispositions, subject matter, objectives, strategies, and pedagogy. The abstracts of the papers
were analysed to support whether they actually highlight the dimension of
hidden diffusion of teachers' personal values into instructional settings. The
combination of the two groups of descriptors guided the author of this paper
to include in this review a total of 24 studies, from which the following patterns
emerged: (i) values infused through teachers' beliefs on what should be taught;
(ii) subject-linked values, that is, values derived from teachers' conceptions of
the subject matter; (iii) values emerging from teachers' strategies, whenever

they teach value-laden issues; and (iv) values resulting from teachers' character and dispositions.

The research under examination could not be subjected to quantitative meta-analysis because of their theoretical and methodological differentiations, nor to detailed description as the latter could weaken the focus of the entire study. Hence, their results are presented in a narrative descriptive way, which is considered appropriate to highlight the emerging patterns.

4.1 Values Infused through Teachers' Beliefs on What Should Be Taught

This pattern of values is the most easily distinguishable and recognisable. Teachers in these studies are bound to make choices regarding the emphasis placed on each aspect of the subject matter taught, as it is impossible to cover the full syllabus, not only because of its quantity, but also due to time restrictions. Such choices are implemented through their teaching goals and objectives, which, despite official guidelines for teaching each unit, often differ, even between teachers within the same school (Gudmundsdottir, 1990). Following the guidelines of the above research study, another study conducted in Greece (Frydaki & Mamoura, 2008) identified that two High School teachers taught the same novel (Stratis Tsirkas' *Ariagne*, the second volume of the trilogy *Drifting Cities*), but driven by their own personal value orientations created two different texts and instructional settings. The first one, devoted her instructional time to a socio-political perspective, and taught the text as historical evidence on the conditions of the expulsion of Greeks from Egypt. The second teacher, addressed classroom issues to her own humanitarian worldview and placed a lot more emphasis on 'the inherent tenderness and sublimeness included in the female soul' (Frydaki & Mamoura, 2008, p. 1494).

Another way in which teachers infuse their values through their beliefs on what should be taught is as follows: Despite the supposed priority of cognitive goals, some teachers have been observed to dedicate up to 50% of their instructional time to the development of social skills (Wentzel, 1991), others on democratic attitudes (Blumenfeld et al., 1979), while others on the discussion of the students' personal problems and the class's collective problems (Prawat, 1980). More recent research (Ennis, Ross & Chen, 1992; Ennis, 1994; Husu & Tirri, 2007) shows an increasing trend of academic goals giving way to social and community goals, including social responsibility, cooperation, responding to the needs of others, respect, and participation. In support of these orientations and rationales, teachers reported the following: (i) student population becomes increasingly heterogeneous; in order to deal with academic content, students first need to obtain a relative social cohesion as members of the school community; (ii) the content of all subject matters should be connected to students' personal, social, and professional life; and (iii) students should be motivated to involve themselves more actively in the class, seeing that interesting, pleasant and meaningful education yields greater opportunities for enhanced student performance (Ennis, 1994, pp. 116–118).

In short, teachers who participated in the above research studies infuse implicitly their social, political, religious, cultural, aesthetic, or other types of values, even if these values are not predetermined as necessary for shaping the students' character. That is, they put into practice various tacit Value Education 'programmes' consistent with their beliefs. In these 'programmes', the shift from the discipline to the responsibility, participation, respect of difference and cooperation is habitually discernible. The question is whether these personal 'programmes' consider values as something to be transmitted once more or as something to be communicated involving students actively in meaning making, that is, taking into account their personal experience, commitments, worldviews and understanding of themselves.

4.2   *Subject-Linked Values*

This pattern concerns values derived from teachers' conceptions of the subject matter taught. Shulman (1986) introduced the notion of pedagogical content knowledge speaking 'of the particular form of content knowledge that embodies the aspects of content most germane to its teachability [...], of the ways of representing and formulating the subject that make it comprehensible to others' (p. 9). According to Gudmundsdottir (1990), teachers transfer their values to their students neither consciously nor intentionally, but rather through their pedagogical content knowledge, that is, through the way they conceive their subject matter and plan their teaching. Indeed, academic disciplines, from which many school subjects are derived, differ in their histories, bodies of knowledge, epistemologies, sets of agreed procedures, and the degree of consensus existing within the field (Grossman & Stodolsky, 1995). Hence, they create a number of subject subcultures, and possibly different subcultures within the field of the same subject.

Relevant research (Gudmundsdottir, 1990; Slater, 1995; Husbands, 1996; Bills & Husbands, 2004) reveals that teachers initially claim to aim beyond the scope of their subject matter, that is, promoting critical thinking, fostering responsible citizens, etc. However, these broader aims often derive from the teachers' own beliefs on the nature and purpose of the subject matter taught. This occurs especially in the case of secondary school teachers who teach broad, less well-defined subjects (such as Literature, History or Social Studies), as these subjects provide them with a greater flexibility and curricular autonomy than more defined school subjects (Grossman & Stodolsky, 1995, p.

6). For example, a Literature teacher who believes that Literature is important for students' self-discovery and growth may organise the class quite differently from another one who teaches a text's established interpretation, to promote the students' 'general education' or 'culture' (Muchmore, 2001; Shaw, Barry & Mahlios, 2008). The two above teachers transfer different values to their students in different ways, that is, through the types of questions asked, the way the class is managed, the points of focus, or the promotion of a single or multiple responses. In the first case, students learn the value of mental and emotional awareness toward literature, while in the second case, students learn the value of conformism, limiting themselves to verbal expressions and 'having something to say'. Other studies revealed that analogous situations seem to apply to other subject matters too. A teacher may think that history teaches us the best human achievements of the past; another one may hold that it teaches us to evaluate facts objectively, so as to reach informed conclusions; a third one may believe that history teaches us to understand the perspectives of others and develop tolerance (Akinoglu, 2004; Bills & Husbands, 2004; Frydaki & Mamoura, 2008).

It should be noted that not all possible teacher attitudes and values appear with the same frequency. Research findings have indicated that teacher beliefs on the nature and purpose of the subject matter are strongly influenced by the dominant values in the subject matter's tradition, which 'embody a notion of the perfection of the intellect' (Pring, 1996, p. 104; Frydaki & Mamoura, 2007). Teachers' priority is to familiarise the students with the subject matter's inherent values, considered critical for their ability to think, reflect and evaluate 'the best that has been thought and said' (Pring, 1996, p. 106). This attitude is often shaped by and within a strong academic tradition of university education, usually reinforced by equally academic curricula and content- and examination-oriented bureaucratic educational systems.

In sum, teachers seem to transfer values to their students through their pedagogical content knowledge and, especially, through the way they conceive and perceive a specific subject matter. The question is: Do teachers hold to a sufficient extent conceptual frameworks and tools that enable them to broaden and critically reflect on their beliefs as a result of the nature and purpose of their subject? Or do they remain confined either to the subject matter tradition or to the prevailing subject's subculture, since these are mainly reinforced by curricula and the school culture as well?

4.3 Values Emerging from Teachers' Strategies, Whenever They Teach Value-Laden Issues

The subjects that inherently contain value-laden issues are mainly the humanistic ones. The ways in which teachers handle these types of issues could reveal their probable orientations toward some of the three aforementioned educational movements. Recent research findings in Greece and elsewhere indicate that Literature and History teachers handle very cautiously, even tentatively, the value-laden issues, especially those that raise reactions from students, opting to maintain their neutrality. Although they reject the predetermined transfer of values and encourage students to exchange their views, teachers avoid expressing their own views, unless their relationship with the students enjoys stability and trust. Even when students express provocative views, teachers refrain from expressing their own, preferring to react more indirectly (e.g., expanding the scope of student discussion, or urging students to exchange arguments) (Frydaki & Mamoura, 2008). This situation seems to endorse other findings on the dilemma between having personal values or educational ideals and publicly expressing them in class (Boxall, 1995; Chater, 2005).

Moreover, teachers in Greece rarely bring into question, while teaching literature, the text's central values, preferring to focus on eternal humanistic values, as expressed in the great texts of literary tradition, including freedom, honour, justice, dignity, and self-sacrifice. For example, the K. Kavafis' poem *Antony's Ending* embodies the value of dignity before a defeat, a frustration, or a dead end. Given the Greek curriculum guidelines and established teaching practices, an observer would note that most Greek literature teachers avoid discussing the text's central value issue and refrain from offering alternative positions, that is, fighting all the way to the end. On the contrary, the same teachers seem to strongly defend similar values while teaching other literary texts, in which this value issue is dominant (i.e., *The Free Besieged* by D. Solomos). In brief, a great majority of Greek teachers seem to avoid either presenting different views or creating moral dilemmas through which students may be encouraged to take a stand and defend their positions.

On the other hand, research conducted by the University of Amsterdam (Veugelers, 2000) revealed that teachers handle value-laden issues by a greater variety of strategies, only the first of which coincides with the pre-mentioned Greek tendency: (i) they try to avoid expressing their personal views, remaining devoted to the 'official' interpretation; (ii) they explicitly clarify which values they find important, that is, they express and defend their position; (iii) they underline the possible views one may hold on the issue under study, avoiding to take sides; and (iv) they present different views, but also express the values they find important. Several participants indicated that they themselves follow a linear sequence of teaching approaches i, iii, and iv; at first, they are neutral, then they present a range of alternative views, while at the end they present their own view for discussion in class. On the other hand, students stated their preference for teachers who present different values and then present their own views, without emphasising them excessively. In other words, students want to know what their teachers believe, but they would not wish to be indoctrinated (Veugelers, 2000, pp. 43–44). These students seem to share Kelly's (1986) notion of 'committed impartiality' according to which the teacher attempts to provide all sides of a topic but does share his/her own views with the class.

In sum, the data at hand revealed that several Greek teachers tend to avoid indoctrinating students; but, contrary to their colleagues from the Netherlands, they tend equally to avoid involving themselves too obviously in the process of value communication either by expressing their own values or by bringing into question the text's central value. The question is whether this stance of value neutrality shows an emerging value orientation that is more critical and eman- cipatory, or an emerging political correctness with conservative overtones.

4.4 *Values Resulting from the Teachers' Dispositions*

Richardson (1993) and Fenstermacher (1999) were among the scholars that dis- tinguished between the three aspects of teachers' behaviour in class: method, style, and manner. Method consists of teachers' intentional actions, aiming at influencing students. Style refers to behaviour reflecting teachers' personal- ity. Manner includes all the characteristics and dispositions that reveal teach- ers' moral and intellectual character. Under the same vein, Fallona (2000), for the purposes of her research, further analysed teaching manner in relation to how teachers express in class each of the 'Aristotelian moral virtues of brav- ery, friendliness, wit, mildness, magnificence, magnanimity, honor, generosity, temperance, truthfulness, and justice' (p. 684). Despite the difficulties inher- ent in observing the distinctions among the above manners, this researcher found it quite important for teachers to realise and study their own teaching manners, so as to enjoy a more fruitful interaction with their students (Fallona, 2000, p. 692).

More recently, Johnson & Reiman (2007) utilise the tradition established by Dewey and the movement of Moral Development, which holds that every action is based on an underlying moral judgment. They define dispositions 'as teacher professional judgment and professional action in the moral/ethical domain' (p. 677), that is, when confronted with situations that can be solved in more than one way. Their qualitative research grouped teachers' values, moral judgments and actions in three distinct patterns, based on how rules are shaped in class. In the first pattern, when confronted with a dilemma, teachers endorse the rules to maintain order, the one 'right' solution to every problem, and the need for students' obedience. In practice, they attribute themselves the role of controlling classroom relationships, and are easily disturbed by the lack of student discipline; they create and modify rules of their own, while their teaching strategies overlook students' perspectives or internal motives, paying no attention to the students' emotional needs. In the second pattern, teachers' judgments are based on rules, which guarantee protection and stability. Although teachers allow no exceptions when applying the rules, they do make an allowance for student perspectives and motives. In practice, they establish explicit and uniform rules, and follow them themselves. Teachers of the third pattern express their judgments and design their activities taking into consideration students' rights, the variety of learning styles, and the situational context; they view rules as relative and changeable, existing only to protect certain rights. In practice, they encourage students to participate in the shaping of rules and in decision-making, they choose individualised and interactive teaching strategies, they are tolerant of provocative student behaviour and committed to facilitating their students on all levels. With reference to the last two patterns, it can be claimed that the quality of teacher-student interaction would be greatly enhanced if teachers were to realise and critically analyse how they shape rules (Johnson & Reiman, 2007, p. 681).

Indeed, little is known about how teachers' dispositions influence how students learn to interact and develop their own values. Nevertheless, in both types of research, the need for the teachers to critically reflect on their manners and choices is crucial for a meaningful interaction with their students. Such meaningful interaction can represent a supportive environment of openness and trust for the students to develop their values with increasing autonomy in an increasingly complex social context.

5 Conclusions and Discussion

The meanings that education attributes to the concept of values have undoubtedly changed. Academic discourse and curricular tendencies seem to have shifted from the value of integration into the environment to the value of the autonomy of the individual, from the adherence to the past to critical thinking, from the discipline to social rules to individual responsibility, respect and cooperation.

Even though educational policies reconsider their orientations regarding values in education, the relevant movements (Value Education, Moral Development and Critical Pedagogy) do not represent integrating approaches to the field. They seem to lack either openness (Value Education) or trust (Moral Development and Critical Pedagogy), which are needed for the development of students' values. On the other hand, the research findings, as revealed in the present study, bring to light some common issues, and draw some major conclusions: First of all, teachers do infuse their values in classrooms through a variety of ways, even if they avoid involving themselves actively in the process of values communication by expressing their own values or bringing into question some values to be taught. Secondly, they seldom have an awareness of what they do in the processes of values communication, since they are deficient in realising and critically reflecting on how they shape their own commitments, beliefs, and values. Finally, although teachers avoid indoctrination, they seem not to adequately take into consideration the need for students to develop their own values and their personal identity with increasing autonomy based on a continuing dialogue with their own experiences as well as the existing societal values. However, some teachers do involve their students in the process of value communication, allowing them to express their own experiences, emotional needs and commitments through an open, supportive and reflective interaction. In this case, the process of value communication seems to become essential and meaningful, reflecting somewhat the Habermasian notion of 'communicative ethics'.

The above point is considered crucial by the author of the present paper. Values are to be developed through an active interaction of students and teachers in meaning making. The relational context promoted by the movement of Value Education, the argument-based moral reasoning promoted by the movement of Moral Development and the emancipatory demands of Critical Pedagogy are useful but not sufficient by themselves to the task of such a development. Although it is rarely articulated as such, a basic issue emerging from most types of research is the demand for an interweaving of openness and trust. Students' value development could be based on the open expression of their own value-commitments, but furthermore it should be ensured by the teachers' self-awareness, 'committed impartiality' (Kelly, 1986), responsibility and continuous reflection on their own practical decision, so that a mutual trust could be achieved. On the other hand, teachers seem to lack the education needed for such a demand.

Bearing in mind the educational needs as set by the current socio-cultural context, the various perspectives on values in education and the research findings, I concur that it is of utmost importance to include 'teaching values' in teacher education. Of course, this does not refer to the normative transfer of any set of values. So far, there is no consensus and a common ground for a shared value system, regardless of how desirable such a system would be. Including 'teaching values' in teacher education simply means that teachers should realise that teaching extends beyond the transmission of academic knowledge, and certainly beyond knowing how students learn. To paraphrase

VALUES IN TEACHING AND TEACHING VALUES 211

Dewey (1964), relying entirely, or even partly, on knowledge and the use of 'methods' is a fatal mistake for the best interests of education.

Whether teachers realise it or not, teaching is a value-laden process; consequently, they ought to learn how to identify and critically reflect on their own values, relating them to the real social contexts in which they live. This is needed specifically in Greece, where, as it has already been noted, the teaching of values 'is fragmentary and it more or less depends on the sensitivity of the educator ...' (CIDREE, 1994, p. 118). They also need to become aware of their own behaviours and choices, incorporating values in the teaching process. Prospective teachers should therefore be encouraged to discuss their experiences and practices, and be urged to identify practical examples of inconsistencies between their stated values and their behaviour or choices (Husu & Tirri, 2007). Moreover, prospective teachers as well as teacher educators need theoretical frameworks and tools, so that they would be able to deal with the issue of values in teaching. These theoretical frameworks and tools can also support them to develop the necessary skills to ensure balance between two orientations, which although seemingly contradictory are actually complementary: defending their own values honestly, without disguising them as absolute truths, and stimulating students to develop and defend their own personal values within a supportive environment of openness, flexibility and trust. If education is a game of continuous meaning making, teachers have to be simultaneously co-players and referees. Both roles call for high degrees of self-awareness, responsibility and professionalism.

Acknowledgement

This chapter originally appeared as: Frydaki, E. (2009) Values in teaching and teaching values: a review of theory and research, including the case of Greece, *Mediterranean Journal of Educational Studies*, Vol. 14(1), pp. 109–128. Reprinted here with permission from the publisher.

References

Akinoglu, O. (2004) *History, Education and Identity*. Paper presented at the Conference History Education and Society, 12–18 July, Ambleside, England.

Ball, A. F. (2000) Empowering pedagogies that enhance the learning of multicultural students, *Teachers College Record*, Vol. 102(6), pp. 1006–1034.

Berkowitz, M. W. (1997) *Integrating Structure and Content in Moral Education.* Paper presented at the Annual Meeting of the American Educational Research Association, 24–28 March, Chicago, USA.

Bills, L., & Husbands, C. (2004) *Analysing 'Embedded Values' in History and Mathematics Classrooms.* Paper presented at the Conference of the British Educational Research Association, 15–19 September, Manchester, England.

Blumenfeld, P. C., Hamilton, V. L., Wessels, K., & Falkner, D. (1979) Teaching responsibility to first graders, *Theory into Practice*, Vol. XVIII, pp. 174–180.

Boxall, W. (1995) Making the private public. In D. Thomas (ed.) *Teachers' Stories.* Buckingham: Open University Press.

Bruner, J. (1990) *Acts of Meaning.* London: Harvard University Press.

Butroyd, B. (1997) Are the values of secondary school teachers really in decline?, *Educational Review*, Vol. 49(3), pp. 251–258.

Chater, M. (2005) The personal and the political: notes on teachers' vocations and values, *Journal of Beliefs and Values*, Vol. 26(3), pp. 249–259.

Cohen, P. (1995) *The Content of their Character: Educators Find New Ways to Tackle Values and Morality.* Alexandria, VA: Association for Supervision and Curriculum Development.

Consortium of Institutions for Development and Research in Education in Europe (CIDREE) (1994) *Values Education in Europe: A Comparative Overview of a Survey of 26 Countries in 1993.* Slough: Cidree & Unesco.

Dewey, J. (1964) *John Dewey on Education: Selected Writings.* New York: Modern Library.

Ellsworth, E. (1989) Why doesn't this feel empowering? Working through the repressive myths of critical pedagogy, *Harvard Educational Review*, Vol. 59(3), pp. 297–324.

Ennis, C. D. (1994) Urban secondary teachers' value orientations: social goals for teaching, *Teaching and Teacher Education*, Vol. 10(1), pp. 109–120.

Ennis, C. D., Ross, L., & Chen, A. (1992) The role of value orientations in curricular decision making: a rationale for teachers' goals and expectations, *Research Quarterly for Exercise and Sport*, Vol. 63, pp. 38–47.

Fallona, C. (2000) Manner in teaching: a study in observing and interpreting teachers' moral virtues, *Teaching and Teacher Education*, Vol. 16(7), pp. 681–695.

Fenstermacher, G. D. (1999) *Method, Style, and Manner in Classroom Teaching.* Paper presented at the Annual Meeting of the American Educational Research Association, 19–23 April, Montreal, Canada.

Flouris, G. (1995) Non-alignment between educational goals, curriculum, and educational means: some aspects of educational inconsistency. In A. Kazamias & M. Kassotakis (eds.) Greek Education: *Perspectives of Reconstruction and Modernization* (in Greek). Athens: Seirios.

Flouris, G. (1997) The case of Greece: human rights in the educational legislation, school curriculum, teachers manuals and textbooks. In D. Evans, H. Grassler & J.

Pouwels (eds.) *Human Rights and Values Education in Europe*. Freibourg: Fillibach-Verlang.

Frydaki, E., & Mamoura, M. (2007) Values in the planned and delivered curriculum: the case of literature and history. In N. P. Terzis (ed.) *Education and Values in the Balkan Countries*. Thessaloniki: Publishing House Kyriakidis Brothers.

Frydaki, E., & Mamoura, M. (2008) Exploring teachers' value orientations in literature and history secondary classrooms, *Teaching and Teacher Education*, Vol. 24(6), pp. 1487–1501.

Gailbraith, R., & Jones, T. (1975) Teaching strategies for moral dilemmas: an application of Kohlberg's theory of moral development to the social studies classroom, *Social Education*, Vol. 39, pp. 16–22.

Gilligan, C. (1977) In a different voice: women's conceptualizations of self and morality, *Harvard Educational Review*, Vol. 47, pp. 481–517.

Gilligan, C. (1982, 1993) *In a Different Voice: Psychological Theory and Women's Development*. Cambridge, MA: Harvard University Press.

Giroux, H. A., & McLaren, P. L. (1989) *Critical Pedagogy, the State and Cultural Struggle*. New York: State University of New York Press.

Grossman, P. L., & Stodolsky, S. S. (1995) Content as context: the role of school subjects in secondary school teaching, *Educational Researcher*, Vol. 24(8), pp. 5–11.

Gudmundsdottir, S. (1990) Values in pedagogical content knowledge, *Journal of Teacher Education*, Vol. 41(3), pp. 44–52.

Halstead, M. J. (1996) Values and values education in schools. In M. J. Halstead & M. J. Taylor (eds.) *Values in Education and Education in Values*. London & Washington, DC: The Falmer Press.

Huitt, W. (2004) *Values*. Available online at http://www.edpsycinteractive.org/topics/affect/values.html

Husbands, C. (1996) *What is History teaching? Language, Ideas and Meaning in Learning about the Past*. Great Britain: Open University Press.

Husu, J., & Tirri, K. (2007) Developing whole school pedagogical values – a case of going through the ethos of good schooling, *Teaching and Teacher Education*, Vol. 23(4), pp. 390–401.

Johnson, L. E., & Reiman, A. (2007) Beginning teachers' disposition: examining the moral/ethical domain, *Teaching and Teacher Education*, Vol. 23(5), pp. 676–687.

Kassotakis, M. I. (2004) The curriculum reform of Greek secondary education during the period 1990–2002: attempts and problems. In T. Papakonstantinou & A. Lambraki-Paganou (eds.) *Study Programmes and Educational Work in Secondary Education* (in Greek). Athens: Athens University.

Kelly, T. (1986) Discussing controversial issues: four perspectives on the teacher's role, *Theory and Research in Social Education*, Vol. 14, pp. 113–138.

Kohlberg, L. (1969) Stage and sequence: the cognitive developmental approach to socialization. In D. Goslin (ed.) *Handbook of Socialization Theory and Research*. Chicago: Rand McNally.

Kohlberg, L. (1984) *The Psychology of Moral Development*. San Francisco, CA: Harper & Row.

Koutselini, M. (1997) Contemporary trends and perspectives of the curricula: towards a meta-modern paradigm for curriculum, *Curriculum Studies*, Vol. 5(1), pp. 87–101.

Linkona, T. (1993) The return of character education (the character education partnership Inc.), *Educational Leadership*, Vol. 51(3), pp. 6–11.

Linkona, T. (1997) Educating for character: a comprehensive approach. In A. Molnar (ed.) *The Construction of Children's Character*. Chicago: University of Chicago Press.

Lockwood, A. (1997) What is character education? In A. Molnar (ed.) *The Construction of Children's Character*. Chicago: University of Chicago Press.

Lovat, T., & Schofield, N. (1998) Values formation in citizenship education: a perspective and an empirical study, *Unicorn*, Vol. 24(1), pp. 46–53.

Maslow A. H. (1970) *Toward a Psychology of Being*. New York: D. Van Nostrand.

Maslow A. H. (1979) Humanistic education, *Journal of Humanistic Psychology*, Vol. 19, pp. 13–27.

Massialas, B. (1975) Inquiry into social values, feelings, and self: new helpful approaches. In B. Massialas, N. Sprague & J. Hurst (eds.) *Social Issues through Inquiry: Coping in an Age of Crises*. New Jersey: Prentice-Hall & Englewood Cliffs.

Massialas, B., & Flouris, G. (1994) *Education and the Emerging Concept of National Identity in Greece*. Paper presented at the Annual Conference of the Comparative and International Education Society, 21–24 March, San Diego, CA, USA.

McLaren, P. L. (1994) Foreword: critical thinking as a political project. In K. S. Walters (ed.) *Re-Thinking Reason, New Perspectives in Critical Thinking*. Albany: State University of New York Press.

Muchmore, J. A. (2001) The story of Anna: a life history study of the literacy beliefs and teaching practices of an urban high school English teacher, *Teacher Education Quarterly*, Vol. 28(3), pp. 89–110.

Noddings, N. (1995) *Philosophy of Education*. Boulder, CO: Westview Press.

Papoulia-Tzelepi, P. (1997) Human and children's rights as part of values education in Greek elementary school: the case of reading textbooks. In D. Evans, H. Grassler & J. Pouwels (eds.) *Human Rights and Values Education in Europe*. Freibourg: Fillibach-Verlang..

Parsons, T. (1951) *The Social System*. Glenchoe, IL: Free Press.

Pedagogical Institute (PI) (2000) *Curricula of Primary and Secondary Education, Theoretical Sciences*. Athens: Ministry of National Education and Religious Affairs.

Prawat, R. S. (1980) Teacher perceptions of student affect, *American Educational Research Journal*, Vol. 17, pp. 61–73.

Prencipe, A., & Helwing, C. (2002) The development of reasoning about the teaching of values in school and family contexts, *Child Development*, Vol. 73(3), pp. 841–856.

Pring, R. (1996) Values and education policy. In M. J. Halstead & M. J. Taylor (eds.) *Values in Education and Education in Values*. London & Washington, DC: The Falmer Press.

Richardson, V. (1993) *Continuity and Change in Teachers' Manner*. Paper presented at the Annual Meeting of the American Educational Research Association, Atlanta, GA, USA.

Rogers, C. (1961) *On Becoming a Person: A Therapist's View of Psychotherapy*. London: Constable.

Rogers, C. (1983) *Freedom to Learn*. Columbus, OH: Charles E. Merrill.

Shaw, M. D., Barry, A., & Mahlios, M. (2008) Preservice teachers' metaphors of teaching in relation to literacy beliefs, *Teachers and Teaching: Theory and Practice*, Vol. 14(1), pp. 35–50.

Shulman, L. S. (1986) Those who understand: knowledge growth in teaching, *Educational Researcher*, Vol. 15(2), pp. 4–14.

Slater, J. (1995) *Teaching History in the New Europe*. London: Cassell.

Thomas, M. R. (1992) The moral identity development in ethnic relations. In K. Schleicher & T. Kozma (eds.) *Ethnocentrism in Education*. New York: Peter Lang.

Veugelers, W. (2000) Different ways of teaching values, *Educational Review*, Vol. 52(1), pp. 37–46.

Veugelers, W., & Vedder, P. (2003) Values in teaching, *Teachers and Teaching: Theory and Practice*, Vol. 9(4), pp. 377–389.

Wardekker, W. (2004) Moral education and the construction of meaning, *Educational Review*, Vol. 56(2), pp. 183–192.

Wentzel, K. R. (1991) Social competence at school: relation between social responsibility and academic achievement, *Review of Educational Research*, Vol. 61, pp. 1–24.

Whiting, J. (1961) Socialization process and personality. In F. Hsu (ed.) *Psychological Anthropology*. Homewood, IL: Dorsey.

Wynne, E. (1997) For-character education. In A. Molnar (ed.) *The Construction of Children's Character*. Chicago: University of Chicago Press.

Xochellis, P. D. (2001) The education and in-service training of teachers in Greece: the present situation – concerns and debate – proposals. In N. P. Terzis (ed.) *Teacher Education in the Balkan Countries*. Thessaloniki: Balkan Society for Pedagogy and Education.

CHAPTER 12

Peace Education in Israel

Encounter and Dialogue

Dov Darom

1   Introduction

Issues of peace and war are not determined in the arena of education. Political, economic, military and even religious interests are far more powerful than 'mere education'. Nevertheless, education can have an impact on young people's ideas, views, beliefs and behaviour vis-à-vis questions such as stereotypic thinking, prejudice, de-legitimisation and even dehumanisation of the 'enemy', violence, the sanctity of human life and others. These are prerequisites of conflict situations and, as such, exert paramount influence on the state of mind of the people involved.

In Israel, some considerable experience has accumulated in the sphere of Peace Education. Ever since its foundation almost 50 years ago—and for many decades before that—Israel has been involved in a severe conflict with its Arab neighbours. This conflict is characterised not only by bloody military clashes and widespread terror, but also by frames of mind in which each side conceives the other as the enemy, as untrustworthy, treacherous, bent on 'our' total destruction and conceives itself as the victim with the monopoly of truth and justice on its own side.

It is this polarised 'black and white' mentality that efforts of Peace Education attempt to cope with. Let us go back in time a few years, before the courageous and wise leaders in our region—Rabin and Peres of Israel, King Hussein of Jordan and Arafat of the Palestinians—began their dialogue and signed partial or total peace agreements. Before this new and hopeful era, the major contact between Arabs and Jews was inside the borders of the state of Israel. Both groups were citizens of Israel, but nevertheless the atmosphere that prevailed was one of mutual prejudice, suspicion, distrust and hostility. Jewish stereotypic thinking considered Arabs as blood-thirsty terrorists, whereas the major Arab stereotype of Jews was one of brutal soldiers and settlers, denying the Palestinian people their land and independence. These stigmas are closely linked with the double role of Israeli Arabs—that of members of the Palestinian nation and that of citizens of the state of Israel.

© THE EURO-MEDITERRANEAN CENTRE FOR EDUCATION RESEARCH, UNIVERSITY OF MALTA, 1998
DOI: 10.1163/9789004506602_012

PEACE EDUCATION IN ISRAEL

Much has been written in Israel on the potentials and difficulties of direct Jewish-Arab encounters. Here are some of the major considerations proposed:

1. Inter-group tension breeds negative psychological frames of mind. Some of their direct expressions are stereotypic thinking, prejudices, attitudes (and behaviours) of discrimination, de-legitimisation of the 'other', hatred (Bar & Bargal, 1995). In an inter-group meeting, Shalvi (1996) said: 'One of the great challenges for education now, for both peoples, is to create a human version of each other to replace those stereotypes: This brings me back to the need for direct encounter, because there is no other way to break down stereotypes'. In the same meeting, Landau (1996) said: 'After decades of dehumanisation, the challenge before parents and teachers today, in both Israel and Palestine, is to find ways to re-humanise the former enemy. We need to develop effective pedagogical methods of confronting the negative stereotypes that have developed because of distance and estrangement between the two peoples' ... 'Simulation exercises and (in mixed encounters) role reversals can be helpful, if facilitated by trained, sensitive group leaders'.

2. Bargal (1992) describes workshops 'for improvement of inter-group relations and minimising prejudice and discrimination'. These are based on theoretical and applied models in fields such as group dynamics, attitude changes in small groups, group therapy, and problem-solving groups (Lewin, 1946; Lippett, 1949; Rogers, 1983).

3. Bar & Idi (1995) wrote as follows: 'The encounter is one of the channels of political education, by means of an inter-group process, that focuses on personal and educational growth of the individual in confrontation with the Jewish-Arab conflict which involves two peoples (in contrast to the erroneous conception, widespread among Jews, that this is a "Palestinian problem".

> The aim of the encounter is often described as dealing with the inter-cultural and inter-ethnic conflict toward the development of a pluralistic culture, based on the legitimisation of the Other and on respect for his culture. (Director General of the Ministry of Education, 1.3.1984)

4. Bar & Idi (1995) sum up their experiences of many years in the field of Arab-Jewish encounters:
   - The encounter is the means not merely to talk about the conflictual issues but to 'live' them directly and concretely.
   - In the live encounter, it is possible to learn (i.e., experience and get to know) what we do not know about ourselves and about the Other,

including emotions, attitudes, prejudices, stereotypes (of ourselves and of the other).

– By means of the various structured and unstructured activities, the participants are exposed to meaningful experiences vis-à-vis concrete individuals in the other group. These confront the individual participant with his/her ability to internalise complex reality.

– The encounter enables individuals to confront the gap between good intentions, statements and headlines in which they believe and their ability to experience the direct implications (on feelings, behaviour and attitudes) of the complex reality on themselves, their group and the other group. The participant experiences the tension of polarity, which is part and parcel of the ability to live with the conflict: thoughts and attitudes/emotions and behaviour; closing oneself/opening up; similarities/differences; uniformity/pluralism; one-dimensional perception/ complex multi-dimensional perception; specific/universal; one-sidedness/mutuality; harmony/conflict; empathic/judgemental; near/far; victim/aggressor; violence/dialogue; powerlessness and despair/hope.

Against such a background, who are the agents for peace education in Israel?

1. The Ministry of Education established the 'Unit for Democracy and Co-existence'. This unit is active in producing curricular material dealing with relevant issues of democracy, peace and co-existence. It should be noted that the Ministry's initiative came after some public opinion research found considerable correlation among Jewish high-school pupils between high hostility to Arabs and low commitment to principles of democracy.

2. Principals and teachers in high schools in general—and in the more progressive Kibbutz schools in particular—who are inspired by their own commitment to peace and education for peace.

3. A number of special institutions, such as the Van Leer Institute, the Adam Institute for Peace and Democracy, the Jewish-Arab 'Oasis for Peace' school and the 'Kibbutz Artzi' Kibbutz-Movement's Jewish-Arab Centre for Peace at Givat Haviva, whose programme 'Children Teaching Children' (CTC) I am about to describe.

I became acquainted with this programme in the summer of 1993, when I was invited to facilitate a workshop at the summer meeting of Jewish and Arab teachers active in CTC. We worked together for 8 hours and for me this was a meaningful experience. I met a group of highly motivated people, profoundly

PEACE EDUCATION IN ISRAEL

committed to Arab-Jewish peace and co-existence, most of them beginning their second or third year in the project.

Ever since, I have been following their work, talking in depth to the project's leaders and recently attending a series of classroom encounters as a participant observer: I am writing this paper as an outside observer of CTC, appreciating their work but not actively involved in the project in any way.

'Children Teaching Children' began in 1987 with two classes. In 1996, it encompassed 28 schools, 38 classes, 80 teachers and 1500 pupils, mainly from junior high schools. This is a two-year programme, based on a series of regular encounters between pupils from two parallel classes—one from an Arab school and one from a Jewish school—as well as teachers. These encounters are run on the following lines:

- Meetings of the teachers—once a fortnight for a complete school year (in the wake of an intensive joint learning experience during the summer);
- A short period of work in the original uni-national homerooms—in preparation for the real encounter;
- During most of the school year, the two parallel groups meet each other one week and meet in their separate homerooms the other week, each meeting lasting for two school lessons.

One of the unique features of the programme is the importance it attaches not only to the bi-national encounters but to the processing of the encounter experience in the children's original homerooms. The present director of CTC thinks that the most important steps in reinforcing the lessons of CTC occur in the subsequent homeroom sessions, where the children process 'their impressions from the bi-national encounter, explore the complexity of their own identity and learn about the other side, while beginning better to understand themselves (Dichter, 1996). Bar & Idi (1995) add that the uni-national homeroom sessions enable the children 'to release pressure, to express more freely their feelings of disappointment, anger, and confusion in a climate of support and reinforcement'. I was told by the coordinator of one of the mixed groups that their joint teachers' group has decided to have bi-national encounters only once a month, which act as a stimulus for the in-depth processing taking place in the three subsequent homeroom activities (Feldesh, 1996).

The objectives of the CTC programme focus on creating personal acquaintance among pupils as well as teachers, promoting deeper awareness of the complexities of the Arab-Israeli conflict as well as of each other's daily existence, internalisation of pluralistic values, and deepening the commitment to democratic principles.

It should be noted that special attention is paid to the educational climate of the meetings. CTC stresses:

- the promotion of an educational environment conducive to openness and personal growth of both teachers and pupils;
- the development of an inter-personal dialogue within the context of an ongoing conflict;
- the exploration of the two different group identities—one's own as well as the other's—and discovering similarities and differences in a supportive climate. This type of climate enables the participants to have meaningful insights of a personal, inter-personal and inter-group nature.

The programme is based on principles of Humanistic Education (Combs, 1974; Rogers, 1983). It is process-orientated and founded on dialogue furthering experiential learning, combining personal and inter-personal emotional experiences, cognitive learning experiences as regard the cultural, social and political aspects of the conflict, confrontation with values dilemmas, dealing with values of empathy, acceptance, pluralism and democracy. Figure 12.1 represents such holistic learning processes, integrating cognitive, affective, values and behavioural domains (Darom, 1988).

The 'curriculum' of the programme is an on-going joint creation. 'The particular curriculum in CTC is to be tailored to the particular schools, teachers and pupils involved. In other words, beyond general guidelines and a given, rather flexible, framework the programme is created locally in the team-meetings, in response to the needs of the pupils and to incidents within or between the classes. The essence of CTC is the on-going creation of an educational programme based on dialogue between its participants' (Hartman, 1994).

The teachers' meetings are in fact an ongoing workshop, processing the issues, needs and difficulties experienced in the previous children's encounters, and planning future meetings accordingly. CTC has resource hand books but has no 'textbook' (Hartman, 1994). Needless to say, not all teachers can adapt themselves to this open approach to classroom activities. At all stages of the planning process, special emphasis is devoted to issues such as stereotypes and stereotypic thinking, conflict resolution, fears and anxieties on personal and group levels, self-image.

The value of holistic educational processes is derived directly from their humanistic nature. If education is to focus on human beings, then educators must relate to learners in their totality. Humans are not divided into separate compartments; rather, cognitive learning, emotional experiences, values and day-ta-day behaviour are deeply intertwined in each learner. These factors mutually influence one another. Any educator who decides to relate selectively

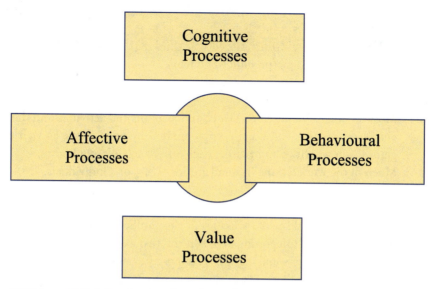

FIGURE 12.1 Holistic learning: interdependence of processes

to portions of these spheres of humanness is likely to render the educational process less effective.

What then are the guidelines of the programme?

1. Teachers adopt the role of group-facilitators. This is not always an easy process. It means finding new balances between democracy and hierarchy, between pupils' initiative and those of teachers, between openness allowing freer expression of emotions as opposed to traditional, primarily cognitive studying. Many teachers—but not all—express their satisfaction at learning new methods and attitudes, which have a positive influence on their teaching far beyond CTC.
2. The on-going teachers' workshop, processing the encounters, planning future activities and deepening their own inter-personal trust and cooperation are the core of the programme.
3. Uni-national and bi-national activities play equally important roles in the total process.
4. The encounters take place in groups smaller than total classrooms. Usually, the two parallel classes are each divided into three sub-groups (approximately 12 to 15 pupils) and the actual encounter takes place in the framework of two sub-groups—one from each national group.
5. The programme goes through a number of stages:
   – Introduction to the CTC programme
   – Beginning of acquaintance
   – Deepening of acquaintance

- Group dynamics
- Image of Self and Other (stereotypic thinking)
- Emotional barriers (prejudice and fear)
- Conflict resolution
- Summing up

6. Most meetings are based on structured, experiential activities and their verbal processing. These are complemented by texts, films, as well as games, 'fun' activities and visiting each other's schools and homes.

7. Much of the work is done in small groups of 2, 3, or 4 individuals.

There are a number of dilemmas continually facing CTC:
- To what extent should political issues of the conflict be dealt with explicitly? The balance of integrating between the two extremes—emphasis on personal and inter-personal matters as opposed to a study-course in political aspects of the conflict—is not always easy to find.
- Should participation be voluntary or should the meetings take place with classes in their entirety? The first has obvious short-term advantages, but what is the point of addressing only the previously convinced. The second alternative is more difficult, but it would bring the message of peace to wider populations in their organic classrooms.
- How can the language difficulty be overcome? Most Arabs have a considerable knowledge of Hebrew, but only few Jews speak Arabic. If the language of the encounter is Hebrew, all participants understand what is said, but the lack of symmetry between Arab minority and Jewish majority is reinforced.

Finally, let us consider some of the outcomes of these encounters (Bar & Bargal, 1995; Bar & Idi, 1995). In pre- and post-programme measurements as well as comparisons with control groups, the results were as follows:

1. Both sides report an increase in inter-personal acquaintance, knowledge and awareness of relevant issues, and a decrease in feelings of mutual strangeness and alienation. On the other hand, there was no significant increase in interaction outside the programme.

2. Both sides gain a more realistic conception of the conflict in its complexity. They report a better understanding of the severity of the conflict, which is painful to both national groups; a significant rise in the legitimation that each side grants to the national aspirations of the other; a growing awareness that each group not only suffers pain but also inflicts pain on the other; a better realisation in the Jewish group that they themselves play an active part in the conflict.

3. A significant decrease was measured in feelings of personal and group hatred toward the other national group.

PEACE EDUCATION IN ISRAEL

4. In addition, there was a rise in feelings of optimism toward finding positive solutions to the conflict, a rise in feelings of similarity with the other group and a decrease in misgivings and anxiety as to future encounters between Arabs and Jews.

5. The ongoing CTC programme is more effective in bringing about positive change than programmes conducting one-time encounter workshops, usually lasting for about three days.

These are some of the outcomes on the macro-research level. I should like to add some of my observations on the micro level representing one particular CTC unit. Eight grade children were asked at the conclusion of the programme: 'What did you learn about yourself? What did you learn about others?' Some of their answers are given in Table 12.1.

Some children summed up their learnings in a more poetic style. One girl wrote 'CTC is a flower, and we watered it'. One of the boys came to a very realistic conclusion: 'There is a crack in the wall, but the wall still exists'. One kid said: 'This encounter should only be a beginning. Now I want to meet other groups, such as new immigrants from Ethiopia and Russia, religious youth, and other sectors of Israeli society, that I have—as yet—not encountered'. Some

TABLE 12.1   Children's answers at the end of CTC programme

About myself	About others
'Not to reach hasty conclusions before examining all aspects'.	'To break stigmas on others'.
'To be open to different points of view'.	'I have met Arabs with whom I found a common language'.
'That I am able to associate with children from diverse cultural background'.	'Not only Jews suffer pain inflicted by Arabs, but Jews also inflict pain on Arabs'.
'That I can freely express my thoughts, as well as understand and even agree with the other side'.	'All in all, they are quite similar to us'.
'Not to hate human beings'.	'They are eager for good relations with us, just as we are'.
'To listen to opinions different from my own'.	'They have fears just like us. It is a good feeling that "we are not alone in this boat"'.
'Some of my prejudices have disappeared'.	'I learned about Jewish women: they are not as free as I had thought previously'.

children related to two especially meaningful encounters, both in extremely painful circumstances—one after Prime Minister Rabin was murdered and one after a particularly severe Palestinian terrorist massacre.

At an end-of-the-year summing up meeting, the teachers also asked themselves: 'What did we learn about our pupils? What did we learn about ourselves? What did we learn about our partners?' Here are some of the points that were made:

- The kids are open, eager for new experiences, motivated to meet children 'from the other group'.
- They learned to listen to each other, to accept people different from themselves.
- The personal and inter-personal issues were more meaningful to them than the political issues.
- Relating to stereotypes gave way to relating to human beings. Our own teamwork—our creating a real support group—was highly important to us.
- The key to positive relationships—in education and otherwise—is openness and sincerity.

One of the Jewish teachers made this poignant comment: 'Some of our emphases, concepts and norms of behaviour are different from theirs. But then we somehow expect them to be similar to us. For instance, at one of the joint meetings at the Arab school, the rooms were not ready, the crayons were not prepared—things that we call 'bad organisation'. On the other hand, the meal they prepared for us and their warm hospitality were just wonderful. At the time I was angry, but in time I have processed my anger and become more accepting. I am learning to accept differences and rid myself of unrealistic expectations for similarity ('they should be more like us')'.

This expresses a higher level of encounter and dialogue. The present director of CTC, Dichter, told me that the coordinators of CTC are at present working intensively on problems such as these. How can we turn the encounters into in-depth processes of accepting diversity—even antagonism—without which real partnership is quite impossible? How much leadership am I prepared to share? In other words—our aim is no longer mere 'co-existence' but real 'co-living'.

There can be two diametrically opposed approaches to peace education. One would be—as one of the CTC activists told me after a visit to North Ireland—along the lines of 'Good fences make good neighbours'. The other is furthering encounter and dialogue, aimed at 'rehumanising' the other side of the conflict. This second direction may be meaningful not only in Israel, but in many of the other warring areas on our troubled globe. Let me conclude with an anecdote quoted by Landau (1996):

PEACE EDUCATION IN ISRAEL

Shuki told a story about his experience in the Lebanon war in 1982, when his unit was ordered to clear a Palestinian refugee camp of PLO fighters. Shuki and his comrades fought their way into the camp, shooting as they went, taking care not to harm civilians. Suddenly two refugees came in their direction carrying an object and yelling at the soldiers. Shuki and his buddies screamed back at them, urging them to get out of the way. Since the two men were only about 20 yards distant, the soldiers could quickly make out that they were carrying a crate of Pepsi Cola and could decipher their screams as invitations to have a drink. Shuki later reflected: "If they had been 200 yards away, we would have shot at them and been glad to hit them." And he asked: "How far away does a human being have to be before he becomes a target? How close must he be before we see he is human?"

Acknowledgement

This chapter originally appeared as: Darom, D. (1998) Peace education in Israel: encounter and dialogue, *Mediterranean Journal of Educational Studies*, Vol. 3(1), pp. 129–139. Reprinted here with permission from the publisher.

References

Bar, H., & Bargal. D. (1995) *To Live with Conflict: Encounter of Jewish and Palestinian Youth, Israeli Citizens* (in Hebrew). Jerusalem: Guttman Institute for Applied Social Research.

Bar, H., & Idi, E. (1995) *The Jewish Arab Encounter* (in Hebrew). Jerusalem: Henrietta Szold Institute for Research in the Behavioural Sciences.

Bargal, D. (1992) Conflict management workshops for Palestinian and Jewish youth: a framework for planning, intervention and evaluation, *Social Work with Groups*, Vol. 15(1), pp. 51–68.

Combs, A. W. (1974) *Humanistic Teacher Education*. Fort Collins, CO: Shields.

Darom, D. (1988) Freedom and commitment – values issues in humanistic education (in Hebrew), *Journal of Humanistic Education and Development*, Vol. 26, pp. 98–108.

Dichter, S. (1996) Private Communication.

Feldesh, D. (1996) Private Communication.

Hartman S. (1994) *Children Teaching Children: Handbook*. Givat Haviva: Givat Haviya Institute.

Landau, Y. (1996) Rehumanising the enemy and confronting ourselves: challenges for educators in an era of peace, *Palestine Israel Journal of Politics, Economics and Culture*, Vol. 3, pp. 67–70.

Lewin, K. (1946) Action research and problems of minority groups. In D. Bargal (ed.) *Conflict Resolution* (in Hebrew). Jerusalem: Keter.

Lippitt, R. (1949) *Training in Community Relations*. New York: Harper & Row.

Rogers, C. (1983) *Freedom to Learn for the 80's*. Columbus, OH: Merill.

Shalvi. A. (1996) Roundtable – education for peace, *Palestine Israel Journal of Politics, Economics and Culture*, Vol. 3, pp. 58–66.

CHAPTER 13

The Birth of 'Citizenship and Constitution' in Italian Schools

A New Wall of Competences or Transition to Intercultural Education?

Sandra Chistolini

1 Introduction: Triads Spanned by System Competences

It seems to have become almost impossible to talk about education and teaching without referring to the abilities which should constitute the new ID, with which a European citizen presents himself to the world. This study analyses the current situation in order to outline the present and future of a Europe that is increasingly trying to communicate, better and better, values drawn from common historical and cultural roots.

Reading the news, aided by telecommunications and the transparency of online documents, often in the various languages of the countries of the European Union (EU), necessitates an initial selection that corresponds with this article's proposed research approach.

Reading, selecting and planning are part of the educational policy we are experiencing and from which emerges clearly enough the intention of achieving ambitious objectives. They are, on the one hand, a logical consequence of the development determined by globalisation, while, on the other hand, they are the 'structures' conceived to manage a multiplicity of elements which have to be dealt with. To convey what the cultures of Europe have produced in the course of time requires not only the structural and formal command of a language, but, more importantly, it questions our willingness to be in a world in which civilisations must meet, even if, historically, they have not always followed the same path. To understand, in a European context, where we are going and which skills we have to develop, as teachers, students, citizens and people belonging to different traditions and cultures, means that our human and professional training should aim at combining our legacy from the past with the present, in order to enrich our common human heritage.

A Europe of knowledge is an urgency, not just a computerised slogan. It is essential to interact with this situation in order to uphold the revitalisation, in European universities, and try to propel them toward a better future. Science and technology are committed to accepting the challenge launched by

© THE EURO-MEDITERRANEAN CENTRE FOR EDUCATION RESEARCH, UNIVERSITY OF MALTA, 2009
DOI: 10.1163/9789004506602_013

This is an open access chapter distributed under the terms of the CC BY-NC 4.0 License.

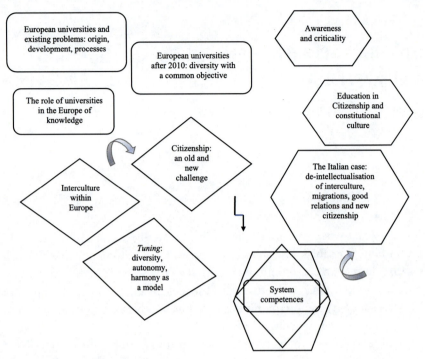

FIGURE 13.1   The fundamental theme

a culture conceived as a connective tissue, uniting peoples and traditions. If interculture involves educating people toward dialogue, citizenship means establishing the rules for living together—valuing each person's capacities—as individuals and as part of a community and a State, to deal with institutions and achieve justice in an ethically sound society.

The rings of knowledge, interculture and citizenship intertwine in the Europe we are building, starting from the universities and aiming to include the whole of society (see Figure 13.1). It is not a question of standardisation, but rather of making the training systems consistent and mutually compatible, thereby avoiding the fragmentation and the limits stemming from multiple approaches. This undertaking is certainly as arduous as it is interesting. Intellectual evaluations and inventions will have to come to terms with the exchange of knowledge made possible through international communications.

2   The European University and Existing Problems: Origins, Development, Processes

Among the oldest universities are Al Karaouine, Morocco University, founded in 859; Al-Azhar, Cairo University, Egypt, founded in 988; the University of

THE BIRTH OF 'CITIZENSHIP AND CONSTITUTION' IN ITALIAN SCHOOLS   229

Bologna, Italy, founded in 1088; Oxford University, England, founded around 1096; and Paris University, founded in 1150. One can observe how the culture of Africa, facing the Mediterranean, was linked to European culture, hereby passing through Italy.

In the 7th century, the Aristotelian system encountered Arabian culture and the intellectual osmosis between West and East, Christianity and Islam, generated a profitable exchange of scientific and philosophical knowledge. The Syrians, disciples of the Greeks, taught the Arabs to appreciate the classics and preserve ancient science. In the East, the Abassid Caliphs created a flourishing tradition with rich university libraries in Baghdad, whereas in the West the Caliphate of Cordova revised and disseminated Greek thought. From India to Egypt to Spain, the Muslim Empire combined elements of Hellenistic and Persian civilisation with Indian culture. In the 12th and 13th centuries, the Crusades and the Turkish and Mongol expansions marked the political and military decline of the great caliphates and the transfer of cultural tradition to the Latin peoples. The Arabian philosophy of Avicenna and Averroës compared Aristotle to the Koran and produced its own perceptions of the universe. Christian scholars translated the major philosophical and scientific works from Arabian into Latin and, in Toledo and Sicily, learned Arabs and Jews met at conferences.

The *universitas magistrorum et scholarium*, the association of students in Bologna and professors in Paris, is one of the most significant hallmarks of higher studies of the 11th and 12th centuries. The students, more than the professors, are the ones who gained autonomy from the Municipalities, by appealing to the Holy See for justice. The Archdeacon of Bologna quickly took on the right to award *licentia*. Also, at the University of Paris, officially recognised by the King of France, the exercise of jurisdiction was assigned to the Bishop's representative, the 'Chancellor'. Quite often, universities appealed to the Pope to assert their rights, sometimes privileges, with respect to local authorities.

The ups and downs that characterised 19th century Europe yielded the great models of English, German and Scottish universities, which were to be exported throughout the world. Models derived from the liberal elites: the English, more concerned with the quality of teaching and teacher-student relations, and the German, more oriented toward knowledge and science (*Wissenschaft*); the university was supposed to serve the professional needs of society and the State, an idea already present in the Universities of Padua and Bologna. But German universities confirmed this function and extended *professional needs* to the economic and industrial world and the technological society.

In 1810, Karl Wilhelm von Humboldt founded the University of Berlin as a place for studying classical culture, pursuing the ideal of the integral, humanistic and harmonious education (*Bildung*) of the inner being; teachers enjoyed teaching freedom and dedicated themselves to study and scholarship.

A different situation developed in universities of North European that were completely swallowed up by the new era. The Scottish universities opened up more to the industrial revolution, by producing engineers and scientists, concentrating on *research* and *teaching*, taking up, to a certain extent, the German meritocratic approach.

In 1896, the Aberdare Report on English universities showed a change in the perception of higher education. The report stated that it was important to adapt university courses to the country's circumstances; and making them more practical meant paying adequate attention to the nation's commercial and professional life, so as to favour the careers of university graduates. Oxford and Cambridge were seen as the ivory towers of knowledge and scholarship. Knowledge, attention and interaction among people are the salient features of British universities, to which are added nobility of spirit and the formation of character. Newman further refined this model, by emphasising the value of aesthetic considerations and the education of feelings. If upholding person-to-person relations was relevant in England, in Germany and Scotland priority was given to objectives such as the development of modern knowledge and need for the correct academic responses to the social demands of the State. A kind of dualism was clearly outlined between individual and social needs for growth. Even today, one asks what a university is and wonders if it is still an institution that educates toward intellectual leadership, if it is a centre in which independent thought and critical judgement are encouraged.

Although many universities broadly pursue these aims, interesting disparities, dependent on the general educational approach, can always be noted. During the decade 1950–1960, strong economic growth soon turned the universities into mass institutions. The growth in enrolments led to the renewal of the university structure and system that could no longer meet the above-mentioned needs. The increased number of courses, the raised expectations and the demand for greater professionalism constituted a call, as well as a duty, for universities to close the gap between theoretical education and the workplace, and define continuous courses for the training and utilisation of human resources. Around 1990, the practical idea spread that those teaching at university must conduct the courses and also do research, without which they would risk remaining at a standstill in relation to theories that had developed and opened new frontiers of knowledge.

3   European Universities after 2010: Diversity with a Common Objective

European youth policies go beyond education. In March 2005, the heads of State and government adopted the *European Youth Pact*, which outlined a series of common principles concerning the creation of youth work opportunities. The basic skills that educational systems should guarantee were specified and the need for a balance between working life and family was emphasised, thereby taking into account the female population. More specifically, the EU 'Youth' programme promotes active participation in society and the project aims at reinforcing the feeling of European citizenship in young people and developing in them the spirit of initiative, creativity and an entrepreneurial vision. Europe's investment in this project is about 0.9 billion euro for the period 2007–2013.

At the end of the second millennium, European universities are in the process of realising the proposals of the Bologna Declaration (1999), as well as attempting to open the national frontiers of academic culture.

It should be borne in mind that the Bologna Declaration represents the goal of the European movement which, in the previous decade through the mobility of Erasmus, had already started fostering a feeling of 'Europeanness' that brought the peoples of the European Community closer together. Even before this, international understanding and contacts, at the university level, were favoured, above all, by the Foreign Ministries, which also permitted free movement even in non-Community countries through agreements between the individual States. For example, Hungary, Poland and Romania entered into the agenda of European Community students and university professors, through the procedures agreed to between the Ministries and the universities.

Between 1970 and 1980, these exchanges (conducted in a third language, often English or French) had already included the study of the local language, participation in university lectures, sharing leisure time, visits to places of particular cultural significance in the host country, and the creation of friendships between European youth, without East or West European divisions.

Agreements set up by the central governments' education systems made the principle of rapprochement of the peoples operative, starting from youth education, in accordance with peace policies, the defence of freedom and democracy and the awareness, among the young, of sharing a common destiny. After the Second World War, with the signing of the Rome Treaties of the European Economic Community (EEC) in 1957 and the European Atomic Energy Community, Euratom, the signatories, inspired by the same ideal, decided on common action to ensure economic and social progress, by eliminating barriers and divisions.

The cultural effect of the economic agreements of the 1950s did not take hold until the Bologna Declaration (1999), recognises the diversities of culture, language and higher education systems in the various countries as a fundamental value, a general reference framework that the creation of a common space must necessarily take into account in the attempt to define new education curricula.

Universities carry out a central role in the Europe of knowledge through research and teaching, together with the equally important and significant task of innovation (European Councils of Stockholm 2001, and Barcelona 2002). The democratic principles that guide the strategy are those of proportionality and subsidiarity, while the basic factor of the Lisbon method for extending European research is the comparative evaluation, benchmarking, of research policies (European Commission, 2002).

4 The Role of Universities in the Europe of Knowledge

European documents reflect on the historical and cultural reasons that made European universities exemplary places of education for the entire world. For over eight hundred years, European universities have encouraged scientific research, worked toward the emergence of a tolerant civil society, far from dogmatism and totalitarianism, prepared the young to take up their social roles for the economic and political improvement of peoples and States. This applied to the past. As for the present and the future, the challenges posed by the 21st century are perhaps more arduous and include the issues of climatic change, the energy crisis, population decrease and aging, and the speed of technical revolutions.

To explain the great upheavals in terms of economic interdependence and social inequality is not, however, enough to guarantee social cohesion. Identifying a problem does not in itself mean knowing, understanding and communicating it. Understanding presupposes experience and precedes communication. Those who focus on a problem pose a question of rationality and, in some cases, ethics. They call other people to collaborate in order to present the solutions, so that others may participate in their experiences, which can become a common cognitive heritage.

With regard to the hermeneutics of understanding, Habermas, in *Knowledge and Human Interests* (published in Italian in 1970), expressed the important concept of the emergence of life and its fundamental significance in the study of the structure of the human sciences. To be involved in life and have an influence over it is the problem of scholars, scientists and politicians. Inevitably, every judgement will be conditioned by a person's individual characteristics, culture and historical context. Awareness of this conditioning helps one to understand the contents of the evaluation and does not eliminate the need for universal validity. W. Dilthey (1883) and C. S. Peirce (1933) had dealt extensively with the contrast between vital relations and scientific objectivity, in order to remain in the context of Habermas's statements, without, nevertheless, leaving aside the objectivism of hermeneutic knowledge. Objectification is part of a symbolic, inter-subjective connection, both binding and unavoidable, and for understanding to occur it is necessary, in a given situation, for two parties to communicate in a language which, in the end, is shared and becomes indivisible (cf. Habermas, 1973, pp. 179–180).

The concept of European Space for Higher Education refers to the knowledge society and the creation of opportunities in science, development, technology and innovation. If we talk about the knowledge society, we cannot avoid discussing the theory of knowledge and, if this is reduced to a theory of science, we would be going back to the old positivism which, according to Habermas, was brilliantly contradicted by Peirce and Dilthey. The return to self-understanding and reflection means taking up again the principle which harmonises language, action and experience, according to the distinction between the instrumental action, of the natural sciences, and the communicative action, of the human sciences. People are interested in regulating their relationships through language that connects symbols, actions and expressions; so that they can determine concepts of the world and give rise to human interactions, in which the protagonists are the socialised persons who communicate their lives.

The problem for science is not so much proclaiming its neutrality as searching for conditions that make research possible and, thus, a priori conditions of knowledge. The two-fold objective of economic success and social stability in Europe cannot disregard the relationship between the sciences, only partially dealt with by encouraging interdisciplinary research.

If we consider science, economy and society as three specific units, we realise that they are only the columns and sentinels of world development. These three factors define the level of competition among groups that have the power of information. Could all knowledge possibly have the same level of significance? No, this does not happen. Instead, there is supremacy of one kind of knowledge over another; this supremacy, called 'par excellence', is defined by science, put into circulation by economy and solidified into society. Institutions and persons reach this excellence when they are within the same set path, shared at the highest levels of social and political consensus. These paths are often selected based on economic assets. Cultural quality and financial quantity do not always agree.

Despite the high quality of scientific publications, the evaluation of the scarcely competitive state of European universities, compared to those of their major world partners, constantly poses questions of a methodological nature about how to:

– reach sustainable financial levels in, and ensure efficient spending of funds by, the universities;

- guarantee autonomy and professionalism in the academic and managerial worlds;
- concentrate sufficient resources and create the necessary conditions so that universities can attain and develop excellence;
- improve the contribution of universities, with respect to their needs and local and regional strategies;
- establish closer cooperation between universities and businesses for a better dissemination and utilisation of new knowledge in the economic market and society as a whole;
- make the European space of higher education, coherent, compatible and competitive, according to the Bologna Declaration, like the creation of a new European space for research.

The Europe of knowledge, based on the economy and society, combines four interdependent factors: production, transmission, dissemination, innovation. These factors influence each other in the sense that production is always in search of vaster markets and markets require new products to feed consumerism.

The new patterns of production, transmission and application propose the enlargement of the international context. The Bologna Declaration generated a process that should not lead to the uniformity or standardisation of the national educational systems, but should respect their autonomy and diversity. That is why one speaks of convergence, to be fostered through: the creation of a framework of excellence; the availability of efficient structures for management and practices; and the development of interdisciplinary skills.

The framework of excellence concerns each subject and is measured on a European, not national, level. As regard the structures, decisional processes should be rendered effective through the remuneration of services, accreditation and going beyond the pure academic tradition. As for interdisciplinary skills and faculty-wide objectives, universities must leave behind the logic of single discipline research and open up to advanced research, necessitated by the complexity of the problems; individual disciplines can offer their specific contributions without omitting the academic comparison between the sciences.

During the annual meeting in London, in July 2007, to review the progress made in relation to the Bologna Declaration, in the *Stocktaking Report,* there was a call for flexible higher education courses, accompanied by procedures for recognising the learning carried out in non-university contexts. As a result of this, we can see that, for some years now in Italy, efforts are being made to accept the principle of flexibility of training careers. Recognition of skills accrued through non-traditional studies are gradually being recognised.

THE BIRTH OF 'CITIZENSHIP AND CONSTITUTION' IN ITALIAN SCHOOLS   235

Since 2005, Italy has started simplifying the transition from the first to the second cycle of university studies; increasing internationalisation; strengthening university-industry contacts; and activating new PhD institutes. The challenges still facing the Italian system: unfocused studies; attainment of a degree within the prescribed times; improving employment levels for those who have 3-year degrees; internationalising the university system (Rauhvargers, 2007).

5   Interculture within Europe

The European Council meeting in Strasburg in 1981 to discuss *L'Éducation des Enfants des Travailleurs Migrants en Europe: l'Interculturalisme et la Formation des Enseignants*, introduced the general character of intercultural education, which was defined as education for all, democratic education, quality education and teaching children to be open-minded toward others (see Porcher, 1981).

The reference to children of migrant workers as a field of action for intercultural education was quite customary at that time and is still a constant in pedagogical studies directed at asserting the principle of equal educational opportunities, to be achieved in multiple forms. There are discussions about the teaching strategies to assess how the principle was pursued, achieved and, possibly, disregarded.

From 1944 to date, four wide-ranging themes have been at the heart of the international scientific debate, which aimed at heightening teachers' awareness of:

– the values of peace, democracy and justice, equal opportunities (around 1960);
– students with specific needs (around 1970);
– multicultural education (around 1990);
– education toward citizenship, starting from about 2000 (Chistolini, 2007).

From a theoretical point of view, the studies of comparative and intercultural teaching mark the rise of a neo-criticism concerned with examining educational systems that define themselves as democratic, although presenting a low level of cultural pluralism. These systems are so monocultural and monoconfessional as to have crossed over into totalitarianism and State ideology, in the most glaring cases in the history of education over the last fifty years.

Subjects such as cultural anthropology, ethnology, and human geography are not sufficient to develop an understanding of other peoples and make knowledge an instrument for overcoming racial prejudices and cultural stereotypes. The comparativist Holmes spoke of eliminating error in the context of comparing educational policies. The critical view of interculture leads to the denunciation of the social injustice produced by the educational systems imprisoned in the selection of excellence, the guiding principle of new educational policies. This is one of the contradictions arising from the comparison of the model produced by the Bologna Declaration and the intercultural dimension of Europe in the preceding decade. From quality education we have sunk to competitive education, from cosmopolitan Europe, we have passed to Europe as the beacon of the world, so we should not be surprised at seeing the ancient ghosts of intolerance and exclusion reappear, just as the globalisation of information and knowledge is being proclaimed.

6   Citizenship, an Old and New Challenge

From cross-cultural studies, the analysis of migratory movements and phenomena and the identification of the interdependence of culture, society and personality emerges the material which provides the acid test for teaching's basic premises.

Breaking with traditional interpretative models is the most interesting challenge facing contemporary education. The children of migrant workers are no longer to be treated interculturally, but rather recognised as citizens of the State; an immigrant and his family do not live in the suburbs and are no longer products of the metropolitan ghetto, they attain social consensus and cultural inclusion; a person does not just belong to the restricted group that favours, or hinders, his/her growth, but is instead part of a world community, without borders; the village is not moving toward the world, it is the world which is becoming a global village; the flow that led from economic poverty to wealth and social success has been overturned; wealth buys shops and services, thereby distorting the identity of continuously changing European cities; recognising oneself is more difficult than knowing oneself, in a context in which the rules are no longer to be presumed, but rather to be totally established.

In 1964, N. M. Gordon published an important book about assimilation in America, revealing the problems of citizenship of new immigrants, who were asked to adhere fully to the United States cultural model, often ignoring the nostalgia for a far-away land and family members, they might never see again. Foreigners had already become citizens of overseas countries, in which the period of interculture had passed rapidly (Taft, 1966). This reference to the United States is interesting as a historical and political antecedent that marks the passage from the season of interculture to that of citizenship. From 'guests' to citizens, one might say.

Today, Europe finds itself discussing a citizenship dealing with civic values, democracy, freedom and human rights. Teaching and educating about citizenship do not refer to uniform concepts in the various EU countries. Diversity is an important opportunity to create a pedagogic debate among teachers and educators to produce practical results. The concept of citizenship has become central and crucial following the expansion of the EU. The European Council of 2004 laid down as the priority objective of the social agenda the development of responsible citizenship, within the regulatory framework of the democratic society for which European youth should be educated.

One should also remember that globalisation makes it necessary to talk to and educate the world citizen. An interconnected, interdependent world interprets citizenship as the harmonious coexistence of different communities in local, regional, national and international contexts (Dooly, Foster & Misiejuk, 2006): this concept expresses the commonly accepted idea of living together in peace and harmony.

The impact of globalisation and the opening of borders does not weaken the feeling of nationality, deemed a distinctive feature of citizenship. The notion of nationality is prevalent in many countries and permits cultural, historical and geographic identification, as well as belonging to chosen groups. The nation State shapes the organisation of contemporary social life and describes the thinking and proposing of education in each country. In this regard, we are confronted by the freedom of the economic market on the one hand and, at the same time, less and less freedom in education, particularly in those States in which the national curriculum has a very strong bearing on educational programmes.

Recent research in British schools highlighted the reluctance to listen to children and students and to allow them to express themselves on issues of daily life, how schools are run and the assessment of human relations. Teachers and educators do not appear to support active participation, considered the essence of citizenship education. This state of affairs encourages attempts to remove the obstacles that prevent young scholars from becoming active citizens (Holmes, 2006).

There is a clear contradiction. On one hand, the individual States are trying to face many internal problems in schools. Both students and teachers complain about the lack of attention to human relations. On the other hand, these same States must seriously take into consideration the standards set forth by European declarations. Attachment to one's own country and positive response to Europe: this is the contradiction to be overcome. Devotion to one's own educational system has to come to terms with what was called for in Bologna and Lisbon.

The new university system is diversifying and interpreting the transition from an elite organisation to one catering for the masses as the coexistence of cultural missions and the strengths deriving from the plurality of study outlines and programmes. The Europe that attracts talent is building citizenship, thereby granting its citizens the skills to take up opportunities in a society in which it is necessary to educate students to be aware of shared values and their belonging to a common social and cultural space.

7 Tuning: Diversity, Autonomy and Agreement as a Citizenship Model

Europe supplies two tools, among others, to identify interculture and citizenship correctly. The first is the *Thesaurus for Education Systems in Europe* (TESE), the latest version being that of 2006, and the second is the so-called *Tuning* methodology.

The glossary contains European terms, while *Tuning* contains the skills that lead to agreement in Europe and which should foster the process of building citizenship. The glossary states that, instead of *multicultural education,* the term *intercultural education* is used and *citizenship education* becomes *civics* with the variations noted below.

– Citizen: population; marital status.
– Citizen participation: civil society, democracy.
– Use 'civics' for 'citizenship education', 'citizenship learning', 'citizenship training' and 'civic education'.
– Civic values: democracy; freedom; human rights.
– Civics: citizenship education; citizenship learning; citizenship training; civic education; education for citizenship; social sciences; community studies; education for peace; law studies.

The term 'civic values' is useful: it refers to the specific skills indicated by the *Tuning process* (see Figure 13.2) designed to harmonise educational structures and programmes based on diversity and autonomy and coordinated by the Universities of Deusto, Bilbao, Spain, and the University of Groningen, Holland.

The term 'tuning' was chosen to convey the idea that universities must not blend together or merge or offer prescribed, final curricula, but should be able to communicate, converge and move toward a common understanding. Respect for educational diversity, independence of subject-matter, and local and national authority are assured.

THE BIRTH OF 'CITIZENSHIP AND CONSTITUTION' IN ITALIAN SCHOOLS

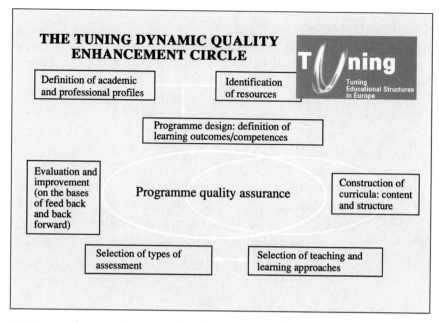

FIGURE 13.2   The 'tuning' dynamic quality enhancement circle (from González & Wagenaar, 2003)

'Tuning' was set up to include the curricula and make them comparable. This approach provides for five lines of discussion and study in the academic disciplines:
- general skills;
- specific skills;
- the role of credits and the system of accumulating them;
- approaches to learning, teaching and assessment;
- increasing the quality of the educational process.

In the list of the 30 general academic skills (for all the subjects) which students should acquire, the ones indicated under numbers 20 (ability to work in an interdisciplinary team), 21 (ability to communicate with non-experts in the field), 22 (appreciation of diversity and multiculturalism), 23 (ability to work in an international context), 24 (understanding of the cultures and customs of other countries) are the closest to interculture, multiculture and citizenship.

However, as regard the specific skills in Teaching, European Studies, and History, the following are indicated:

Education
03. Ability to reflect on one's own value system
15. Ability to adjust the curriculum to a specific educational context

240   CHISTOLINI

European Studies
07. Ability to work in a multicultural team
19. Awareness of the debate about European citizenship and European
identity

History
39. Awareness of, and respect for, points of view derived from other
nations or cultural backgrounds

Pedagogy, translated as *education,* does not use the words interculture, multiculture or citizenship, but refers to the individual's system of values and a context-adjusted curriculum. Surveys show that multiculture and citizenship are deemed a privileged field of European Studies, while History deals with national identity.

8   The Italian Case: The De-intellectualisation of Interculture, Migrations, Civil Coexistence and New Citizenship

In 1992, the drive toward intercultural studies, in their final form, reached the Chairs of General Pedagogy in Italy (Chistolini, 1992). The Ministry of Education actively entered the academic debate with a declaration on intercultural education in schools, signed by Corradini, which then became a ministerial circular (Ministero della Pubblica Istruzione, 1992).

By reconstructing the intercultural situation in training teachers in Italy, we note how interculture as a subject for teacher training, although not unfamiliar in Europe, was unexpected at the Faculty of Education, responsible for training all teachers, regardless of school type or level.

The greatest impact of interculture in European universities was on educationalists with international interests, while schools, bound to the centralised nature of education and sheltered from the as yet calm wind of autonomy, were less concerned with the change. Apart from some rare exceptions, the theoretical and practical experience of interculture could not be said to be a universal, permanent feature of all Italian teacher training.

The initial approach to interculture in Italian universities was not identical with the ministerial and scholastic one. In the universities, one started from the theory of comparative teaching, bearing in mind the numerous international studies which, starting from the 1800s, had concerned themselves with comparing educational systems in order to improve teacher training, from a developmental perspective, which was neither ethnocentric, nor exclusively

European. The issue of international comparisons acted as an impetus for changing educational systems, aiming at a better understanding among peoples, nations and cultures. For the comparison to occur and achieve understanding, even in different languages, it was necessary to meet and discuss teaching concepts and experiences related to the development of education.

The ministerial approach to interculture was striving to augment the planning skills and autonomy of the schools which, on the one hand, looked to the central regulatory-institutional framework and, on the other hand, considered the problem of intercultural teaching, especially with regard to foreign children, who were increasing year by year. The migratory phenomenon tended to reinforce the intercultural approach. The twin themes of cross-cultural studies about migration and interculture were favoured by ministerial and scholastic culture.

The two approaches, the academic pedagogic-comparatist and the socio cultural one of the central and peripheral school policies, influenced each other over subsequent years and produced a comparatist-type teaching literature, in which the socio-cultural factor was considered a dependent variable within the context of historic-systemic analysis. The impact of any one single perspective of study could not be significant considering the wealth of relevant material available.

It was one thing to formulate the theoretical discourse on education, starting with the critical analysis of historical-social processes, such as colonisation, assimilation and integration, and promote interculture as a reaction to isolation, discrimination and unequal opportunity; but it was another thing to start from a comparative theory, as a working hypothesis, and demonstrate the formal, substantial contradictions of educational systems that declare themselves democratic, while falling short of their own objectives by reproducing the selection and neglect which afflicted the deprived categories of the population.

As one can well understand, the two approaches were destined to destroy each other, or feed off each other, not so much because of an obvious ascendancy of one over the other, but rather for reasons of vital space, opportunity to exist and educational realism. By reasons of vital space, we mean the persistence in linking interculture almost exclusively to migration; since 1998, the Ministry has been producing annual reports, referring to 'pupils of non-Italian citizenship' and offering a statistical fact which turns to teaching interpretation for an ample, detailed assessment of the subject. By reasons of opportunity to exist, we mean the need to keep alive the interest in international comparative studies that help us understand what we have left behind and where we are going. If interculture was a source of comparison for Van Daele (1993), for Vico

(1992) it was a theoretical challenge to the fundamentals of general and social teaching, just to give some indicative, but not exhaustive, examples.

Finally, by reasons of educational realism, we mean the commitment to consider the value of the two approaches which are a sign of the intellectual fertility of teaching over the last twenty years and, as such, without cancelling each other out, they have the responsibility to stay alive to enrich the debate and favour the opportune linking of pedagogical theory and practice. Particularly the third group of reasons, those of educational realism, give rise to the eclipse of interculture, to the advantage of the emerging civil coexistence (Corradini, Fornasa & Poli, 2003). Cultural comparisons, accepting immigrant children, the culture of dialogue and tolerance, the resource of ethnic diversity and the discovery of the multiplicity of religions lead back to issues of individual and collective freedom, the correct view of rights and duties, relations with institutions balanced between legitimacy and legality, laboriously intent on having to concur with what the citizen deems is right and what regulations sanction, knowing full well that, in many situations, there is an unbridgeable gap between the individual's sense of personal justice and the application of the law.

As it evolves, intercultural education merges with educating toward civil coexistence and citizenship. In any case, it is necessary to avoid insisting upon identifying interculture with citizenship by means of, sometimes sterile, intellectual twists and turns. The de-intellectualisation of interculture requires that the state of schools should be assessed, in practical terms, and, when the stage of development allows it, the transition can be made from intercultural education to citizenship education, from dialogue to agreement, from acceptance to participation and from rights to duties.

9   Citizenship Education and Constitutional Culture

In the current state of university training of teachers in Italy, interculture, multiculture and citizenship are not always included as independent subjects; they may fall within the teaching of General Pedagogy. They are indispensable transversalities, necessary recommendations that society imposes and the individual takes on.

In the new phase, which we have gradually reached through school reform (Law no. 53 of 28 March 2003) and the *personalised plans*, which provide for pre-school activities and primary school curricula (Legislative Decree no. 59 of 19 February 2004), interculture and multiculture are cited in educating toward civil coexistence that includes citizenship, road and environmental education, as well as health, nutrition and affectivity.

In the fundamental idea of educating everyone, both those who are legally recognised as citizens and those who are not, to accept coexistence, we find the desire to overcome the limits of definitions and affirm the common principles of living together. Teachers' educational responsibility is to foster political awareness, fertile terrain to encourage understanding between different people and lead everyone toward an education which will be a means of freeing the individual.

History, geography, mathematics and art supply the intellectual and technical tools for putting into effect civil coexistence, as well as for demonstrating how the social and natural sciences help a person to live better in the community. To go beyond national borders and bring the moral core of civil coexistence to the fore requires understanding fully all that the term coexistence means and defining educational objectives ever-more clearly.

In 2007, pedagogical concerns turned once again to the issue of citizenship as described in Directive no. 58 of 8 February 1996. The debate in Italy is particularly lively at the moment and tends to interpret citizenship as the political status of citizens, who know how to balance their rights and duties in their relations with institutions, whether in terms of a social culture learnt at school and in the community they belong to, or a knowledge of the constitution, as well as active participation in local, national, European and worldwide levels. The phrase *citizenship education and constitutional culture* is the subject of national discussions among sectorial experts (Ministero della Pubblica Istruzione, 2007, pp. 133–135).

This is a lengthy text that examines citizenship from a broader point of view; it considers the person as having fundamental rights, including the right of citizenship: belonging to a State, a political and social community, in which one learns and shares common values. The decision to belong to the community of a State involves widespread social and political participation, which does not end with voting, but also includes an appreciation of each person's unique value and his/her right to be free from the snares of any kind of discrimination, which would hinder equality and democracy. Let us talk about citizenship as:

- a right and duty of a teacher's professional development;
- the opening of borders and the choice of an intercontinental approach in training working teachers;
- an epistemological transition from interculture to worldwide citizenship;
- a human-spiritual dimension of the educational system;
- civil coexistence;
- a comparison of teaching methods;
- autonomy in Italian schools.

But we are interested in creating the conditions of citizenship as:
- *belonging* to the community of men and women, living together in society;
- *formulating* spiritual values;
- *producing* economic well-being for everyone;
- *participation* in the common good;
- *sharing* rights and duties, based on ethical and institutional considerations;
- *accepting* others;
- *legitimising* a person's right to be seen as a human being in society.

This citizenship does not turn to invisible classifications to alienate the new poor and it does not hide personal views about teachers' training, behind implausible scientificities, under the pretext of generalising them. It deals with the construction of a solid democracy as a common, shared reference point. In his book *On Democracy* (2002), R. A. Dahl considers the following as the minimum requirements of a democracy:
- elected administrators;
- free, fair, frequent voting;
- freedom of expression;
- access to alternative sources of information;
- associative autonomy;
- extended citizenship.

For Dahl, a higher basic level of civic education at school would enable adult citizens to make political choices. However, we must also talk about public discussions and controversies, salient elements of a free society. If institutions are ineffective in forming competent citizens, it is necessary to start from the beginning, according to Dahl, with intrinsic equality: we must consider the good of each human being as intrinsically equal to that of anyone else (Dahl, 2002). The pedagogical viewpoint is perhaps less instrumental than the political one and, therefore, broader, riskier and irreplaceable in educating the person to be part of an open society.

10 Awareness and Criticality

Some overall considerations emerge from the topics dealt with so far. Europe has put forward a rather ambitious regulatory framework, which is putting the various countries to the test, in their efforts to reach targets of excellence, competition and appeal. As could be expected, in a pressing, progressive reform like the one fostered by the Bologna Declaration, not everyone is proceeding at

THE BIRTH OF 'CITIZENSHIP AND CONSTITUTION' IN ITALIAN SCHOOLS   245

the same pace and with the same degree of interest. What is certain is that the process has started and cannot be stopped, while a lot can be done to steer it in the most appropriate direction.

In the assessments of the progress being made, prior to 2010, there are also some elements, known to everyone, which are not always transparent. Students and teachers are evaluated on what they show they have learned and not on what they have actually experienced during their training.

The system of credits also permits this, namely, only to evaluate skills corresponding with some prerequisites and not with others. The correctness of the answer will thus depend more upon the capacity to move technically through the maze of knowledge than on reasoning. Doubt would, by definition, appear to be banished and certainty, so highly criticised by the scientific thinking of the 1900s, re-emerges with the risk of slipping toward new intellectual, if not actually political, dogmatisms.

The comparative research on teachers in Italy and other European and non-European countries points to at least two trends that describe the teacher of the new millennium (Chistolini & Verkest, 2006). For the first trend, a teacher's worth depends upon what he/she teaches; the building up of knowledge and activation of educational processes are derived from the human concepts and the sense of presence of the individual in the universal project of rationalisation and humanisation of the person. All this harks back to the systems of thought, such as Idealism, Neo-idealism, Personalism, Existentialism, Spiritualism and Criticism, that described the feelings of a period and foreshadowed the future in which the individual, at the centre of knowledge, was the maker of the object in which he/she was mirrored.

The second trend is that of the teacher whose value depends totally, or almost, upon the pupils' success; this model, mainly American, based primarily on the philosophy of Pragmatism and learning by doing, values the student's answer more highly if it is part of a clearly defined project.

In some schools, the first model triumphs over the second and Idealism prevails over Pragmatism; in other schools, the opposite occurs. Figure 13.3, concerning the *Identity of the good teacher in the world*, compares eight groups of teachers belonging to various cultural areas.

As may be seen, the didactic concern is common to all the countries, except for Belgium and Libya, where the teachers interviewed stated that a good teacher is above all serious about his/her civic and professional duties. Bearing in mind that we are talking about a strongly Catholic sample (Belgium) and a strongly socialist one (Libya), we must conclude that religion and politics exercise a decisive influence over the evaluation of teachers, while in the other countries the essential criterion is teaching ability. As regard the third item, the students' scholastic results, the distribution of the US sample offers objective confirmation of the pragmatist vision of education, described here as the second trend.

Figure 13.4, concerning the *Definition of the teacher in the world*, indicates the general consensus on considering the teacher an educator. Only in three countries, Turkey, Cyprus and Libya, is the teacher considered more a citizen than an intellectual. It would appear that, once again, the relationship of religion, society and politics results in the teacher's civil function being highly valued. Under conditions of low religious, social and political pluralism, the teacher-citizen carries out the educational task assigned by the centralised State.

The Europe that speaks the language of competences is perhaps better understood by countries that consider students' success praiseworthy, while the Europe that speaks the language of citizenship is presumably better understood by teachers in countries with a centralised educational system. In other words, the era of competences finds fertile ground in a pragmatist mentality, while the construction of European citizenship circulates in the great Mediterranean Sea, the cradle of ancient civilisations.

Although we are aware of treating partial data that might be disproved by other worldwide surveys, we believe the arguments outlined here represent minimum hypotheses that can become material for discussion and in-depth research in the twin fields of study and teaching.

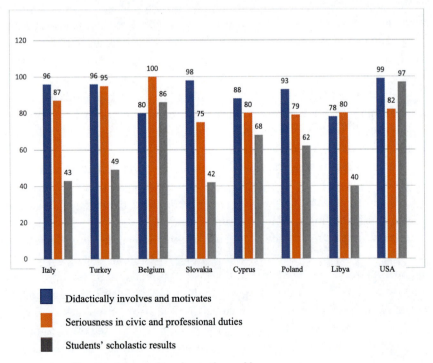

FIGURE 13.3 Identity of the good teacher in the world

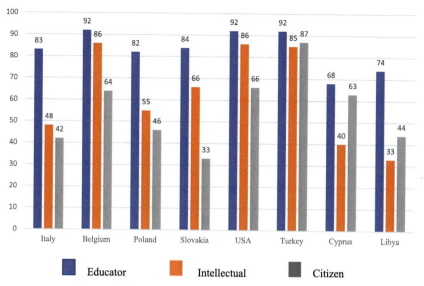

FIGURE 13.4   Definition of the teacher in the world

Acknowledgement

This chapter originally appeared as: Chistolini, S. (2009) The birth of 'citizenship and constitution' in Italian schools: a new wall of competences or transition to intercultural education?, *Mediterranean Journal of Educational Studies*, Vol. 14(2), pp. 93–115. Reprinted here with permission from the publisher.

References

Chistolini, S. (ed.) (1992) *Educazione Interculturale: La Formazione degli Insegnanti in Italia, Gran Bretagna, Germania*. Roma: Euroma-La Goliardica.

Chistolini, S. (2007) *Pedagogia della Cittadinanza: Lo Sviluppo dell'Intercultura nella Formazione Universitaria degli Insegnanti*. Lecce: Pensa MultiMedia.

Chistolini, S., & Verkest, H. (2006) The social deprivation of teachers in Italy, Belgium, Cyprus, Libya. In A. Ross (ed.) *Citizenship Education: Europe and the World: Proceedings of the Eighth Conference of the Children's Identity and Citizenship in Europe Thematic Network*. London: Children's Identity & Citizenship in Europe (CiCe).

Corradini, L., Fornasa, W., & Poli, S. (eds.) (2003) *Educazione alla Convivenza Civile: Educare Istruire Formare nella Scuola Italiana*. Roma: Armando.

Dahl, R. A. (2002) *Sulla Democrazia*. Bari: Laterza.

Dilthey, W. (1883) *Einleitung in die Geisteswissenschaften: Versuch einer Grundlegung für das Studium der Gesellschaft und der Geschichte*. Leipzig: Duncker & Humblot.

Dooly, M. R., Foster, R., & Misiejuk, D. (2006) *Developing A World View of Citizenship Education in Higher Education Programmes*. London: Children's Identity & Citizenship in Europe (CiCe).

European Commission (2002) *Innovation Policy Studies: Status Report of Latest Results, and Forthcoming Tasks*. Brussels: Author.

González, J., & Wagenaar, R. (eds.) (2003) *Tuning Educational Structures in Europe: Final Report – Phase One*. Bilbao: University of Deusto.

Gordon, M. M. (1964) *Assimilation in American life*: *The Role of Race, Religion, and National Origins*. New York: Oxford University Press.

Habermas, J. (1973) *Conoscenza e Interesse*. Bari: Laterza.

Holmes, J. (2006) Participation and whole school improvement, *Reflecting Education*, Vol. 2(2), pp. 38–47.

Ministero della Pubblica Istruzione (1992) Pronuncia di propria iniziativa sull'educazione interculturale nella scuola. In S. Chistolini (ed.) *Educazione Interculturale: La Formazione degli Insegnanti in Italia, Gran Bretagna, Germania*. Roma: Euroma-La Goliardica.

Ministero della Pubblica Istruzione (2007) *Scuola e Legalità* (Primo Rapporto sui lavori del Comitato Nazionale 'Scuola e Legalità'). Roma: 23 Maggio.

Peirce, C. S. (1933) *Collected Papers of Charles Sanders Peirce* (edited by C. Hartshorne & P. Weiss). Cambridge, MA: Harvard University Press.

Porcher, L. (1981) *L'Éducation des Enfants des Travailleurs Migrants en Europe: l'Interculturalisme et la Formation des Enseignants*. Strasbourg: Council of Europe.

Rauhvargers, A. (chair) (2007) *Bologna Process Stocktaking Report 2007* (Report from a Working Group appointed by the Bologna Follow-up Group to the Ministerial Conference in London, May 2007). London: Socrates.

Taft, R. (1966) *From Stranger to Citizen: A Survey of Studies of Immigrant Assimilation in Western Australia*. London: Tavistock Publications.

TESE (2006) *Thesaurus for Education Systems in Europe* (English version). Brussels: Eurydice European Unit.

Van Daele, H. (1993) *L'Éducation Comparée*. Paris: Presses Universitaires de France.

Vico, G. (1992) *Pedagogia Interculturale: Problemi e Concetti*. Brescia: La Scuola.

CHAPTER 14

Private and Privatised Higher Educational Institutions in Jordan

Muhammad Raji Zughoul

1 Introduction

Jordan has witnessed giant strides in the establishment, growth and expansion of higher educational institutions, first at the level of two- to three-year institutes, then at the level of the four-year university granting the first degree or undergraduate diploma. Two major reasons lie behind these strides. First is the strong drive in the country toward 'modernisation', 'development', 'progress' or—in a wider sense—'catching up' with the western standards of living in which education and higher education have been perceived as instrumental since they are a gate for the technological and information revolutions of the modern age. It is also assumed that education provides solutions for challenging problems. The second reason is the fact that Jordan prides itself on being a source of trained manpower, skilled human resources which it 'exports' to neighbouring oil rich countries and other Arab countries.

Before addressing the topic of this paper, namely private and privatised higher education, it pays to have a glance at the development of higher education in Jordan. In both its intermediate degree (2–3 years after high school) and in its first degree (4 years after high school) modes. It is worth noting that these two- to three-year institutes—mostly Teachers' Training Institutes—all became Community Colleges after the decision of The Ministry of Higher Education in 1979.

2 Institutes and Community Colleges

The first two-year institute was established in the country in 1952 and it was a Teachers' Training Institute in Amman. Similar other institutes were established in the country to meet the high demand for trained teachers. Nine such colleges sponsored by the Ministry of Education and later by the Ministry of Higher Education were established by 1982, two Technical Institutes and one hotel management training institute were also established by the Ministry to raise the number

© THE EURO-MEDITERRANEAN CENTRE FOR EDUCATION RESEARCH, UNIVERSITY OF MALTA, 2000
DOI: 10.1163/9789004506602_014

of these institutes to twelve. Other ministries and governmental departments in Jordan felt the need to have institutes of their own to provide the trained manpower needed to work for these ministries in different parts of the country.

Sixteen such colleges were established for the Ministries of Health (Nursing Colleges, professional allied health services), Social Affairs (Institute for Cooperation, College of Social Services), Islamic Waqf (College of Islamic Sciences), and the Department of Statistics (Statistical Training Centre), the Department of Communications (College of Wired and Wireless Communications), the Royal Medical Services (Princess Mona Nursing College), the Aviation Authority (Royal Aviation Academy), the Royal Geographic Centre (College of the Royal Geographic Centre), the Central Bank (Institute of Banking Studies). The United Nations' Refugees and Works Agency (UNRWA) established two colleges between the years 1960 and 1971 for the training of the Palestinian refugees living in Jordan. This brings the number of these official and semi-official colleges to 30. Twenty-two similar colleges were established by the private sector in different parts in the country (all for profit, all in major Jordanian cities and mostly in Amman, and established by individuals, families and companies) bringing the total number of colleges to 52 in addition to 14 colleges in the West Bank which was occupied by Israel in 1967. Jordan kept its pre-1967 supervisory role of the education sector till the signing of disengagement treaty between the East Bank and the West Bank in the year 1988.

The Community Colleges developed extremely rich and varied programmes that cover the needs of the different sectors of Jordanian society. These have included eight major programmes with a range of specialisations within each. These are the Academic, the Educational, Engineering, Social Work, Finance and Business, Paramedical professions, Agriculture, Hotel Industry and Fine Arts programmes. Enrolment in these colleges has gone up dramatically to peak in 1990–1991 to the figure of 40,777 and to drop to half that figure in later years after the spread of private university education which partly replaced community level education.

3 Official (Public) Universities

Jordan has not had a long history of university education. Generally speaking, Jordanian students used to go to other Arab countries for their studies, with Syria, Egypt and Iraq absorbing the largest numbers. I will list the universities in Jordan in their order of establishment.

1.   The first Jordanian university—the University of Jordan—was established in the form of a College of Arts and only in the early 1970s did the

University of Jordan start to take shape as a full academic institution having the outlay for all the faculties offering most of the traditional specialties offered by other universities.

2. As the University of Jordan took shape in the early 1970s, the second major university, Yarmouk University was established in Irbid with the underlying thinking of being much less traditional stressing the Sciences, Engineering, Economics and Business and Languages. It started teaching in 1976. Yarmouk grew into an academically outstanding institution in both teaching and research because of an open-minded administration, a very active scholarship programme which contributed to the training of a good number of Jordanians in some of the best American universities.

3. A third university was established in M'uta (Karak) in 1984, and this offered military education and training beside the traditional academic training.

4. The Jordan University of Science and Technology (JUST) was constructed near a free industrial zone in the northern part of the country with a view to facilitating the transfer of technology and employing it in the development of the country (cf. JUST, 1996).

5. A fifth university is Aal Al-Bayt University (University of the Kinsmen or Relatives of the Prophet—Prophet Muhammad PBUH), established in Mafraq in order to provide Islamic Shari'a education to Muslim students from non-Arabic speaking Islamic states. It started teaching in 1994.

6. The Jordanian University is the Hashemite University in Zarka, the second most important city in Jordan. It was established to respond to the needs of the students in Zarka, and it started teaching in 1994.

7. Balka Applied University was founded in 1997 to oversee the operations of the Community Colleges and Technical Institutes.

8. In addition to these seven universities, there are two three-year colleges that have been changed into four-year colleges and given university status. The first of these is what was previously the Amman University College for Applied Engineering, which was established in 1989.

9. The ninth university embraces what was previously the College of Preaching and the Foundations of Religion. This university is directly supervised by the Ministry of Islamic Waqf, Islamic Affairs and Holy Places. It is the only university supervised by an authority outside the Ministry of Higher Education.

These universities offer Academic specialisations in almost all fields of knowledge. The great majority of these departments and academic specialisations are duplicated in most of the universities. These nine institutions enrolled 15,019 students in the year 1997–1998 and 18,851 students in the year 1998–1999, compared to 6,035 in 1980–1981, 7,645 in the year 1985–1986, and 11,920 in the year 1990–1991 (see Ministry of Higher Education, 1981, 1986, 1991, 1998, 1999).

4 Private Universities: A Preamble

The idea of having a private university in a country like Jordan was unthinkable till recently. One major reason for that is the fact that university education, not only in Jordan but in most neighbouring countries, is monopolised by the state. Only in a few cases were there some exceptions, the most well-known being the American Universities in Beirut and Cairo. It was necessity that triggered the idea of setting up a private university in the country. It so happened that in 1985 there was a conference for Jordanian expatriates or 'emigrants' who were mostly working in the Arabian Gulf States and one major recommendation of the conference was to petition the Jordanian government for permission to establish a private university in the country. This recommendation was motivated by the fact that children of expatriates could not be admitted into Jordanian universities due to a complex quota system which allows only up to 5% admissions to expatriates. In other words, only 5% of the seats are allotted to children of Jordanians who live abroad, a percentage which far from satisfies demand.

The placement of these students in countries other than Jordan is perceived by parents to be problematic or even seriously dangerous politically, financially, socially and culturally. Such a perception was even more strong with regard to the futures of female offspring. As a result, the expatriate community succeeded in establishing their agenda and carried through their recommendation to found a private university in Jordan which catered for the needs of expatriates in the main. This university was to be a non-profit institution. The Council for Higher Education responded positively to the recommendation of the conference and the establishment of the first private university in the country was 'licensed' in principle. The university was named the Applied Science University and it had to start with a capital of no less than eight million Jordanian Dinars (JDs) or approximately US$ 11.4 million.[1]

5 Fast Growth: Other Private Universities

No sooner had the Applied Science University been given a license to operate than other applications began to be submitted to the Council of Higher

Education, to the extent that those authors writing about the private higher education sector in Jordan use the word 'overflow' with reference to the sheer number of applications received. It became clear from the very outset that investors were after money, and that the original idea of justifying the setting up of a private university to cater for the sons and daughters of expatriates vanished quickly into thin air. The Council licensed three private Community Colleges to be turned into full-fledged universities.[2] Other permits were granted to twelve universities, all but two of which are profit-making establishments. As many and even more applications for licensing are still pending and the Council does not seem to be disposed to grant more permits at present. Table 14.1 shows the development of the establishment of these universities chronologically.

A look at Table 14.1 clearly shows that over a period of no more than five years, twelve private universities were established. It is also clear that other than Zarka, Irbid and Jerash, the other nine universities are in Amman or in the very vicinity of Amman. The table clearly shows the implied tough competition: a competition for investment.

TABLE 14.1   Development and growth of Jordanian private universities

No.	Name of private university	Establishment date	Started teaching
1.	Amman Private University	1989	1990–1991
2.	Applied Science University	1989	1991–1992
3.	Philadelphia Private University	1989	1991–1992
4.	Al-Isra Private University*	1989	1991–1992
5.	Princess Sumayya College for Technology	1990	1991–1992
6.	Jordan University for Women	1990	1991–1992
7.	Jordan Academy of Music	1989	1992–1993
8.	Jerash Private University*	1991	1993–1994
9.	College of Educational Sciences	1993	1993–1994
10.	Al-Zaytoonah Jordanian Private University	1990	1993–1994
11.	Zarka Private University	1991	1994–1995
12.	Irbid National University	1991	1994–1995

Note: All but the two asterisked (*) universities are owned by investing companies which are licensed and supervised by the Ministry of Commerce and Industry. Princess Sumayya College is not as profit-oriented as the other institutions, while the College of Educational Sciences is a non-profit establishment belonging to UNRWA.

6 Growth of Student Enrolment

As the Council for Higher Education approved the establishment of private universities, the question directly arose as to who should control, supervise or at least regulate these institutions, and how this was to be done. The first issue that the Ministry of Higher Education had to deal with is whether to allow these universities to exercise an open-door policy of admission or to regulate access in some way or another. The Ministry decided to establish its control by designating the numbers of students that were to be admitted each year and by establishing the minimum average General Secondary School Certificate passes to be accepted. The Law, which was decreed in 1989 for private universities, regulated admission beside several other aspects of administrative matters. Table 14.2 shows the numbers of students enrolled in private universities compared to those enrolled in public universities. The figures for public universities include those enrolled in graduate studies.

Table 14.2 clearly shows that the student enrolment in private universities has been on the increase ever since the first university opened in the year 1990–1991. It has almost doubled every year in the first four years, and then increased by 20%–30% between 1993–1996. Numbers have tended to stabilise over the last three years. The number of students multiplied by almost 25 times between 1990–1991 and 1997–1998. In the first few years, it was only a small fraction compared to enrolment in public universities, but it became close to half of the enrolment in public universities. It should be noted that the figures of enrolment in public universities include all graduate students in these universities. In other words, if graduate students are excluded in order to be in a better position to compare like with like, student enrolment in private universities would amount to more than half the enrolment in public universities. Table 14.2 also clearly shows that private universities have taken a good share of the load of offering university education to the ever-increasing number of Jordanian high school graduates. The capacity of Jordanian public universities has always fallen short of accepting other than a marginal percentage of high school graduates in the country, utilising a complex system of competitive quotas allocated to different geographical, social and occupational sectors in order to regulate access.[3]

TABLE 14.2 Growth of student enrolment in public and private universities

Year	90/91	91/92	92/93	93/94	94/95	95/96	96/97	97/98	98/99
Public	36165	41517	49945	49944	54437	56652	58834	61257	67894
Private	1324	4072	7003	11319	16109	24868	30583	32851	35207

7 Sources and Characteristics

It is important at this stage to consider the profile of students seeking admission into private universities in Jordan. There are as yet no studies available on the characteristics of these students. Nevertheless, several valid observations can be made:

1. Generally speaking, students who are not admitted to the public universities go to the private universities. This is particularly true of two categories of students:
   a. those whose average in the high school leaving examination falls between 60 and 65 and who therefore cannot, by law, be admitted to public universities but may, by law, be admitted to private universities. Averages less than 60% are not acceptable in either. This category, I believe, forms a sizable percentage of those admitted.
   b. those who fail to make it into public universities within the quota established according to competition for places along social, geographical and occupational criteria.
2. A minority of students who have obtained high grades in their examinations but who nevertheless prefer to go to private universities.
3. Students from other Arab and foreign countries. This category has been on the increase in terms of numbers since 1990–1991. The percentages fluctuate because of the increase in enrolment among Jordanians. The numbers—as shown in Table 14.3—grew more than 17 times from 1990–1991 till 1998–1999.

It is generally felt that students enrolling in private universities come from families with a higher income, come from families working outside Jordan (mostly in the Gulf) and, more importantly, have lower averages than their peers in public universities.

TABLE 14.3 Private universities—Arab and foreign student population

Nationality	1990–1991	1992–1993	1994–1995	1996–1997	1998–1999
Jordanians	1006	4888	11839	24929	29624
Arab (A)	318	2092	4182	5415	5583
Foreign (F)	–	23	88	239	–
Total	1324	7003	16109	30583	35207
% of A & F	24.0%	30.2%	26.5%	18.4%	15.8%

8 Faculty Members: Growth and Development

Table 14.4 shows the growth of the numbers of faculty members in private universities according to academic rank. It shows that the number of faculty members in private universities has been steadily increasing since the opening of the first university in 1990–1991. The bulk of the faculty members is at the Assistant Professorial level. The table also shows the percentage of those at the professorial level steadily decreased from 25% in 1990 to 8% in 1998–1999. The decrease, however, was not because their numbers grew less; quite the opposite: their numbers kept growing. Rather, it is because the number of faculty in other ranks increased sharply.

TABLE 14.4   Growth and distribution of faculty members at private universities according to rank

Academic rank	1990–1991	1992–1993	1994–1995	1996–1997	1998–1999
Full Professor	11	40	88	117	127
Associate Professor	10	61	150	195	227
Assistant Professor	17	132	369	597	732
Instructor	6	38	137	231	274
Lecturer	–	82	74	116	61
Teaching Assistant	–	22	98	110	78
Total	44	375	916	1366	1499

9 Sources and Some Characteristics of Faculty

Dahiyyat (1996)—previously a president of a private university, and presently presiding a public university—specified four sources for faculty members for private universities in Jordan:

1. Faculty members from other Arab countries, particularly Iraq, Syria and Egypt.
2. Faculty members who applied for teaching posts at public universities and were not chosen.
3. Faculty members working in public universities but who are either on sabbatical or on leave.
4. Jordanian faculty members who are either retired or occupied key positions in the government and cannot by law be paid a salary in public universities.

PRIVATE AND PRIVATISED HIGHER EDUCATIONAL INSTITUTIONS IN JORDAN 257

TABLE 14.5 Distribution of faculty members according to nationality

Nationality	1990–1991	1992–1993	1994–1995	1996–1997
Jordanians	35	316	655	918
Arabs	9	53	227	411
Non-Arabs	–	6	34	37
Total	44	375	916	1366
Total non-Jordanian	9	59	261	448
% of non-Jordanian	25.7%	18.6%	28.4%	32.7%

These trends reflect rather badly on the standards of education at private universities, as well as on their stability. Table 14.5 sets out the distribution of faculty members in private institutions according to their nationality.

According to the statistical reports published by the Ministry of Education (1991, 1992, 1993, 1994, 1995, 1996, 1997), the number of non-Jordanian faculty members—the overwhelming majority of whom are Arabs—grew from 9 in 1990–1991 to 448 in the year 1996–1997. This represents an increase of about 50 times. Of the 448 non-Jordanian faculty members, 37 carry non-Arab nationalities. Out of a total of 1366 faculty member working at the private universities in Jordan, 32.7% are non-Jordanians, 99% of whom are Arabs. The overwhelming majority of the Arab faculty members are Iraqis who left Iraq for political and economic reasons after the Gulf War. The return of these faculty members to Iraq once the political situation there changes definitely threatens the stability of these universities. The second major source of faculty members for private universities puts the quality of education in these universities at risk because these members are not as well qualified as one would expect at this level. The majority of these members got their degrees from universities with no special distinction in the ex-Soviet Block, India, Pakistan and other countries. They have never lived regular graduate student university life and they did their research in a hurry at a distance. The third and fourth sources form a minority, but they can be considered as assets to the academic level of these universities.

10   Administrative and Technical Staff

Administrative and technical staff include those who work in the administrative and financial departments of any university. Included also are those in services, maintenance, transportation, gardening, cleaning, and so on. Table

TABLE 14.6 Numbers and quantitative growth of administrative and technical staff and their distribution according to qualifications

Qualifications	1990–1991	1992–1993	1994–1995	1996–1997
PhD	–	15	58	34
MA	3	32	36	36
Higher Diploma	2	11	27	38
BA	23	222	274	427
Intermediate Diploma	12	90	220	283
Secondary and below	17	227	431	729
Total	57	597	1164	1547

14.6 shows the quantitative development of the administrative and technical staff in private universities in Jordan, together with their academic qualifications. Of direct relevance, most likely, would be the ratio of administrators and technicians to students.

Table 14.6 shows that there has been a steady and sharp growth of the administrative and technical staff. From the humble figure of 57 in 1990–1991 to twenty-seven times that number in 1996–1997. Those with Intermediate Diploma (i.e., two years after high school) and those with secondary school certificate form the majority of personnel, amounting to about 65.4% in 1996–1997 and 55.9% in 1994–1995. Those with an MA and higher form the minority (about 8% on the average). Those with a BA fluctuated between 38.3% in 1992–1993 to 27.1% in 1996–1997. The ratio of administrative and technical staff to students is about 1:20 on the average which is twice the ratio in public universities (1:10).

11 Fields of Specialisation: Faculties and Departments

It is expected that these private universities offer traditional specialisations that have high market demand (namely courses that are instrumental in getting a job), or focus on offering new specialisations not available in public universities and have high employment market demand. The two universities not owned by companies and that can be considered semi-public, namely Princess Sumayya College of Technology and UNRWA's College of Educational Sciences, do not follow the patterns of private universities.

Table 14.7 provides a summary of the fields of study offered by private universities. One can note that these institutions offer a total of 41 areas of specialisation within the faculties of Arts, Education, Science, Economics and Administrative Sciences, Engineering, Law, Shari'a and Agriculture. The overwhelming majority of these specialisations are traditional fields of study already offered by public Jordanian universities. The innovation has been by introducing new major areas of study in some of these universities to respond to needs in the society not met by other universities. These new major areas include Hospital Administration, Hotel Management (offered at the tertiary level by a two-year Hotel Management Institute), Diplomacy in connection with political science (it is also offered as a major area of specialisation in the Institute of Diplomacy in Amman) and Translation at the undergraduate level (translation is offered as a major area in public universities at the graduate level).

12   Areas of Focus

Other than that, private universities have not contributed to introducing new fields of study. On the other hand, these universities have been keen to offer major areas of study that are in big demand in Jordanian society and in such neighbouring countries as Saudi Arabia and the Arabian Gulf States, which constitute the prospective job market for graduates. An analysis of Table 14.8 shows where the demand is, and shows some major patterns in the selection of an area of specialisation. The following can be concluded.

1. Business Administration, Accounting, and Finance and Banking are major areas that are offered by almost all these universities because they are badly needed, particularly in the private sector. The needs of Jordan and neighbouring countries for specialists in this area is well attested by the high student enrolment in these fields of study, ultimately generating revenue in these profit-making institutions. In the academic year 1997–1998, for example, student enrolment in these major areas of study reached 37.8%, representing the highest percentage of enrolment in all major areas of study in private universities (cf. Ministry of Higher Education, 1998).

2. Computer Studies is offered by almost all universities. It is a relatively new field of study and looks promising in terms of employment opportunities. Figures of student enrolment for the year 1997–1998, for example, show that Computer Sciences attracted the second highest number of students' percentage of enrolment according to major area of study. It reached 13.5%, the second after Economics and Administrative Sciences (Ministry of Higher Education, 1998).

TABLE 14.7   Major areas of specialisation offered by private universities

Number	College	Major Area of Specialisation	Private Universities												No. offered
			Amman	App sc	Women Univ	Zajtoonah	Al-Isra	Jerash	Zarka	Philadelphia	Sumayya	Ed. Science	Irbid	Music Ac	
1.	Arts & Humanities	Arabic	X	X	X	X		X	X	X			X		8
2.		English	X	X	X	X	X	X	X	X			X		9
3.		Translation		X	X	X									3
4.		Psychology	X												1
5.		Sociology		X											1
6.		History							X						1
7.		Journalism			X										1
8.	Education	Fine Arts, Music			X									X	2
9.		Guidance		X	X										2
10.		Child Education			X							X			2
11.		Subject Teacher							X			X			2
12.		Class Teacher							X						1
13.	Science	Computer Science	X	X	X	X	X		X	X	X		X		9
14.		Informatics	X	X											2
15.		Chemistry		X	X			X							3
16.		Mathematics		X	X	X			X				X		5
17.		Physics		X											1
18.		Biology						X	X						2

No.	Group	Subject	1	2	3	4	5	6	7	8	9	10	11	Total
19.	Economics & Admin Science	Business Admin	X	X	X	X	X	X	X	X			X	9
20.		Accounting	X	X	X	X	X	X	X	X			X	9
21.		Finance & Banking	X	X	X	X	X		X	X				7
22.		Marketing		X		X								2
23.		Public Admin						X						1
24.		Economics	X					X					X	3
25.		Hospital Admin	X											1
26.		Hotel Admin		X										1
27.		Political Science/Dip		X										1
28.	Engineering	Computer Engineer	X	X			X							3
29.		Mechanical		X						X				2
30.		Industrial		X										1
31.		Chemical		X										1
32.		Civil		X			X							2
33.		Architecture		X	X		X							2
34.		Com. & Electrical	X	X			X					X		4
35.		Electrical								X				1
36.	Medical Science	Pharmacy	X	X	X	X	X			X				6
37.		Medical Labs	X	X	X	X	X	X						6
38.		Nursing				X								1
39.		Nutrition		X										1
40.	Law	Law		X		X	X		X	X			X	6
41.	Sh	Islam Shari'a		X				X	X				X	4
42.	Agr	Agriculture Econ						X						1
43.		Animal Products						X						1
44.		Plant Products						X						1

TABLE 14.8   Distribution of students according to major area of specialisation and percentage to total

Academic Year and Percentage	Major area of specialisation										
	Educ & Fine Arts	Humanities & Shari'a	Law	Social Science	Economy & Admin Sc	Natural Science	Math & Computing	Medical Science	Engineering	Agriculture	Total
1996/1997	1412	2950	2973	421	11565	245	3988	3960	2288	463	30583
% total	4.6	9.6	9.7	1.3	37.8	0.8	13.0	12.9	7.4	1.5	
1997/1998	1612	3378	3202	498	12444	231	4440	3864	2735	429	32851
% total	4.9	10.2	9.7	1.49	37.8	0.7	13.5	11.7	8.3	1.3	
1998/1999	1749	4067	3239	549	13277	346	5105	3691	2766	409	35198
% total	4.9	11.5	9.2	1.5	37.7	0.98	14.5	10.4	7.8	1.1	

3. The third area of emphasis is medical sciences and particularly Pharmacy and Medical Laboratories. This area, according to the same sources, reached 11.6% of enrolment according to major area, with Pharmacy having the lion's share of 7.7%.

4. The fourth major area of specialisation of attraction to enrolment is Law. This area attracted 3378 students or 10.2% of the overall student enrolment in private universities.

5. The least attractive area of study is Natural Sciences. Natural Sciences attracted no more than 231 students in the year 1997–1998. This raises serious questions about the quality of education in the colleges of engineering and medicine in the absence of a well-developed college of natural sciences.

13   Regulation, Control, and Supervision

The Jordanian government represented by the Ministry of Higher Education and the powerful Higher Education Council felt the need to exercise regulation, control and supervision over private universities. It was realised from the very beginning that these institutions were profit minded and the quest for more money could lead to violations of the tradition of scholarship associated with universities. A temporary law governing the general organisation and administration of these universities was enacted though not strictly enforced.

The Higher Education Council thus determines the number of students to be admitted to each university every year. This is important given that there is always a temptation to take more students than one can cope with in order to increase revenue from fees. In another step, the Council has issued detailed criteria specifying the requirements for two kinds of accreditation, 'general' and 'special'. 'General accreditation' lays down requirements in four areas, namely administrative organisation, academic organisation, buildings and facilities, and finally instruments, equipment and general educational resources. To be clearer, general accreditation requires the availability of convenient and well-equipped classrooms, typing, copying, projectors, tape recorders, computers, study halls, laboratories, workshops, a library, a clinic, a cafeteria, sports facilities, and so on. The 'special accreditation' is intended to accredit different major areas of specialisation offered by private universities. 'Special' and 'specialisation' (i.e., major area of study) accreditation stipulates requirements that must be met in four areas, namely:

a.   the study plan as to its general structure, distribution of credit hours, number of credit hours for each specialisation and the distribution of courses on the different content areas in the specialisation;

b. faculty members and technicians as to their numbers, ratio to students, qualifications and experience;
c. books, references and professional journals as to the number of each that should be available and for each specialisation;
d. instruments, machines, laboratory equipment, workshops and audio-visual aids.

Whenever a private university is ready for general or special accreditation, it files an application. The Ministry/Council of Higher Education forms a team of specialists to visit the university and evaluate it according to very specific forms prepared beforehand.

Despite these regulatory measures taken by the Ministry, these universities have not quite lived up to expectations. In an interview with a Jordanian paper (Al-Nsour, 1996; in Al-Tall, 1998), the Minister of Higher Education did not mince words:

> The Ministry has followed up on the mess in student admissions when these universities accepted twice the number of students allowed by the Ministry. The Ministry asked these universities to take corrective measures and we are going to be strict, but without suppression.

The Minister expressed his conviction that supervision should be strictly maintained after the accreditation process, since some universities rented equipment and machines to meet standards, but returned these once the committees of accreditation finished their report.

14   Profiting or Profiteering

It is obvious in the financial circles in Jordan that private universities have so far proved to be a great success in terms of turning tidy profits, as can be seen from some of the published budget reports of some of the mother companies owning these universities. Al-Tall (1998) gave one example of the profit-oriented nature of private universities. He depended on what was published in *Al-Aswaaq*, a Jordanian weekly economic review. The annual report of the Arab International Company for Investment which owns Applied Science University stated that the company has made 4.5 million JDs in profits in 1995 using a capital of 10.125 million JDs. Of that amount of profits, 2.65 million were allotted for distribution. The writer maintains that these figures are phenomenal.

It is worth noting in this connection that because of the enormous profits made by private universities, public universities have started programmes admitting lower averages and asking for fees matching those of private universities (in some cases 10 times the regular fees paid by regular students in public universities). These programmes have been called 'Parallel Education Programmes' or 'Programmes of Parallel Studies' and some of the profit public universities make goes to solve the acute financial problems of these institutions. In some public universities, a proportion of the revenue goes to faculty members who teach these programmes as compensation for being overloaded. Public universities which complain from over-crowded conditions do not mind accepting more students if they are willing to pay the designated high fees. A Jordanian student who scores a high average but falls short of getting access to, for instance, the department of computer sciences will have to put up with seeing another Jordanian student with a far lower average gaining access to the department because he can pay the fees of 'Parallel Studies'.

15   Assets, Problems and Challenges

The idea of starting private universities is by itself pioneering in this part of the world. In fact, even before the experience is evaluated, several private universities in other Arab countries have been established along the lines of the Jordanian setup and several others in other Arab countries are being contemplated. In Jordan itself, many applications for licensing new universities are pending the Council of Higher Education's approval.

Private universities in Jordan have indeed solved many problems, most important of which is taking some of the burden off the shoulders of public universities whose admission capacities have always been exceeded to accommodate more high school graduates. These universities have also had serious financial problems. Private universities have been placing thousands of high school graduates who would otherwise have either left for another country for their education (spending an estimated 300 million JDs yearly), exercised more pressure to get into public universities, or remained without university education. Responding to the needs of these students could not have come at better time, namely immediately after the Gulf War and the return of hundreds of thousands of Jordanian families from the Gulf. These universities have also been offering education to an increasing number of Arab and foreign students from over forty different countries.

Private education at the university level in Jordan is relatively a big financial investment estimated at 200 million JDs. These universities have offered thousands of jobs for Jordanians, and they are offering more with their expansion.

However, the birth, growth and expansion of these universities have been strewn with problems of all kinds. Taking the right action for each of the big questions raised concerning so many aspects of running and maintaining these private institutions is a big challenge for the future of these universities. The following are some of the major problems/challenges facing private universities.

16 Standards: Balancing Profitability and Quality

As shown earlier, the Ministry of Higher Education and the Council of Higher Education have taken measures to ensure that private universities meet the minimum requirements of the accreditation process which is in direct relationship to the quality of education in Jordan. However, no further measures of control over the quality of education are taken other than what these institutions try to offer in this respect. I have not come across any systematic research studies evaluating the standards of the graduates of private universities. However, if we take individual observations, impressions of many educators, experiences of faculty members who spent a sabbatical in these universities and the scanty evaluative remarks of authors on higher education in Jordan, and if we moreover examine the input of these universities, a very dim picture emerges. Sometimes these universities are called 'shops', and 'supermarkets', due to their excessive emphasis on financial gains. People who call these universities these names do imply that the issue of standards is not of primary concern to these institutions. Al-Tall (1998) addresses this issue daringly and with concern when he states:

> There is a feeling among the students of private universities that the student's mere payment of the high fees makes his graduation almost guaranteed ... because these universities are in perpetual need of students. This kind of feeling has been reinforced by the commercial advertisements about some of these universities in the mass media in a way which showed these universities dying to get 'clients' by all means. These universities should have depended on the quality of education offered as a means to show distinction .... There are cases when shareholders in some of these universities interfered to raise passing percentages and to overlook unexcused absenteeism. (My translation)

The need for striking a balance between profitability on one hand and quality on the other has been lacking and has to be catered for. Attaining higher standards may require raising the admission scores and risking some of the profits. Al-Tall (1998) maintains that standards may be jeopardised even further if the government responds positively to the call of private universities for lowering the admission average down to 50% in order to attract more students. It is imperative in this connection to state firmly that if the private universities think and plan to get this proposal approved, they can do so. Private universities have a lot of influence; they have a strong lobby and they can buy more influence if need be. They can hire people to get them through and they have done so on more than one occasion. It suffices to state here that private universities hire ex-ministers of Higher Education, ex-ministers, ex-public university presidents for their symbolic presidency of their universities. It is also necessary to say that most of these universities are owned by influential people in government and the private sector. The impression of innocent talk about privatisation, democracy, relieving the government of some of its burdens and so on are arguments forwarded by the people who were hired to do the job.

17 Lack of Catering for Excellence, Research and Student and Faculty Development

It follows naturally that because of the preoccupation with profit and, as Nsour (1996) put it, 'the temptation of saving more money at the risk of quality', these private universities have never had academic excellence as one of their objectives. These universities either have a minimal or no budget at all to allocate to scientific research. They do not send students on scholarships (a student on scholarship may cost up to a quarter of a million JDs) and they rarely support their faculty to present research findings in conferences and seminars. These universities do not have plans to cater for the outstanding student and the talented.

18 Duality in Administration

Despite the fact that university administration is spelled out by the law of private universities (Law No. 19 of 1989), these universities have constantly tried to avoid the obligations therein when these regard the power attributed to the academic councils or the president of the university. They prefer instead to resort to the law of companies and corporations reinforced by the Ministry of Commerce and Industry. On the pretext that these universities are private 'economic projects', the 'managerial committee' claims the supremacy of the law governing companies and corporations in running these universities rather than the law of private universities. At all times, there is this 'war' between the representatives of capital on one hand, and the representatives of 'academia' on the other. The winner has always been capital. The duality in administration has always weakened these universities since the university presidents' hands are tied, given that the chief controller in the university is not the president—as is the case in public universities—but the owners of the capital.[4]

19 Deformation of a Concept

When the proponents of private higher education in Jordan are faced with questions regarding the validity of their profiteering ventures, they always invoke the American higher education example, pointing out that private universities in the USA have better standards than public ones. They refer to such highly esteemed American universities as Princeton, Harvard and Yale, reminding one and all that these institutions are private ones. What is conveniently forgotten is that these universities are non-profit organisations, that they are extremely well-supported by charitable organisations, individuals, companies and corporations, and that they have the funds they need in order to ensure that the quest for academic excellence, creativity, the advancement of human knowledge and the actualisation of human potential is successful. Their admission policies are extremely competitive and stringent. They are the pride of the American system of education. Private universities in Jordan are a mere distortion of this noble ideal.

The concept of a private university on the lines of Princeton and Yale has excellent chances of flourishing in Jordan, in a context of Arab-Islamic culture which glorifies learning and the learned. In this culture, the support for learning and the learned comes from the creed and from a very long tradition supporting the quest for knowledge. In that sense, the private university in Jordan is simply antithetical to this culture and tradition.

20 Conflict with Building National Character

If profitability remains a major criterion for these universities, it may prove detrimental when taking the collective formation of the personality of the incoming student from an ideological point of view. If the most important thing in a private university is the payment of fees, the country is putting a large percentage of its student population at stake. Lack of discipline, the lightening of academic requirements, toleration of absenteeism, carelessness in testing, relaxation of seriousness, aversion to hard work, and so on may become a welcome change to attract more students into these institutions.

21   Suggestions for Improvement

There has been an attempt in this paper to outline the major assets and weaknesses of private and privatised higher education in Jordan. Some of the shortcomings of private higher education are detrimental to the national character and some are fatal to creativity and excellence. However, these are institutions which have invested money, effort and a lot of struggle for power. They have powerful lobbies and they can hire (and have hired) people to buy influence and to shape the decisions of such overpowering institutions as the Council of Higher Education. In short, they are there to stay and the best way to deal with them is to try to improve them. Improving these institutions is good for all the 'stakeholders'. The following is a list of suggestions for improvement, mostly based on the arguments and points presented earlier.

These institutions should, at this juncture in their history, redress the issue of quality because it is pivotal for their long-term survival. They should reconsider the following:

1. Their admission policies, in such a way as to improve the quality of intake as much as possible. Accepting a majority of those whose averages in high school is in the low 60s is not going to give an index of quality at any time in the history of these institutions.
2. Accepting the idea of striking a balance between profitability and offering good quality education for the new generations of Jordan.
3. Showing a sense of commitment to establish, reinforce and maintain good teaching practices in these universities, even though they might conflict with the interest of some shareholders.
4. Avoiding cheap publicity like advertising in the papers about themselves like any other commodity in the market.
5. Avoiding commercial practices, such as that of cutting costs to raise the profits.
6. Changing the decision-making process by granting enough responsibilities to the university councils and committees. The presence of a very strong Deans' Council is a necessity for the proper running of these institutions. The 'Council of Managers' which has been running these institutions according to the law of companies in the Ministry of Commerce and Industry is no substitute to the Deans' Council.
7. The spirit of a university is research. Private universities in Jordan need to allot funds to research budgets.
8. These universities should have more strict conditions for the recruitment of faculty members. They should not accept mediocre applicants even though they might be easier to manage, manipulate and mould.

9. These universities should have long term plans for securing faculty members. As soon as the Iraqi problem with the Western powers is solved, the Iraqi faculty members will go back to Iraq in a flux similar to their coming into Jordan. The question as to how they will be replaced remains.
10. Private universities have to start a scholarship programme which is effective and long term, so that bright students are sent abroad to complete their education and go back to teach in these universities.
11. They should have programmes that respond to the creativity of students, encourage it and enrich it.

Acknowledgement

This chapter originally appeared as: Zughoul, M. R. (2000) Private and privatised higher educational institutions in Jordan, *Mediterranean Journal of Educational Studies*, Vol. 5(1), pp. 95–117. Reprinted here with permission from the publisher.

Notes

1 See, for example, *Applied Science University: A Proposed Project* (unpublished manuscript circulated to all founders, 1989). According to this document, the objectives of the Applied Science University were perceived to be, in this order: (i) cultural (Arab-Islamic identity); (ii) raising the cultural and thought levels of students; (iii) supporting the civilising aspect of society; and (iv) ensuring social affinity. In no way was profitability even discussed. Or even hinted at.
2 I think that the Council of Higher Education was under the influence of the strong lobbying of the owners of these three private Community Colleges. It is my personal estimation that these very Community Colleges turned universities have been behind the 'commercialisation' of private higher education, and indeed have been behind many of the practices of private universities.
3 It has always been a valid question raised at the national level as to why the national educational institutions do not take in all the graduates of high school. It was impossible throughout the years till the country witnessed the establishment of 12 private universities. With more pressure exercised on public universities for admitting more and more students and the availability of so many Community Colleges, it has become possible for all these institutions to take in up to 98% of high school graduates. Al-Su'oud (1995), who was the Minister of Higher Education then, gave the following figures of admission. Jordanian public universities accepted 11,488 students or 36.5% of Tawjiihi graduates:

Private Universities	7734	24.6%
Public Community Colleges	6261	19.9%
Private Community Colleges	3949	12.6%
Grants and Scholarships	1496	4.7%
Total	**30928**	**98.3%**

4 It is a fact that the most influential decision-making body in private universities is the 'Managerial Committee' or the 'Committee of Directors'. There are so many anecdotes on how those with money direct those with the mind. The biggest of these universities, which is now practically wholly owned by a semi-illiterate Jordanian who made a fortune working in the Gulf, has been pioneering in this direction. It has always hired Jordanian celebrities to be on the board of trustees and then, when they turn against the conspicuous treachery of 'capital', are unceremoniously replaced.

References

Al-Tall, A. (1998) *Higher Education in Jordan Amman: The Committee on the History of Jordan* (in Arabic). Amman: Aal Al-Bayt Foundation.

Al-Su'oud, R. (1995) *The Admission Policies of Jordanian Public Universities* (in Arabic). Paper presented at the conference on 'Higher Education in Jordan: Problems and Solutions', Amman, Jordan.

Dahiyyat, E. (1996) *Private Universities in Jordan* (in Arabic). Amman.

Jordan University of Science and Technology (JUST) (1996) *Jordan University of Science and Technology: Facts and Figures.* Irbid: Author.

Ministry of Higher Education (1981) *The Annual Statistical Report on Higher Education.* Amman: Author.

Ministry of Higher Education (1986) *The Annual Statistical Report on Higher Education.* Amman: Author.

Ministry of Higher Education (1991) *The Annual Statistical Report on Higher Education.* Amman: Author.

Ministry of Higher Education (1998) *The Annual Statistical Report on Higher Education.* Amman: Author.

Ministry of Higher Education (1999) *The Annual Statistical Report on Higher Education.* Amman: Author.

Nsour, A. (1996) An interview: an interview on issues in higher education. *Al-Ra'i* (Jordanian newspaper), 17 July.

CHAPTER 15

The Implications of Lebanese Cultural Complexities for Education

Linda Akl

1 Introduction

Lebanon has managed to survive numerous wars and internal conflicts. Its geostrategic position as a small country lying between Syria and Israel makes incursions by these opposing foreign powers inevitable. Lebanon still exists on the map but the fundamental quandaries remain. The consequences of the multiple Lebanese cultures and the ways in which they relate to one another and impact on the Lebanese educational system are unique and complex.

This paper provides a brief overview of the various entangled elements that underlie the Lebanese culture and explores their influence on the educational system. The purpose is to set a framework for future empirical research on the issues of equality within the Lebanese educational system. Since there is a limited amount of published research within the Lebanese context on this topic, this paper draws on constructs created by western cultural theorists. The author of this paper draws upon her own and others' personal experiences to exemplify some of these theories.

Culture symbolises the specialised lifestyle of a group of people (Devito, 2004) and 'can be thought of as a blueprint that guides the ways in which individuals within a group' (Biehler & Snowman 2003, p. 145) perceive, believe, evaluate, value, share and work (Arends, Tannenbaum & Winitzky, 2001; Eggen & Kauchak, 2003; Femiano et al., 2005). In addition, when religion plays a prominent role in culture, it is difficult to separate the impact of religion from other cultural influences. Berger's (2003) comment that 'as soon as one looks at culture one is looking at religion' (p. 4) applies particularly to the Lebanese situation. Furthermore, language and culture are deeply intertwined and 'one cannot separate the two without losing the significance of either language or culture' (Iskold, 2002, p. 103). Thus, culture is a dynamic phenomenon that encompasses numerous, usually covert, variables. These underlying components appear to be the reason why cultural problems are not easily identified and solved. The importance of religion and language, and their effect on the formation of a culture, vary from one community to another. Lebanon is a

© THE EURO-MEDITERRANEAN CENTRE FOR EDUCATION RESEARCH, UNIVERSITY OF MALTA, 2007
DOI: 10.1163/9789004506602_015

good example of a country in which religion and language profoundly affect the evolution of the culture which, in turn, influences the educational system.

The Lebanese Republic is one of the most unusual states in the world, encompassing a melange of cultures. It is a conglomeration of paradoxes and contradictions. Lebanon as a polity is archaic, inefficient and divided; it is also democratic, traditional and modern (Hudson, 1985). As described by Harris (2006):

> Lebanon's story is a particularly rich and varied tapestry, encompassing sectarianism and class conflict, secularism and religious radicalism, Islam and Christendom, the Orient and the West, Sunni and Shi'a, Israel and the Arabs much else besides. (p. 9)

Lebanon is a country with a mosaic of cultures, a linguistic kaleidoscope and a vivacious population. Lebanon is difficult to classify according to the usual typologies, it is a democracy, but it is also an oligarchy (Hudson, 1985).

The infrastructure of Lebanon and the coordination of its highly articulated subcultures create fundamental problems on various levels and in many organisations, including the educational system. Most of the research that deals with multicultural education has been designed by western writers who are guided by a liberal-secular ideology which fits into the cultural formation of their respective societies. In order to look at multiculturalism from an insider's point of view it is important to look at the various components of the Lebanese educational system. These include:

1. The foundation of the school system and its cultural implications.
2. The formal and the hidden curriculum.
3. The infrastructure of the Lebanese universities and their affiliations within a cultural context.
4. The politico-religious events that are taking place within educational settings.

Furthermore, this paper will look at Lebanon's politico-religious history and Lebanese multilingualism in order to explore how they influence the development of a Lebanese national cultural identity.

2 The Influences of Culture on Educational Systems

It is difficult to challenge the view that culture impacts on learning (Evans, Schweingruber & Stevenson, 2002; Eggen & Kauchak, 2003; Armstrong, Henson &

Savage, 2005). However, each culture influences pedagogy in a different way. Hofstede & Hofstede (2005) generated a framework for defining some of the ways in which educational relationships are constructed in different cultural situations. At opposite ends of the continuum are the collectivist cultures and the individualist cultures. Collectivism pertains to societies where the interest of the group prevails over the interest of the individual, whereas individualism pertains to societies where the interest of the individual prevails over the interest of the group (Hofstede & Hofstede, 2005). Western cultures tend to be individualistic, whereas most non-western cultures tend to be collectivist (Hogg & Vaughan, 2002; Anjum et al., 2005).

In individualistic societies, multicultural education is dealt with by constructively using students' diverse backgrounds as enhancements instead of impediments (Eggen & Kauchak, 2003; Armstrong, Henson & Savage, 2005). In addition, the teacher's role is viewed as a mediator of cultural diversity (Arends, Tannenbaum & Winitzky, 2001; Biehler & Snowman, 2003). This western perspective on multicultural education can be labelled a 'liberal-secular ideology'. Many multicultural educational programmes for students are built upon this ideology (Kluth & Straut, 2001; Barth, 2002; Gay, 2003; Schaps, 2003; Wolk, 2003; Shields, 2004; Albright & Kugler, 2005; Bazron, Fleischman & Osher, 2005; Bismilla et al., 2005; Napoliello & Powell, 2005).

Furthermore, the liberal-secular ideology is a significant feature of national identities. For example, there is arguably a hegemonic culture evident in the UK and the USA. The dominant populations are white Anglo-Saxon, and English is the basic language. Therefore, it can be argued that there is a power-dominant view of what it means to be a citizen of the UK or the USA. Even though many subcultures exist within these two countries, there appears to be a dominant, albeit sometimes contested, national identity and language. Accordingly, the subcultures are at a disadvantage. This puts pressure on minority groups to integrate to the cultural hegemony. It is possible that this hegemonic culture drives liberal-secularists to deal with multicultural education in a way that is compatible with their cultural perspective. Therefore, these liberal-secular approaches to the educational field are easily applied in western cultures.

In contrast to western individualistic cultures, Lebanon is characterised by collectivist cultural values (Hofstede & Hofstede, 2005). Lebanese multiculturalism is fragmented to the extent that the notion of a national identity is highly contested. This is because there is no single dominant faction which promotes the development of a central Lebanese identity. When national identities are weak, national unities are threatened. In the absence of a hegemonic culture, conflict is difficult to resolve. The equivocal dominance of the Lebanese cultures lack constructive interaction except on functional levels. There are difficulties in communicating thoughts about the various cultural differences, which are at the core of the Lebanese quandaries. In exploring these issues, the author will refer to Barth's (2002) concepts of 'non-discussables'. Some western concepts on multicultural education are of questionable value to Lebanese educational concepts. The reason being the liberal-secular argument that the diversity of students is something to be highlighted, acknowledged and explored rather than ignored.

The following are central to Hofstede & Hofstede's (2005) account of the construction of educational relationships in collectivist societies:
- Students tend to speak up in class only when sanctioned by the group.
- Students from different ethnic backgrounds often form subgroups in class.
- Students from the same ethnic background as the teacher or other school officials tend to expect preferential treatment.

Whereas, these authors argue that in individualistic societies students expect to be treated as individuals and preferential treatment of students is considered nepotism. In addition, Hofstede & Hofstede (2005) point out that collectivist cultures usually tend to have 'large power-distance' cultural dimensions. Power-distance is defined as 'the extent to which the less powerful members of institutions and organisations within a country expect and accept that power is distributed equally' (Hofstede & Hofstede, 2005, p. 46). Thus, in terms of relating the power dimension with educational relationships, these authors highlight the following features of educational settings in collectivist cultures:
- Authority resides with the teacher.
- The parent-child inequality is perpetuated by a teacher-student inequality.
- The educational process is teacher centred.
- In the classroom, there is strict order with the teacher initiating all communication.
- Teachers are never publicly contradicted or criticised and are treated with deference, even outside the school.

There is a difference between the way multiculturalism is defined in western cultures and the way it is defined in eastern cultures. The use of the term multiculturalism in the West often refers to ethnic minorities, religious and racial differences, foreign students, and challenged or gifted students (O'Brien et al., 2003; Schaps, 2003; Albright & Kugler, 2005; Bazron, Fleischman & Osher, 2005; Bismilla et al., 2005; Napoliello & Powell, 2005). In Lebanon, multiculturalism refers to similar types of diversity with the additional category of related political affiliations. Paradoxically, the Lebanese culture is characterised by the absence of a single dominant culture. In this paper it is argued that the Lebanese culture is in fact characterised by the presence of diverse and un-integrated subcultures. However, within these subcultures, the ethnic, religious and political components are deeply interwoven in such a way that ethnic identification is associated with linguistic identity and political and religious affiliations. Appendix A shows how the key elements of the Lebanese culture overlap. Furthermore, education systems are main functions of cultural reproduction. Their role is not to change the culture but rather to reproduce it harmoniously (Bernstein, 1970). Central to this paper is the argument that there is an absence of a national Lebanese identity to promote within schools. So each faction in the Lebanese society tends to reproduce its own culture in the schools that it organises in the diverse Lebanese educational system.

3 Key Historical Cultural Influences in Lebanon and the Lebanese National Identity Confusion

There are deeply entrenched historical reasons that underlie the confusion about Lebanese national identity. After the First World War, the Middle East was divided according to the Sykes-Picot Agreement of 1916, by which France and Great Britain each took responsibility for the governance of a country (Ismail, 1972). Great Britain was allocated control of several areas including some Arab countries. France was allocated control of several countries, Lebanon included. When French forces landed in Beirut, Christians cheered their arrival whereas the Muslims watched the arrival of the French with grave apprehension (Salibi, 1988). This welcome presaged the acceptance of the French mandate which was enthusiastically accepted by the Christians and adamantly rejected by the Muslims (Salibi, 1988). This conflict was the result of the earlier occupation of Lebanon by the Muslim Turks (the Ottoman Empire) who had fought against the victorious western powers during the First World War (Ismail, 1972). Lebanese Muslims had been privileged under the Ottoman occupation, whereas under the western occupation the Christians were favoured by the then dominant power (Hudson, 1985).

The Lebanese government and the French authorities decreed the creation of the State of Greater Lebanon (Picard, 2002). Leaders from the Christian majority, in consultation with the French mandate authorities, wrote the Constitution in 1926 (Hudson, 1985). This led in turn to the creation of the Lebanese Republic (Grafton, 2003). It is sometimes referred to as the Franco-Maronite[1] creation of Greater Lebanon; a Maronite concept for Maronite purposes (Harris, 2006). It left the Muslims feeling alienated because they aspired to Arab unity (Hudson, 1985; Dagher, 2000).

Consequently, from the 1920s onward the Lebanese have developed contrasting ideas regarding the role and identity of the Lebanese polity (Dagher, 2000). At the two ends of the spectrum are what have been termed 'Lebanonism' (proponents being exclusively Maronite Christians) which views Lebanon as something detached from its Arab neighbourhood and 'Arabism' (proponents being Muslims) which views Lebanon as an integral component of the Arab world (Salibi, 1988; Harris, 2006). Lebanonism implied asserting the mythology of Phoenician origins and of attachment to the West, which could be labelled 'Maronite Nationalism' (Harris, 2006). Consequently, the two forces collided on every fundamental issue, impeding the normal development of the state (Salibi, 1988). In 1991, the word 'Lebanonisation' emerged, meaning the 'process of fragmentation of a state as a result of confrontation between diverse communities' (Harris, 2006, p. 1). This one word basically describes the disjointed infrastructure of Lebanon.

Christians and Muslims disagree on major concepts, such as Arabity, pluralism and cultural differences (Dagher, 2000). Even though Christians and Muslims remain in strong disagreement on how the Lebanese Republic ought to be generally interpreted and run, both sides have become equally convinced that there can be no viable alternative to Lebanon as territorially constituted (Salibi, 1988). 'Geography has constrained their coexistence while history has taught them that living together—for better or worse—was an irrevocable fate' (Dagher, 2000, p. 6).

The legacy of the confused national Lebanese identity is that 'both doctrinaire Christians and Muslims feel superior to and threatened by each other' (Hudson 1985, p. 91). The Muslims and the Christians of Lebanon did not exhibit a common identity in 1920, or in 1943 when the Lebanese Republic gained its independence on the basis of a 'polite fiction' (Salibi, 1988) of national unity among its people, or in 1958 when the Muslim and Christian Lebanese were in conflict with each other for six months over the issue of pan-Arab unity (Salibi, 1988). Clearly then, culture is not synonymous with nationality because even if individuals of a certain country are taught similar beliefs, attitudes and values, enormous differences will emerge (Devito, 2004). As Salibi (1988) described the Lebanese situation: 'to create a country is one thing, to create a nationality is another' (p. 19).

4 The Influence of Lebanon's Multilingualism on Its Culture and Educational Systems

Multicultural societies often 'contain a single dominant high-status group whose language is the lingua franca of the nation and a number of other ethnic groups whose languages are subordinate' (Hogg & Vaughan, 2002, p. 427). This is what the current author refers to as cultural hegemony. Lebanon's multicultural society has equivocal levels of multilingualism, yet there is a distance between the various factions as a result of the aforementioned historical reasons. Although language is the most obvious sign of cultural difference within Lebanon, it is merely the symptom of a deeper symbolic rift. The root of the rift is religion, which is based on the historical clashes, which in turn resulted in the Lebanese national identity confusion.

Christian groups adopted the French language, traditions and customs. Muslim groups preferred to speak and to teach their children the Arabic language. Nevertheless, they adopted English as their second language since many came from Arab countries at a time during which Britain had power of authority. Given that language is one of the most distinct and clear markers of ethnic identity (Hogg & Vaughan, 2002) and speech styles cue ethnic identity, each factionalised Lebanese culture conveys its individuality and its distinctiveness by the language it has adopted. For example, at a shop in the western side of Lebanon the salesperson would say the price in English or Arabic, whereas in the eastern side the price is mostly spoken in French or in Arabic. Interestingly, national greetings are almost always spoken in French: *'bonjour'*, *'bonsoir'*, or on the phone *'allo'*. A good example of the complexity of the Lebanese culture is a common phrase used by the Lebanese, which combines all three languages: English, Arabic and French: *'Hi, kifak, ça va?'* Translation: 'Hi, how are you, fine?'

4.1 *The Lebanese Language*

English began surreptitiously to seep into Lebanese-Arabic, leading to a fusion of languages into what is now referred to as 'Arabinglizi' (Al-Yousef, 1999). The grammatical structure of these words is derived from English roots and 'Arabified' (for examples see Appendix B). Hence, in addition to the already existing words with French roots, English words mutated into 'Arabic' words. These changes led to the following significant question: 'What is the language of Lebanon and what implications does it have for education?' Thonhauser (2001) researched this issue and reported that this simple question turned out to have not as simple an answer as might have been thought. The following example further elucidates the complexity of the linguistic divisions. A student coming to Lebanon from the University of Cambridge, UK, with the intention of strengthening her Arabic language, ended up leaving Lebanon without any improvement in her Arabic language, while polishing her English and French languages. She expressed her dismay by asking: 'Why don't the Lebanese like to speak their own language?' (cited in Al-Yousef, 1999). The question should not be generalised, as this is not the case with *all* Lebanese.

For historical reasons, the Lebanese Christians preferred to speak French and English instead of Arabic, as they tried to ignore the Arabic culture in order to strengthen their lifelong quest for independence from the Arab world (Dagher, 2000). The link between Arab and Islam is clear, however the link between Christians and Arabs is vague. The overwhelming majority of Arabs happen to be Muslims, hence Islam naturally underlines the sense of common ethnicity among most Arabs (Salibi, 1988). In addition, the foundation of the Arab world's identity and the expression of its specificity is the Arabic language. This coincides with the language of Islam, which can only be fully learned and embraced in Arabic (Dagher, 2000). This association between the Arabic language and Islam presents the real dilemma for eastern Christians (Dagher, 2000).

When a population perceives its ethnic identity to be a source of self-respect and pride, it accentuates it (Hogg & Vaughan, 2002). It is common for some Christian Lebanese to de-emphasise their Arabic native language because of its connotations. Some Lebanese Christians refer to their language as Lebanese and not Arabic to emphasise the distinction. According to Salibi (1988), the Lebanese Christians have no doubt about the matter, they remain 'Lebanese regardless to which extent the outside world might choose to classify them as Arabs, because their language happened to be Arabic' (p. 27). Conversely, Muslims value their Arabic language. They are in a position where it is pragmatic to learn alternative languages to succeed in this modern era. Further, historic friction between Muslims and the French language seemed to have declined by the late 20th century (Dagher, 2000). However, it is possible that this symbolic convergence has been interrupted by the most recent war that took place in July 2006.

Another example of Lebanon's multilingualism is provided on the streets where most placards combine languages (Al-Yousef, 1999; Thonhauser, 2001). This includes the colloquial Arabic, which follows no rules or grammar and is usually written in English script. Appendix C provides an example of a placard in Lebanon. A further uniqueness of the Lebanese multilingualism is in informal writings. For instance, 'ana mnie7' translates to 'I am fine'. Obviously, numerical numbers replace letters (e.g., the number '7' is used to replace the stressed 'H' sound). The numbers chosen resemble the letters in the Arabic language (e.g., '7' is ح and '3' is ع in Arabic). However, official documents are usually written in Arabic, the official language, before being formally presented.[2]

4.2   *The Implication of Language for the Educational System*

Most private schools in Lebanon require students to learn two main languages (Arabic and either French or English) and a third minor language (English or

French). Some even implement a curriculum containing all three languages with equal importance. In addition, schools implement formal Arabic which is different from spoken Arabic. Hence students are introduced to yet another new language, which ignores all prior experiences that have shaped the student's identity and cognitive functioning. Within a constructivist approach, educators would argue that teachers with students from linguistically diverse backgrounds should explicitly activate their students' prior knowledge. This knowledge embraces not only the information or skills previously acquired in formal instruction, but also the totality of the experiences that have shaped the learners' identity and cognitive functioning (Bismilla et al., 2005).

'The study of language in society illustrates how the members of a culture use verbal expression to define themselves and others in relation to one another' (Block & Lemish, 2005, p. 154). Furthermore, the manner in which a person speaks (accent or language) affects the way s/he is evaluated by others. The reason does not envelop the probability that 'certain speech styles are intrinsically more pleasing than others, but rather because speech styles are associated with particular social groups that are consensually evaluated more or less positively in society' (Hogg & Vaughan, 2002, p. 427). Similarly, in educational settings, students coming from diverse backgrounds are distinguished by their primary language (Au & Blake, 2003). This is particularly true in a Lebanese classroom where students' ethnic backgrounds will be recognised by the manner in which they speak. Consequently, teachers will identify the social group to which students belong and, if the teachers hold preconceived biases and prejudices, discrimination for or against those students might occur. Not only could students be subjected to unfairness because of their language and ethnicity, but a teacher's perception of students' academic abilities could also be influenced by the students' language use (Galguera, 1998).

5   Religious Cultural Factors Underpinning Educational Institutions

Lebanon is dominated by its religions. Religion is not only part of the Lebanese culture, it is the catalyst that binds the individual subcultures internally. Casual or professional encounters between Lebanese people often entail indirect questions, with the intention of finding out the religion of the other person. The Lebanese population comprises different religious communities: the Christian (mainly Maronite, Greek Orthodox, Greek Catholics) and the Islamic (Sunnite Muslims, Shiite Muslims and Druze) (Salibi, 1988).

A research article by Jamali, Sidani & Safieddine (2005) reported that 'the Muslims are estimated to comprise 70 per cent of the total resident population, with the remaining 30 per cent Christians' (p. 584). However, this is not entirely accurate because although Jamali, Sidani & Safieddine (2005) claim that these figures are based on 2002 data from the United Nations Develoment Programme (UNDP) website,[3] the present author found that the UNDP website does not break down the Lebanese population by religion and only reports that the total Lebanese population was 3.5 million in 2003. In addition, several authors (Hudson, 1985; Dagher, 2000; Harris, 2006) assert that the demographic figures of the Lebanese population are considered a taboo, the belief being that if the actual numbers of people within different religions were known, those with the highest number might use this information as a basis for seeking greater political power. Thus, recently quoted demographic figures for Lebanon are usually spurious and often biased, because the latest available official figures date back to the 1932 census. Jamali, Sidani & Safieddine's (2005) report tries to promote the idea that the Lebanese culture is characterised by the Muslim religion, however this might not actually be the case.

Religious symbols are part of everyday classroom life. Students identify themselves by using verbal or non-verbal expressions that typify their cultural background. This presents a problem if individuals hold negative bigotry views about others. Some Christian students often make the sign of the cross before taking an examination and some Muslim students often say 'Allah Akbar' meaning 'God is Great' when hearing the prayer from the Mosque. Therefore, teachers can easily identify the religious backgrounds of their students. Thus, if the teacher is able to recognise the students' ethnicity, it is possible that preconceived biases or prejudices could emerge. The solution is not easily found. The educational paradox is that there is an absence of the opportunity to acknowledge or discuss these differentials. Then again, discussing these locally controversial issues could have major consequences.

6   The Lebanese School System: The Formal and the Hidden Curriculum

In Lebanon, the public (i.e., the government) school system is poorly established. Across Lebanon, public schools suffer due to political interference, a spiralling number of students and dwindling government funds (Hajj, 2000). Hajj (2000) reports that the president of the public secondary school teachers' league addressed the following aspects during a seminar that took place in 2000:

- The issue of sectarianism being the most difficult obstacle standing in the way of public education.

- The concern for national unity is being jeopardised since rampant spread of sectarian politics is prevailing in schools all over Lebanon.
- The confessional troubles which are not being solved by the government.
- The suffering of students due to political interference in the administration of public education.

There are more Lebanese private sectarian schools than non-sectarian schools. In most cases, the geographical location of a school indicates the religion to which it subscribes. Parents choose a school for their children based on the types of values, ethos and traditions they want their children to follow.

Schools across Lebanon teach different versions of its history. Each community has its own collective memory, its own history, its own heroes, its anthem and its flags (Salibi, 1988; Dagher, 2000). Hence, Lebanon is permitting the young to be educated using highly selective and contradictory versions of its history (Picard, 2002). The Druze schools teach a new version of the history of Lebanon, which is radically different from the official version, as well as changing the curriculum to parallel the political ethos of the Druze community (Salibi, 1988). In contrast, the Sunnite schools follow the official government curriculum, upholding all the established symbols and traditions of their version of Lebanon (Salibi, 1988). As a result, students across Lebanon are acquiring their national citizenship in diversified ways, which causes intercultural conflict when they interact together academically and socially.

Most schools in Lebanon follow either the French baccalaureate model of the curriculum or align themselves with the American High School system. However, some schools adopt a mixture of the two. Each private school implements its own curriculum alongside the formal national Lebanese curriculum, which public schools are compelled to follow. The hidden curriculum encompasses a wider range of learning experiences than the formal curriculum. It will thus be discussed in more detail.

A new curriculum was legally established in Lebanon in 1997.[4] Because religion and culture are interwoven and culture influences education, a religious-cultural educational conflict emerged. In 1999 Muslim intellectuals criticised the new school curriculum (Kayali, 1999). One general argument was that the curriculum copied the texts from western countries, neglecting to include Arabic traditions and customs. A specific debated issue was that the civic education textbooks emphasised the woman's role as an income earner and marginalised her role as mother and wife. Another complaint was that the science textbooks promoted improper sex education. Finally, the omission of the Islamic school of thought in the economic learning materials was considered a personal insult to the Islamic religion and totally disgraceful (Kayali, 1999).

One of the common factors in the many different curricula in Lebanon is that they rarely overtly address social issues. The liberal-secular ideology argues that if a school curriculum does not systematically include important information about the diversity of the society, it then causes major gaps in students' academic achievements (Gay, 2003; Brooks & Thompson, 2005). Douglas (2002) claims that one profound source of unrest in this world is the failure of educational systems to bypass narrow ethnic and national interests and to provide teaching about differing belief systems and shared common values. In Lebanon, the curriculum lacks cohesive and general guidelines which would direct students on how to deal with the political and religious quandaries that are inherent in the ways in which cultural factors are negotiated in Lebanon.

Central to this paper is the argument that in Lebanese educational settings, individuals rarely converse about 'non-discussable' issues. According to Barth (2002),

> non-discussables are subjects sufficiently important that they are talked about frequently but are so laden with anxiety and fearfulness that these conversations take place only in the parking lot, the rest rooms, the playground, the car pool, or the dinner table at home. (p. 8)

Major Lebanese 'non-discussables' entail political and religious subjects. There is great fear that open discussions of these controversial issues will produce severe consequences. Some kind of harmony is maintained by not discussing the very issues that are at the heart of the Lebanese predicament. However, it seems that this type of harmony is only maintained inside the classroom. Substantial student arguments take place elsewhere. However, within school grounds, the confrontations are not severe, possibly because of the formation of the school system which is based on a hierarchical authority structure. Another explanation could be that it would depend on the school system into which the parents enrol their children. If the school parallels communal regional cultural values, then the students would maintain homogenous beliefs and customs. Whereas on university campuses all over Lebanon, students' constantly clash with each other over political and religious events (Tuttle, 1998; Zaatari, 1998; Ibrahim, 1999a; Abdul-Hussain, 2003; Abou Nasr, 2004; Hatoum, 2005, 2006; Ghazal, 2006a, 2006b). Appendix D provides a chronological list of some of the conflicts that occurred between university students in Lebanon.

A possible interpretation of these discords is that although students are sheltered from divergent cultures during school years, the exposure to diverse cultures is inevitable when they go to university because the choice of high-quality university education is limited. The educational dilemma is that it is unclear whether the discussion of these taboo topics in school would have led to positive consequences or not. When some views are exclusive and entrenched in a culture, productive dialogue is not only difficult to produce, but is also delicate in its nature because the unwrapping of some topics might lead to open hostilities and major ruptures.

From the liberal-secular perspective, it is argued that teachers' deficiency in openly discussing taboo topics leads to a lack of collective classroom coherence (Tatum, 2000; Barth, 2002; Shields, 2004). Thus, the liberal-secular ideology encourages teachers to develop classroom cultures that create shared student values (Kerfoot, 2004) by taking students' cultural differences into account (Shields, 2004). Shields (2004) points out that 'a successful education leader must attend to both social justice and academic excellence because one implies the other' (p. 38).

Tatum (2000) offers some reasons behind teachers' avoidance of provocative topics in the classroom. These include a lack of skill at discussing them, or a limited opportunity to explore these issues in their own education or a reluctance to lead such discussions for fear that they will generate classroom conflict. Barth (2002) asserts that giving these 'non-discussables' such incredible power as to govern the school culture indicates that the same underlying problems will continue. The proposition to interrupt the cycle of biased behaviours, according to Tatum (2000), is that students need to understand how they operate in their society.

One would assume that the liberal-secular ideology would resolve social and academic problems in Lebanon, since hiding behind the taboo issues apparently did not resolve the quandaries. Then again, scrutinising the complexity of the Lebanese situation, coupled with the consideration of the consequences of the war that broke out in July 2006, leads to the inference that the liberal-secular ideology challenges what would be the obvious interpretation of the situation. The divergent factions differ sharply over the national interests and hold totally opposing views of what Lebanon is or should be. Thus, the quandary remains on how the educational system could unite the Lebanese multicultural students.

7   Politico-Religious Events in the Educational Field

There is a rigid link between politico-religious events and the educational field in Lebanon. The Lebanese academic landscape reflects the confessional mosaic of the country in the way in which prominent universities were established by religious foundations. For example, as pointed out by Dagher (2000):
- The Shiites Supreme Council founded its Islamic University.
- The Sunni community established the al-Makassed.

THE IMPLICATIONS OF LEBANESE CULTURAL COMPLEXITIES FOR EDUCATION   285

- The Greek Orthodox administered the Balamand University.
- The Greek Catholic and Maronites founded Notre Dame University, Kaslik University, Law School of La Sagesse, and the Haigazian and Homenetmen Armenian institutions.

Lebanon 'currently accommodates 18 officially recognised private universities that are mostly patterned after the American credit system of higher education' (Abouchedid & Nasser, 2002, p. 198).

The first example comes from the Lebanese University (LU), a public institution. 'During the war, its various branches were geographically, confessionally and ideologically divided between 'East' and 'West' and were the hotbed of political militancy' (Dagher, 2000, p. 129). In 1999, a plan was initiated to merge east and west campuses (Ibrahim, 1999b). In 2001, the proposal came into effect (Darrous, 2001). The proposal received mixed reactions from both LU academics and LU students. Members at Beirut branches (Muslims) generally supported the cabinet's decision, whereas Mount Lebanon-based staff and students (Christians) opposed the merger. The latter believed that merging the campuses would have dangerous political aspects and that the merger was aimed at suppressing students' and academics' political freedoms. Although students from the Progressive Socialist Party, which is a mostly Druze party, did not politically approve of the Christian opposition bloc, they supported them in their plan to fight the cabinet proposal. They justified their support on the basis that the decision entailed a political dimension and not an academic one. However, their long internal strife with the Shiites of Beirut, who happened to support the merger, is recognised (Darrous, 2001).

Another example from the school system consists of anecdotal information. Recently, in the eastern side of Lebanon, a Christian inter-sectarian conflict between the Lebanese Forces and the Free Patriotic Movement (FPM) has been escalating. The FPM has adopted orange as its colour, resulting in the whole country linking the orange colour with that movement. Accordingly, this gives rise to easy differentiation between people on political lines. Now, to avoid being politically differentiated, it appears that some people are avoiding wearing any orange garment. It is argued that this behaviour has contaminated school grounds. The affiliation of teachers or students who wear the orange colour could be recognised, and thus biased behaviours could emerge toward and from the opposing group. This is in line with Hofstede & Hofstede's (2005) theory that in collectivist cultures, students tend to expect preferential treatment when they share common ideologies with the teacher. Taking into account that 'prejudices and stereotypes influence teachers' perceptions of and behaviour toward students but also that similar attitudes influence students' perceptions of and behaviour toward teachers' (Galguera, 1998, p. 412).

If these kinds of events are generalisable throughout Lebanese classrooms, then it is possible that there is an absence of healthy teacher-student relationships where teachers promote learning (Wolk, 2003), establish rapport (Mendes, 2003) and enhance student achievements (Marzano & Marzano, 2003). As a consequence, the concept of educating the 'whole' child (Wolk, 2003) fails since it depends on school bonding, a healthy school climate, teacher support, and student engagement (Blum, 2005).

Some liberal-secular ideologists would argue that students require unconditional acceptance to flourish (Kohn, 2005), and claim that education that is just and caring provides opportunities for students to make sense of complex topics such as religion and ethnicity (Shields, 2004). Brooks & Thompson (2005) emphasise that teachers have a 'professional responsibility to see the diverse cultural value systems of their students with an open mind, as free as possible from their own value systems' (p. 50). Accordingly, it is suggested that toxic school cultures that are monopolised by politics and religion are not only preserving hostile discriminatory feelings in the new generation, but are also affecting students' learning and personal growth.

A logical conclusion to be drawn from the preceding arguments is that, on the one hand, there are the 'non-discussables' and, on the other hand, there are individuals who are parading their political affiliations. This is a threatening combination and a potential source of conflict. The problems are there for everyone to see, yet they cannot be discussed within the formal educational context. This suggests an unhealthy state of affairs in the classroom. The very things that divide people are the exact things that are not allowed to be discussed. Although multiple sources of variations exist within cultures, one's early experiences tend to become organised into definite systems of thought (Jackson & Wasson, 2002). Even more, in a multicultural country such as Lebanon, one would assume that education is multicultural, which means 'education that promotes educational equity for all learners' (Armstrong, Henson & Savage, 2005, p. 115). Evidently, this is not the case.

8 Conclusion

This paper recognised the fragmentation of Lebanon. 'Lebanonism' became a byword that describes the disjointed infrastructure of Lebanon. During the writing of this paper, another war broke out in Lebanon which changed its whole panoramic view. Political alliances shifted and were reconstructed on the bases of political and personal gains rather than religious grouping. The war's implications for the educational system are countless. Other than reintegrating bias and prejudice feelings in the older generation, the younger generation is now living the harsh reality of intolerance which were previously just anecdotes passed on to them. Multiple Lebanese cultures continue to exist, but in a volatile state. This has produced serious consequences which will lead to future political and social conflicts. These, in turn, will undoubtedly have significant implications on the educational system. The Lebanese quandary is, among other things, an educational challenge.

The aim of education in general is bound by a universal purpose—to educate the students, but each particular society has specific aspirations and methods which make it unique (Noddings, 2005). A liberal-secular argument is that for successful teaching and learning in multi-linguistic and multicultural societies, students must gain an understanding of the differences and similarities of the various cultures. As Brooks & Thompson (2005) stated, 'it is crucial to help students consider diversity, understanding, and the places where the two intersect and clash' (p. 48). In order to promote a unified national culture, students who are prospective teachers need to encounter more cross-cultural experiences so that they can develop favourable personal and professional beliefs about diverse learners (Garmon, 2004). However, the application of liberal-secular educational theories in Lebanon is contestable.

The history of Lebanon is marked by conflict and filled with turmoil, dismay and suffering. It is difficult to read one book or one paper that captures the whole Lebanese picture. Many books have been written about Lebanon and yet none capture the reality. Lebanese writers portray the view of the aspect with which they are or choose to be aligned, thus failing in their efforts to be unbiased. No Lebanese person who has lived in Lebanon can be truly unbiased. Each group, having observed the death and suffering of its own members caused by an opposing party, cannot be totally objective when claiming facts and events. Foreign writers, unfamiliar with the Lebanese culture, also fail to convey a view of Lebanon that is free from bias. They might investigate many issues, interview different political parties, but there is something about Lebanon that a person cannot fully comprehend unless s/he has lived there.

This paper has illustrated the difficulties in attempting to describe Lebanese culture. The Lebanese people are, on the one hand, united by a common fate, yet, on the other hand, are separated by religious doctrines and political ideologies. Although the profound and negative influences of the culture on the educational system are recognised, solutions have yet to be determined.

Acknowledgement

This chapter originally appeared as: Akl, L. (2007) The implications of Lebanese cultural complexities for education, *Mediterranean Journal of Educational Studies*, Vol. 12(2), pp. 91–113. Reprinted here with permission from the publisher.

Notes

1 Maronite is a dominant Christian sect in the Middle East.
2 Source: personal communication with a senior civil servant in the Lebanese government.
3 See http://www.undp.org/
4 Public Law number 10227.

References

Abdul-Hussain, H. (2003) Student polls show support for pro-government groups: FPM sees setbacks at most universities. *The Daily Star* (Lebanon), 30 December.

Abouchedid, K., & Nasser, R. (2002) Assuring quality service in higher education: registration and advising attitudes in a private university in Lebanon, *Quality Assurance in Education*, Vol. 10(4), pp. 198–206.

Abou Nasr, M. (2004) LU campus sealed after fight breaks out between Amal and Hizbollah students: three injured in fracas; conflicting stories circulating. *The Daily Star* (Lebanon), 7 February.

Albright, E., & Kugler, E. G. (2005) Increasing diversity in challenging classes, *Educational Leadership*, Vol. 62(5), pp. 42–44.

Al-Yousef, Y. (1999) The very resistible rise of Arabinglizi. *The Daily Star* (Lebanon), 15 June.

Anjum, A., Baarsen, B. V., Boratav, H. B., Carson-Arenas, A., Gibbs, M. S., Goodrich, C., Hsu, D., Pan, K., Perrino, C. S., Rashid, T., Sigal, J., & Van der Pligt, J. (2005) Cross-cultural reactions to academic sexual harassment: effects of individualist vs. collectivist culture and gender of participants, *Sex Roles: A Journal of Research*, Vol. 52(3–4), pp. 201–216.

Arends, R. I., Tannenbaum, M. D., & Winitzky, N. E. (2001) *Exploring Teaching: An Introduction to Education* (2nd edition). New York: McGraw-Hill Higher Education.

Armstrong, D. G., Henson, K. T., & Savage, T. V. (2005) *Teaching Today: An Introduction to Education* (7th edition). Upper Saddle River, NJ: Pearson Prentice Hall.

Au, K. H., & Blake, K. M. (2003) Cultural identity and learning to teach in a diverse community: findings from a collective case study, *Journal of Teacher Education*, Vol. 54(3), pp. 192–206.

Barth, R. S. (2002) The culture builder, *Educational Leadership*, Vol. 59(8), pp. 6–11.

Bazron, B., Fleischman, S., & Osher, D. (2005) Creating culturally responsive schools, *Educational Leadership*, Vol. 63(1), pp. 83–84.

Berger, P. L. (2003) Religions and globalisation, *European Judaism*, Vol. 36(1), pp. 4–11.

Bernstein, B. (1970) Education cannot compensate for society, *New Society*, Vol. 15, pp. 344–391.

Biehler, R., & Snowman, J. (2003) *Psychology Applied to Teaching* (10th edition). Boston: Houghton Mifflin Company.

Bismilla, V., Chow, P., Cohen, S., Cummins, J., Giampapa, F., Leoni, L., Sandhu, P., & Sastri, P. (2005) Affirming identity in multilingual classrooms, *Educational Leadership*, Vol. 63(1), pp. 38–43.

Block, L. R., & Lemish, D. (2005) "I know I'm a *Freierit*, but...": how a key cultural frame (en)genders a discourse of inequality, *Journal of Communication*, Vol. 55(1), pp. 38–55.

Blum, R. W. (2005) A case for school connectedness, *Educational Leadership*, Vol. 62(7), pp. 16–20.

Brooks, J. G., & Thompson, E. G. (2005) Social justice in the classroom, *Educational Leadership*, Vol. 63(1), pp. 48–52.

Dagher, C. H. (2000) *Bring Down the Walls: Lebanon's Post-War Challenge*. New York: Palgrave.

Darrous, S. (2001) LU students deeply divided by plan for proposed merger. *The Daily Star* (Lebanon), 15 May.

Devito, J. A. (2004) *The Interpersonal Communication Book* (10th edition). Boston: Pearson Education.

Douglass, S. L. (2002) Teaching about religion, *Educational Leadership*, Vol. 60(2), pp. 32–36.

Eggen, P. D., & Kauchak, D. P. (2003) *Learning and Teaching: Research-Based Methods* (4th edition). Boston: Pearson Education.

Evans, E. M., Schweingruber, H., & Stevenson, H. W. (2002) Gender differences in interest and knowledge acquisition: the United States, Taiwan and Japan, *Sex Roles: A Journal of Research*, Vol. 47(3–4), pp. 153–168.

Femiano, A. C., Ludlow, L. H., Mahalik, J. R., Morray, E. B., Slattery, S. M., & Smiler, A. (2005) Development of the conformity to feminine norms inventory, *Sex Roles: A Journal of Research*, Vol. 52(7–8), pp. 417–436.

Galguera, T. (1998) Students' attitudes toward teachers' ethnicity, bilinguality, and gender, *Hispanic Journal of Behavioural Sciences*, Vol. 20(4), pp. 411–429.

Garmon, M. A. (2004) Changing preservice teachers' attitudes/beliefs about diversity: what are the critical factors? *Journal of Teacher Education*, Vol. 55(3), pp. 201–214.

Gay, G. (2003) The importance of multicultural education, *Educational Leadership*, Vol. 61(4), pp. 30–35.

Ghazal, R. (2006a) NDU students overcome security to get advocacy group onto campus. *The Daily Star* (Lebanon), 23 March.

Ghazal, R. (2006b) PSP-Amal brawl forces LAU to shut down: instigators to face expulsion. *The Daily Star* (Lebanon), 27 May.

Grafton, D. D. (2003) *The Christians of Lebanon: Political Rights in Islamic Law*. London: Tauris Academic Studies.

Hajj, J. D. (2000) 'Sectarian influence' is harming schools. *The Daily Star* (Lebanon), 31 March.

Harris, W. (2006) *The New Face of Lebanon: History's Revenge.* Princeton, NJ: Markus Wiener Publishers.

Hatoum, M. (2005) Violence erupts at Arab University: fight between opposition and loyalist students leaves 2 wounded. *The Daily Star* (Lebanon), 24 March.

Hatoum, M. (2006) Seven injured in LF-FPM student clashes. *The Daily Star* (Lebanon), 4 May.

Hofstede, G., & Hofstede, G. J. (2005) *Cultures and Organizations: Software of the Mind.* New York: McGraw-Hill.

Hogg, M. A., & Vaughan, G. M. (2002) *Introduction to Social Psychology* (3rd edition). Frenchs Forest, Australia: Pearson Education Australia.

Hudson, M. C. (1985) *The Precarious Republic: Political Modernization in Lebanon.* Boulder, CO: Westview Press.

Ibrahim, A. (1999a) LU fistfight thought to have political undertones. *The Daily Star* (Lebanon), 3 December.

Ibrahim, A. (1999b) University unity addressed at forum. *The Daily Star* (Lebanon), 4 June.

Iskold, L. V. (2002) Integrating culture, language and technology, *Academic Exchange Quarterly*, Vol. 6(4), pp. 103–108.

Ismail, A. (1972) *Lebanon: History of a People.* Beirut: Dar Al-Makchouf.

Jackson, M. H., & Wasson, D. H. (2002) Assessing cross-cultural sensitivity awareness: a basis for curriculum change, *Journal of Instructional Psychology*, Vol. 29(4), pp. 265–277.

Jamali, D., Sidani, Y., & Safieddine, A. (2005) Constraints facing working women in Lebanon: an insider view, *Women in Management Review*, Vol. 20(8), pp. 581–594.

Kayali, I. (1999) Textbook mistakes cause Muslim ire. *The Daily Star* (Lebanon), 14 October.

Kerfoot, K. (2004) Attending to weak signals: the leader's challenge, *Pediatric Nursing*, Vol. 30(1), pp. 79–82.

Kluth, P., & Straut, D. (2001) Standards for diverse learners, *Educational Leadership*, Vol. 59(1), pp. 43–46.

Kohn, A. (2005) Unconditional teaching, *Educational Leadership*, Vol. 63(1), pp. 20–24.

Marzano, R. J., & Marzano, J. S. (2003) The key to classroom management, *Educational Leadership*, Vol. 61(1), pp. 6–13.

Mendez, E. (2003) What empathy can do, *Educational Leadership*, Vol. 61(1), pp. 56–59.

Napoliello, S., & Powell, W. (2005) Using observation to improve instruction, *Educational Leadership*, Vol. 62(5), pp. 52–56.

Noddings, N. (2005) What does it mean to teach the whole child?, *Educational Leadership*, Vol. 63(1), pp. 8–13.

O'Brien, M. U., Payton, J., Resnik, H., & Weissberg, R. P. (2003) Evaluating social and emotional learning programs, *Educational Leadership*, Vol. 60(6), pp. 46–50.

Picard, E. (2002) *Lebanon: A Shattered Country* (revised edition). New York: Holmes & Meier Publishers.

Salibi, K. (1988) *A House of Many Mansions: The History of Lebanon Reconsidered*. Los Angeles, CA: University of California Press.

Schaps, E. (2003) Creating a school community, *Educational Leadership*, Vol. 60(6), pp. 31–33.

Shields, C. M. (2004) Creating a community of difference, *Educational Leadership*, Vol. 61(7), pp. 38–41.

Tatum, B. D. (2000) Examining racial and cultural thinking, *Educational Leadership*, Vol. 57(8), pp. 54–57.

Thonhauser, I. (2001) Multilingual education in Lebanon: 'Arabinglizi' and other challenges of multilingualism, *Mediterranean Journal of Educational Studies*, Vol. 6(1), pp. 49–61.

Tuttle, R. (1998) LAU altercation before students' right victory. *The Daily Star* (Lebanon), 16 May.

Wolk, S. (2003) Hearts and minds: classroom relationships and learning interact, *Educational Leadership*, Vol. 61(1), pp. 14–18.

Zaatari, M. (1998) University poll ends in faculty brawl. *The Daily Star* (Lebanon), 21 February.

Appendix A: Schematic Illustrating the Key Elements of the Lebanese Culture

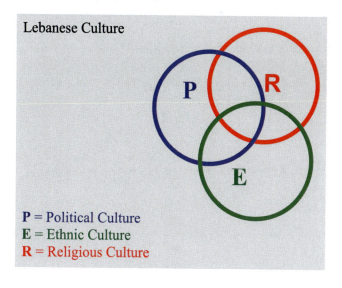

Appendix B: Glossary of Arabinglizi

Word	Meaning
angarit	to become angry
golargi	goalkeeper
hawvaret	to 'hoover' (to clean—from the vacuum cleaner brand 'Hoover')
sayyiva	to save something on a computer
dapris	to get depressed
reglij	to regulate
cancil	to cancel
jagal	gigolo
cdeeyet	plural of CDs
emaiyilla	to e-mail
fawella	to fill it up

Appendix C: An Example of Lebanon's Multilingualism Taken from Thonhauser (2001)

'Yeprad Amseyan & Sons. Repair – Frigidaires & Woching Machines'

The sign addresses customers with essentially the same message in two different languages and two different scripts. There is even a French word (Frigidaires), which is simply a brand name in a somewhat plural feature of Lebanese communication. The spelling of 'Woching Machines' reflects the dominance of spoken discourse in everyday language use. Orthography seems to rank second. The visual representation of a familiar combination sound is enough.

Appendix D: Conflicts between University Students in Lebanon as reported by *The Daily Star*, a Leading English Language Lebanese Newspaper

1998	A fistfight broke out between the two competing blocs; one holds supporters of the Communist Party and Hizbollah and the second bloc groups supporters of the Amal Movement, the Baath Party, and the Syrian Social Nationalist Party during the election of a new student council at LU (Zaatari, 1998).
1998	Students clashed over the election of the student council at LAU Beirut (Tuttle, 1998).
1999	Students from the Amal Movement clashed with students from PSP at the LU Beirut campus (Ibrahim, 1999a).
2003	Students from the LF and the FPM clashed at NDU over election seats (Abdul-Hussain, 2003).
2004	Students clashed between proponents of Amal and Hizbollah at LU Sanayeh (Abou Nasr, 2004).
2005	Students from the opposition and pro-Syrian factions clashed at the Arab University in Beirut (Hatoum, 2005).
2006	Students from the FPM overcame the security checkpoint at NDU to direct a political meeting, which the administration had banned (Ghazal, 2006a).
2006	Students from the Amal Movement brawled with students from the PSP movement at LAU Beirut campus (Ghazal, 2006b).
2006	Students from the LF clashed with students representing the FPM at LU over election seats for the student council (Hatoum, 2006).

Abbreviations:
- Lebanese University (LU)
- Lebanese American University (LAU)
- Notre Dame University (NDU)
- Lebanese Forces (LF)
- Free Patriotic Movement (FPM)
- Progressive Socialist Party (PSP)

CHAPTER 16

The Maltese Bilingual Classroom

A Microcosm of Local Society

Antoinette Camilleri Grima

1 Introduction

Malta presents an interesting case of societal and educational bilingualism. The Maltese nation can be described, by and large, as a mono-ethnic and mono-cultural community that operates in two languages: Maltese and English. Maltese is the first language of about 98% of the population (Borg, Mifsud & Sciriha, 1992) for whom it functions as the means of everyday communication. Maltese is designated as the national language in the Constitution of the Republic of Malta; it is the official language of Parliament, of the Law Courts and of the Church. English, on the other hand, is spoken as a home language by a minority, and simultaneously used for a variety of purposes by everyone: in public administration and industry, for written communication, by the mass media, and in education.

2 Historical Background

Maltese is a mixed language of Semitic origin. It has been spoken by the people inhabiting the Maltese Islands for many centuries. Unfortunately, little is known about language in Malta prior to Arab rule (870–1090 AD). It seems clear, however, that the Semitic foundations of Maltese are similar to North African Arabic, and were firmly established locally during Arab rule. The Arabic stratum forms the basis of the phonology, morphology, and to a lesser extent the syntax of Maltese, while the lexis of Semitic origin constitutes a nucleus of basic concepts related, for instance, to life in the home and realms of manual work.

Maltese has subsequently been shaped by a Romance superstratum. For many centuries following Arab rule, roughly until the 19th century, European cultural and linguistic influences became extensive (cf. Mifsud, 1995). A Romance superstratum, especially in the lexicon of Maltese, continues to hold its ground in many cultural domains. This is especially due to the influence of

© THE EURO-MEDITERRANEAN CENTRE FOR EDUCATION RESEARCH, UNIVERSITY OF MALTA, 2001

DOI: 10.1163/9789004506602_016

numerous Italian television stations accessed in Malta, geographical proximity to Sicily and Italy, and other cultural ties.

The English adstratum is a relatively recent phenomenon. During the latter half of the 20th century English became the main medium of international communication in Malta, of acculturation, and was promoted intensively in education. Under British rule (1800–1964) English became increasingly important and its use widespread among the Maltese population. Although it took English almost a century to be introduced in schools at a time when a significant sector of the Maltese professional elite were pro-Italian, once English found a secure place in the civil service and was promoted to official status alongside Maltese in the 1934 Constitution, then it steadily replaced Italian as the language of education. As time went by, English took over as the language of more and more domains, especially as a written medium. Nowadays, English is practically the exclusive linguistic source of new terminology connected with modern life, such as in the fields of science, technology and sport.

Maltese can be described as a 'Young Standard Language'. It has been codified with dictionaries, grammatical studies, and other volumes describing its history and development. A literature for both children and adults, as well as texts of literary criticism in Maltese, are available. It is a compulsory subject at school.

Furthermore, it is pertinent to point out that Maltese is not a heterogeneous reality, but consists of a number of geographically-defined varieties, with the main distinction being that between the Standard variety and the dialects. Standard Maltese is socially prestigious, and a superposed variety for all the population. Dialects, on the other hand, are many since every town and village practically boasts its own variety. These varieties are different from each other on most linguistic levels, and although the phonetic distinctions are the most obvious, differences have also been recorded on the lexical and grammatical levels (see, for example, Aquilina & Isserlin, 1981; Camilleri & Vanhove, 1994).

In Gozo, for example, the dialects play an important role in the classroom. Buttigieg (1998) provides evidence about the kind of problems that dialect-speaking children face in school. Although all Gozitan dialects are linguistically related to Standard Maltese, when pupils are faced with a standard speaking teacher, and hence a different mode of communication from that experienced so far at home, they face a psycho-linguistic barrier. This results in a phase referred to as 'silencing' (Simon, 1990) during which, for a number of years at least, children choose to shut up rather than loose face by uttering anything in a dialect which is stigmatised by the standard speaking community represented in class by the teacher.

Furthermore, dialect-speaking pupils face a number of additional problems when it comes to learning to write. Written Maltese is very closely related to the standard variety, and is phonetically-based on it such that almost every vowel and consonant corresponds to a phoneme. Thus, non-standard speakers need to first learn to speak the standard variety prior to learning how to spell the written language. Buttigieg (1998) puts forward a number of practical pedagogical proposals that she tried out herself with a third-year primary class in Gozo. These consist of tasks that help pupils become aware of the value of possessing more than one language variety, thus leading them to feel confident in using their own dialect as appropriate, while developing a positive attitude toward the acquisition of Standard Maltese.

The relation between dialectal and Standard Maltese can be described as one of *diglossia*, where two language varieties exist side by side in a community, and where one has a higher status than the other (cf. Ferguson, 1959). On the other hand, Standard Maltese and English co-exist in a context of bilingualism without diglossia, where two languages compete for use in the same domains (cf. Fishman, 1967). The Maltese bilingual context is a rather complex one given that there is only one speech community that uses a number of dialects, a standard variety of the national language, and English in very similar, and sometimes the same spheres of activity (for a more detailed account see Camilleri, 1995).

3 The Functional Distribution of Maltese and English in Local Society

Maltese and English come together within the Maltese speech community at two levels: (i) the level of the bilingual individual who learns and uses both languages from childhood; and (ii) at the societal level where, although there are domains in which one language dominates, there are many others in which both languages are used interchangeably.

The only two domains that could probably claim exclusivity for the Maltese language in both spoken and written forms are: Parliament, where proceedings are only recorded in Maltese; and the Law Courts, where the Maltese version of the Law is binding. This does not mean, however, that an individual's speech in these domains may not be coloured by some code-switching into English, even if not as frequently as in the other domains. In addition, it is interesting that Italian terminological influences abound in these two contexts.

Two important official domains are the Catholic Church and the Public Service. The Catholic Church declared Maltese its official language following Vatican Council II (1964) when the vernaculars replaced Latin as the language of the Church. Since then, Standard Maltese (henceforth Maltese) has been used for spoken purposes, for communication with the people, and for spreading

THE MALTESE BILINGUAL CLASSROOM

297

the teachings of the Church through many publications. Yet again, within this domain, there are a few contexts where prayers and religion classes are held in English. The argument put forward is that the participants are English-speaking, as is the case in some localities or in some families in Malta. Written Church documents for international communication are in English.

Similarly, in the Public Service, spoken interaction takes place largely in Maltese, with some code-switching into English depending on the topic and the interlocutor. Written documents are either in Maltese, in English, or bilingual.

The media is one of the greater influential domains on language. There are seven Maltese television stations, all of which broadcast programmes in both languages. Normally, films and documentaries are transmitted in English, while the main news bulletins, discussion programmes, day-time entertainment, and children's programmes are broadcast in Maltese. Radio stations are numerous, and amount to about fifteen which are Maltese-speaking, and three with an English-speaking policy. In contrast to this, there is, more or less, a balance in the publication of both daily and Sunday newspapers in both languages. It is not rare to find bilingual journals and magazines. To mention two in the education domain, *Education 2000*, the journal of the Faculty of Education of the University of Malta, and *The Teacher*, the journal of the Malta Union of Teachers, are bilingual.

4   Bilingual Education in Malta

Classroom language practices are to be understood in the light of the specific societal background in which they are embedded. Teachers and learners continually interact in the classroom. Societies are made up of interacting individuals; people and language are continually changing through such interactions. Interaction implies human beings acting in relation to each other, taking each other into account, acting, perceiving, interpreting and acting again.

Any instance of bilingual use needs to be understood in terms of the use of language in that particular lesson, and as embedded in a series of concentric circles of increasingly larger (more 'macro') contexts. If we move from the micro-context of specific instances of language use (for example, a specific instance of code-switching in a particular lesson) outward, these rings will include other interactions during the lesson taken as a whole, and their dependence on participants' classroom characteristics, the school, the society and its linguistic repertoire.

The following examples of bilingual usage in the classroom reflect the major patterns observed within this micro-context embedded, as it is, within the larger societal context.

4.1 The Choice of Medium of Instruction

There is an opportunity to use either Maltese or English as media of instruction across the schooling system. There has, as yet, been no legal obligation for schools or teachers to use any particular language for any subject. What normally dictates the choice of medium is the availability of textbooks, and the language of the national examinations. Mid-yearly and annual school examinations are held nationally for state schools starting from the fifth year of primary school. All subjects are examined through written papers in English, except for Maltese, Religion, Social Studies and Maltese History. At a later stage, when sitting for School Leaving, Intermediate and Advanced Matriculation Examinations, students are allowed to respond to questions in the Religion, Social Studies, Maltese History, and Systems of Knowledge papers in either language. In the latter paper examinees are to answer at least one question in the other language.

The extensive use of English in examinations has been in place since the introduction of examinations at these levels, which, until the 1980's were British based. The continued use of English is justified due to the availability of textbooks and other pedagogical materials in English. Furthermore, it allows students the possibility of further studies in that subject that are carried out in English both locally and abroad. The use of English for examination purposes does not seem to be contested as it is understood by the Maltese population as a necessary window to the field of world knowledge.

In fact, the use of a second or foreign language for non-language subject instruction is a method that is recently being emulated in a number of schools across Europe (cf. Marsh, Bruce & Maljers, 1998). In most cases it is English that is chosen as the new medium of instruction since this language has become widely acknowledged, in practice, as a world language.

The use of Maltese for a few subjects, on the other hand, helps to give the language additional status and value in the education domain, and ensures that students acquire a desirable level of competence in it as a language of study and knowledge.

As has been explained earlier, Maltese and English share roles in many societal domains. The allotment of different languages to different subjects in the written mode reflects a societal reality where the two languages are used within any one domain, are valued almost equally, and thus render the situation close to one of bilingualism without diglossia.

4.2 The Spoken-Written Distinction and Terminology-Switching

The most conspicuous division of labour between the two languages is the spoken/written distinction. English is largely a written language, Maltese the major spoken means of interaction. Education in Malta is heavily associated with subject-teaching that relies almost exclusively on the written text established by the syllabus. In the classroom, there is continual interaction between the written text in English as the basic point of reference, and the oral discussion in Maltese through which participants reiterate and reinterpret the written text. By using Maltese, participants reason out problems for themselves and find their ways to the solutions required.

The discussion of a written text in English through Maltese motivates code-switching. The international literature reports several kinds of code-switching that result from this interaction between the written word in one language, and the spoken discourse in another (e.g., Taha, 1989; Lin, 1990; Ndayipfu-kamiye, 1991; Merritt et al., 1992).

The use of technical terms in English amid what can be otherwise considered as Maltese discourse, amounts to two-thirds of all code-switching taking place in the classroom (cf. Camilleri, 1995). Considering that almost all textbooks used throughout the school day are in English, and that the majority of learners come to class with Maltese as their first language, then it becomes clear why the participants resort to English terms all the time, and why the teacher very often needs to translate terms from English to Maltese.

The translation of technical terms, in fact, has been investigated in detail in Camilleri (1996, 1998, 1999). Not every code-switch related to technical terminology is carried out in the same way. For instance, translation-switching could be explicit or non-explicit. The explicit translation of terms means that a literal equivalent in Maltese is given, and this may or may not involve a metalinguistic marker such as *jiġifieri* ('this means'). On the other hand, non-explicit translation of terms or phrases involves the use of other linguistic devices, such as: an amplification in Maltese on the meaning of the term in English, without an exact translation; the elicitation of a response from the learners following the introduction of a term in English by calling out on them in Maltese to indicate that a response explaining the term is expected from them; a relatively lengthy explanation in Maltese is given by the teacher, again without giving a precise equivalent for the term.

The following examples should serve as illustrations of terminology-switching, very frequent both in the classroom and outside it (see Table 16.1). The first two examples show how the speaker translates an English phrase or term into Maltese. In the classroom extract there is no metalinguistic marker, while in the example from a television documentary there is a metalinguistic marker *bil-Malti* ('in Maltese').

Another type of translation-switching involves the elaboration in Maltese of new information given in English. When new information is introduced

TABLE 16.1   Examples of terminology-switching

In the classroom	Outside the classroom
In the following extract from a Social Studies lesson (students aged 11), where a poem in English is discussed in Maltese, the teacher translates a phrase into Maltese.	During a television programme in Maltese on nature and ecology, the presenter translates the term from English to Maltese. At this stage he does not explain that the phrase refers to the name of a flower (23.11.99):
T: **Jack in the pulpit is preaching today,** għax qisu qiegħed jippriedka fil-pulptu.	P: Il-**legumes** bil-Malti legumi.
(T: Jack in the pulpit is preaching today, because he looks like he is preaching in the pulpit).	*(P: Legumes, in Maltese are called legumi).*

through an English term or phrase, it is sometimes discussed further in Maltese in a way that the speaker explains what he meant by what he said in English without giving a translation equivalent. One important reason for this is the lack of an exact equivalent in Maltese, especially since technical terms are introduced in English at the same time as the concept they represent. Occasionally, however, as one Biology teacher explained, even if there are Maltese equivalents, they do not carry the academic connotations necessary for their use in a classroom setting, and therefore are sometimes avoided.

The following two examples, one from a Home Economics lesson, and the other from a Minister's speech, illustrate how an English term, once introduced, is further described and explained in Maltese (see Table 16.2). In both cases there is no one term in Maltese that could have been used as a translation equivalent.

Another interesting case of terminology-switching occurs when the speaker quotes or refers to the written text in English during an exchange in Maltese. This is related to what was termed 'situational switching' by Gumperz (1982)— only in this case, rather than a change in situation, there is a change in focus of medium, from the spoken to the written. It is different from translation-switching in that it does not involve an explanation or elaboration in Maltese on the information given in English. In these cases, bilingual speakers simply make use of noun phrases in English within a context of Maltese discourse, without obvious signs that they are distinguishing between the two languages,

THE MALTESE BILINGUAL CLASSROOM

TABLE 16.2   Example of how the meaning of English terms is elaborated in Maltese

In the classroom	Outside the classroom
During a Home Economics lesson (students aged 15), the teacher explains a term in English by giving more information rather than simply translating the term.	During his budget speech, the Minister of Finance (22.11.99) is not simply content to use technical terms in English as read out from his text, but resorts to an explanation:
T: **Fast colour** means fejn il-biċċa drapp tkun tal-kulur u mbagħad wara li naħsluha ma tibqax bħal qabel, tiċċara jew titlef il-kulur.	M: Hemm bżonn li tidħol il-mentalità ta' **cost-consciousness** fost kulħadd. Ma nistgħux nibqgħu nippermettu l-ħala. Kulħadd irid iwieġeb għall-infiq li jsir.
(*T:* **Fast colour** *means where a piece of coloured cloth that is washed becomes different, loses its colour*).	(*M: There's a need for a mentality of* **cost-consciousness** *among everybody. We cannot permit waste. Everyone has to become responsible for the expenses carried out*).

unlike what happened in the examples explained above. It is interesting to note that this occurs most of the time with noun phrases in English, or more rarely with adjectives, but not with verbs. In the case of English verbs, these are usually inflected using a Maltese (Semitic) structure as in *niddrajklinjaw* ('we dry clean'), *tispelli* ('she spells'), and *tibbukkja* ('she books'). This phenomenon needs further analysis, but an overview of Maltese-English crosslinguistic influence is given in Camilleri (1995). The two examples below illustrate how bilingual speakers make use of English phrases and terms within Maltese discourse as they refer to the written text in English (see Table 16.3).

5   Conclusion

From a linguistic point of view, specialists do not express any worries in relation to the survival of Maltese as a language. First of all, it has to be appreciated that Maltese is a heterogeneous reality, and the first language of the vast majority of the population. It is valued by them as an important aspect of their identity. Its contact with, and the influence it receives from English, is understood

TABLE 16.3   Example of the use of English phrases/terms in Maltese by bilingual speakers

In the classroom	Outside the classroom
During a Mathematics lesson (pupils aged 11), the teacher switches to English when pointing to a drawing on the blackboard that represents the written text.	During a beauty programme in Maltese on television (20.11.99), a beautician refers to a number of beauty products, and switches to English as she shows each one.
T. Meta ngħidu **the circumference of the circle** x'inkunu qegħdin nifhmu?	B: Ħa nitkellmu fuq il-**powder**. Din tista' tkun **loose** jew **semi-loose**.
(*T: When we refer to **the circumference of the circle**, what do we understand?*)	(*B: We are going to talk about the powder. This could be **loose**, or **semi-loose**.*)

in the light of the various influences Maltese has gone throughout its history and explained/accepted as a natural evolution and sign of its vitality. Similarly, in education, there can be no doubt about its relevance, it being the native language of the majority of the learners who, as has been discussed, need to make sense of the written text in English through oral discussion in Maltese.

At the same time English is seriously valued. It is a world language, the language of education and international communication also very important locally due to the tourist industry, and undeniably has extended its use to local contexts.

Code-switching is one way of managing a bilingual reality, in fact, of embodying and expressing such reality in the most spontaneous and resourceful of manners. In the classroom, undoubtedly, it becomes a pedagogically efficient way of communicating, of solving the difficulty of making sense of a 'foreign', new and academic text in English, by liberally and uninhibitedly discussing it in one's native language.

Acknowledgement

This chapter originally appeared as: Camilleri Grima, A. (2001) The Maltese bilingual classroom: a microcosm of local society, *Mediterranean Journal of Educational Studies*, Vol. 6(1), pp. 3–12. Reprinted here with permission from the publisher.

References

Aquilina, I., & Isserlin, B. S. J. (eds.) (1981) *A Survey of Contemporary Dialectal Maltese – Volume 1: Gozo*. Leeds: Leeds University Printing Service.

Borg, A., Mifsud, M., & Sciriha, L. (1992) *The Position of Maltese in Malta*. Paper presented at the Meeting for Experts on Language Planning, July 1992, Malta.

Buttigieg, L. (1998) *Id-Djaletti u l-Malti Standard: Hemm xi Problemi fit-Tagħlim?* MEd dissertation, Faculty of Education, University of Malta.

Camilleri, A. (1995) *Bilingualism in Education: The Maltese Experience*. Heidelberg: Julius Groos Verlag.

Camilleri, A. (1996) Language values and identities: code switching in secondary classrooms in Malta, *Linguistics and Education*, Vol. 8, pp. 85–103.

Camilleri, A. (1998) Codeswitching: an added pedagogical resource. In J. Billiez & D-L. Simon (eds.) *Alternances des Langues: Enjeux Socio-culturels et Identitaires*. Grenoble: Université Stendhal.

Camilleri, A. (1999) Speaking in two tongues, *Multiethnica*, Vol. 24/25, pp. 25–27.

Camilleri, A., & Vanhove, M. (1994) A phonetic and phonological inventory of the Maltese dialect of Mġarr, *Zeitschrift für Arabische Linguistik*, Vol. 28, pp. 87–110.

Ferguson, C. (1959) Diglossia, *Word*, Vol. 15, pp. 325–340.

Fishman, J. (1967) Bilingualism with and without diglossia, diglossia with and without bilingualism, *Journal of Social Issues*, Vol. 23(2), pp. 29–38.

Gumperz, J. J. (1982) *Discourse Strategies*. Cambridge: Cambridge University Press.

Lin, A. (1990) *Teaching in Two Tongues: Language Alternation in Foreign Language Classrooms* (Research Report No. 3). Hong Kong: City Polytechnic of Hong Kong.

Marsh, D., Bruce, M., & Maljers, A. (eds.) (1998) *Future Scenarios in Content and Language Integrated Learning*. Jyväskylä: University of Jyväskylä.

Merritt, M., Cleghom, A., Abagi, J. O., & Bunyi, G. (1992) Socializing multilingualism: determinants of code switching in Kenyan primary schools, *Journal of Multilingual and Multicultural Development*, Vol. 13(1&2), pp. 103–121.

Mifsud, M. (1995) *Loan Verbs in Maltese: A Descriptive and Comparative Study*. Leiden: E. J. Brill.

Ndayipfukamiye, L. (1991) *The Transitional Year: Code Alternation in Primary Classrooms in Burundi*. Papers from the First Dar es Salam Colloquium on Language in Education in Africa (Lancaster/Dar es Salaam Link Programme – Working Papers Series).

Simon, R. I. (1990) The fear of theory. In T. Eagleton (ed.) *The Significance of Theory*. Cambridge: Blackwell.

Taha, A. M. T. (1989) *The Arabicisation of the Higher Education Curriculum: The Case of Khartoum University*. PhD thesis, Lancaster University, United Kingdom.

CHAPTER 17

Multiculturalism, Citizenship, and Education in Morocco

Moha Ennaji

1 Introduction

This paper discusses the close linkage between multiculturalism, citizenship, and education in Morocco. It deals with the changing role of education, the concept of citizenship inherent in it, and the relation of multiculturalism to wider society from the early years of French occupation in 20th century Morocco to the present. These complex concepts are discussed through an analysis of the policies of education without losing sight of their impact on the concepts of knowledge and power in Morocco.

The language-culture interface is commonly acknowledged as an important symbol of citizenship and group identity, often engendering solidarity among communities and feelings of belonging to larger populations. In the Moroccan context, highly interesting issues arise in the construction of an adequate system of education and of national identity in the interaction of different languages, namely Arabic, Berber, French, Spanish, and recently English.

The approach that I adopt is that of anthropological linguistics, based on the relationship between bilingualism, biculturalism, and education. This approach takes for granted the strong link between language, education, and culture as well as the idea of concurrence of multiple variables like class, gender, attitude, and the channel of communication. The paper is also inspired by studies on multiculturalism and society by Bourdieu (1982), Eickelman (1985), Fairclough (1989), and Kymlicka (1995), which are applied to investigate the relationship between multilingualism, multiculturalism, citizenship, and education in Morocco. In line with Kymlicka (1995), I argue that group-specific rights are consistent with citizenship and liberalism. Minority rights should be protected in order to promote equality. I propose that societies need to become more welcoming and inclusive than they are currently in respect of group rights. I am mostly supportive of the recognition and preservation of the distinctive patterns of 'minority' cultures. In this framework, a genuinely multicultural community would seek to promote the recognition of national ethnic difference through education and other means.

© THE EURO-MEDITERRANEAN CENTRE FOR EDUCATION RESEARCH, UNIVERSITY OF MALTA, 2009
DOI: 10.1163/9789004506602_017

This is an open access chapter distributed under the terms of the CC BY-NC 4.0 License.

The construction of common cultures of difference at the national level remains one of the key objectives of multiculturalism. In cultures where citizenship is predominantly formulated through national institutions such as education and government, these perspectives remain important. Yet the debate thus far presupposes that multicultural concerns are questions exclusively for national contexts. Such formulations are inadequate in that modern societies have become marked by globalisation and migrations of people that defy the exclusive role of citizenship (Stevenson, 2002).

The paper also aims to demonstrate that multiculturalism in Morocco—and in the world at large—has reached a significant level in terms of scale and importance. While adopting Sklair's (1999, p. 154) idea that 'it is absolutely fundamental that we are clear about the extent to which the many different structures within which we live are the same in the most important respects as they have been or different', I would like to argue along the lines of Fishman (1998) and Maurais (2003), among others, that multiculturalism today is developing within the context of globalisation and is in fact 'qualitatively different' from what it was before, as it represents in effect a new cultural and social trend with increasingly deep effects on citizenship and education (Aronin & Singleton, 2008).

The paper asks the following questions: First, how far are ideas of the national community inclusive or exclusive? To what extent does the state generate and how does it sustain definitions of citizenship? How important are factors like social movements, politics, and education in constructing a sense of identity?

This paper is divided into a number of sections. The next section deals with multiculturalism and citizenship in the global and national contexts. The following section, then, focuses on the historical background of Morocco. Next comes a section that is concerned with the sociolinguistic context, more particularly aspects of multilingualism. This is followed by a section that discusses the challenges of Arabisation and bilingual education. Finally, the last two sections deal respectively with the role of Berber education in the development and management of multiculturalism and citizenship and offer a conclusion to this paper.

2   Multiculturalism and Citizenship

Before embarking on issues relevant to multiculturalism, citizenship, and education, it is useful to provide some definitions. I want to acknowledge immediately that terms such as 'multiculturalism' and 'citizenship' are ambiguous. In fact, there appears to be a clear relation between these concepts. For the purposes of the present paper, I define 'multiculturalism' in its inclusive sense, as the acquisition and use of a plurality of cultures. Multiculturalism acknowledges that cultures are characterised by a range of distinctive values and attitudes; it can disrupt processes of assimilation or globalisation by protecting the specificity of individual cultures from absorption into more dominant ones. The concept of multiculturalism can be descriptive and refer to an actual condition of a society, namely that a multiplicity of cultures is present and represents a significant proportion of the population. Or it can be normative and refer to a desired state of a society. As a normative concept, it can refer to an official government policy, as in the Canadian or Australian contexts, or it can refer to an idea that is instantiated to a greater or lesser extent in actual societies. The ideas can be stronger or weaker but, in all cases, would demand that cultural differences found in a society be accepted and respected by both societal institutions and members of the public alike.

As for the term 'citizenship', it refers to the rights and obligations that define an individual's membership of the political community. The study of citizenship needs to engage with both multicultural and educational questions. Bringing these issues together is possible if citizenship opens questions of cultural identity, and multiculturalism decouples itself from specifically national concerns. My argumentative strategy is that such questions are both central to any contemporary consideration of citizenship, and vital for future debates of educational issues and social and political theory.

In whichever way one seeks to define concepts of citizenship and national identity, 'imagined communities' attain an extraordinary impact as real social phenomena in which people believe and on which they act. The French sociologist Émile Durkheim's injunction to 'treat social facts as things' becomes brutally relevant when people are looked down upon because of (imagined) 'racial inferiority', or when diversity is disrespected.[1]

Multiculturalism need not be considered exclusively as a device for integration. It could just as well be considered as an instrument for bringing about a form of preserving cultural, religious, racial, ethnic, linguistic, or other forms of diversity.

The discourses of human rights have created an alternative need and source for the legitimation of individual and collective rights other than membership of a nation. For example, the International Labour Organisation defines and monitors the observance of the rights of migrant workers, demanding and obtaining for them entitlements which at one time only citizens of a country might customarily have expected to receive. What we have is a trend toward a new model of membership anchored in de-territorialised notions of persons' rights. Classical conceptions of citizenship are no longer adequate in understanding the dynamics of membership and belonging to a country or a community.

Entitlement to citizenship carries with it a host of specific rights and responsibilities: rights to residence, education, and work, assorted benefits, political representation and participation and, often, associated obligations to the wider community.

Citizenship has wider, affective connotations too: the sense of belonging to a broader community, expressed in symbols and values, and the often quite vehement emotional identification which may be associated with that wider community of belonging. Conversely, exclusion from citizenship may be associated with lack of entitlement to vote or with marginalisation in undemocratic countries.

Trends such as globalisation, global migration, and the technological revolution along with uncertainty about the future all contribute to the view that schools must do more than prepare students for jobs, that citizenship education must be re-conceptualised and re-instituted as a centrepiece of public education.

The current multicultural situation in Morocco has a number of distinctive features. Since independence in 1956, global processes of the internationalisation of the economy, enhanced communication networks, and cultural currents have been changing the character and functions of the society, and a person's identity as a member of the nation has been uncoupled from their rights.

Since Morocco's independence until very recently, citizenship education has not been a central purpose of public education. This view is supported by the neglect of social studies education over the past three decades, which has begun to have the effect of leaving a large proportion of the student population without a sufficient knowledge base to make informed decisions regarding public affairs or civic responsibilities.

The national charter of education has recently raised concern about the appropriateness of curricula and the necessary development of resources. Today, it appears that interest is spreading into the wider education community, especially with the potential introduction of citizenship courses like 'asha?n al maHalli' (local affairs). Public education, as a cornerstone of democracy and citizenship education, should be central to the provincial education programme.

The concept of citizenship should be broadly defined to encompass multiple dimensions applied locally, nationally, and globally and based on such values as respect, tolerance, acceptance, open-mindedness, non-violence, equality, commitment to social justice, and concern for the common good.

Responsibility for citizenship education rests with the school, the family and community, and with society at large through government support for public education. Citizenship education is relevant to students' interests and involves active engagement, critical thinking and advanced levels of literacy. Citizenship education should include community service work that would help draw school and community closer together.

3 Historical Background

Since the 8th century, an Islamic traditional system of education was prevalent in Morocco. Qur'anic and religious schools offered an Islamic traditional style of education. They taught mainly the Arabic language and the holy Qur'an for centuries; the University of Qarawiyyine at Fès, built in the 8th century, helped students to pursue and deepen their knowledge of Arabic and Islamic thought (see Grandguillaume, 1983, p. 70).

Moroccan sultans encouraged education and Islamic studies. Sultan Moulay Hassan (1873–1894) incited scholars (*ulamas*) to debate modern issues, and his interest in higher education was basically aimed to modernise the society and to introduce reforms. Men of learning played a great role in the community (Burke, 1972), and Morocco's sultans used scholars' support to bestow legitimacy on their power (Al-Fassi, 1954, pp. 276–277).[2] Educated people enjoyed a great deal of prestige in the *Makhzen* (government) and in Moroccan society at large (see Eikelman, 1985, p. 4). Religious knowledge remained highly viewed by the Islamic '*Umma*' (nation) throughout the Islamic world; it was and still is indeed the most culturally valuable knowledge (Rosenthal, 1970), and is considered a valuable form of cultural capital (Bourdieu, 1973, p. 80).

The universities Qarawiyyine and Yusufia continued to receive students from intellectual, religious, and political circles from different parts of the country. In the 1920s, reformists introduced subjects like Classical Arabic literature, theology, Islamic law (*shari'a*), and history. Although the main objective was to teach and learn the religious sciences, the studies also helped the graduate to attain positions in the government as a judge (*qadi*), a secretary (*katib*), a teacher (*fqih*), an *imam* in the mosque. These skills were equally used to engage in political and social activities and establish social networks and economic advantages.

Morocco was colonised by two European powers in the 20th century: France and Spain. The French colonial power justified its existence by claiming that it had a mission to civilise and develop the region. But politically the real reason was that the French wanted to dominate Morocco and subjugate its population. Economically the intention was to exploit the raw materials and use cheap labour to the advantage of the European market. The main objective of colonialism was to perpetuate the political and economic dependence of the indigenous people. Concerning education and science, the kind of colonial education reserved for the local populations (whose objective was to train people for low-level jobs) and the economic policy adopted meant that Moroccan natives would remain dependent and under-developed in these fields.

The French colonial presence in Morocco provoked two different processes: first, the spread of French language and culture, and the acculturation or alienation of the masses, and second this caused anti-colonial feelings among nationalists. The latter reaction took violent forms in the struggle for independence, and was based on religious motives which are still strong among the population. After independence, almost the opposite tendency resulted, as many young people and intellectuals seemed to insist on learning French language and culture for pragmatic goals (for the reasons of social promotion and openness to the West). Today, there is a rush to the French schools and classes especially in urban centres (see Ennaji, 2005, p. 105).

During the colonial period, the French colonisers made great efforts to dissociate Moroccan society from its indigenous languages and cultures. The French endeavoured to divide the country into ethnic groups to facilitate the colonisation process. This act was not arbitrarily implemented; rather, it was carefully planned because the colonisers were aware of the strong feelings of ethnic group membership in the region.

On 16 May 1930, the French issued the Berber *Dahir*, which formally put Berber-speaking zones under the customary law courts instead of the Islamic jurisprudence. Both Berberophones and Arabophones stood against this decision. Demonstrations spread all over the country, from Sale, to Fès, to Rabat, in order to express Moroccans' utter condemnation of this decree which sought to divide and rule Moroccans.[3] The *Dahir* was presented as an attack on Islam and a threat to Muslim values and principles. From that period onward, the French efforts in education, scarce as they were, were viewed with scepticism, and people started to understand French rule as a menace against Islam. Many nationalist meetings were held in mosques. The nationalist movement gained momentum in the mid-1930s, and the moment the French authorities arrested Kind Mohammed V and exiled him and his family to Corsica and then to Madagascar on 20 August 1953, the beginning of the end of the French occupation started (Eickelman, 1985, p. 102).

The French introduced modern education but only in favour of their own children and at best in favour of the children of the Moroccan elite and collaborators. Education continued to be elitist under the French rule, and standards were high. For lack of large numbers of university graduates, primary certificate holders were appointed in high positions. According to Waterbury

(1970, p. 84), between 1912 and 1954, only 530 Moroccan students passed the end of high school certificate (French *Baccalauréat*). Mass education started after independence; only 25,000 students were registered in primary education in 1955, and 130,000 new students entered the primary cycle in 1956. Popular enthusiasm for modern education grew as the link between socioeconomic mobility and educational achievement was strong.

Despite the decline of Islamic higher education during the French occupation, cognitive studies remained the main style of learning, influencing the nationalist movement and the political action in the country. The pursuit of religious knowledge among Arabic and Berber speaking people was commendable although it did not necessarily lead to social promotion or economic advantages.

At the beginning of the 20th century, religious scholars were basically the only Moroccans with full literacy in Classical Arabic. Until recently, literacy has been possessed only by a minority in Morocco. Educated people had such a great social respect that, without their cooperation, the French colonisers would not have succeeded to pacify Morocco and expand their administrative power all over the country. However, when the French authorities used violence and direct intervention, many intellectuals and scholars joined the resistance and the nationalist movement for independence led by Allal El-Fassi and Mohamed Hassan Ouazzani and many others.

According to Laroui (1967, pp. 19–28), Arab intellectuals can be divided into three categories. First, there are the religious scholars and clerics who seek to improve the society while maintaining the dominance of Islamic thought and values. Second, there are the liberal politicians, who aim to modernise society by adopting Western norms and ideas and political reforms. The third category is that of Western-educated technocrats and apolitical intellectuals, who seek the betterment of society through the adoption of socialist or Western know-how and rational thinking. I agree with Laroui when he notes that the clerics are usually less interested in establishing dialogue with Westerners. However, Laroui's division is vague and not 100% correct since there is a large overlap between the three categories; furthermore, the elite's attitudes change over time, and the first category, which is the most complex, is vaguely defined.

Religious knowledge in Morocco is characterised by orality, especially in the Berberophone areas; religious scholars venerate the words in the Qur'an which they memorised by heart with the purpose of spreading and transmitting the Holy Book and the traditions of Prophet Mohammed, without alteration or falsification, from generation to generation. Until very recently, literacy in Morocco entailed religious schooling, with the first years of study emphasising memorisation and recitation of the Qur'an; the subsequent years consisted of

MULTICULTURALISM, CITIZENSHIP, AND EDUCATION IN MOROCCO 311

learning reading and writing. The literacy estimates of the early 20th century are indicative of the scale of traditional education in Morocco. In the 1930s, the rural areas witnessed a literacy rate of 4% of the adult male population and 20% of the adult male urban population (Geertz, 1979, pp. 470–487). As to the overall rate of literacy among women, it was less than 1% (cf. Eickelman, 1985, p. 60; Ennaji, 2005, p. 219).

Qur'anic teachers (*fqihs*) played an important role in the memorisation of the Qur'an; up until the beginning of independence *fqihs* taught Arabic and Islamic thought in mosques, *medersas*, and elementary schools. The fact that they were not generally rich did not preclude their respect and high esteem of society as carriers of the Qur'an (Waterbury, 1970, p. 32).

For most students, this was the only form of education they could achieve. Only the fortunate few could access Qarawiyyine or Yusufia University. Both universities were also used by the community as spaces for worship and other pious meetings in such a way that the university was both a mosque and a learning centre. Lessons, which were held five times weekly, were organised around 'the daily cycle of prayers' in the form of circles of teachers and students, and were open to the public, which indicated popular support to these lessons. The teaching and learning activities were related to the needs and expectations of the community. For accommodation, hostels were reserved to students of these institutions (Geertz, 1979, p. 469).

From the 1930s onward, and well after independence, the shift went in favour of modern Western-type of education, and religious scholars were no longer re-produced in large numbers, although they continued to enjoy considerable respect in the community. Higher Islamic education lost its vitality because the French colonisers imposed reforms to the two major universities and appointed salaried teachers, whom they controlled. Gradually, religious education was left to students from poor socioeconomic backgrounds or of rural origins. For comparison, according to Marty (1924, p. 337) and Berque (1974, p. 173), in 1924 there were 300 students from the city of Fès and 419 from rural areas at Qarawiyyine University. In 1938, only 100 students from Fès and 800 from poor or rural backgrounds were registered. As to the Yusufia University in Marrakesh, estimates mention that in the early 1930s there were about 250 students from the city of Marrakesh, and 150 from neighbouring villages; these numbers dropped in 1935 to a few dozens of students. Islamic education after independence became less sought for because it lacked analysis and it did no longer meet the needs of the job market. The post-independence governments had to focus their efforts on modernising education and society. Moroccans regarded their children's futures as dependent on their training in French and their acquisition of certification that only French education could offer.

This shift in interest shows the close link between education and society in the Moroccan context and the way in which value is placed on various forms of learning, traditional or modern. For this reason, religious scholars and traditional 'ulamas' sent their own children to Francophone schools rather than to religious schools and universities. Even nationalist leaders from prominent urban families like Allal El-Fassi, Mohamed Hassan El-Ouazzani, and King Mohammed v, all sent their children to French-run schools (Waterbury, 1970, p. 44).

Until the 1960s, students attended religious classes in mosques and memorised the Qur'an by heart, but today very few educated Moroccans could recite but a few verses from the Qur'an. Religious education is referred to officially by the terms 'lettres originales', which is reminiscent of the strong influence of French-style education, as the word 'original' does not seem compatible with 'modern' education. However, the fact that Islam is the state religion coupled with the affinity between popular thinking and religious education allowed the latter to keep its important place in society until today. As a consequence, Islamic higher education never actually disappeared. Being conscious of the important role of Islamic education, and of the necessity to control it, the government decided to preserve religious education and to open Islamic schools and institutes, the most important of which is Dar Al Hadith Al-Hassania in Rabat.

Today, Yusufia University is called the 'Faculty of Arabic Language', and its staff is totally Moroccan. Qarawiyyine University in Fès continues to be an important centre of Islamic learning with the main language of instruction being Arabic, although French and English are also taught as foreign languages. One of the consequences of these Islamic schools was the transformation of religiosity in the late 20th century, with the expansion of Islamic associations like *Al-Adl wa Al-Ihsan* (extreme right NGO that challenges the establishment) and the Party of Justice and Development, which is a legal Islamist party, and who call themselves as Islamists (*Islamiyyun*) in sign of their self-description as the true carriers of Islamic values. The growth of these Islamist organisations is also the result of the success of the Iranian revolution, the fall of the Berlin wall, and the economic difficulties of post-independence, resulting in the strong social gap between the poor and the rich (see Eickelman, 1985, p. 175; Ennaji, 2005, p. 29). For the Islamists, independence did not bring development and progress, and Islam can lead to a profound transformation of society and to real progress and social justice.

After the proclamation of independence, the French were successful in influencing the Moroccan system of education, hence the reinforcement of French language and culture in the curricula. The country's leaders recognised

MULTICULTURALISM, CITIZENSHIP, AND EDUCATION IN MOROCCO

the need to place education at the centre of Morocco's socioeconomic and political future (see Damis, 1970).

Classical Arabic was declared the official language and French the second language. Since then, French has been used alongside Classical Arabic. The former has been adopted for purposes of modernisation and development, and the latter for preserving the country's cultural identity and authenticity. In this respect, Al-jabri (1973, p. 45) notes that the Moroccan elite is in full favour of keeping the essence of the educational system of the French colonisation and developing it on the basis of the French model.

Post-independence officials endeavoured to spread French in fields like trade, administration, education, and the media. In the name of achieving modernity and preserving cultural identity, the ruling elite opted for Standard Arabic-French bilingualism in most active sectors (cf. Grandguillaume, 1983).

Free education is provided to all children in public schools; the technical track offers subjects like engineering, economics, and agricultural sciences. Vocational training courses are also offered. English is introduced into the state curriculum in Grade 10 (first year of secondary school). English, however, is becoming popular in the private schools in Morocco (Clark, 2006).

Two different educational systems in Morocco have always co-existed. As mentioned earlier, the first one is the Islamic model of instruction at Qur'anic schools, which concentrates on Islamic studies and Arabic literature. The second is the modern model, adapted from the French type, to serve the needs of Modern Morocco. Although only a small percentage of students follow the original track, the government stresses its importance as a means of maintaining a sense of national and regional identity (Wagner & Lotfi, 1980).

4   Sociolinguistic Context

Morocco is characterised by multilingualism in the sense that many languages and varieties are used, including Classical Arabic, Standard Arabic, Moroccan Arabic, Berber, French, Spanish, and recently English. This multilingual dimension has a direct impact on the sociocultural life and education and brings about sociolinguistic problems that must not be overlooked in language planning and in education.

The most salient sociolinguistic feature of Morocco is the emergence of three forms of Arabic: Classical, Standard, and Moroccan Arabic (cf. Ennaji, 1991). Classical Arabic is the language of Islam, which is the vehicle of a great literary tradition and enjoys immense prestige among the population. Classical Arabic is culturally conceived as a sacred language because it is the language in which the Muslim holy book, the Qur'an, was revealed, and because it is a written code unlike the Arabic dialects.

Like Classical Arabic, Standard Arabic is a written Arabic variety which has no native speakers. Classical and Standard Arabic are both learnt at school only, as they are not spoken languages. Standard Arabic, which is structurally less rigid than Classical Arabic, is both codified and standardised; the policy of Arabisation has led to its modernisation and to its use as a vehicle of modern culture. It is widely made use of in education, administration, and the media. The expansion of free education has led to the spread of Standard Arabic and to favourable attitudes toward it (see Ennaji, 2005, pp. 53–58).

Moroccan Arabic is the mother tongue of at least 60% of the population, which unlike Classical and Standard Arabic, is unwritten but spoken. It is generally acquired by Arabophones as a native language, and learnt as a second language by Berberophones. Moroccan Arabic can be divided into several regional varieties, which are often mutually intelligible unless they are geographically distant from each other. However, Moroccan Arabic is usually stigmatised and treated as a corrupt form of Arabic (cf. Ennaji, 1991).

Berber is the mother tongue of approximately half the population, but it is looked upon by many Arabophones as debased essentially because it is not fully standardised as yet (although the process has started), has no religious connotations, and no great written literary tradition. These issues are dealt with in greater detail in the section on Berber education below.

Moroccan Arabic is spoken as a *lingua franca* by many Berberophones. Through it, the latter sometimes express their beliefs and feelings. Moroccan Arabic is used by both Arabophones and Berberophones as a means of expression of affective and cognitive experiences.

French is widely used as a second language. Despite its being a colonial language, it is still prestigious. Its chief domains of use are education, administration, government, media, and the private sector. It is employed to achieve efficiency, wider communication, and socioeconomic development.

Spanish is made use of to a lesser extent in the north and south of Morocco. It is optionally taught as a foreign language. By contrast, English is widely taught in high schools and universities. It is perhaps the most popular foreign language in the country because it has no colonial overtones (cf. Sadiqi, 1991; Errihani, 2008).

Morocco is also characterised by Arabic-French code switching, which occurs when there is a juxtaposition of strings of words formed according to the patterns and grammatical systems of both languages. Educated bilinguals code switch regularly between Moroccan Arabic and French (for example: '*aji shuf l'ordinateur est bloqué*'; meaning: 'come see the computer is stuck'). This code switching takes places mainly in informal situations during daily verbal interactions among schooled or highly educated people. In formal settings, however, Moroccan bilinguals use only one of these codes since formal contexts or specialised topics call for the use of one language exclusively.

Studies of Moroccan Arabic-French code switching have been developing since the 1970s. They have dealt with bilinguals' choice to switch between Moroccan Arabic and French from sociolinguistic, psycholinguistic, and grammatical perspectives (Ennaji, 2005, pp. 139–156).

Sociocultural factors like geography, education, age, gender, and class determine the nature and extent of code switching. Code switching tends to be an urban phenomenon (see Caubet, 1998; Sadiqi, 2003, pp. 257–271) in the sense that most code switchers are usually educated city dwellers; however, people who code switch differ in their competence in the two languages concerned. There are different types of code switchers depending on the languages they switch, their linguistic ability and the topics dealt with. On the other hand, code switching entails informality, intimacy, or solidarity between code switchers. Myers-Scotton (1993) calls this phenomenon 'solidarity syndrome'. Code switching shows precisely the 'innovative accommodation' in engaging with both languages, both traditions, both mind-sets *at the same time* (Zughoul, 1978).

There are administrative factors which regulate the degree of code switching. Given that the Moroccan administration is bilingual, there is a tendency to shift from French to Standard Arabic in formal situations. In less formal contexts (administration meetings, social address, etc.) there is more shift from Moroccan Arabic to French or Standard Arabic. But most of the written work is done in Standard Arabic or French. In most of the above situations, code switching between Moroccan Arabic, Standard Arabic and French takes place.

Moroccan Arabic-French code switching is stigmatised (cf. Ennaji, 1988; Lahlou, 1991; Caubet, 1998). Despite being negatively viewed by most Moroccans, code switching is part and parcel of the multilinguistic panorama of the country, and the Maghreb in general.

Educated people are not all favourable to code switching. The Arabic-educated intellectuals (*Arabisants*) loathe this form of speech which they consider corrupt and a sign of loss of identity. However, the French-educated people tend to be in favour of code switching, which they regard as a symbol of high social status (see El-biad, 1991; Lahlou, 1991; Moatassim, 1992). In education, code switching is quite common, especially in science classes; many teachers mix Moroccan Arabic and French to explain scientific and technical phenomena.

For many intellectuals, code switching is one of the residues of cultural colonisation and a sign of lack of pride in Arabic language and culture. Moatassim

(1974) qualifies code switching as a poor form of expression, and Guessous (1976) states that it is a 'bastard language' in the Moroccan multilingual and multicultural context. Code switching is in fact the most salient feature of the Arabisation policy applied since independence with the overall goal of generalising the use of Standard Arabic to all domains as a language of wider communication instead of French, which is considered by conservatives to be a threat to the linguistic and cultural identity of the country.

5 Arabisation and Bilingual Education

Given the connection between Standard Arabic, Islam, and nationalism, Arabisation may be considered a sign of the revival of the Arabic language and culture. Arabisation is strongly supported by religious groups and fundamentalists. Abdelaziz Benabdallah, ex-director of the permanent office of Arabisation, highlighted the invaluable role of Classical and Standard Arabic in an interview which appeared in the Moroccan daily *Le Matin* of Sunday 2 November 1997.

Furthermore, most scholars support bilingualism or mastery of foreign languages in addition to Arabic. The eminent Moroccan lexicographer, Lakhdar Ghazal, (ex-director of the Institute of Arabisation in Rabat, Morocco) argues that if Arabisation is a duty, Arabic-French bilingualism is a necessity as far as it serves the enrichment of Standard Arabic.

Arabisation is not only a language problem, but also a political and ideological matter. Right-wing political parties like the *Istiqlal* party and the Justice and Development party advocate total Arabisation at the expense of mother tongues (cf. Al-jabri, 1995). Progressive and modern scholars advocate bilingualism and the revival of mother tongues (cf. Boukous, 1995; Ennaji, 1997 and the references cited there). The Arabisation policy has in a way been turned against the public authorities, as it is often used by the opposition parties and by Islamists as a tool in their fight for power.

Despite four decades of Arabisation, French is still widely used in education, administration, and the private sector. The efforts of Arabising the educational system have not fully succeeded for three main reasons: (i) the place of French is still very strong in key socioeconomic factors; (ii) the ruling elite holds negative attitudes toward Arabisation and the way it has been politicised and implemented; and (iii) the official language policy has been inconsistent, and as a result there seems to be no plan to Arabise higher education.

The unfair dichotomy between written languages, that is, Classical Arabic, Standard Arabic, English, and French, on the one hand, and spoken languages like Moroccan Arabic and Berber, on the other hand, is sharpened by the policy of Arabisation whose aim is to introduce Standard Arabic in all fields of activity, as it is the symbol of cultural independence.[4]

Arabisation has had negative consequences on the Berber language because it has led to its marginalisation and to the assimilation of the Berber culture and people. However, in 2001 the government decided to revitalise Berber and introduce it in the educational system.

The fact that the post-independence government opted for Arabic-French bilingualism in education was certainly a pragmatic choice. However, this type of bilingualism is more imposed by historical, political and economic factors than chosen. The major reforms after independence have been the omission of French from the first two years of public primary schools and the increase of the teaching load of Arabic and the strengthening of the position of French in university, especially in science faculties.[5]

This kind of bilingualism and biculturalism is the source of difficulty for learners in schools because of the different and at times conflicting roles of Arabic and French. This difficulty is translated in reality by the high rate of failure and dropouts in primary, secondary, and higher education, hence the adoption of the Arabisation policy whose aim is to reduce the number of dropouts and the failure rate at school (Grandguillaume, 1983). In 1973, the government decided to Arabise mathematics and the sciences in the primary and secondary education, and philosophy and the social sciences at all levels of education; French thus became *de facto* a second language, and Arabic the language of instruction of all disciplines in primary and secondary education. However, up until now, the sciences are taught in French in higher education, whereas the faculties of science, medicine, engineering, and private institutes use French as the language of instruction.

The political leaders' stand on Arabisation and bilingualism has evolved since independence. While the enthusiasm for Arabisation was very strong immediately after independence, nowadays, it is waning as a result of unemployment among Arabised university graduates.

The ambiguity and hesitation that have characterised the educational system and the language policies adopted in a way reflect the painful acculturation and alienation that a whole generation of politicians, officials, and people have suffered in the post-colonial era.

The expansion of bilingual and bicultural education to masses of pupils and students from different sociological backgrounds after independence has led to their alienation and consolidated acculturation.

Bilingual education is a political option which has a serious impact on education and citizenship, and fosters communication with the West and the rest of the world (see Fitouri, 1983). However, after decades of the implementation of the Arabisation policy, the degree of mastery of French has regressed; yet, the prestige of French prevails and attitudes toward it remain for the most part favourable.[6]

The multicultural context in Morocco hides a class struggle, group competition, a clash of interests of the different sociocultural categories, as well as ideological tensions, which pose problems for citizenship. These tensions and conflicts reflect also the fight for power at various levels (cf. Grandguillaume, 1983; Ennaji, 1991; Boukous, 1995 among others). The multicultural context is instrumentalised by the progressive forces to consolidate democracy, citizenship, and minority rights, while the traditionalists (particularly the Islamists) use it as a political tool to give vent to their ideology and their political agenda with the aim of re-Islamising the country and ruling in the name of Islamic religion and culture.

Thus, the debate about Arabisation and bilingual education implies a larger debate on citizenship, government policy, ideology, politics, religion, culture, and identity. Arabisation policy is a hidden fight for social promotion used by opposition political parties and the lower social classes in the hope that Arabisation will re-establish collective rights, social justice, and equal opportunities for all.

As mentioned above, Berber, considered by many as a 'minority' language, has been marginalised by Arabisation and by French-Arabic bilingual education. However, since 2001 the authorities have called for the revival of Berber language and culture as a sign of reinforcing citizenship. In the following section, I discuss the impact of Berber on education.

6 Berber Education

Historically, although at least half of the population speaks Berber, preference has always been given to Latin and later on to Arabic as the official language of the nation. Berber has never been recognised as the official language, nor introduced in the educational system, until 2003.

After independence, Berber was excluded from schools in the name of state-building and in search of a unified national identity. This forced a whole generation of children to enter school in a language they had never spoken before, contributing to a higher dropout rate among Berber children. Trouble for Berber-only speakers did not stop in the educational system. Many continued to face other difficulties communicating in hospitals and the court system, where Arabic and French dominated.

The frustration led to two major Berber revolts—one in 1973 and a second in 1994—both of which the Moroccan government suppressed. But by mid-1990s the Berber movement was strong enough to catch the attention of King Hassan II, who on 20 August 1994 publicly vowed to integrate the indigenous tongue into the education system. However, there was little progress until King Mohammed VI, whose mother is Berber, took over. In 2001, he announced a programme to teach all schoolchildren Berber and declared the creation of a research institute, The Royal Institute of Berber Culture in Rabat, to develop a curriculum and promote the study of the Berber language. This initiative gave the teachers the chance to spend three hours a week teaching Berber to their students, in addition to Arabic and French.

The official recognition of Berber as part of the national heritage and cultural authenticity, and its introduction in Moroccan primary schools are good examples of the revival of this language. This revival is due mainly to the fact that both Arabic and Berber cultures play a strong symbolic role in strengthening the national identity, multiculturalism, and citizenship.

As a result of this move, the authorities have tentatively introduced Berber in a number of primary schools and plan to generalise its teaching and its use in the media. On television, the new move is the broadcasting of news bulletins, films, and advertising in Berber language. Attitudes to Berber have changed favourably since the royal speech of Ajdir on 17 October 2001 when the king announced the policy for the promotion of Berber language and culture. Attitudes toward Berber have in general become favourable (see Ennaji, 2003), and Berber academics and associations are working on how to standardise and unify their language. The number of Berber cultural associations has multiplied (more than 60 exist in Morocco). Their objective is to revitalise Berber language and culture, and sensitise people and government to the cultural value of Berber as part of and parcel of the national legacy and Moroccan citizenship.

In the field of education, one may state that the teaching of Berber is spreading steadily; Berber is taught in over 900 public schools and in many private schools, including the French Institute in Agadir and NGOs working for the dissemination and protection of this language both in Morocco and Europe, where there is a large Moroccan immigrant community (see Quadéry, 1998; Kratochwil, 1999). In 2007, nearly 300,000 students—native Arabic speakers as well as Berber speakers—were enrolled in Berber courses, according to the Ministry of Education (cf. Errihani, 2008).

Since the creation of the Royal Institute of the Berber Culture, the existing multilingual and multicultural dimension of Morocco has been recognised, and a new language planning, codification, and standardisation policy has been launched so as to integrate this language not only into the educational system, but into the different sectors as well.

In 2000, the National Charter for Education and Training was adopted with the aim to restructure the Moroccan educational system and language policy in order to upgrade the standards. The Charter outlined the role of Berber in society and the need to introduce it in education, as well as the need to have a good command of Arabic and foreign languages.

However, it would be interesting to find out whether the type of language policy set out by the Charter is compatible with the country's sociolinguistic and multicultural reality. Moreover, it would be of paramount importance to investigate the extent to which multilingualism and multiculturalism can be a source of conflict in language teaching and learning.

The official support for Berber has helped fuel a larger revival of Berber culture and life in the kingdom, where the country's native people have long been shunned, and sometimes imprisoned, for public expressions of their heritage. Nowadays, summer arts festivals are commonplace, Berber newspapers are thriving, and a long-blocked translation of the Qur'an into Tamazight finally made it into print.

Of course, the transformations have been far from uniform, and there are signs that the slow pace of change is beginning to exacerbate the tension between the government and Berber activists. Yet the story of the Berber project and the challenges it has faced from politicians, parents, and Berber natives is in many ways symbolic of the broader struggle Morocco faces as it tries to balance the competing interests of a multicultural country of over 30 million (Schwartz, 2008).

Though the government initiative calls for adding a new level of Berber each year, many schools have offered only the first level for the past three years. Many still have no Berber teachers, and the Ministry of Education will not allocate money to recruit new ones—a position that many Berber people see as a sign that the Arab-dominated government has not fully accepted the initiative. Textbooks are not always sent to rural areas, where Berber speakers are often the majority. Other promises, such as plans to launch an all-Berber television station and develop university-level programmes on Berber culture, have not materialised either. As a result, many Berber activists are beginning to criticise and distance themselves from the officials' efforts. In 2005, for instance, seven of the 30 board members of The Royal Institute of Amazigh Culture (IRCAM) resigned because of the constant pushback from the state.

Despite all the obstacles, Berber is no more a forgotten national dialect, but a subject in its own right in Moroccan primary schools. Different positions arise concerning its introduction in education. The attitudes range from those of Berbers advocating the promotion of Berber to some Arabophones who are opposed to the idea of revitalising it. Many refute Berber as a mandatory subject in primary schools, claiming that it is useless in the job market.

Proponents of the teaching of Berber argue that it will motivate Berber-speaking students to continue their education and facilitate their socioeconomic integration and strengthen their sense of citizenship in a multicultural society (see Jackson, 2004, p. 21; Ennaji, 2005, p. 217).

7 Conclusion

Fifty-three years after independence, the multicultural situation and the educational system in Morocco have witnessed many changes. Although French remains important especially in higher education and in the private sector, Arabic has been consolidated through the Arabisation process. English has emerged as the most popular foreign language with no colonial connotations, and Berber has finally been introduced in elementary education. Moreover, the presence of Islam, which constitutes a fundamental cultural component side by side with Western culture, must also be taken into account, as a symbol of unity and a token of Morocco's cultural diversity.

One of the major hurdles faced by the Moroccan system of education since independence has to do with the ambivalence and the indecisiveness of decision-makers with regard to the management of multiculturalism and its impact on citizenship. The hesitation is flagrant specifically with regard to the officials' attitude toward Berber and its introduction in the educational system. Although Berber is taught in elementary schools, it is not yet recognised in the constitution as an official language, nor as a national language. The ambivalence equally concerns the Arabisation policy, which has been implemented in primary and secondary education, but not in tertiary education for ideological and political reasons. This reveals the complexity of the post-colonial Moroccan society.

Thus, the national community's ideas have not always been inclusive of all the cultural components of Moroccan society, and despite new efforts, the state does not strongly sustain modern definitions of citizenship. Factors like social movements, politics, and education, however, play a key role in constructing a sense of citizenship and identity.

A judicious reform of education is badly needed in order to achieve sustainable development, tolerance, social cohesion, and the preservation of Moroccan cultural identity. Integrating multiculturalism and citizenship issues may develop critical thinking, empower students to take action for problem-solving, and develop their awareness of citizen issues and global issues (cf. Ennaji, 2004).

Citizenship ought to be consistent with democratic values, namely respect for human rights, multiculturalism, and the rule of law. Educational authorities and decision-makers must adopt a multicultural approach as an efficient tool for addressing pluralism and cultural diversity and for enhancing multicultural education and citizenship, which include students' right to be prepared appropriately for life as citizens playing a full part in democracy.

All in all, the nature of the political institutions, the political processes and governmental policies to a great extent structure the kinds of social and political relationships that ensue in a multicultural society. In such a society, individuals naturally prefer and promote the interests of their own group. By negligence and mismanagement, this attitude could degenerate into tension and conflict. Democratic culture and good governance have proven to be capable of changing the outcome of the social, political, and economic processes from being confrontational to national accommodation.

Acknowledgement

This chapter originally appeared as: Ennaji, M. (2009) Multiculturalism, citizenship, and education in Morocco, *Mediterranean Journal of Educational Studies*, Vol. 14(1), pp. 5–26. Reprinted here with permission from the publisher.

Notes

1 France in the modern era pioneered the definition of an active citizenship that was inclusive of all who accepted the principles of the Revolution and French culture. The availability of French citizenship to the children of immigrants on condition of their education in, and identification with, French culture expresses the idea of the French nation as a 'daily plebiscite'. Yet the very presence of immigrants who utilise the right to be different against the universalism of the rights of the citizen has caused French people to reassess the nexus between citizenship and ethnic nationality.

2 To encourage education, annual celebrations for religious students were held at Qarawiyyine University in Fès and Yusufia University in Marrakesh. Students chose a 'mock' sultan among them and other students constituted the crowd and the whole procession walked in a parade in the main streets of the city (this was called in Arabic '*Sultan Tolba*', i.e., the sultan of students). The Sultan sent gifts to the best students. However, in 1925, this tradition was discontinued by the French rulers who feared that this event had political implications.

3 People read the *latif* in the mosques, 'a collective invocation to God in times of disaster'.

4 Today, the *Tifinagh* alphabet is used to write Berber, and efforts are made to generalise its use to the whole Maghreb region. In Morocco, short stories and novels are nowadays written in Berber.

5 In addition, the government applied four principles in education: the generalisation of schooling to all the population which led to an extension of education; the unification of

MULTICULTURALISM, CITIZENSHIP, AND EDUCATION IN MOROCCO

education (the same programmes have been adopted all through the country); free education to all (no tuition fees are paid); and Moroccanisation and Arabisation of education, which implied hiring Moroccan teachers to replace foreign ones, and progressively consolidating Modern Standard Arabic as the language of education, instead of French.

6 This is due to the fact that French is still the language of scientific, technical, and business studies, whereas Arabic and Berber remain the language(s) of cultural authenticity and ethnic identity expressing intimate, emotional, and spiritual values and beliefs (Gill, 1999).

References

Al-Fassi, A. (1954) *The Independence Movement in Arab North Africa* (translated by Hazen Zaki Nuseibeh). Washington, DC: American Council of Learned Sciences.

Al-jabri, M. A. (1973) *On the Question of Education in Morocco* (in Arabic). Casablanca: Dar Annashr Almaghribiya.

Al-jabri, M. A. (1995) *The Question of Identity* (in Arabic). Beirut: Publications of the Center for Arab Unity Studies.

Aronin, L., & Singleton, D. (2008) Multilingualism as a new linguistic dispensation, *International Journal of Multilingualism*, Vol. 5(1), pp. 1–16.

Berque, J. (1974) Lieux et moments du réformisme Islamique. In *Maghreb: Histoire et Sociétés*. Paris: Editions J. Duculot.

Boukous, A. (1995) *Société, Langues et Cultures au Maroc*. Rabat: Publications de la Faculté des Lettres.

Bourdieu, P. (1973) Cultural reproduction and social reproduction. In R. Brown (ed.) *Knowledge, Education and Cultural Change*. London: Tavistock Publications.

Bourdieu, P. (1982) *Ce que Parler Veut Dire*. Paris: Fayard.

Burke, E., III (1972) The Moroccan ulama, 1860–1912: an introduction. In N. R. Keddie (ed.) *Scholars, Saints, and Sufis*. Berkeley & Los Angeles: University of California Press.

Caubet, D. (1998) Alternance de codes au Maghreb: pourquoi le Français est-il Arabisé?, *Plurilinguismes*, Vol. 14, pp. 121–142.

Clark, N. (2006) Education in Morocco, *WENR*, Vol. 19(2/3), pp. 5–16.

Damis, J. J. (1970) *The Free-School Movement in Morocco* (translated into Arabic by Said Moatassim in 1991). Casablanca: Tansift Publishers.

Eickelman, D. (1985) *Knowledge and Power in Morocco*. Princeton: Princeton University Press.

El-biad, M. (1991) The role of some population sectors in the progress of Arabization in Morocco, *International Journal of the Sociology of Language*, Vol. 87, pp. 27–44.

Ennaji, M. (1988) Language planning in Morocco and changes in Arabic, *International Journal of the Sociology of Language*, Vol. 74, pp. 9–39.

Ennaji, M. (1991) Aspects of multilingualism in the Maghreb, *International Journal of the Sociology of Language*, Vol. 87, pp. 7–25.

Ennaji, M. (1997) The sociology of Berber: change and continuity, *International Journal of the Sociology of Language*, Vol. 123, pp. 23–40.

Ennaji, M. (2003) Attitudes to Berber and Tifinagh. In M. Peyron (ed.) *Proceedings of the Conference on Amazigh Language and Culture*. Ifrane: Al-Akhawayn University Press.

Ennaji, M. (2004) Teaching citizenship in the Moroccan context. In A. Zaki (ed.) *Proceedings of the 21st MATE Conference*. Rabat: MATE Publications.

Ennaji, M. (2005) *Multilingualism, Cultural Identity, and Education in Morocco*. New York: Springer.

Errihani, M. (2008) *Language Policy in Morocco: Implications of Recognizing and Teaching Berber*. Saarbrücken: Vdm Verlag Dr. Müller.

Fairclough, N. (1989) *Language and Power*. London: Longman.

Fishman, J. (1998) The new linguistic order, *Foreign Policy*, No. 113 (Winter), pp. 26–40.

Fitouri, C. (1983) *Biculturalisme, Bilinguisme et Education*. Paris & Neuchatel: Delachaux & Niestlé.

Geertz, C. (1979) Suq: the bazaar economy in Sefrou. In C. Geertz, H. Geertz & L. O. Rosen (eds.) *Meaning and Order in Moroccan Society*. New York & Cambridge: Cambridge University Press.

Gill, H. (1999) Language choice, language policy and the tradition-modernity debate in culturally mixed postcolonial communities: France and the 'Francophone' Maghreb as a case study. In Y. Suleiman (ed.) *Language and Society in the Middle East and North Africa*. London: Curzon.

Grandguillaume, G. (1983) *Arabisation et Politique Linguistique au Maghreb*. Paris: Maisonneuve et Larose.

Guessous, M. (1976) Bilingualism and biculturalism (in Arabic), *Al-Mouharrir*, Vol. 2(5), pp. 11–12.

Jackson, R. (2004) *Rethinking Religious Education and Plurality: Issues in Diversity and Pedagogy*. London: Routledge Falmer.

Kratochwil, G. (1999) Les associations culturelles Amazighes au Maroc: bilans et perspectives, *Prologues: Revue Maghrébine du Livre*, No. 17, pp. 31–40.

Kymlicka, W. (1995) *Multicultural Citizenship: A Liberal Theory of Minority Rights*. Oxford: Oxford University Press.

Lahlou, M. (1991) *A Morpho-Syntactic Study of Code Switching between Moroccan Arabic and French*. PhD thesis, University of Texas at Austin, USA.

Laroui, A. (1967) *L'Idéologie Arabe Contemporaine*. Paris: François Maspéro.

Marty, P. (1924) L'Université de Qaraouiyne. In *Renseignements Coloniaux, Supplément de l'Afrique Française*. Paris: Presses Universitaires de France.

Maurais, J. (2003) Towards a new linguistic world order. In J. Maurais & M. Morris (eds.) *Languages in a Globalizing World*. Cambridge: Cambridge University Press.

Moatassim, A. (1974) Le bilinguisme sauvage, *Tiers-Monde*, Vol. XV, pp. 619–670.

Moatassim, A. (1992) *Arabisation et Langue Française au Maghreb*. Paris: Presses Universitaires de France.

Myers-Scotton, C. (1993) *Social Motivations for Code Switching: Evidence from Africa*. Oxford: Oxford University Press.

Quadéry, M. (1998) Les berbères entre le mythe colonial et la négation nationale: le cas du Maroc, *Revue d'Histoire Moderne et Contemporaine*, Vol. 45(2), pp. 39–47.

Rosenthal, F. (1970) *Knowledge Triumphant: The Concept of Knowledge in Mediaeval Islam*. Leiden: E. J. Brill.

Sadiqi, F. (1991) The spread of English in Morocco, *International Journal of the Sociology of Language*, Vol. 87, pp. 99–114.

Sadiqi, F. (2003) *Women, Gender, and Language in Morocco*. Leiden: Brill.

Schwartz, E. (2008) Morocco's Berbers reclaim their language and their indigenous culture. *U.S. News & World Report*, 13 March.

Sklair, L. (1999) Competing conceptions of globalization, *Journal of World-Systems Research*, Vol. 5(2), pp. 143–162.

Stevenson, N. (2002) Cosmopolitanism, multiculturalism and citizenship, *Sociological Research Online*, Vol. 7(1), pp. 172–188.

Wagner, D. A., & Lotfi, L. (1980) Traditional Islamic education in Morocco: sociohistorical and psychological perspectives, *Comparative Education Review*, Vol. 24(2), Part 1 (June 1980), pp. 238–251.

Waterbury, J. (1970) *The Commander of the Faithful: The Moroccan Political Elite*. New York: Columbia University Press.

Zughoul, M. R. (1978) Lexical interference of English in Eastern Province Saudi Arabia, *Anthropological Linguistics*, Vol. 20(5), pp. 214–225.

CHAPTER 18

Conflict and Democracy Education in Palestine

Maher Z. Hashweh

1 Introduction

Democracy can be viewed as an important means for the peaceful resolution or management of conflict in a society. It is also a means, for individuals and groups, to influence decision making, that is, to affect change in reality through the use of dialogue and rational debate in order to persuade others and to defend positions, as well as through political participation and activism. Democracy education, to be authentic, has to use these processes of democracy as processes of teaching and learning. However, whereas democracy advocates have largely stressed the role of democracy in the resolution of already-existing conflicts, this article shows that teaching and learning about democracy in Palestine, within a case-based approach that encourages problem-solving, critical thinking, and active participation, emphasises the creation of conflict, in an already conflict-laden area. The role of those involved in democracy education, students and teachers alike, becomes to face these external and internal conflicts. In some important cases, the protagonists undergo radical change in attempting to resolve these conflicts. The main aim of the present paper is to describe how courageous, dedicated, and tactful teachers can surmount the obstacles to teaching democracy in a generally undemocratic context, and to show how teachers who were involved in a democracy education project in Palestine, as well as their students, faced conflict situations that sometimes facilitated radical change in their knowledge, beliefs, or behaviour. The paper also aims to underscore the importance of internal cognitive and emotional conflict, in addition to external conflict, in learning, as well as to draw attention to the dialectical relation between teachers' efforts to introduce educational change and their own change and professional development.

The study was based on the assumption that democracy can be taught in the basically undemocratic context of developing countries, and more specifically the Arab States. The situation in Palestine is even the more exceptional one of teaching democracy in a stateless and colonised society. To what degree is this assumption justified? There is a long debate in the educational literature about the causal relationships between educational and societal change. Many, if not most educators, have argued that social change leads educational

© THE EURO-MEDITERRANEAN CENTRE FOR EDUCATION RESEARCH, UNIVERSITY OF MALTA, 2002
DOI: 10.1163/9789004506602_018

CONFLICT AND DEMOCRACY EDUCATION IN PALESTINE

change, and that education, and schools in particular, play an essentially conservative role of maintaining the status quo and recreating the socio-economic structure in societies. Arab educators (Watfah, 1996, for example) have seen educational institutions, in Durkheim's (1956) perspective, as microcosms of the larger society that produced them, and consequently, they carry society's characteristics and act as tools to sustain that social order. Bowles & Gintis' (1976) seminal study showed how schools in America served to reproduce the economic and social capitalist structure. Watfah (1996) reviewed other French studies in the same strand. That schools play a conservative role in maintaining the status quo is largely accepted now. Accepting this position leads to a pessimistic view about the role of education in inducing change, and to a sceptical position about attempts to teach democracy in undemocratic societies.

Most of the writings about education and child-raring practices in the Arab States can be classified in this strand since they analysed Arab culture and society to identify its undemocratic 'character' and revealed how this culture affects schooling on the one hand, and how schooling, on the other hand, helps maintain the present culture and society. The leading intellectuals who have criticised Arab culture, home-rearing practices, and schools as barriers to democracy have been Sharabi (1975, 1987) and Barakat (1984). Sharabi, for example, pointed out to the patriarchal structure of Arab society, and identified child-rearing and schooling practices that reflect and maintain this society. Barakat identified many traditional values that are in dissonance with democratic values, attitudes and habits of mind. More recently, Watfa (1996, 1999) has shown how the authoritarian culture is reflected in, and maintained by, the family and the school relations and practices. Watfa (1999), additionally, reviewed a diverse and rich literature in the Arab States that addresses these issues. Watfa concluded that authoritarianism is closely related to the patriarchal structure of Arab societies, that Arab culture emphasises obedience of the young to the old, that schools train students to become obedient and submissive by embodying these values in student-teacher relations. Al-Naqib (1993) agrees that the role of schools is to develop blind obedience in students and, consequently, to facilitate their acceptance of prevalent societal values and ideology. Other educators have gone further to empirically study the effects of patriarchal relationships on student learning outcomes, for example, on the scientific attitudes of school students (Heidar, 1996).

However, other educators have pointed to the liberating and progressive role of education. There is an important aspect of education that addresses the mind, and that aims to develop intellectual abilities even in a predominantly conservative education context. This, sometimes unintended, by-product of education leads to the development of critical individuals who can reflect on the status quo and work for change. The role of education in promoting social mobility, economic and political development, and modernity in the Developing World in general is known (e.g., Fagerlind & Saha, 1989). Bahlool (1997), in one of the very few books that addressed education and democracy in the Arab States, took this more optimistic position, and argued that 'every change in society or the political system presupposes change at the individual level' (p. 82). He opposed revolutionary or radical instantaneous changes because some members of the new élite will be prone 'to the same shortcomings that were present in the society that produced the élite and in the social culture which the élite is trying to overcome' (pp. 82–83). The alternative, according to Bahlool, is in education: 'positively affecting any individual in the society is like lighting a candle ... [because] the individual is the starting point just as he is the end point' (p. 83).

It is unnecessary to accept either of the two positions in this dualism concerning the relations between social and educational change in order to teach about democracy in predominantly undemocratic contexts. Indeed, it is unuseful to ask the question at this level of generality. The relations are far more complex. For example, most studies assume the existence of one Arab culture. Knowing that there is one dominant culture and many sub-cultures in most societies, the question becomes: which culture is the educational system reflecting and maintaining? In Jordan, for example, can we neglect the differences between a rich private school in West Amman and another rural one in the Jordan Valley? Can we speak, also, about one culture in Palestine, Yemen and Morocco? Can we also reliably assert that the Arab culture is predominantly patriarchal, and take this as our starting point in the study of education and society in the Arab world? Heidar's (1996) aforementioned study revealed that students in this 'patriarchal' society nevertheless believed that there was no intellectual authoritarianism, that is, they could express their differences of opinions with their parents and elders. Hence, there were no clear relations between some of the proposed components of patriarchal relations. Additionally, this dualism assumes that powerful forces in the society completely control schooling practices and other means of enculturation, which is not completely true. Schools can be considered as sites for struggles between different groups in society, representing different interests and ideologies. Finally, the individual in these studies is portrayed as a passive receiver of culture and not as an active and selective constructor of his or her knowledge, a learner who is autonomous and who learns in collaboration with others and through acting on the world, that is an individual who acts and interacts in society and not merely an end-receiver of knowledge and values. In light of these considerations, and in light of the world interest in democracy, and the pro-democracy official discourse in many Arab States, educators and teachers have a significant margin of freedom to experiment with teaching democracy in these States. In my opinion, this debate about the causal effects between societal and educational change will not be resolved at the academic level, but rather will be determined by the results of struggles at the concrete level of practice in schools and other institutes of learning, and it is in this spirit that the study was undertaken.

2 The Democracy Education Project

The Democracy Education Project was a three-year project that started in September 1998. During the first year of the Project nine high school teachers from private, public, and UNRWA (United Nations Relief and Welfare Agency) schools in the Ramallah area of the West Bank participated in a year-long workshop that met on a weekly basis. During the first semester of the academic year, the teachers were exposed to the philosophy, theoretical bases, and teaching methods of a case-based approach to democracy education. They collaborated, under the leadership of a university-based researcher, in designing a case-based unit. During the second semester they taught the unit in their respective ninth grade classrooms, and continued to meet on a weekly basis to reflect on the teaching of the preceding week, and to plan for the teaching of the forthcoming week.

The teaching unit presented a case about punishment of students in schools, and used it as an anchor for collaborative student learning about various elements of democracy, such as citizenship, the rule of law, the separation of powers, the legislative process, accountability, and basic rights. The teachers agreed upon a set of design criteria to guide the development and teaching of the case. Among these were the necessity of building the case using local events or issues, the use of a problem-based approach, the need for the case to provide a base for creating a community of learners, and the requirement that students explicitly plan their investigations before conducting any research. In teaching the unit, students started working as one group to identify problems and questions raised by the case. Consequently, the students worked in small groups to answer questions related to certain elements of democracy, such as the rule of law, or citizenship. Using the jigsaw method (a method that allows regrouping of students so that each of the students in the new group is an 'expert' on a subtopic, but knows very little on other subtopics), the students were finally re-arranged in new groups to propose solutions to the original problems raised by the case. The teaching of the case lasted for about 16 class periods—a detailed description of this phase of the Project is found in Hashweh & Njoum (2001).

In the second year of the Project the teachers collaborated in designing five more case-based teaching units. During the first semester of the third year each of six teachers taught one case-based unit in one of the grades 9 to 11. During the second semester each of the teachers wrote a documentary case to describe and analyse some aspects of her or his experience in teaching the case-based unit. The teachers continued to meet on a weekly basis throughout the two academic years to reflect and deliberate on their work.

The six teachers who participated in the three-year Project held a bachelor's degree (two held a master's degree), had teaching experiences ranging from 5 to 14 years, and their ages ranged from 27 to 38 years. They were teachers of Arabic, English, Social Studies, Mathematics or Physics at grades ranging between 7 and 12. The teachers taught in coeducational schools, except in one case where the school was a girls' school. Whereas in the kind of quantitative work used in this study the aim is not to test generalisations, and hence, there is usually no effort to choose representative samples of a certain population, I was conscious of the need to choose schools that are not unique in the Palestinian context as well. The inclusive private schools and the UNRWA school that were selected had students representing the different religious and socioeconomic diversity found in Ramallah. Additionally, there is no reason to believe that there is a local particularity to Ramallah, in the sense that its teachers and students would be different from those in other areas of the West Bank.

The main source for data for this paper came from the six teacher-written documentary cases. I also used my notes and experience as a participant observer in the Project to supplement the accounts portrayed in the teachers' cases. I chose accounts that portray conflict situations faced by students and teachers, that describe how they confronted these situations, and that depict the results of these confrontations. I start by describing the emotional conflict described by teachers participating in the Project. I then describe conflict situations at three levels, starting with the community and system level, moving to the school level, and finally to the classroom level, concentrating at this last level due to its importance in influencing the learning and development of both students and teachers.

3   Teacher Emotional Conflict

While the educational literature has described teachers' prior beliefs and conceptions (for example, Prawat, 1992; Hashweh, 1996), and the cognitive conflict that sometimes faces teachers during learning and professional development, there is almost no mention of the emotional conflict and anxiety that seem to accompany (or underlie) learning when teachers are involved in educational reform. Most of the six teachers mentioned their fears, hesitations, or anxieties in the cases they wrote. One of the teachers wrote almost at the beginning of her case: 'I felt afraid from the new experience about which I was to embark'. Another wrote: 'I could not reveal my fears to my students, but informed them that I was not an expert on the different facets of democracy'. One of the main reasons for the anxiety was that the teachers were not very familiar with the subject-matter that they were to teach, as the last quote reveals; only the social studies teacher felt she was well-prepared to teach democracy. The same teacher quoted above started her case by writing: 'The beginning of the Project was very difficult for me. As a teacher of physics I did not have the necessary background to teach democracy. I felt I was the least qualified person to teach this subject'.

However, others were anxious about using the new student-centred teaching methods, methods that were in contradiction with the traditional teacher-centred methods that they usually used, and that required new roles for students and teachers, and new beliefs about these roles. A third teacher wrote:

> I was highly hesitant ... I was not familiar with the new teaching methods, teaching through the use of self-learning, or self-service classrooms as I like to call them, where you divide students into groups, re-divide these groups and re-group them in new groups, and additional groups until you lose your mind ... I was highly sceptical about the efficiency of this method, thinking that it is not appropriate for our school students. It might be appropriate for graduate students, or maybe for special students who are serious, industrious and motivated.

He added later:

> We agreed to use the new methods to teach democracy. And I saw a similarity between using the small group approach and the teaching of democracy; both ideas were somewhat alien to our society. Learning in small groups, when the educational system has made the use of traditional teaching methods in languages, social sciences, mathematics and science scripture, will meet the same degree of surprise and estrangement as teaching about the concept and meaning of democracy, with its related elements such as accountability, separation of powers, and diversity, under an [Palestinian] authority that has not heard about such terms, or an [Israeli] occupation that has not the slightest regard to democracy and human rights.

With such hesitation, scepticism, and anxiety among the teachers the question arises as to what motivated them to participate in such a Project. The main motivation seems to have come from the desire of these self-selected teachers to develop professionally. Many simply wanted to improve their practice. One teacher wrote: 'Curiosity and the desire to change my teaching style that has not changed since I became a teacher in the present school six years ago motivated me to risk joining this Project'. However, the more important motivation seems to have occurred when the teacher realised a gap between his or her existing practice and some ideals and goals that she or he held (see also Atkin, 1992). Another teacher, Afaf—who had a black-belt in karate—wrote that she had successfully used coercion and intimidation to control her students, and later realised that this is not how she wanted to treat her students. She added: 'This situation began to bother, even suffocate, me'. This motivation, expressed as a desire to resolve a conflict between the actual and the ideal, set off a variety of emotions such as guilt and apprehension among some teachers. These emotions are depicted most clearly in two cases by two female teachers who co-taught a unit. One of the cases described the teacher's experience in teaching the unit, while the other described the first teacher's development as observed and perceived by the other. The two teachers confess to each other about their mutual hesitations and apprehensions at the beginning of the Project, and offer mutual support to deal with these emotions. One of them, for instance, wrote about the other:

> Afaf told me she could not sleep last night. She was particularly troubled because she believed her students did not have the abilities necessary to succeed in the required activities. "Can they learn autonomously? Can they use the democracy concepts to understand and analyse reality, or to take positions and defend these positions? Can they debate and convince others about their views? I do not believe ninth grade students can analyse cases, pose questions, and come up with recommendations" she asked.

We notice from the case that the other teacher's confidence helped Afaf gain confidence. Afaf also used her colleague to express her ideas and emotions, and to think aloud in order to organise her thoughts, and to reflect on these ideas and emotions, and not necessarily to seek answers from her colleague.

Afaf, as shown in her colleague's case, realised right from the beginning a discrepancy between the way she treated her students and the teaching of democracy. She expected her students to confront her with this contradiction, and indeed, she wrote in her own case that one of her students exclaimed: 'Are *you* going to teach us about democracy! You are the last person who could do that. As a teacher you only order us around. Your gaze is enough to frighten us, and no student dares to stand up to you. You are a dictatorial teacher'. This serves to heighten her sense of guilt. The other teacher wrote in her documentary case that Afaf became greatly critical of her behaviour toward her students. She adds that Afaf whispered to her: 'Why am I feeling that I have committed a crime? All other teachers do the same. Maybe I was a little bit stricter, but they did the same. I should take the whole thing more lightly'.

The weekly meetings that the participant teachers attended helped to provide the mutual support to face these emotions; each discovered that she is not the only one with apprehensions or problems, and that 'we're all in this together'. We often were also able to jointly discuss different solutions to the problems faced by the teachers. The professional climate that characterised these meetings, with emphasis on openness, constructive criticism, and provision of help, facilitated this process, although teachers varied in their willingness to put their thoughts, feelings, and practices on the 'examination table'. The long period of the Project also helped in building trust between the participants. This sense of trust was very important to the learning process of the teachers, since it allowed them the opportunity to express their ideas and feelings, to discuss them, and to construct or accept new ones when needed (see also Brown [2001] and Maria [2000] who emphasise the importance of trust in learning in very different contexts).

This process of expressing one's ideas and feeling to others became even more difficult for some when they started writing their documentary cases. One teacher told us that writing the case made her feel like getting naked in front of others. In spite of this, this particular teacher saw great value in the discussions during the weekly meetings. When a teacher posed a problem that she faced for discussion and saw how another views it from a different perspective or a third proposes solutions that she had not thought about, this allows her to reconstruct her experience and to deepen her understanding, and, simultaneously, this allows her to realise the importance of discourse in knowledge creation, or the social construction of knowledge.

Although the initial motivation to join the Project was a desire to develop professionally, at later stages it appears that the nature of this motivation might have changed. In light of the profound difficulties that some met at the initial stages of implementation, the main motive to continue was perhaps the sense of obligation to continue or the avoidance of the embarrassment of withdrawing. One teacher wrote: 'I did not know whether there was any point to what I was doing or whether it was all in vain—periods lost with nothing achieved. I had no choice: I had started the Project, and I had to complete it'.

When the same teacher achieved success at the end of the Project, she was exuberant: 'Samer (one of her students who had initially displayed negative attitudes toward democracy and its study) has changed his mind, and this was something I had never expected. This was a great achievement for me, and I felt the delight of success'. The final motivator for all teachers was sensing indicators that their students had learned, better understood a concept, became more skilful, or developed positive attitudes toward the subject matter they were teaching. Although monitoring student involvement in classroom activities was initially used by teachers to assess their teaching effectiveness, student learning was finally the main yardstick with which they assessed their success or failure.

The cases were revealing in illuminating the emotional states, goals and motivation of the participant teachers, and they indicate that teacher learning, like student learning, is warm and whole, and quite different from the cold cognitive learning that is usually described and analysed.

4 Conflict at the Educational System and Community Level

The six teachers involved in the Project were granted permission to teach the democracy unit using class periods that were usually assigned to civic education, social studies, or library. Nevertheless, the teachers felt under enormous pressure to finish teaching the unit in the minimal amount of time in order not to affect the coverage of the curriculum they were usually teaching. Education Ministry supervisors, principals, and parents expected teachers to teach the official curriculum, and to use the textbooks authored and published by the Ministry, as in many other countries in the area, and attempts to change this status quo were sometimes perceived as subversive. Since we had secured permission from the administration of the different school systems and the principals for the Project, the teachers met few problems with the administration. However, some teachers failed to communicate well with the parents about the goals and methods of the Project, and this created some conflict situations for them.

This conflict is well documented in Afaf's case:

> One day Farah, one of my students, started crying in class. I learned, upon questioning her, that her father had found out she was studying about democracy. He wanted to forbid her from going to school, and tore up all the materials and papers she had for the Project. He said he did not send her to school to study such principles. When she argued with him, he

became more furious, attributing her willingness to argue with him and to disobey him to the Democracy Education Project. She added that her father was coming to see me and the school principal.

The second day Farah's father came to the school, accompanied with some of the members of the executive committee of the Parent's Council (the Parent-Teacher Association). I and the principal met with them. The father was very angry and spoke in an offensive and harsh manner. He accused me of inciting the girls to rebel against their parents. He explained that democracy is in contradiction with our Islamic faith, and that it helps girls stand up to their parents and to do what they wish. Finally, he added that he thinks I should concentrate on teaching the basics, language and mathematics, rather than this democracy stuff.

The teacher continues to describe how a member of the Executive Committee, an Islamic cleric who had come to the meeting upon the father's request but who had not been previously informed about the nature of the problem, disagreed with the father, and showed how Islam is compatible with democracy and women's rights. At the end of a long meeting the father reluctantly agreed to allow his daughter to continue studying the democracy unit.

While this case describes how some parents objected to the content of the unit, other cases describe how they objected to the teaching methods used. One teacher wrote that students and parents accused him of not teaching any more:

I heard one student say that this method of teaching is easy for teachers since we now have to do all the work while the teachers take the credit for our learning. In other schools, parents complained to the administrations, and questioned the teacher's role, and even cast doubt on the teacher's competencies in some cases.

5   Conflict at the School Level

The conflict situations at the school level were no less serious than those at the larger context level. Afaf's case describes how she managed to convince her principal to grant her permission to teach the democracy unit without affecting the principal's sense of grandiose, after the later was offended that the teacher knew about the Project before her. The same case describes how Afaf got in trouble with her students in other classes who accused her of bias in selecting one particular section to study about democracy and neglecting other sections. She also described how she was able to change her behaviour when interacting with students in the class section that studied the democracy unit but not with students in other sections, and the dilemma that she faced. Another teacher described how she was put in a conflict situation with one of her colleagues:

> Democracy is still freedom to most of the students even after all they had studied about the principles and elements of democracy. Whenever they wanted to do whatever they liked, they justified it by saying that this is democracy—being free, complete freedom with no accountability or constraints by law. This caused a big problem with the history teacher. He had planned to discuss democracy as part of the history course he was teaching. When he reached that unit, they accused him of treating them in an undemocratic manner. They insisted that as part of democracy they should decide on what they should study and how to learn it. The teacher talked to me about this incident in the teachers' room, and accused me of inciting his students to rebel against him. Although he was initially harsh, he mellowed down when I told him about the Project, about the tenacious misconceptions that the students held about democracy, and about my efforts to confront these misconceptions.

While the cases describe these external conflict situations that the teachers were put into, they also show how tactful and dedicated teachers can manage to face these situations, and reach resolutions that break down the barriers to educational innovations.

6 Conflict at the Class Level

Conflict at the class level was the most difficult for teachers and students alike, and while it was sometimes manifested as external conflict between teachers and students or among students, the more important kind of conflict was internal. Teaching and learning about democracy introduced internal conflict and sometimes necessitated radical changes in the thoughts and behaviours of students and teachers alike. Learning, in this context, was not solely additive and cumulative, but was occasionally characterised by qualitative changes in the learners' thoughts and behaviours. I shall start by briefly describing one conflict situation that affected student learning, and later describe situations that affected teacher learning in more detail.

6.1   *Students' Conceptions about Democracy*

I have chosen to describe and discuss one illustration of a conflict situation that faced students and teachers resulting from the students' prior conceptions about democracy and attitudes toward it. It is revealing that most of the six documentary cases show that students came to the study of democracy with already-held ideas about and attitudes toward democracy. Some of these conceptions were sophisticated. In the case written by Afaf she described how her students equated democracy with freedom and freedom of choice. They were also adept at seeing the gap between the reality at home, the school, and the larger society on one hand, and how things should be in a democracy on the other hand. However, the cases also reveal that many students held inaccurate conceptions and negative attitudes. Many, for example, thought democracy means complete freedom unrestrained by law or accountability. They believed that the only restraint should be internal, that is self-control. This, of course, makes many of the elements of democracy, such as legislation, the rule of law, and accountability, unnecessary.

When the students started to discuss the teaching cases presented to them, and to read about the different element of democracy, many faced conflict between their prior inadequate conceptions of democracy, on the one hand, and reality as described in the case and the readings about democracy on the other hand. One teacher wrote her case focusing on these prior conceptions, the ensuing conflicts, and the results of these conflicts. Samer, one of her outspoken students, initially defined democracy as 'the freedom of a person to do whatever he likes within a certain framework'. When she asked him to explain what he meant by that, he answered that there are certain persons who do not know where the boundaries on their freedom lie. He made it clear that restrictions on behaviour should be internal only. When discussing the political process in Palestine he saw no need for accountability: 'As long as we have chosen our authorities through elections, they are authorised after that to do what they deem appropriate, to choose the means that they find suitable'. The case that this particular class studied was about consuming expired canned food (sardines), and the health problem that this caused. Students discussed the causes of the problem, and how to solve it, discussing issues about who should be held responsible for the presence of expired food in food stores, the separation of power, the adequacy of legislations and how to influence legislation, and the rule of law. One important piece of information in the case, that some middle-level person in the Palestinian Authority might have had some connections with the distribution of expired food products, caused conflict for Samer. Toward the end of studying the unit, the teacher was surprised by the change in Samer's position:

The most important result was that Samer discarded his belief that democracy is freedom. When we were discussing the separation (and balance) of powers Samer said: "No authority should have absolute power". I replied, repeating what he had said a few weeks earlier: "As long as we have chosen our authority and government through elections, aren't they free to do what they like after that?" Samer answered passionately, "No. democracy is not absolute freedom. What if these rulers abandoned the principles they were proclaiming during election? Do we leave them to play havoc with our society? Do we leave them to import expired food products for the poor people who believed in them?"

6.2 *Teachers' Beliefs about Students*

Most teachers held two prior beliefs about students, as evidenced by the cases they wrote, beliefs that they were required to reconsider when they faced cognitive conflict during the teaching of the case-based democracy unit. The first belief was that students' characteristics were stable across time and domain. A 'smart' student will stay smart in the future, and if he/she is smart in languages then he/she will be smart in other subjects, such as mathematics, as well. These stable characteristics or traits might be intelligence, motivation, effort, or distinction. In one case the teacher worried that a student displayed negative attitudes toward democracy, and expected that he would not change his attitudes. In another story the teacher candidly describes her surprise when a student, who was poor in mathematics, demonstrated strengths in other areas when working in a small group:

> As I had expected, the students in each group chose one of the good students as a group coordinator except for one group, where the students chose Samar who was a very poor student in mathematics. I couldn't but express my surprise to this group asking: "*You* have been chosen by the group?" I was curious, and asked each group what criteria they had used to choose the coordinator. Each group answered that they chose the student because she was a good student, except for Samar's groups. They told me that Samar was a good student in Arabic, and that she wrote short stories and poems, and that is why they had chosen her. I did not know what to answer. I had thought she doesn't understand anything. ... I kept a close eye on Samar's group to observe how she conducts herself. I wasn't sure why I did that. Was I feeling guilty about my hasty judgment and the way I had treated her in the past? Or did I want to prove to myself that I was right?

Samar surprised the teacher again by proving to be the best coordinator in the class. In a third story a teacher described his scepticism about small group work. He added that he expected students 'who are industrious and study under traditional teaching methods will maintain the same standards under any other teaching method'. He was surprised when he saw three 'poor' students, who hardly participated in any class activity during his Arabic periods, the stars of an after-school basketball game to which he went for the first time.

In all three cases we find that what initiated the conflict was the discrepancy the teacher discovered between his or her beliefs, or the expectations based on these beliefs, and a certain incident that occurred while teaching (a student changing his attitude toward democracy, a poor student in mathematics excelling in Arabic, inactive students in Arabic periods becoming the centre of activity and attention in a basketball game). This conflict led the teachers to reconsider their initial beliefs about one-dimensional stable intelligence and to appropriate the theory of multiple intelligences that was presented to them in the workshop. In the first case, when she realises that her student had changed his attitudes toward democracy the teacher wrote: 'I realised that making prior judgments about the outcomes of teaching is not correct'. In the second case, the teacher not only changed her beliefs about Samar's abilities, but used the theory of multiple intelligences to direct the attention of students in another small group to the talents of a girl with low status, in an effort to raise her status and, thus, to engage all students in work. The third teacher displayed an emotional reaction, in addition to the conceptual change that he underwent:

> This compelled me to reconsider my theories and repertoire of teaching methods ... If this energy is available here in the basketball court, why can't it be available in my class? God how much time I have lost in front of silent, stiff and lifeless benches. Please forgive me God. ... I should avoid making prior judgments on behalf of any student. A student can be a good achiever in one area and a poor one in another, or vice versa.

This change in teachers' beliefs about student abilities was the most profound change that occurred in their thinking, and we find evidence for its occurrence in five out of the six cases written by the teachers. Two factors facilitated this change: the anomalous events that contradicted with the teachers' prior beliefs, and the presence of an alternative belief—the theory of multiple intelligences that was presented to the teachers. The importance of teachers actually engaging in practice and learning from practice has to be stressed, and in particular the dual role of anomalous events—they simultaneously contradict with prior conceptions and lend support to new ones.

The second belief about students that many teachers held was that their students have low abilities. One teacher described them as 'academically poor', while a second described them as 'not having the intellectual skills necessary for the activities suggested by the Project'. A third claimed they were unmotivated and not serious. Since the teachers believed their students had low abilities or motivation to begin with, and since these 'traits' do not change with time (the first belief above), then they concluded that they will not learn anything worthwhile as a result of the Project. In this case, the teachers' beliefs changed when they conflicted with reality. One teacher expressed this change best: 'The outcomes that I got with this class was different from what I had expected. I had thought that I would never succeed with this class no matter what teaching method I use. In reality, I was astounded by the results. How is it that these students who never understand what I explain in class now understand and analyse? How is it that these students, who had never heard a word of praise from me, achieve so well and disprove my hypothesis?'

6.3   Teachers' Beliefs about Democracy and about Discipline

Some teachers shared with their students the belief that democracy means total freedom, and that only self-control should be used to regulate behaviour, with no need for external constraints and mechanisms for monitoring and guiding behaviour. This does not mean that the teachers did not simultaneously hold sophisticated and accurate conceptions of democracy, but these will not be discussed here. These beliefs interacted with the teachers' beliefs about classroom management and discipline, and, consequently, are described together in this section. In the first conflict situation I describe, I use the case of Afaf to show how she had to reconsider her beliefs about discipline in light of the contradiction she realised between these beliefs and her beliefs about democracy.

Afaf initially held two salient beliefs about her students and classroom discipline. She believed that student should be well disciplined in class for learning to be effective. She also believed that students do not have adequate self-control to behave properly in class. She used these beliefs to rationalise her initial intimidating behaviour toward her students. However, as we saw earlier, she soon realised a conflict between her practice and the implications of her new conceptions of democracy. To treat her students in a more 'democratic' manner, she had to change her initial belief about students and believe that they can exercise self-control. Examination of the two cases written by Afaf and by her colleague reveal the important role of dialogue, reflection, and deliberations in allowing Afaf to make the necessary changes in her beliefs, and, accordingly, in her practice. Afaf's colleague described how Afaf was hesitant throughout the teaching of the democracy unit to allow her students latitude in behaviour or expression. Afaf was especially appalled by the criticism that her students made of the school discipline policies and practices, and the alternatives they proposed. She considered them rude. It took her colleague some effort to convince her that this was eventually in the teacher's own interest:

> Don't you see that they have developed a good understanding of the rights and duties of citizens? You will find it easier to deal with them in the future because they have developed and discussed rules and policies that will act as guidelines for their behaviour. They have accepted them, and you will have little discipline problems in the future.

Afaf, convinced by now that the teaching of democracy would help her students exercise more self-control, changed her behaviour. 'I started to allow them to take part in decision making, especially in issues that were closely related to them', she wrote. She added later, 'The relation between me and my students became a friendship relationship, and we started to deliberate and debate using our minds and logic'. However, she changed her practice only in that particular section:

> I could not interact with students in other sections in the same manner because they had not studied the principles of democracy. If I treat them in a manner similar to the one I used in this class I believe they will go overboard in their behaviour because they do not know their rights and obligations, and there will be no constraints to check their behaviour. My students would be committed to the school regulations because they internally believe in them and not out of fear of me or of punishment. Fear can temporarily induce discipline, but internal self-control, which results from students knowing their rights and duties, is more lasting.

Another conflict situation occurred when some teachers, upon using small group work, found the sound level in the classroom irritating and unacceptable. Having been used to traditional teacher-directed classrooms, they expected very low noise levels. This conflict between beliefs or expectations and classroom reality again triggered thinking on the teachers' part. However, and in contrast to the last conflict situation, this conflict did not lead to a change in the teacher's beliefs or expectations. One teacher discussed this issue in her case at some length. She had problems with the high noise level, especially at the beginning of the period. However, she attributed the high noise level to the use of inappropriate furniture, heavy desks that were hard to move in order to arrange them for small group work. She wrote at the end of her case:

> All my efforts failed to change the chaos at the beginning of each class period. I realised that the real problem lay in the physical set up of the classroom, and that this should be taken into consideration to provide the necessary environment in the future.

She did not entertain the idea that a higher noise level, compared to that during traditional teaching, is acceptable, and desirable—no genuine group work can occur without dialogue. This lost opportunity for teacher development occurred because she did not have an alternative to her prior beliefs or expectations. People will not abandon an idea if they do not have an alternative one (see Hashweh [1986] and Posner et al. [1982] for a discussion of conceptual change in science).

The third conflict situation occurred when teachers wanted their students to express and defend their ideas, and to have the courage to defend their rights as part of democracy education, yet often found students 'rude' when they actually engaged in such practices. The teachers set goals and expectations for student behaviour when learning about democracy. However, when the students acted in accordance with these expectations, teachers felt uncomfortable because these new student behaviours contradicted teachers' prior expectations about student behaviour. Some of them were not able to draw a line between desirable courageous behaviour and rude behaviour.

This conflict is evident in Afaf's case. She wrote: 'I hated this weakness, docility, and submissiveness to orders that characterised my students ... Fear controls their minds and tongues. ... How can I make these girls demand that their rights be respected?' Yet when these girls submitted a proposal that evaluated the existing school discipline policy and demanded amendments, she found them, according to her colleague, radical and rude. Another teacher punished a student when he asked about the final use of the report that his group wrote. The teacher felt that the student was rude, and did not see that the student was worried about his intellectual rights as a co-author of the report. He could actually have used the incident to discuss intellectual property rights in a democracy rather than punish the student. Again, this is an example of a lost opportunity for teacher learning and development since this teacher did not have the chance to discuss this incident with his colleagues in spite of the design of the Project that included weekly meetings to discuss teaching and to plan for it.

Some teachers believed that democracy entailed that students be engaged in decision making regarding all aspects of teaching, including a say in the content and methods of teaching. I have already pointed out that some students shared the same belief. Some teachers experienced a conflict between this interpretation of the implications of democracy for teaching and learning,

CONFLICT AND DEMOCRACY EDUCATION IN PALESTINE

and the necessity of teaching a specific unit on democracy using a specific approach, and grouping students in heterogeneous small groups. In many cases the teachers could not resolve this conflict, and we find that they ended their cases struggling with these dilemmas.

Afaf's case describes how she faced this problem when she tried to divide her students into heterogeneous small groups. High achievers wanted to work together, and refused to have poor achievers in their groups, claiming that the latter will not work hard, and that the group's grades will consequently be lowered. She informed the students that the way she had grouped the students was final, and not open for discussion. Some students answered, 'How are we going to study about democracy while you are using your authority as a teacher to enforce decisions from the beginning of the Project?' The teacher added in her case: 'In spite of the fact that I completely agreed with what they said, I answered that this grouping was for their own interests, and I ended the discussion'.

Again, we notice that when the teacher, Afaf, did not have a chance to discuss this problem with others, that is to deliberate and reflect on her practice, and to be exposed to alternative ideas, she did not change her prior ideas, in this case her beliefs about democracy its implications for teaching. However, as we have seen earlier, the same teacher changed her ideas about student ability to self-control their behaviour when she had the chance to discuss the issue with her colleague. As for Afaf's (and some other teachers') misconceptions of democracy, she assumed that democracy means providing freedom for choice for every individual in every situation that requires decision making. She was not cognizant that democracy entails freedom of choice within certain constraints. She, and other teachers, could have used such opportunities to discuss the nature of democracy in class, to provide for alternatives within constraints, and to show that the Project actually provides these alternatives. Students, for example, could choose which democracy subtopic (element of democracy, such as rule of law) they wanted to study, what problems and questions to define and pursue, how to answer these questions, and what format their final project should take. She could also have allowed students to have some choice in joining the different groups, as long as each group remained heterogeneous.

6.4   *Teachers' Beliefs about Democracy Education*

Teachers held many beliefs about the aims of democracy education that I shall not try to identify here in full. I shall only emphasise the conflict that some teachers faced when they sensed the gap between the principles of democracy and the Palestinian reality. Teachers faced with such a conflict questioned the value of teaching students about democracy. The teacher who was particularly affected by this conflict was Afaf, who entitled her case 'Democracy in a Refugee Camp?' The title reflects the teacher's doubting the possibility of democratic life or democracy education in a camp. In spite of this initial hesitation, she taught the democracy unit, and was greatly surprised by the success she met. Her students became daring in asking for their rights and defending these rights, which was the most important goal of democracy education for Afaf. We have already mentioned how she found them almost rude when they daringly criticised the status quo regarding school discipline in their school, and suggested modifications in the school policy and regulations. She described incidents that also show the benefits of democracy education for her students.

In the first incident the students wanted to leave school to join in a rally against occupation on a certain day that celebrated a national occasion, but the principal refused to allow them to leave the school. The teacher intervened, and asked her students to discuss the issue with the principal. The students elected some representatives who negotiated a solution with the principle that allowed the students to join the rally after the fourth period that day. The class discussion after this reflected how students have internalised many of the democracy ideas discussed in class, and how empowered they felt. The episodes provide evidence that the case-based approach had succeeded in helping students acquire knowledge that they can use in their personal and social life, in contrast to the knowledge that they keep in 'cold storage' to use only in examinations during traditional teaching. The second episode described how one of the students mentioned that they had stopped cheating in mathematics examinations after studying the democracy unit, and did not need the teacher to proctor these examinations. Afaf seems to have been greatly successful in achieving her important goal of democracy education—inducing student self-control.

Afaf, due to this success she met in teaching democracy, became worried that she had provided her students with a disservice; she believed that her students who were all female, now adamant about protecting their rights, would be faced with problems in the future in a male-controlled and undemocratic society. In reality, these questions reflect Afaf's views of the aims of education in general: to prepare the individual to adapt to society and maintain the status quo or to change and transform her or his society? Due to her adherence to the first aim she faced a conflict, a dilemma that remained unresolved.

7 Conclusion

This last incident about Afaf worrying about the future of her students ironically reveals that after three years of participation in the Project, and in spite of the sometimes drastic changes that occurred in her thinking and practice, she has still not realised an important aspect of the Project—mainly, that teachers should and can participate in the struggle in their society to change the status quo. As mentioned in the beginning of this paper, many Arab intellectuals and educators (e.g., Barakat, 1984; Sharabi, 1975, 1987; Watfa, 1996, 1999) have criticised Arab culture and society as patriarchal and authoritarian, and have identified cultural values, home child-rearing and school practices that are barriers to democracy in the Arab World, but have not clearly explained how changing this state of affairs should occur. The main premise of the Project, still not completely realised by the teacher Afaf, is that schools, like other social organisations, are arenas for the struggle between conservative and progressive movements in the society.

Students and teachers have approached democracy education with prior ideas, experiences, and expectations that sometimes stood in contradiction with the ideas concerning democracy and pedagogy that they were exposed to. This had occasionally triggered cognitive and emotional conflict, and prompted them to undergo examination and reorganisation of their mental structure. When teachers faced conflict, and were able to reflect on their prior ideas and to entertain new ideas with the support of their colleagues and Project leader, they underwent important qualitative changes in their ideas and practices, and, therefore, developed professionally. On other occasions, the teachers did not have the chance to think through these conflicts or to consider new alternative ideas, and the conflict did not lead to radical change.

In this article I have emphasised the emotional and cognitive conflicts that the students and teachers faced when learning and teaching about democracy. The cases, however, also replicate the findings of previous studies about the relations between culture, society and schools in the Arab States. In agreement with Al-Naqib (1993) and Watfa (1996, 1999), we found that students and teachers sometimes initially held beliefs about student-teacher interaction and appropriate classroom behaviour, and about democracy that reflected an authoritarian culture. Teachers like Afaf continued to struggle with the implications of democracy for student-teacher interactions until the end of her case, and still was uncomfortable with student honest expression of their ideas because she did not completely give up her old emphasis on obedience. She has still not finally resolved the differences between rudeness and civility. It is precisely because the Project necessitated the introduction of new content, pedagogy, and student-teacher relations that were in dissonance with prior practices and beliefs that conflict was created. In contrast to previous studies that emphasised how schools reflect and maintain the culture and the social structure, the cases show how students and teachers were able to undergo important changes in their ideas and behaviour. The cases describe classes that did not reflect authoritarian values, but exemplified democratic relations, and were enhancing the process of democratisation in Palestinian society.

We have found that teaching democracy occasionally creates conflict. If we view democracy as a tool for struggle, a means of changing reality through resistance and dialogue, then the contradiction between learning and practising democracy disappears—in either case, conflict is a major component of the process. Struggle for democracy, justice and freedom is necessarily characterised by conflict. The importance of the teacher written cases in this Project lies in revealing the deep, rather than the surface, aspects of this conflict— the internal emotional and cognitive conflict that accompanies external visible conflict. Their strength also lies in bringing to our attention that changing reality dialectically interacts with personal change. Additionally, the use of teacher-written cases has allowed teachers to tell their own stories, to sketch their own accounts of their attempts at educational innovation and change. These stories show that while teaching democracy in Palestine is a very difficult process, it can be successfully undertaken. They are stories of courageous and dedicated teachers who tactfully surmounted the obstacles to teaching democracy in an essentially undemocratic context. It may be striking that all six cases turned out to be mainly stories about conflict and struggle. But should we have expected that stories about attempts to change the status quo, even the educational one, in a context of a society struggling to achieve statehood, to build its own civil society and democratic institutions, and to achieve independence from a foreign military occupation to be any different?

Acknowledgement

This chapter originally appeared as: Hashweh, M. Z. (2002) Conflict and democracy education in Palestine, *Mediterranean Journal of Educational Studies*, Vol. 7(1), pp. 65–86. Reprinted here with permission from the publisher.

References

Al-Naqib, K. H. (1993) The educational dilemma and the silent revolution: a study in the sociology of culture (in Arabic), *Al-Mustaqbal Al-'Arabi*, Vol. 16(174), pp. 61–74.

Atkin, J. M. (1992) Teaching as research: an essay, *Teaching and Teacher Education*, Vol. 8(4), pp. 381–390.

Bahlool, R. (1997) *Education and Democracy*. Ramallah: Muwatin.

Barakat, H. (1984) *Contemporary Arab Society* (in Arabic). Beirut: Centre for the Study of Arab Unity.

Bowles, S., & Gintis, H. (1976) *Schooling in Capitalist America: Educational Reform and the Contradictions of Economic Life.* New York: Basic Books.

Brown, J. S. (2001) *Storytelling: Scientist's perspective.* Paper presented at the weekend symposium at the Smithsonian Associates on 'Storytelling: Passport to the 21st Century', 20–21 April, Washington, DC, United States of America.

Durkheim, E. (1956). *Education and Sociology.* Glencoe, IL: Free Press.

Fagerlind, I., & Saha, L. (1989) *Education and National Development: A Comparative Perspective.* New York: Pergamon.

Haidar, A. L. (1996) Patriarchal relations and their effects on scientific attitudes of secondary school students in Yemen (in Arabic), *Al-Mustaqbal Al-'Arabi,* Vol. 19(214), pp. 86–106.

Hashweh, M. Z. (1986) Toward an explanation of conceptual change, *European Journal of Science Education,* Vol. 8(3), pp. 229–249.

Hashweh, M. Z. (1996) Palestinian science teachers' epistemological beliefs: a preliminary report, *Research in Science Education,* Vol. 26(1), pp. 89–102.

Hashweh, M. Z. & Njoum, I. (2001) A case-based approach to education in Palestine. In R.G. Sultana (ed.) *Challenge and Change in Euro-Mediterranean Region: Case Studies in Educational Innovation.* New York: Peter Lang.

Maria, K. (2000) Conceptual change instruction: a social constructivist perspective, *Reading & Writing Quarterly,* Vol. 16(1), pp. 5–22.

Posner, G. J., Strike, K. A., Hewson, P. W., & Gertzog, W. A. (1982) Accommodation of a scientific conception: toward a theory of conceptual change, *Science Education,* Vol. 66(2), pp. 211–227.

Prawat, R. S. (1992) Teachers' beliefs about teaching and learning: a constructivist perspective, *American Journal of Education,* Vol. 100(3), pp. 354–395.

Sharabi, H. (1975) *An Introduction to the Study of Arab Society* (in Arabic). Jerusalem: Salah Eddin Publications.

Sharabi, H. (1987) *The Patriarchal Structure: A Study of Contemporary Arab Society* (in Arabic). Beirut: Dar Al-Tali'a.

Watfa, A. (1996) The social backgrounds of educational interactions in Arab universities: the University of Damascus as an exemplar, *Al-Mustaqbal Al-'Arabi,* Vol. 19(214), pp. 74–85.

Watfa, A. (1999) Manifestations of authoritarianism in contemporary Arab culture and education (in Arabic), *Al-Mustaqbal Al-'Arabi,* Vol. 22(247), pp. 54–71.

CHAPTER 19

Navigating Religious Boundaries at School

From Legitimate to Specious Religious Questions

Maria Esther Fernández Mostaza, Gloria García-Romeral and Clara Fons i Duocastella

> Le bricoleur est apte à exécuter un grand nombre de tâches diversifies; mais, à la différence de l'ingénieur, il ne subordonne pas chacune d'elles à l'obtention de matières premières et d'outils conçus et procurés à la mesure de son projet: son univers instrumental est clos, et la règle de son jeu est de toujours s'arranger avec les « moyens du bord », c'est-à-dire un ensemble à chaque instant fini d'outils et de matériaux, hétéroclites au surplus, parce que la composition de l'ensemble n'est pas en rapport avec le projet du moment, ni d'ailleurs avec aucun projet particulier, mais est le résultat contingent de toutes les occasions qui se sont présentées de renouveler ou d'enrichir le stock, ou de l'entretenir avec les résidus de constructions et de destructions antérieures. L'ensemble des moyens du bricoleur n'est donc pas définissable par un projet (ce qui supposerait d'ailleurs, comme chez l'ingénieur, l'existence d'autant d'ensembles instrumentaux que de genres de projets, au moins en théorie); il se définit seulement par son instrumentalité, autrement dit, et pour employer le langage même du bricoleur, parce que les éléments son recueillis ou conservés en vertu du principe que « ça peut toujours servir ».
>
> CLAUDE LÉVI-STRAUSS (*La Pensée Sauvage*)

∴

1 Introduction: From Engineering to *Bricolage*

Claude Lévi-Strauss (1962) in *La Pensée Sauvage* contrasts the tasks of *bricolage* to those of an engineer. In the case of *bricolage*, it is a question of re-using what is left (the 'residues' or 'leftovers') of previous constructions and demolitions; in the case of engineering, however, the elements and the tools are conceived

© THE EURO-MEDITERRANEAN CENTRE FOR EDUCATION RESEARCH, UNIVERSITY OF MALTA, 2009

DOI: 10.1163/9789004506602_019

This is an open access chapter distributed under the terms of the CC BY-NC 4.0 License.

and constructed according to the specifications of each problem. Continuing this same analogy, the 'engineering' work of which we shall take advantage of the 'residues' is a report sponsored by the Religious Affairs Department of the Generalitat of Catalonia. For this report we designed a number of instruments to ascertain and illustrate the main elements that were outlined as sources of conflict for the teaching staff in Catalan educational centres as well as for the various religious representatives. We gave special attention to those situations that are commonly seen as responses to certain religious practices or concepts. This investigative work was based on an exhaustive analysis of religious diversity in different educational fields. Equal emphasis was given to that which passed as collective evidence as to that which tended to go unnoticed. The information used came from a detailed analysis of 26 interviews with staff from different Catalan education centres. The interviewees were selected according to the following criteria: type of centre (infant, primary, secondary), the status of the centre (public, private, state assisted), territorial diversity, and a significant proportional presence of students from minority religious traditions.

Consequently, and keeping with the original analogy, our paper becomes a *bricolage* job due to the fact that we have sought to make use of pre-conditioned and specific 'residual materials' viewed from a sociological perspective. We set out by taking a step backward to see things from a different angle so that what is usually taken for granted or normal will be questioned. So, when we asked about the existence of religious plurality in educational centres, the staff, for example, often spoke of the collective immigrant group to refer to it, or to identify those who practised a religious confession *different* from what has been for decades taken as the norm, that is to say, the Catholic faith, although it is almost never actually named. It is a question of taking a step beyond the simple documentation of what is called 'common sense' and thus accepting that social reality is much more complex than we dared to imagine. We think, to a certain extent, that is what sociology is all about.

In order to understand the current situation, there is a need to briefly turn to: (i) the legislative framework that regulates the curricular situation of the subject of Religion; and (ii) the fact that Catalonia is today a geographical region in which more than 13 religious traditions are represented.

1.1 *Legal Context or What Legislators Imagined in 1979*

The Spanish Constitution (1978) combines the non-denominational nature of the State with certain cooperation between religious confessions. Article 16.3 states,

> No religion shall have a state character. The public authorities shall take into account the religious beliefs of Spanish society and shall consequently

maintain appropriate cooperation relations with the Catholic Church and other confessions.

This specific mention of the Catholic Church is interpreted in some sectors as being the remnant of undercover confessionality. Article 27.1 says, 'Everyone has the right to education. Freedom of teaching is recognized'. This announcement of the right to education, understood to therefore mean the creation of schools, the right for parents to choose their children's education and academic freedom, did not appear in the draft and was added to the document with an amendment agreed by various groups. This article is understood to mean the end of the classic struggle that from the early 19th century (cf. The Spanish Constitution of 1812 that was promulgated by the Cádiz Cortes) had been going on between those that defended the Church's monopoly on education and those that supported public and lay schools, like in France. The Constitution thereby guaranteed ideological pluralism both in the public and the private system. But this does not mean that as regulations have developed since, there have not been criticisms both of public aid awarded to private centres or the belief that it privileges in an unbalanced way the rights of the owner of a private centre, and the belief that it restrictively interprets parental rights. Article 27.3 says, 'The public authorities guarantee the right of parents to ensure that their children receive religious and moral instruction in accordance with their own convictions'.

In terms of the 1979 Agreements between Spain and the Holy See, the state recognises the fundamental right to religious education, and the Church admits that it should coordinate its educational mission with the principles of public freedom regarding religious affairs and the rights of families and all pupils and teachers, avoiding any discrimination or situation of privilege. In fact, the agreements made the right to freedom in education a provisional right, whose organisation was entrusted to the ecclesiastic hierarchy and whose cost was financed by the State. The ecclesiastic hierarchy proposes the teachers that will provide this teaching, as well as its academic content.

What legislators imagined in 1979 was that there would still be Catholic Religion classes in schools, but they would no longer be compulsory. Absolutely no legislation was issued that considered the possibility that the alternative might have been another religion that was different to Catholicism. Later equivalent agreements were established with the Federation of Evangelical Entities, the Islamic Commission and the Israelite Community.

From the moment when the State signed, in 1992, a series of agreements with the Jewish, Islamic and Evangelical communities, we enter into what is to a certain extent a contradictory situation. It is the situation we find ourselves in today: in application of the agreements that have been signed with these communities, on the one hand it seems that the State has made it possible for there to be confessional religious teaching of all these religions at schools; but at the same time such a situation is not viable, because there are relatively few schools that have a large enough number of pupils that require it, and if there were a lot of these schools, then there would not be enough teachers with the right training or the resources to pay for it.

To summarise, the situation the Catholic Church finds itself in is one of unashamed privilege, in that the confessional teaching of the Catholic religion can be provided whenever a group of parents request it. And if this model continues, we will find ourselves faced either by an unfair situation of inequality, which will become increasingly more patent, as in the future there will be many more schools at which the parents of Muslim children request the teaching of the subject of the Islamic religion, or otherwise by a situation in which pupils are segregated when it comes to Religion classes. Something that would make the subject of Religion not a unifying factor, but one that could cause segregation.

1.2   *Minority Religions within a Majority Catholic Context*

The first indications of diversity go back to the early 20th century, when we find clear signs of a large number of Protestants and the opening of the first synagogue in Catalonia, founded in 1918 (Estanyol, 2002). However, the Franco dictatorship made it an obligation for minorities to become clandestine and it was not until the beginnings of the transition to democracy (1975) that many of the minorities now living in the country (such as Orthodox, Mormons, Buddhists, Hindus, etc.) started creating their own places of worship in our country.

Not until 1967, the year of the fist law on religious freedom, was it possible for the religious groups that had had to hide themselves during the Franco dictatorship to start coming out in public and not have to face any apparent obstacles to joining the religious 'market'. These groups were the posit for a diversity that would increase exponentially, partly as a result of the increase in international migration.

The migratory flows originating from outside of the State started increasing from the 1980s and have especially increased over the last 16 years (1992–2008). So, if we observe the data[1] we note how from 65,533 foreign residents in 1989, there was a rise to 183,736 in 1999, and more than 860,000 foreign residents in 2007. In other words, from amounting to 1% of the total population in the late 1980s, the foreign population resident in Catalonia is now almost 12% of the total.

This population comes from a very diverse variety of nationalities, the majority being Moroccans (currently making up 20% of the foreign population resident in Catalonia). Nevertheless, it has also been noted that in recent years this migratory group has diminished in Catalonia, while there have been increased arrivals of people proceeding from other countries. This change has been referred to as the 'tendency for the Latin Americanisation' of the foreign population (Domingo & Gil, 2006).

Catalonia today is a geographical region in which more than 13 religious traditions are inscribed (see Table 19.1). Of these, as indicated by Griera (2007), we can only show that two are the result of the arrival of newcomers: Islam and Sikhism; the other traditions already existed before, although they have been affected by the incorporation of new migratory flows. With the increase in immigration there has not only been an increase in religious diversity, but also diversity within the groups that make up the religious confessions.

2 Two (Re)constructions of Hypothesis about Religious Pluralism at School

To understand the 'great theatre that is the world' is a difficult task, but such an understanding might be achieved, according to Mills (1987), by those who possess 'sociological imagination' with reference to the private life as well as

TABLE 19.1   Number of places of worship per religious tradition

Religious tradition	Places of worship
Brahma Kumaris	5
Buddhism	41
Adventists Churches	16
Latter-Day Saints	13
Evangelic Churches	435
Orthodox Churches	21
Baha'i Faith	14
Hinduism	25
Islam	167
Judaism	4
Sikhism	6
Taoism	6
Jehovah's Witnesses	146
Others	5
Other Christians	12
Total	**915**

SOURCE: DATABASE OF RELIGIOUS CENTRES IN CATALONIA, ISOR (2007)

the public life of a great number of individuals. With the idea of exercising sociological imagination, starting from the information collected in the sixty-odd interviews carried out, plus the bibliographical sources used during the initial research phase (Carbonell, 2000; Franzé, 2002: Montón, 2003; Terrén, 2004), we would like to make a note of several significant questions related to the Catalan educational sector.

Before enumerating and presenting the areas we refer to, it is important to bear in mind that each centre is a unique case, and that the singularities of educational centres are based on three interrelated factors. Firstly, despite the fact that all the centres interviewed share the same general intercultural context and religious pluralism, each one has one or more particular approach depending on the length of time that the centre has been involved with immigration or religious diversity; the type of immigration and/or religious diversity that affects the centre, and the density in which 'the others' have arrived at the centre, etc. Secondly, with regard to the specific situation of each centre, discussions and justifications are generated that help to legitimise the specific procedures and attitudes that the centre adopts. Finally, each centre responds in a different way to similar situations—a fact observed in each one of the areas presented—because each centre uses or has different tools on hand to manage religious and cultural pluralism.

2.1 *From 'It's Always Been Done Like That' to 'Things Can Be Done in a Different Way'*

Hypothesis 1: It is common to translate literally and apply the term 'religious pluralism' to most present-day societies to the point of making modern society synonymous with 'plural society'. A plural society is one where diverse systems of legitimation exist in equality of conditions, and where none may succeed in imposing themselves absolutely, thereby establishing a monopoly. A plural society is one then in which there is no totalitarian ideology, no single party and no single official religion. Given that the Roman Catholic Church has ceased to hold its position of protected religious monopoly that has always typically represented our country, we may describe Catalonia as pluralist. But if by 'pluralism' we mean a formal open market embracing competing religious systems, then we have to opt for the term 'pseudo-pluralism'.

2.1.1 School Calendar and Catholic Celebrations

The development of school activities throughout the course includes diverse celebrations and festivities that take place in the centre. Apart from the celebrations that mark the end of a specific scholastic period (end of term, beginning of a holiday period, etc.), there are others that do not relate to the school calendar *per se*, but take place every year and all members of the school community are expected to take part in them. From a generalised set of norms, each centre chooses the content and the manner of doing things. Nonetheless, the majority of these festivities have a Catholic foundation, both historically and culturally. Most probably, therefore, those students who have been socially nourished in Catholicism will experience these celebrations with greater ease and comfort and would not question them taking place in their centre. Whereas those students who, by family or cultural tradition, have no Catholic roots will simply have to adapt to the situation. So, on the one hand, we can state that it is not normal to consider the possibility of non-attendance at class for religious reasons. On the other hand, we verify that there is discrimination provoked through ignorance or lack of attention to the customs of certain student groups. A case in point could be, as occurs in many other countries, that it is not considered justifiable for a Muslim child to be absent from school during the Celebration of Sacrifice or the End of Ramadan, but at the same time, for example, the centre tolerates the lack of active participation in the Shrovetide celebrations of a Jehovah's Witness child.

2.1.2   Sporting Activities and Related Scenarios

With regard to sporting activities there are basically two areas of conflict. One concerns the fact that it is obligatory to shower sponge bath in shared spaces after taking part in physical activities, especially swimming classes, and the student simply does not wish to show his or her naked body in public. The other area of conflict is related to the norm that requires participants to dress in a certain way in order to take part in games and sports. This second conflict is particularly relevant to girls from Islamic traditions. What usually happens will be that some of these students either do not reconcile themselves to wearing a short-sleeved vest as recommended by the centre, or because the student wants to wear a veil during the physical education class and the centre considers this inappropriate. In short, we wish to underline two aspects: firstly, the physical activity in itself is not the cause of the conflict, but rather aspects related to it. Secondly, the point is that the conflicts resulting from the physical activity have more to do with cultural traditions than with religious precepts.

2.1.3   Dinosaurs in Eden

One common feature of almost all the interviews carried out with the staff of public educational centres was to consider normal an understanding of the origin of human life based on the Theory of Evolution and with the resultant feeling that it needed to be explained. At the same time, a common feature of most of the religious representatives interviewed was their interest in informing the children in their centres about the different theories regarding the origin of human life. They were thinking, of course, of an explanation in class of Creationism,[2] Intelligent Design,[3] and the Theory of Evolution.[4] Therefore, it should be mentioned that it appears to be an aspect that does not generate conflict *per se*, but has indeed many religious implications. (It would not be irrelevant to point out that Charles Darwin concluded his *The Origin of Species* with this famous sentence: I see no valid reason why the opinions expressed in this book should hurt anyone's religious feelings. Obviously, if he saw 'no valid reason', the sentence was superfluous. But no doubt he wanted to be ready for the criticisms and counteract possible accusations, as far as he could. Darwin was right when he said that the opinions expressed in his book should not hurt the feelings of anyone, however, the problem was not what he said—and Darwin knew it—but rather at what he was hinting: the biological origins of man.)

2.1.4   That Which Cannot Be Eaten

In most cases, the alimentary precepts contemplated by religious traditions are not obligatory for minors. In spite of that, however, it is quite normal to find students in educational centres who follow some type of alimentary prescription related to their beliefs, for example, vegetarianism for Hindus. These prescriptions appear in the centre in very diverse ways. For example, when the students need or want to stay in the school dining-room; when they take part in activities that require them to eat away from home (school trips, camps, celebrations, etc.); when some students are not present at the centre due to fasting periods, as in the case of Ramadan for Muslim students; and when birthdays are celebrated, as in the case of Jehovah's Witnesses. Although all this is true, it is also true that questions related to alimentation have a very important cultural element. To a certain point it may be said that the process of adaptation of newly arrived students also passes through a period of adaptation to different culinary tastes and family models which are not necessarily related to religious precepts.

2.1.5   From Compulsory to Optional Out-of-School Activities

When we speak of out-of-school activities we refer to those activities that take place outside the centre's physical space or outside the normal school timetable. School trips, cultural visits or certain types of games could be examples of this. The educational centres consider these out-of-school activities to be part of the formal or implied curriculum and that participation is 'normal' and expected. This 'normality' is considered the main justification for the efforts the staff makes to convince families that all students should take part in them. Although our field work showed that many students from different cultural or religious backgrounds—and not necessarily newly-arrived ones—do not take part in these activities, it proved to be impossible to identify any religious confession that had prescriptions or regulations relating to participation in these events. The non-participation of the newly arrived student in these activities, therefore, could be for other reasons, such as, economic inequality, differences in interpretations of what is considered 'educational', questions of social class, or lack of trust in the staff assigned to control activities outside the centre. If the activity lasts for more than a day, it means the child will be spending the night out of parental control. Thus, we confirm that the fact of non-participation in the out-of-school activities is very often due to the family model, and *not* belonging to a certain religious confession.

2.1.6 Pink Veil Versus Blue Turban

One of the most visible distinguishing characteristics that mark the increasing diversity in Catalan classrooms is attire that responds to religious precepts and recommendations. This is as much owing to its nature as an external sign as to the fact that it becomes a characteristic feature that identifies and indicates the singularity of one community with respect to others. It is precisely because it makes the differences visible and at the same time holds ideologies together, plus as well as echoes the subject causes in the media, that this behavioural area is distinct from the rest. It is important to underline, firstly, that wearing the traditional veil or headscarf (*hijab*) should not be seen as fundamental obedience of a religious precept. It is one interpretation:

> Children of Adam, We have sent you down clothing with which to conceal your private parts and to dress up in. Yet *the clothing of heedfulness is best*! That is one of God's signs, so that they may bear it in mind. (Surah 7, verse 26; emphasis added)[5]

In fact, it is worth mentioning that the veil was, and in certain parts still very much is, an unmistakable feature of the Mediterranean tradition, whereas in the majority of Islamic countries women are under no obligation to wear it. (Legislation in certain countries, however, such as Iran or Saudi Arabia do require women, Islamic or not, nationals and foreigners, to cover their heads.) Secondly, this problem does not only involve girls wanting to wear the headscarf. As one teacher informed us, 'Some students ask why they cannot wear caps, hats and hoods'. Thirdly, and quite curiously, we do not know of a single case where Sikh boys wearing turbans were involved in such difficulties. It would seem that problems arise exclusively with adolescent girls. And lastly, those who interpret the veil as a symbol of male repression would be well-advised to refrain from dissuading the girls from wearing it. For would not those well-meaning discourses prove to be another type of repression?

2.2 *Some Further Views on the Question of Women and Veils*

> **Hypothesis 2:** Two results of religious 'pseudo-pluralism' in the Catalan context are as follows: (i) From the viewpoint of religious convictions, the emergence of pluralism in the Catalan/Spanish society has supposed a significant increase in religious indifference; and (ii) From the viewpoint of religious culture, the religious indifference brings Catalan/Spanish society closer to religious illiteracy (especially in the younger generation).

Now we will dedicate a deeper look at the issue by referring, firstly, to the interpretations that the educational centre staff makes of dressing differently: whether the interpretations are uniform and critical ... whether they try to convince and justify why students dress in certain ways, and/or to determine whether they are doing so for religious reasons or not.

Before entering into sociological interpretations of these matters, we consider it appropriate to report the classification of positions taken by educational centres when referring to the 'question of the veil'. The first case to attract public attention in Spain was in San Lorenzo del Escorial (Madrid) in 2002, when a state-assisted school refused to admit Fatima, a Moroccan student, because she wore a *hijab* (Moreras, 2007). Five years later, in Catalonia, the Generalitat compelled a centre to re-admit Shaima, an eight-year-old student who had been expelled in Girona for failing to comply with an internal norm that prohibited the use of the *hijab*. Along the same lines, but arriving at different conclusions, Terrén (2004) showed that for Moroccan girls in Catalan schools, the *hijab* could be considered a religious symbol, or as a sign of maturity, responsibility, and indeed, coherence. Thus it may be said that the *hijab* should not necessarily be interpreted as an imposition—either directly (by father, elder brother or mother) or indirectly (by the imam or the community)—but may be understood as an environmental imposition or a differentiating symbol of identity. These questions clearly have been amplified and made problematical through echoes and reverberations of similar situations in other European countries like France or Great Britain. Although different from each other (Molokotos, 2000), they have helped to create a climate of alarm due to the high likelihood of a repetition of such cases.

When it came to citing cases, we found a range of views from those radically opposed to the use of the veil and also, though to a lesser degree, those opposed to the use of the Sikh turban, to those in favour. Far from considering this question to be problematical, the latter felt the veil to be a differentiating characteristic which might even foster the integration of the collective since it demonstrates the singularity of certain communities with respect to others. In the following text we shall refer exclusively to the interpretations that the centre staff gave to the use of clothing with religious connotations though, however, not only religious. A classification of attitudes emerged that: (i) directly forbid it; (ii) openly criticise it as discriminatory; (iii) try to establish a dialogue to convince; or (iv) justify it as part reinforcement of identity, be it Muslim, Sikh or other. (We shall take a number of excerpts from the interviews carried out to illustrate these attitudes, knowing that an understanding of these phenomena is elusive and irksome, but unavoidable. From the sociological perspective that runs through this document we maintain that a proper understanding of the situation calls for descriptions that are non-judgemental and not over-eager to qualify as exhaustive and final.

2.2.1   As an Obstacle to Integration the Veil Should Be Forbidden
In a number of the cases collected there is justification of prohibition of the veil on the grounds that certain ways of dressing are an obstacle to the integration of students of that religion. The arguments in support of this view and the cases that illustrate it are quite diverse. However, we could point out that a young Sikh's turban, though often considered to be an 'ostentatious' element, is curiously respected and problems seem to be avoided. On the other hand, the adolescent Muslim's veil is interpreted as 'problematical', and consequently, it is in many cases explicitly forbidden. This dissimilar attitude is paradoxical since the Sikh youth wearing a turban and the Muslim girl with a veil are of course identical actions, that is, they are covering their heads with a piece of cloth. Here are a few excerpts from our interviews.

> The first Sikh to arrive came as a shock: The students didn't know whether it was a boy or a girl, but now he has integrated well with his companions and nobody takes any notice of it [the turban]. (Director, public infant and primary education centre, Olot)

> It's a difficult subject [i.e., Muslim girls and the veil], because ethically everyone is free to do as they want, but when you are in a centre with 600 adolescents, it's often difficult to stick to your principles. Actually, this could finish up as a source of conflict for the girls themselves. It could end up as a too strongly differentiating feature that does not encourage integration at all, and might produce the opposite effect. Integration is not possible when there is such an obstacle. This is the big problem.

(Director, public compulsory secondary education centre and centre of high school level, Terrassa)

In fact, more than a few centres, when referring to conflicts directly or not related with religious pluralism, place all the blame on the 'the question of the veil'. They present it as a 'complex and confounding' matter to deal with. For sure, questions related to Muslim children and adolescents cause dilemmas and debate among the centre staff themselves revealing the contradictory nature of the issue. Obviously, this diversity of opinion among staff can make it more than difficult to establish a clear consensus of opinion on the matter. Some members of staff consider it to be a characteristic that 'exaggerates' the difference with regard to other students. A closer look at the following extracts from interviews should be helpful:

> Personally the question of the headscarf is a subject that annoys me, and it annoys me because at some time or other it will provoke conflicts, won't it? (Headmistress, public secondary and higher education centre, Terrassa)

> ... because that person faces an integration problem. When you look up at the group [she gesticulates as if looking panoramically at students in a class] it doesn't matter whether they are white or black, does it? But when you are faced with the headscarf, you stop, you analyse and you look. (Headmistress, public secondary and higher education centre, Terrassa)

In short, most of the school staff members interviewed considered the question of the young Muslim girl's veil to be perplexing in the extreme. Practically, half of them are against its use in the classroom. The inference is that the veil is seen as a symbol of restriction, and only in a few exceptional cases is it considered a possible symbol of belonging, a reinforcement of identity, and indeed a symbol of liberation.

2.2.2 Permitting the Use of the Veil Is Discriminatory against Those Who Are Not Muslims

One situation that occurs quite frequently in centres that allow the use of the veil is, strangely enough, the question of possible contradictions or complaints about the differential treatment that this tolerance creates within the classroom. We were able to verify that in several educational centres some students, alongside classmates wearing veils, claim the right to wear caps or hoods. We also found cases where mothers and fathers of students justified their children's claims as a re-affirmation of equal treatment for all. The most frequent remark posed by the teaching staff and picked up by some students and their parents may be expressed as follows:

> Why does one student have to take off his cap, whereas, a Muslim girl can wear the veil? (Headmistress, Infant and primary state school, Canovelles)

Behind this question then lies another: Is there any justification for prohibiting everyone the use all clothing that covers the head in order to avoid differential treatment? If we accept this solution in order to treat everyone equally, are we not being discriminatory toward the religious minority?

In other cases, the use of the veil is interpreted as a patriarchal imposition, as pointed out by De Botton, Puigvert & Taleb (2004),[6] and not as a personal choice made by a Muslim girl. From this angle the veil is seen as a symbol of male chauvinism and oppression of women:

> The question is really not whether they wear the veil or not, but whether they want to wear it or not. What they see as a sign of identity is seen by us as a sign of machismo. This is a question of mental attitude that we should all try to change. That is to say, not to change their beliefs but, in this case to respect the dignity of the women in question. (Headmaster, public compulsory secondary education centre, Reus)

This interpretation is clearly relative to the age of the girl. If she is quite young, the staff of some centres (mainly in primary education) tends to think that the use of the veil is not a personal choice, but a result of family imposition. In other centres, however, this same interpretation is applied to all cases where girls wear the veil, regardless of age, and even when the girls themselves express the wish to wear it freely of their own will.

2.2.3 Has Open Discussion on the Use of Veil Favoured Deification of the Dialogue?

Equally significant, although not representative, are the cases where there is an attempt to convince female students to 'decide' not to wear the veil. Sometimes this is undertaken by the course tutor, at other times through the figure of a mediator or by a person in charge of student reception duties (it should be added that this person is not usually a Muslim).

> Up to now we have not had any student wearing a veil. We have been able to convince them that it would not be appropriate. Nevertheless, it is a question that presents teachers with the dilemma of deciding whether

NAVIGATING RELIGIOUS BOUNDARIES AT SCHOOL

they approve of the veil or not. (Headmistress, public centre of compulsory secondary education, Terrassa)

However, there are cases, of course, in which these attempts to convince female students 'do not work' or only work partially from the perspective of the teaching staff. For example, we might illustrate the situation with the case of a girl who refused to follow the centre's recommendations and so wore the veil. As a result, all the other girls who had previously opted not to wear the veil, in accordance with the centre's criteria, decided to wear it again. On other occasions, the use of the veil has become a question of negotiation where priority is given to finding intermediate 'solutions'. It could be rules applying to different places within the centre itself (veils may not be worn in the classroom, but may be worn in other places such as the centre's playground). Other centres made their regulations according to age, explaining that it could only be by personal choice after a certain age. This meant that it could not be worn by the young ones in primary, but would be allowed in secondary levels. As a result of these negotiations arose the notion of 'peaceful veils' that Massignon (2000)[7] writes about. This is a reference to intermediate agreements made between the educational centres and the Muslim families or students (the girl wears it everywhere except in sports class; or the girl wears it to school, but takes it off when she arrives at class). Moreover, it should be pointed out that the justification for convincing a Muslim girl not to wear the veil is, in certain cases, due to reasons of safety or hygiene.

So, in some educational centres the veil is allowed in the centre and in the classrooms, but with restrictions such as in the case of sporting activities where it is explicitly forbidden. It is argued that because of the very characteristics of the physical activity the veil should not be allowed for reasons of hygiene and that, in some cases, it could be detrimental to their health. In this respect there are centres that have opted for the use of a wide ribbon for physical education classes instead of the veil. This solution has been widely accepted as opposed to leaving the head uncovered.

Finally, in our re-interpretation of the subject there is the underlying idea that dialogue demands reciprocity: There cannot be a dialogue if one party does not wish to take part. Dialogue also calls for respect—it should not be used to nullify or neutralise the other. At times, dialogues are used to exclude, to marginalise or shame the other party; that is to say, using all ways imaginable for what Bourdieu & Passeron (1969) so accurately call *symbolic violence*.

2.2.4   The Veil Is the Vindication of an Identity (or It Will End up so Being)
Although this situation does not occur too frequently, it should be pointed out that some educational centres evaluate the veil as the most visible sign of a vindication of identity. Of course, these pieces of clothing are divisive and

restrictive, but, at the same time, they integrate members of a community whether the origins be cultural or religious or both. The following examples illustrate M'Chichi's (2004) interpretation that '... the use of the veil is not a sign of integration rejection. In fact, it could be just the opposite. It may represent the desire of the girls to integrate by living peacefully and at the same time participating in a movement that reaffirms their community's values' (p. 30). In a wider context, Arab-Muslim women are presented in society as being reduced to male submission and oppression. From this perspective, the Muslim woman is represented as being associated with obligatory maternity and exclusive dedication to the family while remaining fully dependent on the male. She is a person to whom fate has attributed this division of labour. Perhaps for this reason, the teachers usually give their personal support, either implicitly or explicitly, to the successes achieved by Muslim girls, and especially to those who have adopted the model of 'invisibility'.

Consequently, our proposal has been to demonstrate how multifaceted the problem of the veil is and suggest that it would be better to stop talking about religious pluralism at school as problematic. In this way we recognise implicitly that the question that most interests the sociologist does not necessarily coincide with what others usually consider to be a 'problem' and that, even supposing they do coincide, the sociologist does not usually create 'solutions', but rather tries to understand how the whole system works; to understand the foundations on which it is based, and what it is subject or tied to. Nevertheless, we coincide in the interpretation that places the Islamic veil or *hijab* as one of the most evident elements of religious pluralism in educational centres. This is due to its very nature as an external sign as well as the fact that it has been converted into an identity feature that differentiates and recognises the singularity of certain communities from others.

According to what has gone before, we cannot doubt that use of the *hijab* makes certain differences visible. This in spite of the fact that there are numerous types of veils and headscarves, and choices can be made. In addition, the evidence of the social construction of an Islamic threat, in relation to the division between 'conflictive cultures' and cultures that can be integrated, becomes visible through external symbols and give rise to a stereotyped Muslim woman.

In conclusion, from a sociological perspective we must not reproduce and repeat other people's interpretations, but rather force ourselves to construct paradoxes and this is why we consider that the issue of women using veils reaffirms the 'modernity' of western societies.

2.3   *Concluding Comment*

The results of the above-mentioned hypotheses have led to a singular state of affairs in the case of Catalonia/Spain: The indifference in respect to religious

NAVIGATING RELIGIOUS BOUNDARIES AT SCHOOL 363

convictions and to religion in general has brought about a society that is less antagonistic, less unkind to all aspects regarding religion.

3 Tools for a Sociological Investigation of *Other* Religions

A century ago, anthropology was dedicated to finding the ordinary aspects of what was considered exotic. In fact, we could say that this discipline and sociology were created to look in an understanding way at what could be considered unusual and strange. But the distance between what is strange and what is normal is the same as that between an observer and what is observed. In short, it is a question of accepting that the exotic (meaning strange or incomprehensible) can be in one sense just the ordinary. For the purpose of our article, we are going to adapt the question of what is 'normal' and what is not.

3.1 When a Man's Finger Points at the Moon, the Idiot Looks at the Finger (Chinese Proverb)

For a start, it is clear that we cannot simply define as normal the 'common acts of the majority' if we do not first designate them to a certain group or society and to a particular time in history. This statement of the obvious leads us to the main characteristic of a norm, of any norm, namely its relativity. That is to say, just as social concepts of abnormality are relative, so too are 'normal' social concepts. Normality, just like deviation, is a question of social definition. Moreover, between behaviour that can be socially condemned and that which is socially approved, there is a very wide zone of permissiveness. Therefore, deviation can only be present when, with regard to a particular social situation, there is a high degree of consensus about how 'things should be' and what is 'correct'. It may be because 'God decrees it', reason dictates, it is the way of 'good people', it is fashionable (or not), and so on. In short, one characteristic of the concept of deviation is that it depends on what is considered the norm.

There is another and more significant characteristic of social deviation that, remote from the sociological perspective, could appear to be contradictory; if social deviation provokes social alarm—being seen as an attack on the socially acceptable norm—it is at the same time upholding and reaffirming the norm. There is no doubt that certain forms of conduct, behaviours, ideas, etc., at a particular moment and in a defined society, provoke unrest as they question what is considered to be 'normal' behaviour and the right way of doing things. Nevertheless, at the same time and paradoxically, the action that is considered to be a deviation carries within itself the implicit function of protecting the feelings of reality of members of that society, and in that sense, holds together those who follow the norm. Another way of expressing it would be: Defining what is not normal reaffirms our sense of what is normal (Cardús & Estruch, 1981, p. 29).

Who defines an action as deviation? From what point of view is this definition made? And to what end? In order to answer these questions, we turn to the Theory of Labelling (Goffman, 1989). We would like to briefly examine Goffman's inversion, which proposes that in order to understand differences, we should not look at what is different but at what is current and routine, what is obvious and is 'naturally so'. And even when stigmas have, for Goffman, an important general function (i.e., that of achieving help for society among those that are not helped by it), and at this level are extremely resistant to change, there are also additional functions, which vary depending on the type of stigma being dealt with, and that can also function as a means of formal social control.

From the perspective we adopt, the importance and significance of the rules appear much more evident when these are transgressed and interactions are consequently seen to be threatened, than when they are observed and when adhesion to the same means everything goes ahead normally. For Goffman, deviation, violation or transgression of rules is something endemic; it is the normal condition of the habitual framework of interactions. In this respect, he warns us that rules always involve what is 'normal' and its 'deviations', and even when widely accessible norms are implied, their multiplicity has the effect of disqualifying many individuals.

So, the handling of the stigma is a general feature of society, a process that arises anywhere where there are norms regarding how one should be. From this approach, stigma does not imply a set of specific individuals separated into two groups, those that are 'different', 'strange' or 'deviant' on the one hand, and those that are 'normal' on the other, as a penetrating social process composed of two roles in which each and every individual represents one or other, at least in certain contexts and some phases of life. As the Goffman stresses, 'normal' or 'different', what presents in a certain context a difference on the basis of which it is considered 'distinct' or 'strange', are not people, but perspectives.

This theory does not interpret deviation as a set of particular characteristics of groups or people, but as a process of internalisation between those who wear the label of deviators and those who do not. From this perspective it is more important to know who are the ones who stick on the labels, and on whom they stick them, and why. Or, what amounts to the same thing, the labels we use to designate or name the 'marginal' groups say more about those who have the power to stick on labels than it does about those who have been labelled.

In conclusion, social divergence is interpreted as the label hung on certain people and/or their actions. The acceptability of this label will depend on the power of those labellers to define a specific situation as *abnormal* and the impetus they have to define it. In these cases, those that are presented as divergent, that is to say those *stigmatised*, will strive for a level of acceptability, both socially and psychologically, to preserve their identity. It is in this respect that our study raises many more questions than it answers: If being an immigrant cannot be considered as a hereditary characteristic, why is the label of 'immigrant' used so often to refer to second generations? Does immigration necessarily contain *per se* diversity or pluralism? How can diversity be treated at school if the school system aims at a homogenous solution as a means of solving what is considered problematic? Should it be the school system to provide 'solutions' to society's problems? And referring exclusively now to the 'problem of the veil': Does the pressure over the *hijab* at school transform it into a sign of identity for Muslims girls? How can it be interpreted that some girls who wear the veil here do not use it in their families' native villages? And finally, should the religious pluralism of immigrants be considered a problem at school? Perhaps the core problem is the uncertainty created by that pluralism.

3.2 *Religious Pluralism in Catalonia: Yes, But ...*

We live in a society where social classes, ethnic groups, nations or religions unite and at the same time separate. In fact, many solutions may be applied to our dilemma that might range from a desire to eradicate any sign that would suggest that one religion is alien to another,[8] to the opposite extreme of maximum permissiveness represented by what some have termed 'management of diversity'.

Although it may seem obvious to characterise today's society using the term pluralism—be it religious or of another sort—pluralism is not a characteristic exclusive to our times, neither is religious pluralism evident in all contemporary societies. In this respect it is essential to point out that in Catalonia there exists, on the one hand, an increase in expressions of religiosity distinct from Roman Catholicism, and, on the other, the generalised view that religion has been losing its influence among the general public. It is not our intention to reproduce the debate on theories of secularisation or, de-secularisation as Berger (1999) pointed out with reference to Europe. We want to point out what we consider the special features of pluralism in our times: (i) Some social institutions are greatly strengthened, but others, as Religion, are very much weakened; and (ii) Different religions compete with each other in a more or less open market context, but the hegemony over the rest is still held by the Roman Catholic Church. This will help us to present the situation of religious pluralism in Catalonia today.

Regarding the first appraisal above, it is clear that there is a gradation between strong institutions and weak ones, and as one approaches either of the extremes, the differences become ever more visible. Examples of the first would be the great structures of a modern state and its economy or its school system; while in the section of the 'weak', or, more accurately, of 'those that are weakening', we would find religion. Moving further along this line may help to argue that a plural society can be properly represented as that in which there is no ideological totalitarianism, no single party, and no exclusive model of religion. Such a representation should be accompanied by a warning: liberation from any type of totalitarianism in society does not of course necessarily imply liberation, or anything like it, for the individual.

To clarify the second assessment, we will follow Berger's idea which maintains that pluralism may be understood as co-existence among different groups in civic peace, within a single society. It may be important to point out that the term co-existence 'does not only mean abstaining from reciprocal carnage; it denotes rather a degree of social interaction' (Berger, 1994, p. 54). It is true that throughout history there have been numerous periods in which different groups have succeeded in coexisting. However, in general, this desirable state of affairs was maintained by raising barriers on social relations between these same groups (it was not normally the result of tolerance and high ideals, but rather of restriction on power). But the pluralism we are interested in studying in this section is of another sort; the one that appears when the barriers are broken: 'The neighbours look over the fence, speak to each other, and have a reciprocal relationship' (Berger, 1994, p. 54). After this, and in an inevitable way, what Berger has called 'cognitive contamination' starts to occur, which is to say, the different life styles, values and beliefs begin to intermingle.

It should be clarified following Berger's thesis that this sort of pluralism is not exclusive to the modern world. It has appeared periodically throughout history, but what characterises modern pluralism is the fact that people belonging to radically different cultures find themselves compelled to live shoulder to shoulder with each other over long periods of time. Moreover, urbanisation has been transformed into a mental phenomenon and not just a physical one, and this peculiarity is certainly exclusive to our day. Furthermore, by virtue of enormous advances in mass literacy and through modern mass communication, people come into contact with different cultures and concepts of the cosmos without necessarily abandoning their geographical place of birth. Obviously, it is clear that the consequences of 'pluralising' factors in modern times are intensified even more by market economies and democratic systems.

We adapt these reflections to our more immediate context when we affirm that the religious situation existing in Catalonia is plural, given that the

Catholic Church no longer professes to be (at least in theory) the unrivalled protected religious monopoly that was formerly the case in our country. There is no religious pluralism, however, if by that we mean the existence of a formally open and competitive market of legitimate religious confessions.

Another special feature in the Catalan case is that the *appearance* of pluralism has given rise not only to a very significant increase in religious indifference, but this mentioned indifference is turning Catalan society into one approaching religious illiteracy. For example, the euphemism of speaking of 'African children' when those interviewed referred to black Muslim children, indicates, firstly, that being an immigrant is considered hereditary when it is not and, secondly, that 'Muslim' is a label which, generally speaking, is not used by the teaching staff, but when used, it is applied pejoratively. Moreover, the adjectives employed to replace it ('Moor', 'Maghrebi' or 'Arab') either reflect ignorance or show little respect for origins which can only be understood when viewed from a western standpoint. (Thus, we would confirm the argument of the Labelling Theory presented previously, that is, that labelling tells us more about the labeller than about the one who has to wear it).

Hence, according with the above, we are facing a situation in Catalonia in which we move from an environment of religious monopoly to one of pseudo-pluralism, where one religion can no longer stand up firmly as the exclusive one, that is to say, the official one, because alongside it (although not in direct competition) *other* religions exist and are practised.[9] However, this exposition should not leave us with a binary interpretation (the 'others' versus 'us') in which the *others* with their diverse religious manifestations give meaning and reality to the 'us'; and even more so when it is advisable to escape from expressions like 'natives' as opposed to 'foreigners'. The important point, however, is that what has become twisted or has been lost in 'us' remains right or valid in the 'others'. Consequently, under the shadow of the self-invented other, not only ethnic-centralism and xenophobia, but also, and in an ambivalent way, there may be present self-criticism and even *xenophilia* (i.e., a kind disposition toward the foreigner).

Acknowledgement

This chapter originally appeared as: Fernández Mostaza, E., García-Romeral, G., & Fons i Duocastella, C. (2009) Navigating religious boundaries at school: from legitimate to specious religious questions, *Mediterranean Journal of Educational Studies*, Vol. 14(1), pp. 69–90. Reprinted here with permission from the publisher.

Notes

1. Source: Ministerio de Trabajo y Asuntos Sociales. Permanent immigration observatory.
2. Opinion, philosophical or religious doctrine that upholds an explanation of the origin of the world based on one or more acts of creation by a personal God, as found, for example, in the case of the Great Book-based religions.
3. A belief that states that the origin or evolution of the universe, life and man, or of creation was the result of rational actions deliberately undertaken by one or more agents.
4. Biological evolution is the continuous process of transformation of the species through changes taking place in successive generations and is seen in the changes of genetic frequencies in a population. The theory of evolution is the scientific model that describes evolutionary transformation and explains its causes.
5. *The Noble Qur'an* (in Arabic; translated with commentary by Dr Thomas B. Irving in 1992). Amana Books.
6. The *hijab* worn by Muslim women is always viewed with suspicion. It is reduced to being considered as an imposition by man, whether this is the head of state, the father, the husband or the brother. It is an imposition on women to hide or silence their voices (De Botton, Puigvert & Taleb, 2004, p. 102).
7. 'Cependant, les affaires de voile permettent le mieux de mettre en évidence l'existence d'une prise en compte négociée des expressions religieuses à l'école publique. Notre enquête nous a permis de voir qu'il existe des "voiles tranquilles", qui n'entraînent aucune crise dans les établissements, très différents des exemples médiatisés. Des accords sont mis au point, portant sur la forme du voile (plus petit, coloré, coiffe alternative sans signification religieuse: bonnet, large bandeau, turban) et les lieux de son port (interdit dans les salles de classe, voire dans la salle de documentation et à la cantine, mais autorisé dans la cours de récréation)' (Massignon, 2000, p. 358).
8. We agree with the interpretation of Lurbe & Santamaría (2007) for whom immigrants can be seen as the incarnation of the alien. They state this with a double meaning: Firstly, they give them a distant, external character of inappropriateness or social inadequacy; and then secondly, they show how the effects of this alienation are incorporated subjectively so as to be perceived as out of place or living as if out of place.
9. This pluralistic dynamic applied to religion can also be traced in language; in the Catalan case a person is 'a believer' or not, and in this context one can be 'practising' or 'non-practising'. They are expressions that, in the end, serve to underline the peculiarities of this pluralism in which the Catholic Church no longer has a monopoly, but whose influence is still felt.

References

Berger, P. (1994) *Una Gloria Lejana: La Búsqueda de la Fe en época de credulidad.* Barcelona: Herder.

Berger, P. (1999) The desecularization of the world: a global overview. In P. Berger (ed.) *The Desecularization of the World: Resurgent Religion and World Politics.* Washington, DC: Ethics and Public Policy Center.

Bourdieu, P., & Passeron, J. C. (1969) *Los Estudiantes y la Cultura.* Barcelona: Labor.

Carbonell, F. (coord.) (2000) *Educació i immigració: Els Reptes Educatius de la Diversitat Cultural i l'Exclusió Social*. Barcelona: Mediterrània.

Cardús, S., & Estruch, J. (1981) *Plegar de Viure: Un Estudi Sobre els Suïcidis*. Barcelona: Edicions 62.

De Botton, L., Puigvert, L., & Taleb, F. (2004) *El Velo Elegido*. Barcelona: El Roure.

Domingo, A., & Gil, F. (2006) L'evolució recent de la població estrangera a Catalunya. In M. J. Larios & M. Nadal (eds.) *L'Estat de la Immigració a Catalunya, Anuari 2005: Anàlisi Jurídica i Sociodemogràfica, Vol. I*. Barcelona: Fundació Jaume Bofill.

Estanyol, M. J. (2002) *Judaisme a Catalunya, Avui*. Barcelona: Pòrtic.

Franzé, A. (2002) *Lo que Sabía no Valía: Escuela, Diversidad e Inmigración*. Madrid: Consejo Económico y Social.

Goffman, E. (1989) *Estigma: La Identidad Deteriorada*. Buenos Aires: Amorrortu.

Griera, M. M. (2007) Diversitat religiosa i immigració a Catalunya, *Via*, Vol. 3/2007, pp. 103–119.

Lévi-Strauss, C. (1962) *La Pensée Sauvage*. Paris: Agora.

Lurbe, K., & Santamaría, E. (2007) Entre (nos)otros ... o la necesidad de re-pensar la construcción de las alteridades en contextos migratorios, *Papers, Revista de Sociología*, Vol. 85, pp. 57–70.

Massignon, B. (2000) Laïcité et gestion de la diversité religieuse à l'école publique en France, *Social Compass*, Vol. 47(3), pp. 353–366.

M'Chichi, H. A. (2004) Los jóvenes inmigrantes construyen su identidad, *Afkar Ideas: Revista Trimestral Para el Diálogo Entre el Magreb, España y Europa*, Vol. 3, pp. 27–30.

Mills, C. W. (1987) *La Imaginació Sociològica*. Barcelona: Editorial Herder.

Molokotos, L. (2000) Religious diversity in schools: the Muslim headscarf controversy and beyond, *Social Compass*, Vol. 47(3), pp. 367–381.

Montón, M. J. (2003) *La Integració de l'Alumnat Immigrant al Centre Escolar*. Barcelona: Graó.

Moreras, J. (2007) *Els Imams de Catalunya*. Barcelona: Editorial Empúries.

Terrén, E. (2004) *Incorporación o Asimilación: La Escuela Como Espacio de Inclusión Social*. Madrid: Libros la Catarata.

CHAPTER 20

Human Rights Education

A Comparison of Mother Tongue Textbooks in Turkey and France

Canan Aslan and Yasemin Karaman-Kepenekci

1   Introduction

The topic of human rights increasingly attracts the attention of the general public in the world (Donnelly, 1989; Akıllıoğlu, 1995; Buergental, 1995; Çeçen, 1995; Gemalmaz, 2001; Reisoğlu, 2001). The term 'human rights' implies all the ideal rights that are required to be granted to everyone theoretically at a certain age. When human rights are considered, what comes to mind mostly are the rights that are 'required' and the rights under the 'objectives to be reached' statements (Kapani, 1981, p. 14). However, today, most of the human rights are contained by positive law and guaranteed with material sanctions (Mumcu, 1994).

Whether human rights can exist and bear a practical value depends on people's awareness and practise of those rights, and their protection and improvement of those rights. This can be ensured with education in human rights field. Human rights education can be defined as 'education offered in order to arouse awareness for the cognition, protection, use and improvement of human rights, and for respect of these rights by everyone in a general sense and by students within the ambience of formal education' (Gülmez, 2001, p. 49).

The most crucial point in human rights education is definitely to transform the knowledge acquired in this field into behaviour. The process to realise this begins with the offering of human rights education *via* a content that is suitable for the person's level. The presence of specialised lessons that will teach human rights systematically and methodically is required. But this is not enough since this field is so comprehensive that it cannot be contained simply in such lessons. Actually, one of the objectives of general education is to give information required for life and ensure the intellectual and moral development of the student with courses in social fields (Vandenberg, 1984).

In order to ensure sustainability in human rights education, the human rights topic should be given place in other courses that are found in the curriculum such as history, geography, sociology, psychology, literature and philosophy (UNESCO, 1969, 1987; also Gülmez, 1998; Karaman-Kepenekci, 2000). The

---

© THE EURO-MEDITERRANEAN CENTRE FOR EDUCATION RESEARCH, UNIVERSITY OF MALTA, 2008
DOI: 10.1163/9789004506602_020

This is an open access chapter distributed under the terms of the CC BY-NC 4.0 License.

HUMAN RIGHTS EDUCATION

Council of Europe (see Annex of Recommendation No. R(85)7) has suggested that when adolescents' learn about fields that are of abstract quality—such as human rights—courses such as history, geography, social sciences, religious and moral education, language, literature and economics could be made use of.

2 Textbooks and Their Place in Human Rights Education

A textbook is the fundamental tool that allows the teacher to use his/her position in a better way and to offer what he/she would like to teach in a more systematic manner; it also allows the student to revise what the teacher explains anywhere, at any time and at any speed. The textbook is prepared or chosen in relation to the teaching of a certain course and it is recommended as the fundamental resource for teachers and students in a certain school, grade and course upon examination of specific criteria. Today, textbooks are undergoing a radical change with respect to form, content and method (Garner et al., 1986; Oğuzkan, 1993; Aycan et al., 2001; Gérard, 2003; Ceyhan & Yiğit, 2004; Karaman-Kepenekci, 2005).

Textbooks are but one piece of the education puzzle that needs to be reviewed and critiqued (Giannangelo & Kaplan, 1992) and delineate what behavioural objectives can be covered in the course. This can include recommending the structure of the setting in which these objectives are to be achieved. It is a compact, economical, practical device for storing a huge amount of visual stimuli (Baykal, 2004).

At present, although textbooks are not the sole available teaching tool, as a result of the influence of technological developments, they are still the first and the most important tool used in lessons (Coşkun, 1996). According to a UNESCO project, textbooks provide the main resource for teachers, enabling them to animate the curricula and give life to the subjects taught in the classroom (UNESCO, 2007a). In recent decades, UNESCO has developed activities aimed at textbook revision as textbooks are seen as a key component for improving the quality of education and as one of its main strategies in promoting dialogue among and between nations and peoples, and a better knowledge and appreciation of their different cultures, as well as respect for, and acceptance of, cultural diversity (King, 2004). Revision of the school textbooks, or of the teaching materials in a wider sense, is the primary objective of UNESCO.

Today, while resources used in reaching information are greatly diversified, textbooks still play an important role in the development of forms of thinking and mentalities. Textbooks should support the preservation and continuation of cultural traditions, shaping of the identity sensation, realisation of linguistic resemblance and preservation of the national bond by offering the same contents to the entire youth population, using the same language and disseminating the same system of values, and the same historical, literary and even religious references (UNESCO, 2007b).

There is literature that examines the importance of textbooks in human rights education (Power & Allison, 2000; Tibbits, 2002; Kirisika, 2003). A number of studies were conducted to investigate the contribution of some of these textbooks (e.g., of history, social studies etc.) in human rights and citizenship education. For example, Karaman-Kepenekci (1999) examined the level of allocation of the citizenship and human rights issues in 16 Turkish high school textbooks. She found that intensity score of citizenship and human rights issues were higher in the religion, sociology and philosophy high school textbooks than in the other textbooks analysed. In another study, Karaman-Kepenekci (2003) analysed the level of human rights and responsibility issues in three life studies textbooks and four social studies textbooks used in Turkish primary schools. This study concluded that the intensity scores of human rights issues were higher than those of the responsibility issues in these textbooks.

The History Foundation (2003) carried out a project entitled *Promoting Human Rights in Primary and Secondary School Textbooks* in partnership with the Human Rights Committee of the Turkish Academy of Sciences and in collaboration with the Human Rights Foundation of Turkey. This project proposed the re-writing of textbooks so that future citizens would be more aware of the underlying issues.

The United Nations Association of the United States (see Sewall, 2002) carried out a study entitled *Textbooks and the United Nations*. This study revealed that information about United Nations was almost non-existent in some textbooks in American schools and, where present, was often unclear and superficial. Sewall (2002), the author of the report, explains that the United Nations and its agencies are misunderstood, and that textbooks do not clear up this misunderstanding: the information they provide is often arcane and sketchy.

3   The Place of Mother Tongue Textbooks in Human Rights Education

Turkish language courses are of vital importance in formal education in Turkey. Their main objectives are to teach the mother tongue in the most complete manner, to create awareness with respect to the mother tongue, and to bring up democratic and sensitive individuals with well-developed understanding/expression skills. In recent years, many studies have examined

HUMAN RIGHTS EDUCATION

Turkish textbooks in relation to human rights education as well as linguistics (Polat, 1991; Baysal, 1996; Coşkun, 1996; Yörükoğlu, 1996; Esen & Bağlı, 2002; Bora, 2003; Ceylan-Tarba, 2003; Çotuksöken, 2003; Gemalmaz, 2003; Tanrıöver, 2003; Timur & Bağlı, 2003; Karaman-Kepenekci, 2005; Aslan, 2006). French textbooks in France and in French schools—with their use of rich texts and contents—have similar objectives and they are considered as the basic teaching course (Programmes de 2002, 2004; Camenisch & Serge, 2006; Centre National de Documentation Pédagogique, 2007; Humanité, 2007).

When mother tongue textbooks, the priority of which is to improve the language and communication skills of individuals, are prepared carefully, they may become one of the most significant tools in offering human rights education. Human rights-related poems, memoirs, diaries, anecdotes, novels and works that speak of struggles to obtain rights and freedom at various times and places may be included in these books. One can also make use of works related to children's and adolescents' rights (Karaman-Kepenekci, 2000). The Universal Declaration of Human Rights and texts of international contracts on human rights may be analysed, and then students may be asked to write their own universal declarations on human rights and children's rights (UNESCO, 1969).

The texts selected for use in mother tongue textbooks can play an important role in the implementation of human rights education. Literary texts, with their versatile nature that comes from their contents, educate people in terms of sensitivity. A person with educated feelings manages to comprehend what is felt and, as a result, understands the meaning of humanitarianism and equality. One can also offer an indirect human rights education to students by including works of foreign writers and artists. It is important in mother tongue teaching that students meet with different writers, and thus with different styles (tastes). The fine feelings acquired through sensitivity education provide the person with the skills to go into details, to comprehend humans and the world (Binyazar, 1996).

Texts that question the violation of human rights should be included in textbooks to be then submitted to students' review and assessment. For instance, students may be asked to empathise with the protagonists in those texts and interpret the situation within the context of human rights. Extracts from newspapers and magazines that recount real and dramatic stories about human rights may be included in textbooks or students may be asked to find such articles. These acquired texts then may be exhibited in classroom literature corners or school notice boards for the benefit of other students (Sever, Kaya, & Aslan, 2006).

Comprehension questions may be used to highlight the importance of human rights and citizenship. The textbook may include questions and activities that allow students to share in class their own or their relatives' experiences in connection with violation of human rights. The questions should create environments where different opinions can be expressed with composure; they should trigger critical thinking by the child, particularly on human rights (Aslan & Polat, 2007). The prepared questions should be directed toward the objectives of human rights education, such as expressing oneself, generating authentic thoughts, developing positive relationships, etc. For an effective human rights education, preliminary textbook exercises may include thought provoking and analysis-requiring questions developed by the authors to assist teachers in preparing students for the lesson (Çayır, 2003).

Visual stimulants—such as comic strips, pictures and photos about human rights—may be included in the books and students may be asked to talk about their messages. Text content-related pictures, photographs, illustrations or cartoons by foreign artists might also be included in the books. According to Sever (2007), interpretation of a cartoon from different points of view, and the analysis and expression of its contents from different perspectives prepare natural settings for the formation and acquisition of a democratic culture in an educational environment. They enable students to perceive the fact that people may generate different thoughts on the same or various life situations. For this reason, the visual features of mother tongue textbooks should not be undervalued.

In order to determine the contribution of mother tongue courses in human rights, the level of allocation of topics related to human rights in the textbooks of these courses should be examined. In Turkey, the new primary education curriculum was adopted in 2004. In line with this, the curricula of all the courses, including that of the Turkish language course, taught at elementary level were changed and the new curriculum was implemented at the beginning of the 2005–2006 scholastic year. With regard to France, the textbooks that were prepared in accordance with the new primary education curriculum have been in use since 2002. The Turkish language textbooks prepared according to the new primary education curriculum have still not been examined in terms of their human rights component. Neither has this aspect of these books been compared to that of other mother tongue textbooks used in other countries.

4   Objective of the Study

The general objective of this study is to make a comparison between the mother tongue textbooks in Turkey and France in terms of their level of allocation to human rights issues.

HUMAN RIGHTS EDUCATION 375

5 Method

5.1 *Selection of Textbooks*
In Turkey, compulsory education consists of primary education, which spreads over eight years to cover ages 6–14; the first five years being the first level and the next three years being the second level. In France, compulsory education covers the education of children between the ages of 6–16; the first five years of compulsory education are called the primary education level (see Ministère de l' Education Nationale, 2006).

In the study, ten mother tongue textbooks recommended by the Turkish and French Ministries of Education for use by students in the first five years of primary education level were selected for the purpose of examination. These textbooks (five Turkish and five French) are listed in Appendix A.

5.2 *Data Analysis*
Textbooks have been analysed through 'content analysis', a qualitative research method frequently used in this type of study. The main purpose in content analysis is to attain concepts and connections, which can serve to explain the collected data (Yıldırım & Şimşek, 2005).

5.3 *Procedures*
The first things to determine in content analysis are the subcategories of analysis (Strauss & Corbin, 1990). For the present analysis we made use of the subcategories previously defined by Karaman-Kepenekci (1999). These were:
- Rights: Authorities and benefits recognised and protected by law. Rights are divided into civil, political and social rights.
- Freedom: Non-existence of constraints and compulsion; having the power of doing anything that is allowed by independence, sovereignty and law.
- Democracy: Administration of a country by the public, where the majorities in power reflect public popular vote (i.e., power is administered through representatives elected through a free and fair election system by the public).
- Justice: Being fair, punishing the guilty, and making sure that administrators act in accordance with the law, honesty and conflict resolution.
- Tolerance: Showing tolerance, respect and liking toward others (including those of different origin), not applying force or pressure, and ability to compromise and forgive.
- Peace: Orderly and peaceful living, brotherhood, social integrity, safe environment, conflict resolution, and non-existence of anarchy, assault, disorder or tension.

To determine the inter-rater reliability of the content areas, two subcategories and a textbook were randomly chosen (namely the 'Rights' and 'Tolerance' subcategories and 'Turkish Textbook 4') and coded by the co-authors of the paper. An average of 87.5% consistency was noted, implying a good inter-rater reliability (Hall & Houten, 1983). All the reading and comprehension texts, including poems, in the textbooks (i.e., a total of 144 texts in Turkish textbooks and a total of 281 texts in French textbooks) were examined. In other words, we did not use sampling while examining the textbooks. On the other hand, the table of contents, chronology, questions, bibliography, glossary, prepositions, pictures, and photos were excluded.

'Sentence' has been chosen as the unit of analysis while analysing textbooks. We determined the frequency of occurrence of the designated subcategories in each sentence. At this stage, the sentences with words matching the subcategories, or explaining designated subcategories, or sentences directly conveying the meaning were taken into consideration. The weight of each aspect was valued as a point. In order to find out the total number of words in the texts, the words in all the texts in the books were counted one by one. The values of subcategories in the textbooks have been indicated in the tables as frequency, percentage and intensity values.

For each textbook, the subcategory percentage and the subcategory intensity score were obtained using the formulas given below:

Subcategory percentage = (subcategory frequency / total frequency of all subcategories) × 1000

Subcategory intensity score = (subcategory frequency / total word number of the texts) × 1000

The intensity scores of all subcategories were multiplied by 1000 because the resulting figures while calculating the intensity scores were too small, and dealing with small figures causes difficulty while interpreting. In other words, the multiplication by 1000 was a matter of convenience.

6 Findings

6.1 *Analysis of Turkish Textbooks*

The first grade Turkish Textbook 1 (TTB 1) is made up of four themes and 16 texts. The second grade Turkish Textbook 2 (TTB 2), the third grade Turkish

HUMAN RIGHTS EDUCATION

Textbook 3 (TTB 3), the fourth grade Turkish Textbook 4 (TTB 4) and the fifth grade Turkish Textbook 5 (TTB 5) are each made up of eight themes and 32 texts. The titles of some of the themes in Turkish textbooks are as follows: 'Individual and Society', 'Production, Consumption and Productivity', 'Health and Environment', 'Imagination', 'Games and Sports', 'Our Values' and 'Educational and Social Activities'.

When looking at the dissemination of the subcategories of human rights, it can be seen from Table 20.1 that in TTB 1 the subcategories of 'Peace' (60.4) and 'Rights' (49.3) have the highest intensity scores. These are followed by the subcategory of 'Tolerance' (13.6). The lowest intensity scores in this textbook belong to the subcategories of 'Freedom' (7.0), 'Democracy' (5.5) and 'Justice' (4.5)—all three having quite close ratios.

In TTB 2, the subcategory with the highest intensity score is 'Rights' (77.3). The subcategory of 'Rights' is followed by the subcategories of 'Peace' (19.1) and 'Tolerance' (11.5). The lowest intensity scores in this textbook belong to the subcategories of 'Democracy' (4.4), 'Freedom' (2.2) and 'Justice' (0.2).

In TTB 3, the subcategory with the highest intensity score is 'Rights' (41.9). The subcategory of 'Rights' is followed by the subcategories of 'Peace' (34.2) and 'Tolerance' (16.4). The lowest intensity scores in this textbook belong to the subcategories of 'Democracy' (4.4), 'Freedom' (3.0) and 'Justice' (1.7)—again all three having quite close ratios.

In TTB 4, the subcategory with the highest intensity score is 'Rights' (95.6). The subcategory of 'Rights' is followed by the subcategories of 'Peace' (34.2) and 'Tolerance' (15.3). The lowest intensity scores in this textbook belong once again to the subcategories of 'Democracy' (8.4), 'Freedom' (7.6) and 'Justice' (4.3).

In TTB 5, the subcategory with the highest intensity score is 'Rights' (83.6). The subcategory of 'Rights' is followed by the subcategories of 'Peace' (25.0) and 'Tolerance' (8.1). In line with the findings for the other four textbooks, the lowest intensity scores in this textbook belong to the subcategories of 'Freedom' (5.7), 'Democracy' (3.7) and 'Justice' (0.8).

The statements below, quoted from the Turkish Textbooks, can be given as examples of the 'Rights' subcategory:

> Children, if you encounter a producer or a vendor-related problem with the products you have purchased, call 175 Consumer's Line ... A responsible consumer is the one who seeks remedy. Never abstain from seeking remedy .... (TTB 4, p. 62)

TABLE 20.1 Dissemination of all the categories in Turkish textbooks according to frequency (f), percentage (%) and intensity score (IS)

Subcategories		Turkish textbooks					
		TTB 1 (1,988)[a]	TTB 2 (6,587)[a]	TTB 3 (8,091)[a]	TTB 4 (10,401)[a]	TTB 5 (9,903)[a]	Total
Rights	f	98	509	339	994	828	2768
	%	35.1	67.4	41.2	57.8	65.9	57.3
	IS	49.3	77.3	41.9	95.6	83.6	347.7
Freedom	f	14	14	24	79	56	187
	%	5.0	1.9	2.9	4.6	4.5	3.9
	IS	7.0	2.2	3.0	7.6	5.7	25.5
Democracy	f	11	29	36	87	37	200
	%	3.9	3.8	4.4	5.1	2.9	4.1
	IS	5.5	4.4	4.4	8.4	3.7	26.4
Justice	f	9	1	14	45	8	77
	%	3.2	0.1	1.7	2.6	0.6	1.6
	IS	4.5	0.2	1.7	4.3	0.8	11.5
Tolerance	f	27	76	133	159	80	475
	%	9.7	10.1	16.2	9.2	6.4	9.8
	IS	13.6	11.5	16.4	15.3	8.1	64.9
Peace	f	120	126	277	356	248	1127
	%	43.0	16.7	33.7	20.7	19.7	23.3
	IS	60.4	19.1	34.2	34.2	25.0	172.9
Total	f	279	755	823	1720	1257	4834
	%	100	100	100	100	100	100
	IS	140.3	114.7	101.6	165.4	126.9	648.9

a   Total number of words in textbook.

Student: Why do women not have the right to be elected? Why cannot they become members of parliament?

Atatürk asked: What is the main right and duty of a citizen?

Student: The main right is to vote, the main duty is military service. (TTB 5, p. 41)

The statements below, again quoted from the Turkish Textbooks, can be given as examples of the 'Rights' and 'Democracy' subcategories:

HUMAN RIGHTS EDUCATION

... That is, where there is democracy, people have rights. Old or young, poor or rich, women or men, everyone can think, express and do whatever he/she wants to .... (TTB 2, p. 107)

... In democracies, people have to respect others' rights when using their own rights. They cannot violate others' rights .... (TTB 2, p. 108)

The statements below, quoted from the Turkish Textbooks, can be given as examples of the 'Rights' and 'Justice' subcategories:

... Well done, my girl! You did not do us wrong. Just like you, people should always respect each other's rights .... (TTB 4, p. 19)

O Sinan, chief architect Sinan! You have done the right, fairest thing. That is what I would expect from you. (TTB 5, p. 79)

The statements below, quoted from the Turkish Textbooks, can be given as examples of the 'Peace' subcategory:

... He initiated the Turkish War of Independence against the enemies who occupied our country. This war, of which he was the commander-in-chief, resulted in victory .... (TTB 2, p. 27)

... Friends, peace is essential in this world; peace at home, peace in the world! Follow every call for peace .... (TTB 4, p. 31)

... Look, we have not lived through a war. But we learn some things about the war in the movies we watch at the cinema, and on television ... That is not what real war is like .... (TTB 4, p. 26)

... Secure life is to know that we can eat when we are hungry and to sleep in our beds comfortably. It is to be in peace .... (TTB 5, p. 112)

The poem quoted below, from one of the Turkish Textbooks, can be given as an example of the 'Tolerance' subcategory:

Tolerance,
Be tactful, with a smile on your face;
Do not aggrieve anyone with bitter words.
Hoping that you have nice days ahead,
That is how each citizen should be; tolerant. (TTB 4, p. 16)

The statements below, quoted from the Turkish Textbooks, can be given as examples of the 'Freedom' subcategory:

... He always worked for the freedom of the nation .... (TTB 2, p. 26)

It was not easy to come to this point, children. It was not easy to reach the commonwealth, and our independence .... (TTB 4, p. 26)

... We all knew that the most important thing for human kind is freedom and independence .... (TTB 4, p. 29)

6.2   *Analysis of French Textbooks*

French Textbook 1 (CP) consists of four units and 60 texts; French Textbook 2 (CE 1) consists of 12 units and 38 texts; French Textbook 3 (CE 2) consists of six units and 68 texts; French Textbook 4 (CM 1) consists of six units and 22 texts; and French Textbook 5 (CM 2) consists of six themes and 93 texts. The titles of some of these units are as follows: 'Welcome to CP', 'Day by Day' and 'From Invention to Invention' (CP); 'Mystery and Peanuts', 'Fany and her Dream', 'Plants Living in Wetland Environments', 'On the Saint-Malo Beach' and 'Bread for Friends' (CE 1); 'Grammar', 'Conjugation', 'Orthography', 'Vocabulary' and 'Reading' (CE 2); 'Monsters and Stories', 'Detective Stories', 'Various Stories' and 'Stories of Metamorphosis' (CM 1); and 'Grammar', 'Vocabulary' and 'Text Grammar' (CM 2).

When the dissemination of the subcategories is considered, it can be seen from Table 20.2 that the 'Rights' subcategory (69.0) has the highest intensity score in CP. This subcategory is followed by the subcategories of 'Peace' (19.2), 'Tolerance' (13.8) and 'Democracy' (13.6). The lowest intensity scores in this textbook belong to the subcategories of 'Freedom' (3.6) and 'Justice' (1.0)—both scoring very low.

In CE 1, the subcategory with the highest intensity score is 'Rights' (50.8). This subcategory is followed by the subcategories of 'Peace' (21.5) and 'Tolerance' (10.8). The lowest intensity scores in this textbook belong to the subcategories of 'Freedom' (5.5), 'Democracy' (2.8) and 'Justice' (2.3).

In CE 2, the subcategories with the highest intensity scores are 'Rights' (46.6) and 'Peace' (20.9). These subcategories are followed—quite at a distance—by the subcategories of 'Tolerance' (7.1), 'Democracy' (6.7), 'Freedom' (5.5) and 'Justice' (2.4).

In CM 1, the subcategories with the highest intensity scores are 'Rights' (33.3) and 'Peace' (25.6). These two are followed by the subcategories of 'Democracy' (11.3), 'Tolerance' (9.9), 'Freedom' (2.2) and 'Justice' (1.7).

HUMAN RIGHTS EDUCATION

TABLE 20.2 Dissemination of all the categories in French textbooks according to frequency (f), percentage (%) and intensity score (IS)

Subcategories		French textbooks					
		CP (5,013)[a]	CE 1 (6,870)[a]	CE 2 (11,638)[a]	CM 1 (8,078)[a]	CM 2 (7,890)[a]	Total
Rights	f	346	349	542	269	412	1918
	%	57.5	54.2	52.2	39.6	52.9	51.3
	IS	69.0	50.8	46.6	33.3	52.2	251.9
Freedom	f	18	38	64	18	54	192
	%	3.0	5.9	6.2	2.7	6.9	5.1
	IS	3.6	5.5	5.5	2.2	6.8	23.6
Democracy	f	68	19	78	91	37	293
	%	11.3	3.0	7.5	13.4	4.7	7.8
	IS	13.6	2.8	6.7	11.3	4.7	39.1
Justice	f	5	16	28	14	15	78
	%	0.8	2.5	2.7	2.1	1.9	2.1
	IS	1.0	2.3	2.4	1.7	1.9	9.3
Tolerance	f	69	74	83	80	51	357
	%	11.5	11.5	8.0	11.8	6.5	9.5
	IS	13.8	10.8	7.1	9.9	6.5	48.1
Peace	f	96	148	243	207	210	904
	%	15.9	23.0	23.4	30.5	27.0	24.2
	IS	19.2	21.5	20.9	25.6	26.6	113.8
Total	f	602	644	1038	679	779	3742
	%	100	100	100	100	100	100
	IS	120.2	93.7	89.2	84.0	98.7	485.8

a Total number of words in textbook

In CM 2, the subcategories with the highest intensity scores are 'Rights' (52.2) and 'Peace' (26.6). These are followed at some distance by the subcategories of 'Freedom' (6.8), 'Tolerance' (6.5), 'Democracy' (4.7) and 'Justice' (1.9).

The statements below, quoted from the French Textbooks, can be given as examples of the 'Rights' subcategory:

> You have just one right, and that is the right to remain silent … When her father told her so, her grandmother remained silent with displeasure. It

was not surprising since children did not have the right to speak during meals. (CM 2, p. 130)

Until 1848, only very wealthy people had this right (the right to vote) ... It was necessary to pay taxes to be able to vote. France is the first country that granted the right to vote to all its male citizens over 21 ... but only to males. It was considered that instead of dealing with politics, women had other duties. They waited until 1945. (CM 2, p. 213)

In the Middle Ages, the king granted some city states the right to organise their own commune lives such as fighting against fire, ensuring the security of the residents, maintaining and illuminating the streets, establishing a market ... That is how the first communes arose .... (CM 2, p. 72)

The statements below, quoted from the French Textbooks, can be given as examples of the 'Tolerance' subcategory:

Bread, a type of food found in many parts of the world: in North America, Europe ... In those places, bread is the symbol of unity and cooperation among people. A friend is someone with whom you share your bread. Friendship is strengthened with this basic gesture: To split your bread to eat together. (CE 1, p. 164)

Tolerance helps to establish friendship. Everyone is different at school as in anywhere else. Why do we cast them out and make fun of them? We surely do not have to love everyone. But everyone has the right to live on earth honourably, and without being treated contemptuously and suffering wrong. Being tolerant means respecting others, and the way they live and think. It is to see the things that bring us closer more than those that distinguish us from each other. (CP, p. 165)

The statements below, quoted from the French Textbooks, can be given as examples of the 'Peace' and 'Freedom' subcategories:

Once upon a time, a kingdom in China was facing the danger of a civil war and a foreign war. The King had a wise man brought to his palace and asked him to bring reconciliation and peace back to his kingdom. (CM 2, p. 132)

Verdun War caused such pain that it is one of the most commonly known and most murderous battles of the First World War ... More than 300,000 French and as many Germans lost their lives in that war. (CM 2, p. 125)

HUMAN RIGHTS EDUCATION

Our understanding of war is different than that of the Indians. They consider war not as the combat between two nations to gain the respect of other nations; instead, a regular display of their own warriors' courage is in question. That is, for them a war consists primarily of small raids. (CM 2, p. 32)

When the savage man and women take shelter in the cave and light a fire, the savage animals get round to see what is going on. The dog, the horse and the cow traded in their freedom for some food they were offered. (CM 1, p. 154)

The statements below, quoted from the French Textbooks, can be given as examples of the 'Freedom' and 'Democracy' subcategories:

We are in 1794. It is late in the Revolution. In all villages in France, a Liberty tree is being planted as the symbol of the new Republic. (CM 2, p. 24)

Thank you, Prince! You gave me back my old physical fitness and freedom. (CM 1, p. 141)

6.3 Comparison between the Turkish and French Textbooks

When the sum of the dissemination of all subcategories are considered, it is observed that the human rights issue is more frequently mentioned in Turkish textbooks (648.9) than in French textbooks (485.8). When a comparison among all course textbooks is made, one notes that the human rights issue is mentioned most frequently in TTB 4 (165.4), TTB 1 (140.3), TTB 5 (126.9) and CP (120.2).

When the subcategories are considered separately, it can be observed that in both French textbooks and Turkish textbooks, the 'Rights' subcategory attains the highest position with regard to intensity score. In both countries, this subcategory is followed by the 'Peace' and 'Tolerance' subcategories. The 'Democracy' subcategory is more intense in French textbooks than it is in Turkish textbooks. It can also be observed that the 'Rights', 'Peace', 'Freedom' and 'Tolerance' subcategories are given more prominence in Turkish textbooks. Another striking finding is the fact that the 'Justice' subcategory is the least present, and at an almost equal rate, in the textbooks of both countries.

7 Discussion

In this comparative study, the first thing to note is that human rights education is given more prominence in Turkish textbooks than in French textbooks. This largely results from the understanding adopted by the new primary education curriculum and the subsequent obligation to prepare textbooks that take this curriculum into consideration (Ceyhan & Yiğit, 2004). In the new primary education curriculum—which was piloted during the 2004–2005 scholastic year and then implemented at the first level of all the primary education schools in Turkey during the following scholastic year—the inclusion in each textbook of the human rights topic as an intermediary discipline was accepted as a principle. One reason for this may be the lack of a discipline on human rights education and related textbooks in the first five years of primary education in Turkey. In other words, the human rights education topic is interspersed in educational curricula and, thus, in textbooks. This situation is explained in the introduction to the new primary education curriculum:

> Curricula attach importance to the improved awareness regarding human rights. Personal inviolability, which is accepted as the essential human right within the philosophical and practical context, takes free-thinking rights, rights for the security of rights, social and economic rights and political rights into consideration. Besides, the curricula do not allow for discrimination against differences such as race, colour, sex, language, religion, nation, origins, political views, social class and physical/mental health states of persons. (Ministry of National Education, 2005, p. 29)

The most important reason for the lesser inclusion of human rights education in French textbooks may be that human rights education is offered directly in the 'Living Together' courses taught for half an hour each week in the first and second grades; in 'Collective Life' courses taught again for half an hour each week and in 'Civic Education' courses taught for one-and-a-half hours each week in the third, fourth and fifth grades. This means that in French schools, out of a total of 26 hours per week, human rights education is allocated half an hour in the first and second grades and two hours in the third, fourth and fifth grades.

Civic education is the other major area of education at this level. It is during the last years of primary school that a pupil truly learns how to build relationships of mutual respect and thoughtful cooperation with his or her friends and teachers. This leads to an initial awareness of civic values. During regular meetings in the timetable (one hour every fortnight), this type of education tries to inculcate the habit of envisaging the problems posed by living together. In these courses, the primary objective is not the acquisition of knowledge, but the application of learned behaviour. This course has to enable the integration of each student to the classroom and school environment, and the realisation of character development and freedom. Besides, it orients the student to think about abstract problems that come up in school life. This would ensure that students have a clearer consciousness about personal freedom, the pressures of social life and the verification of common values. Through the use of the acquired knowledge, this course encourages the child to expand his/her views of other communities, communes, nations, Europe and the rest of the world. In this course, concepts such as citizenship duties, commonwealth and commitment, rights, authority, legality, justice and democracy are also accentuated. Civic education is not only offered in a single one-hour lesson, but in all fields of school life.

As a melting pot for equal opportunity, school fulfils this role even more so when it builds a shared common culture; this means, first of all, acquiring an essential preliminary common store of knowledge. That is, the mastery of the basic skills of reading, writing and counting—a simple yet demanding priority which, further down the line, enables college to fulfil its role. The school, as the melting pot for the elaboration of responsible and united citizenship, must encourage the building of shared values by making these values known, understood and practised.

In fact, the underlying guideline behind 'Living Together' is to accompany the child in his/her gradual acceptance of living with other persons and its restrictions, as well as building up his/her personality. In 'Living Together' courses, students begin to accept the evaluation of their own behaviours from the points of view of their friends or in a more general sense. They discover that the constraints of living together are the warranty of their own freedom. They learn to reject violence; to prevent conflicts and disagreements and to fight against the problems confronted in daily life; to approve themselves and others; to respect the rules, others and common life; to interact and communicate with their friends and with adults; to take part in group activities and to take the first step toward citizenship.

It was observed that in both countries, the 'Rights' subcategory was included the most textbooks (except TTB 1). A study conducted by Karaman-Kepenekci (1999), in which she examined high school textbooks, reached a similar conclusion. Along the lines of the present study, in Karaman-Kepenekci's study, the intensity score of the 'Rights' subcategory in Turkish language and literature textbooks was found to be much higher than those of the other subcategories.

The intensity score of the 'Democracy' subcategory comes toward the bottom end in the textbooks of both countries (except in CM 1). This makes it more important for the teacher to discuss at appropriate times in mother tongue courses, which have an artistic dimension as well as a social dimension, what democratic government is. In other words, when texts related to this category are being studied, the significance of democracy, what democratic values mean and the advantages that democratic governments bring to people can be discussed with the assistance of the teacher. In French textbooks, for instance, when the texts 'The Action of the Sage' (CM 2, p. 132), 'I am Writing a Historical Document' (CM 2, p. 24), 'The Prince and The Noble Girls' (CM 1, p. 141) and 'Right to Vote' (CM 2, p. 213) are being studied, the teacher may spend more time on the 'Democracy' subcategory. In Turkish textbooks, especially in TTB 2 (p. 105), when the story 'Democracy is Everywhere' is being studied, the significance of democracy and of living with democratic beliefs at home, at school and at work may be emphasised. By doing so, even though democracy holds a relatively small place in textbooks, one ensures the internalisation of the democracy topic by students.

It emerged from this study that the 'Democracy' subcategory is slightly more intense in French textbooks than it is in Turkish textbooks. This finding may be related to the French Revolution in 1789, when the French citizens rose in rebellion against the oppressive feudal system. This event set the social ground of democratic life in literary texts, including textbooks. The social and literary impact of this revolution, which paved the way for fundamental concepts such as freedom and democracy, is well known (Kapani, 1981). In most of the textbooks, the protagonists include a prince, princess, king and queen—the underlying implication however is the 'Democracy' subcategory. In addition to such stories, the French textbooks include short texts that directly assist students to understand the concept of democracy and its importance.

Although the 'Freedom' subcategory does not hold a prominent place in the textbooks of both countries, it is included more in Turkish textbooks. This Turkish prevalence results from the frequent mentioning in all Turkish textbooks, except in TTB 1, of the freedom topic in texts with an 'Atatürk' theme which recall the Turkish struggle for independence.[1] It can thus be seen that the relative frequent mentioning of the 'Freedom' subcategory in Turkish textbooks can be explained with the historical facts that the Turks lived through.

Another striking finding is the fact that 'Justice' is the least included subcategory in both Turkish and French textbooks. This result is not consistent with Karaman-Kepenekci's (1999) high school study, involving Turkish language and literature textbooks, which reported higher levels of inclusion for this subcategory. Still, mother tongue textbooks, in which mostly literary texts are found, may offer nice opportunities for human rights education by including examples of justice-related works from the Turkish and world literature. Although the textbooks examined in this study pay only minimal attention to the 'Justice' subcategory, a mother tongue teacher who believes in the importance of justice in society can do much to rectify this seemingly, at least at first, disadvantageous situation. For instance, when studying texts included in this 'forgotten' subcategory (e.g., 'Gift' [TTB 4, p. 17] and 'Getting the Best and the Most Favourable' [TTB 5, p. 77] in Turkish textbooks, and 'Hameln' [CE 1, p. 93] and 'The Musicians

HUMAN RIGHTS EDUCATION

of Bremen' [CE 1, p. 161] in French textbooks), more time can be dedicated and, furthermore, a genuine discussion environment may be created using real-life related events or texts from other books. Students need to realise that, even though their textbooks seem to give little importance to the 'Justice' subcategory, it still constitutes a fundamental step in human rights education. Students may be further helped to learn about this subcategory by making use of different tools, such as, role playing, question-answer methods and cartoons (Sever, 2007), pictures, newspaper articles, poems, memoirs, diaries, anecdotes and novels (Binyazar, 1996; Karaman-Kepenekci, 2000). Another possibility would be to ask students questions that will make think, question, criticise, solve problems presented in class, generate authentic thoughts and develop positive relations especially about the 'Justice' subcategory (Çayır, 2003; Aslan & Polat, 2007).

It is also worth pointing out that the intensity scores of the 'Rights', 'Peace' and 'Tolerance' subcategories hold the first three ranks in all the textbooks, except in CM 1 and CM 2. The fact that the 'Peace' and 'Tolerance' subcategories hold the second and third ranks in most textbooks, apart from being an indication of their generally high intensity scores, results from the sufficient inclusion of subjects such as humanitarianism, tolerating and respecting diversity, peace, friendship, tolerance, solidarity and cooperation in the selected textbooks.

The 'Peace' subcategory is included more in Turkish textbooks than it is in French textbooks. This can be explained with the inclusion in Turkish textbooks of texts that reflect positive opinions of Atatürk and of the peace protagonists in literary texts within the 'Atatürk' theme. In fact, Turkish textbooks frequently quote Atatürk's 'Peace at home, peace in the world' statement and also very frequently emphasise that peace is very important for people, society and the world we live in.

Acknowledgement

This chapter originally appeared as: Aslan, C., & Karaman-Kepenekci, Y. (2008) Human rights education: a comparison of mother tongue textbooks in Turkey and France, *Mediterranean Journal of Educational Studies*, Vol. 13(1), pp. 101–124. Reprinted here with permission from the publisher.

Note

1. Following the defeat of the Ottoman Empire at the hands of the World War I allies, and the subsequent plans for its partition, Mustafa Kemal Atatürk, a Turkish army officer, established

a provisional government in Ankara and subsequently defeated the forces sent by the allies. His successful military campaigns led to the liberation of the country and to the establishment of the Republic of Turkey.

References

Akıllıoğlu, T. (1995) *Human Rights: The Concept, Resources and Systems of Protection* (in Turkish). Ankara: Ankara Üniversitesi İnsan Hakları Merkezi Yayınları.

Aslan, C. (2006) A study on the use of 'non-Turkish words' in Turkish textbooks (in Turkish), *AÜ TOMER Language Journal*, Vol. 133, pp. 7–19.

Aslan, C., & Polat, D. (2007) *Content Analysis on Primary Education Turkish Course Books from the Point of Acquiring Critical Thinking Skills.* Paper presented at 9th International Conference on Education, Institute for Education and Research, 28–29 May 2007, Athens, Greece.

Aycan, Ş., Kaynar, Ü., Türkoğuz, H., & Arı, E. (2001) *Analysis of Science Textbooks used in Primary Education according to Certain Criteria* (in Turkish). Paper presented at the Science Education Symposium (in Turkish), 16–18 September 2002, Ankara, Turkey.

Baykal, A. (2004) Statistics from primary and high school textbooks. In D. Ceylan-Tarba & S. Irzık (eds.) *How Are We Educated?* Istanbul: International Symposium on Human Rights Education and Textbook Research.

Baysal, J. (1996) Analysis of elementary level Turkish textbooks in Turkey in terms of content. In H. Coşkun, İ. Kaya & J. Kuglin (eds.) *Primary Education Textbooks in Turkey and in Germany* (in Turkish). Ankara: Türk-Alman Kültür İşleri Kurulu Yayın Dizisi.

Binyazar, A. (1996) Realisation of emotional education making use of literary texts in mother tongue books: examples from mother tongue books prepared in Germany. In H. Coşkun, İ. Kaya & J. Kuglin (eds.) *Primary Education Textbooks in Turkey an in Germany* (in Turkish). Ankara: Türk-Alman Kültür İşleri Kurulu Yayın Dizisi.

Bora, T. (2003) Nationalism in textbooks. In B. Çotuksöken & A. Erzan-Silier (eds.) *Human Rights in Textbooks: Results of Browsing* (in Turkish). Istanbul: Tarih Vakfı Yayınları.

Buergental, T. (1995) *International Human Rights*. USA: West Publishing.

Camenisch A., & P. Serge (2006) *Actes du XXXIIe Colloque COPIRELEM: Lire et Écrire des Énoncés de Problèmes Additifs: Le Travail sur la Langue*. Available online at: http://publimath.irem.univ-mrs.fr

Centre National de Documentation Pédagogique (2007) *Qu'Apprend-on à l'École Maternelle? Les Nouveaux Programmes*. Available online at: http://www.cndp.fr

Ceyhan, E., & Yiğit, B. (2004) *Subject Field Textbook Analysis* (in Turkish). Ankara: Anı Yayıncılık.

HUMAN RIGHTS EDUCATION

Ceylan-Tarba, D. (2003) The place of human rights and students in elementary level Turkish textbooks and high school level Turkish and literature textbooks. In B. Çotuksöken & A. Erzan-Silier (eds.) *Human Rights in Textbooks: Results of Browsing* (in Turkish). Istanbul: Tarih Vakfı Yayınları.

Coşkun, H. (1996) Content problems of Turkish and German textbooks of primary education second level within the context of education technology and intercultural education. In H. Coşkun, İ. Kaya & J. Kuglin (eds.) *Primary Education Textbooks in Turkey and in Germany* (in Turkish). Ankara: Türk-Alman Kültür İşleri Kurulu Yayın Dizisi.

Çayır, K. (2003) Improvement of human rights and democracy culture: writing textbooks. In M. T. Bağlı & Y. Esen (eds.) *Human Rights in Textbooks: For Textbooks that are Sensitive to Human Rights* (in Turkish). Istanbul: Tarih Vakfı Yayınları.

Çeçen, A. (1995) *Human Rights* (in Turkish). Ankara: Gündoğan Yayınları.

Çotuksöken, B. (2003) Education philosophy and critical thinking in textbooks. In B. Çotuksöken & A. Erzan-Silier (eds.) *Human Rights in Textbooks: Results of Browsing* (in Turkish). Istanbul: Tarih Vakfı Yayınları.

Donnelly, J. (1989) *Universal Human Rights in Theory and Practice* (translated by M. Erdoğan & L. Korkut). Ankara: Yetkin Yayınları.

Esen, Y., & M. T. Bağlı (2002) A study on pictures of women and men in primary education textbooks (in Turkish), *Ankara University Faculty of Educational Sciences Journal*, Vol. 35(1–2), pp. 143–154.

Garner, R., Slater, W. H., Weaver, V. P., Cole, M., Williams, D., & T. Smith (1986) Do pre-service teachers notice textbook flaws?, *Education*, Vol. 106(4), pp. 429–433.

Gemalmaz, S. (2001) *Introduction to the General Theory of Supranational Human Rights Law* (in Turkish). Istanbul: Beta.

Gemalmaz, M. S. (2003) Evaluation of the data obtained through browsing of the textbooks in terms of human rights criteria. In B. Çotuksöken & A. Erzan-Silier (eds.) *Human Rights in Textbooks: Results of Browsing* (in Turkish). Istanbul: Tarih Vakfı Yayınları.

Gérard, F. M. (2003) *Les Manuels Scolaires d'Aujourd'hui, de l'Enseignement à l'Apprentissage*. Available online at: http://www.fmgerard.be/textes/option.html

Giannangelo, D. M., & Kaplan, M. B. (1992) *An Analysis and Critique of Selected Social Studies Textbooks* (Reproductions supplied by EDRS, Memphis City Schools, TN).

Gülmez, M. (1998) Continuous human rights education in primary education (in Turkish). *Cumhuriyet*, 16 February, p. 22.

Gülmez, M. (2001) *Human Rights and Democracy Education* (in Turkish). Ankara: TODAİE.

Hall, R. V., & Houten, R. V. (1983) *Managing Behavior, Behavior Modification: The Measurement of Behavior*. Austin: Pro-ed.

History Foundation (2003) *Human Rights in Textbooks: For Textbooks that are Sensitive to Human Rights* (in Turkish). Turkey. Istanbul: Tarih Vakfı Yayınları.

Humanité (2007) *Nouveaux Programmes pour le Primaire*. Available online at: http://www.humanite.fr

Kapani, M. (1981) *Public Freedoms* (in Turkish). Ankara: A. Ü. Hukuk Fakültesi Yayınları.

Karaman-Kepenekci, Y. (1999) *Human Rights Education in Turkish High Schools* (in Turkish). PhD thesis, Institute of Social Sciences, Ankara University, Turkey.

Karaman-Kepenekci, Y. (2000) *Human Rights Education* (in Turkish). Ankara: Anı Yayıncılık.

Karaman-Kepenekci, Y. (2003) Human rights and responsibility education in primary education (in Turkish), *Educational Administration in Theory and Practice*, Vol. 34, pp. 280–299.

Karaman-Kepenekci, Y. (2005) Citizenship and human rights education: a comparison of textbooks in Turkey and the United States, *International Journal of Educational Reform*, Vol. 14(1), pp. 73–88.

King, L. (2004) UNESCO's Work in peace and human rights education. In D. Tarba-Ceylan & S. Irzık (eds.) *How Are We Educated?* Istanbul: International Symposium on Human Rights Education and Textbook Research.

Kirisika, Y. (2003) *International Human Rights Standards in High-School Textbooks: Human Rights in Asian Schools*. Available online at: https://www.hurights.or.jp/english/education/2002/03/international-human-rights-standards-in-high-school-textbooks.html

Ministère de l'Education Nationale (2006) *Le Système Éducatif, les Niveaux d'Enseignement, L'École Élémentaire*. Available online at: https://www.education.gouv.fr/

Ministry of National Education (2005) *Primary Education Turkish Course Educational Curriculum and Guide*. Ankara: Devlet Kitapları Müdürlüğü Basımevi.

Mumcu, A. (1994) *Human Rights and Public Freedoms* (in Turkish). Ankara: Savaş Yayınları.

Oğuzkan, F. (1993) *Dictionary of Educational Terms* (in Turkish). Ankara: Emel Matbaacılık.

Polat, T. (1991) *Turkish Language in Secondary Schools: Turkish Courses 1 Textbooks in Turkey* (in Turkish). Istanbul: Cem Yayınevi.

Power, S., & Allison, G. (2000) *Realizing Human Rights: Moving from Inspiration to Impact*. New York: Palgrave Macmillan.

Programmes de 2002. (2004) *La Dimension Culturelle de l'École*. Available online at: http://www.diplomatie.gouv.fr

Reisoğlu, S. (2001) *Human Rights with Their International Dimensions* (in Turkish). Istanbul: Beta.

Sever, S. (2007) *Use of Cartoons as an Artistic Stimulus in Turkish Teaching* (in Turkish). Paper presented at VIth National Symposium on Form Teaching Education, 27–29 April 2007, Eskişehir, Turkey.

Sever, S., Kaya, Z., & Aslan, C. (2006) *Teaching Turkish through Activities* (in Turkish). Istanbul: Morpa.

Sewall, G. T. (2002) *Textbooks and the United Nations: The International System and What American Students Learn about It.* USA: UNA.

Strauss, A., & Corbin, J. (1990) *Basics of Qualitative Research: Grounded Theory Procedures and Techniques.* Newbury Park: Sage.

Tanrıöver, H. U. (2003) Gender discrimination in textbooks. In B. Çotuksöken & A. Erzan-Silier (eds.) *Human Rights in Textbooks: Results of Browsing* (in Turkish). Istanbul: Tarih Vakfı Yayınları.

Tibbits, F. (2002) Understanding what we can do: emerging models for human rights education, *International Review of Education,* Vol. 48(3–4), pp. 159–171.

Timur, Ş., & Bağlı, H. (2003) Visual quality and design in textbooks: human rights in terms of image-text relationship. In M. T. Bağlı & Y. Esen (eds.) *Human Rights in Textbooks: For Textbooks that are Sensitive to Human Rights* (in Turkish). Istanbul: Tarih Vakfı Yayınları.

UNESCO (1969) Trends in teaching about human rights. In *Some Suggestions on Teaching about Human Rights.* Paris: Author.

UNESCO (1987) Human rights: an ethical and civic education for our time, *Human Rights Teaching,* Vol. 6, pp. 175–184.

UNESCO (2007a) *Basic Learning Materials.* Available online at: http://www.unesco.org

UNESCO (2007b) *Étude Comparative de Manuels Scolaires dans le Cadre du Dialogue Euro-Arabe* (Coordonnée conjointement par les Commissions Française et Marocaine pour l'UNESCO, document préparatoire). Available online at: http://www.diplomatie.gouv.fr

Vandenberg, D. (1984) Human rights in the curriculum. In *The Teaching of Human Rights* (Proceedings of the Conference held by the Human Rights Commission and UNESCO). Canberra: Australian Government Publishing Service.

Yıldırım, A., & Şimşek, H. (2005) *Qualitative Research Methods in Social Sciences* (in Turkish). Ankara: Seçkin Yayınevi.

Yörükoğlu, A. (1996) *Primary Education Level Textbooks in Turkey and in Germany, Volume II* (in Turkish). Ankara: Türk-Alman Kültür İşleri Kurulu Yayın Dizisi.

Appendix A: The Textbooks Used in This Study

Turkish Textbooks

1. Erol, A., Bingöl-Özger, M., Yalçın. Ç. S., Demiroğlu, R., Irmak, A., & Ceylan, M. (2006) *Primary School Turkish Textbook 1* (in Turkish). Istanbul: Kelebek Matbaacılık.
2. Coşkun, O., Emecen, M., Yurt, M., Dedeoğlu-Okuyucu, S., & Arhan, S. (2006) *Primary School Turkish Textbook 2* (in Turkish). Istanbul: İhlas Gazetecilik AŞ.
3. Ardanuç, K., Çökmez, A., Küçüktepe, B., & Toprak, G. (2006) *Primary School Turkish Textbook 3* (in Turkish). Ankara: Cem Web Ofset.
4. Çanakcı, H., Yardımcı, S., Yetimoğlu, E. B., Taşdemir, K., & Özaykut, S. (2006) *Primary School Turkish Textbook 4* (in Turkish). Istanbul: Star Medya Yayıncılık AŞ.
5. Gören, N., Yener, Z., İldeniz, A., Aksal, H. S., & Sarıöz, N. (2006) *Primary School Turkish Textbook 5* (in Turkish). Ankara: Pelin Ofset.

French Textbooks

1. Camo, M., & Pla, R. (2006) *Je Lis avec Dagobert,* CP. Paris: Hachette Livre.
2. Assuied, R., Buselli, D., & Ragot, A. M. (2006) *Parcours, Maîtrise de la Langue,* CE *1.* Paris: Hatier.
3. Lucas, J. L., & Lucas, J. C. (2005) *A Portée de Mots,* CE *2.* Paris: Hachette Livre.
4. Schöttke, M. (2006) *Facettes Littérature/Ecriture Observation Réfléchie de la Langue,* CM *1.* Paris: Hatier.
5. Léon, R. (2005) *Français Des Outils, pour Dire, Lire et Ecrire,* CM *2.* Paris: Hachette Livre.

Printed in the United States
by Baker & Taylor Publisher Services